Computers and Information Processing

Computers and Information Processing

Floyd Fuller · Stan Wilkinson
Department of Decision Sciences
Appalachian State University

West Publishing Company
St. Paul   New York   Los Angeles   San Francisco

Copyediting Educational Challenges, Inc.
Cover and interior design John Edeen
Composition Carlisle Communications
Illustration Rolin Graphics
Photo research Judy Mason
Cover artwork Delor Erickson/Studio West

Library of Congress Cataloging-in-Publication Data

Fuller, Floyd.
  Computers and information processing / Floyd Fuller, Stan Wilkinson.
    p. cm.
  Includes index.
  Summary: Examines various aspects of computers and data processing, including the components and functions of computer hardware, the applications of software, information processing systems, and the legal and social issues involved.
    ISBN 0–314–31356–7
  1. Computers–Juvenile literature. 2. Electronic data processing—Juvenile literature. [1. Computers. 2. Data processing.]
I. Wilkinson, Stan. II. Title.
QA76.23.F85 1988
004—dc19

(Acknowledgments and Photo Credits follow Index.)

To my wife Edith, whose love, support, confidence, and encouragement provided me with the motivation and continuing desire to move forward with this book; and to my daughter Cindy, and son Michael, who supported and encouraged me throughout this work in ways that only a father can appreciate, I proudly and gratefully dedicate this book.

Floyd Fuller

I wish to dedicate this textbook to all the persons that made this writing project possible—to the users of this textbook, and my family and friends that supported me throughout the entire process. Without their support and encouragement this textbook would not have been a reality.

Stan Wilkinson

CONTENTS

PART II

Computer Hardware: Components and Functions   57

PART III
Microcomputers
177

PART IV
Software and
Applications   231

CHAPTER 10
Computer Software   254

CHAPTER 11
Programming Languages   273

CHAPTER 12
Computer Applications   293

MODULES

PREFACE

The idea for *Computers and Information Processing* originated in the summer of 1982 while the authors were attending a computer institute. Many teachers and students attending the institute expressed a need for a student-oriented, highly readable, and complete textbook learning package. *Computers and Information Processing* represents a response to the need stated by many educators. From the birth of the idea to the final textbook, the goal of everyone involved has been to help students learn. We believe you will agree that this book represents the achievement of that goal.

This book is written for students who want to learn about computers. The text assumes no prior computer courses or training. Further, knowledge of programming or mathematics, other than basic mathematics, is not assumed.

Content and Organization

This book contains sixteen chapters divided into 6 parts, and two modules. This provides convenient flexibility in the order in which chapters can be covered.

Part I, Information Processing, provides important basic information the student needs before becoming involved in the study of modern computers. Chapter 1 explains what information is, and distinguishes between information and data. Methods of processing data are examined, the "information processing cycle" is explained, and characteristics of useful information are identified. Chapter 2 covers the historical evolution of computers, culminating in the development of modern electronic computer systems.

Part II, Computer Hardware, covers computer hardware devices. Chapter 3 explains the central processing unit and its components. Chapter 4 introduces and explains input devices and media. Chapter 5 explains output devices and media. Chapter 6 explains and illustrates storage devices and media with special sections devoted to microcomputer storage devices and media.

Part III, Microcomputers, is a unique two-chapter explanation of microcomputers. Chapter 7 is a comprehensive explanation of microcomputer technology. Chapter 8 covers recommended procedures for using microcomputers.

Part IV, Software and Applications, provides detailed coverage of computer software and identifies specific computer applications. Chapter 9 is a description of how to logically solve problems using a computer. Chapter 10 explains what computer software is and identifies different kinds of software. Chapter 11 is an overview of programming languages. Chapter 12 describes many specific uses of computers in all areas of society.

Part V, Information Processing Systems, focuses on data communications and remote data processing, and on database processing. Chapter 13 is a simplified explanation of how computers can communicate with each other, and how data is sent from one geographic location to another. Chapter 14 explains database concepts and the main differences between various types of databases.

Part VI, Legal and Social Issues, identify important legal and social issues and controversies involving computers. Chapter 15 identifies modern procedures and methods for protecting computers, computerized information, and computer facilities. Chapter 16 is a look into the future.

Realistic, yet imaginative and interesting, predictions are made about future computer technologies and uses.

The book concludes with two modules. Module A, A Guide to Selecting and Evaluating A Microcomputer System, identifies factors that should be considered when purchasing a microcomputer system, including hardware, software, and peripheral devices. Vendor selection, training courses, and other important considerations are presented to help a prospective buyer make intelligent buying decisions.

Module B, the BASIC Programming Language, begins with an explanation of the operating system and commands. Operating system functions are explained, and activities are included allowing students to use many important DOS functions. Next, BASIC commands and statements are explained in a logical and systematic order. Sample programs illustrate the use of each statement and command.

Flexibility

The book offers almost unlimited flexibility in coverage. It is recommended that Chapter 1, Information, be covered first. Afterwards, the remaining chapters can be presented in virtually any order. They can be covered in sequence, or those who prefer early coverage of microcomputers can skip immediately to part III, Microcomputers. The order of coverage of the remaining chapters is optional. Chapters 15 and 16 include valuable information but may be omitted if desired. Modules A and B can be covered at any convenient time during the course.

Features

Several important learning features are included within each chapter. **Learning objectives** and a **chapter outline** are presented at the beginning of each chapter, followed by a computer **application** related to chapter material. Included in each chapter are **"DO YOU REMEMBER?"** questions to emphasize important concepts students should have learned. A unique feature of this book is the **summary** at the end of each chapter that provides answers to "DO YOU REMEMBER?" questions. Another unique feature is the inclusion of a **"The Computer Didn't Do It!"** insert in each chapter. These inserts are entertaining, and help dispel the myth that computers make mistakes. Each chapter includes information about a **computing career** presented in a form similar to a newspaper advertisement. Most were taken from actual sources. **Key terms, questions,** and **activities** are included at the end of each chapter.

Supplements

A complete Teacher's Resource Manual is available to adopters. Included are class lecture outlines, a three-version set of tests for each chapter, answers to end-of-chapter questions, transparency masters, and answers to study guide questions.

Supplements for students include study guide/application manuals with sample data disks. The disks are available for the Apple IIe, IBM-PC, and compatible computers. Applications for computer lab exercises enable students to gain hands-on experiences with computers. For complete information about these and other supplements and learning aids, contact West Publishing Company.

Acknowledgments

Many individuals and companies have been actively involved in the development of this book. While their hard work and complete dedication helped to make this book a reality, the responsibility for any errors in content belongs to the authors.

Many people reviewed the manuscript at various stages of development, and offered helpful comments and suggestions, many of which were incorporated in the final manuscript. For their contributions, we wish to acknowledge the following reviewers:

High School Reviewers

Margarita Cervantes
Edinburgh High School
Edinburgh, Texas

Charlotte Denton
Rogers Area Vocational Center
Gardendale, Alabama

Dick Dumais
Gilford Middle High School
Gilford, New Hampshire

Beverly Farris
Diboll High School
Diboll, Texas

Bobbi Gelpi
Harrison High School
Bristol, West Virginia

Carroll Harr
Adams City High School
Commerce City, Colorado

Alva Hartry
Decatur High School
Decatur, Georgia

Barbara Herzog
Sahuaro High School
Tucson, Arizona

Ethel Holladay
DuQuoin High School
DuQuoin, Illinois

Gary Langer
Shawnee Mission High School
Shawnee Mission, Kansas

Susan Lathbury
Boyd Anderson High School
Lauderlake, Florida

Ceil Lazarski
Rich Township High School
Richton Park, Illinois

Diane Losiniecki
Bowen High School
Chicago, Illinois

Kathy Parker
Glenrock High School
Glenrock, Wyoming

Larry Peterson
Bonnieville High School
Roy, Utah

Karen Pilon
Willow Run High School
Ypsilanti, Michigan

Faye Rampley
Silverton High School
Silverton, Texas

Charles Schultes, Jr.
Lehighten Area High School
Lehighten, Pennsylvania

Katherine Shortt
Prince George County Schools
Owings, Maryland

Saundra Stisher
Arab High School
Arab, Alabama

Marion Weeks
Fred T. Foard High School
Hickory, North Carolina

Daryl Weir
Education Computer Consortium of
   Ohio
Cleveland, Ohio

Kenda White
Marshall High School
Marshall, Texas

College Reviewers

Barbara Greim
University of North Carolina
Wilmington, North Carolina

Lorinda Hite
Owens Technical College
Toledo, Ohio

Earl Jackson
North Texas State University
Denton, Texas

Walter Leffin
University of Wisconsin at Oshkosh
Oshkosh, Wisconsin

Robert Schmiederer
Los Angeles Valley College
Van Nuys, California

Janet Van Dam
Oakland Schools
Pontiac, Michigan

The authors owe a special debt of gratitude to the following who deserve special recognition: Becky Tollerson, our developmental editor, for her helpful suggestions and diligent work in manuscript development; Pam McClanahan and Barbara Fuller, our production editors, for overseeing the final production of the book; Marilyn Sue, our secretary, for assisting us in meeting schedules; Louis Bourne, Rick Purcell, and David Blalock, for their valuable assistance; Dr. Paul Combs, Dean of the College of Business, Appalachian State University, for providing University resources; and West Publishing Company for providing the authors the opportunity to pursue and complete this book. For his professional assistance and dedication to this project, words cannot adequately convey our appreciation to our editor, Peter Marshall.

PART I
Information Processing

Introduction

The extent to which American society has become dependent upon computers is truly amazing! People marveled at the world's first computer, the Electronic Numerical Integrator And Calculator (called the ENIAC), which was built in 1946. It weighed 30 tons and covered 15,000 square feet. By 1981, there were 3.5 million computers in the world. Between 1981 and 1982, that number doubled. By the end of 1983, the number of computers in the world had doubled again, to more than 13 million.

International Data Corporation (IDC) publishes statistics on the number of computers in the world. According to a recent IDC forecast, there will be 400 million computers in the world in the year 2000—one for every person in the United States. Crazy!, we might think. Maybe about as crazy as thinking there would ever be more telephones than people, more TVs than families, or more cars than adult drivers. Crazy? Maybe we'd better think again!

Equally amazing is the vast amount of information processed by computers. Collectively, computers perform one hundred thousand calculations per person every second. The average American citizen's name appears thirty-five times daily in computers.

Computers come in many sizes and capacities and are used for many different purposes. They are used in businesses, in schools, in homes, and in a wide variety of products people use.

The popularity of computers is increasing rapidly in every segment of society. Recent reports indicate that the number of small computers bought and used by small businesses doubled between 1983 and 1984. Thousands of computers are also being ordered by schools. Some computer manufacturers have difficulty keeping up with the demand.

We are now in the midst of an exciting and challenging era in American history. Some call it the *computer revolution*. Others call it the *technological revolution*. Whatever term is used, it is a time when every American citizen will have access to the technology that will enable them to do things thought to be impossible a few years ago. Millions of people will accept the challenge and learn about this technology and how it can be used to improve their lives. Those who do will find the rewards immeasurable. **This book is written for those who accept the challenge!**

The fun and excitement of computer games and arcades are enjoyed by people of all ages.

Many retailers now use computerized Point of Sale (POS) terminals for efficient sales operations.

In addition to receiving computer instruction during the day, this student is using a computer for preparing his homework assignments.

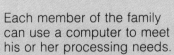

Each member of the family can use a computer to meet his or her processing needs.

Computers are finding new homes down on the farm. Here, a computer is being used to increase farming and ranching efficiency.

Many colleges and schools use computers.

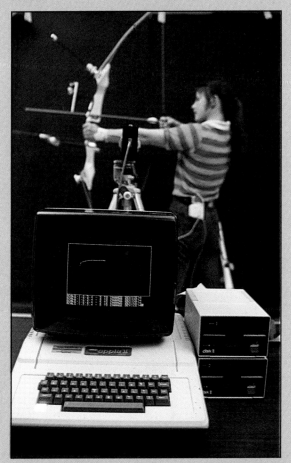

This young athlete's performance is being measured by a computer.

Law enforcement agencies use computers to obtain information, to verify drivers' licenses, and to meet other needs.

A salesperson uses a small computer and modem to send orders via a telephone.

Computers have become important information tools for young executives.

With the "computerized simulation and feedback system" developed by Dr. Jerrold Peltrosky at Wright State University, Nan Davis, a WSU student paralyzed from the waist down, has taken several steps.

Computers are becoming an integral part of business. Here, computers guide industrial welding robots in automobile manufacturing.

A view of computers in the mission operations control room at the Johnson Space Center's Mission Control Center.

Automobile manufacturers have begun installing computers in some models. This computer can alert the driver of approaching traffic, display a map showing the automobile's location, or alert the driver of engine problems.

CHAPTER 1

Information

Learning Objectives

After studying this chapter carefully, you will be able to:

1. Define key terms introduced in this chapter.

2. Explain why information is important and identify some specific groups that need and use information.

3. Explain the difference between data and information.

4. Identify the main characteristics of good information.

5. Identify four methods of processing data.

6. Identify the steps in the information processing cycle.

7. Name the activities included in each phase of the information processing cycle.

8. Identify key historical figures who made important contributions to the development of early computing devices.

Chapter Outline

WHY INFORMATION IS IMPORTANT
Who Needs and Uses Information
What Information Is . . . and Is Not!
Characteristics of Good Information

METHODS FOR PROCESSING DATA
Manually
Mechanically
Electromechanically
Electronically

THE INFORMATION PROCESSING CYCLE
Input
Processing
Output
Storage

DATA PROCESSING CAREER: Service and
    Repair Technician

Application

Marilyn Allison walked straight to one of the two new computer terminals at Service Merchandise's East Independence Boulevard store last week, glanced at her list of items to buy, and started punching the keyboard numbers. "I love it," she said of the new ordering system. "The first time I used it, a lot of people were waiting in line to order from the clerks. I noticed the computer terminals and nobody was at them."

Service Merchandise installed the terminals, nicknamed "Silent Sam," as a convenience for their customers. The terminals are connected to the store's main computer system, which provides the most current inventory and price information.

Instructions on the computer screen tell customers to type in the order number for any item they want. If the item is out of stock, the computer refers the customer to a desk clerk.

If the item is available, the computer confirms the description and price of the item and asks how many the customer wants. The machines can handle any number of items in an order and automatically compute the sales tax and the total bill.

To complete the order, the computer asks the customer's last name and zip code. As soon as the last button is pushed, the order is printed out in the warehouse area of the store. There employees pull the merchandise from stock and send the order to the pick-up desk.

The new system is not perfect, however. "Sometimes, a customer will think he has placed an order, but he hasn't finished the transaction," says assistant store manager Ray Wright. "And sometimes kids will think it's a video game and start playing with it," says another assistant manager, Charita Justice.

Why Information Is Important

Every day we must make decisions—and information helps us do this. The warehouse employee at Service Merchandise, needed the information Marilyn Allison typed into the computer terminal before he could fill her order.

Information helps us make wise decisions and also enables us to function more effectively. For example, if we hear that the daily weather forecast is calling for rain, this information will most likely prompt us to take a raincoat or umbrella on any trip outside.

Who Needs and Uses Information

Everyone makes decisions—students, teachers, school administrators, businesspeople, lawyers, doctors, politicians, and military leaders. Try to imagine living in a society without information—without radio, television, newspapers, or other means of communication. There would be no schools, hospitals, movie theaters, businesses, postal service, or government. This type of society would, in fact, not be a true society because a "society" is a group of individuals who share interests, roles, institutions, and a common culture. Instead, there would be only individuals, each having to provide himself or herself with everything needed for survival.

Fortunately, our Western information-based society makes it possible for us to have at least most of the information we need. We have information about television and movie schedules, civic events, recreational events, world events, and many other activities that affect our lives.

Students.   Students are among the biggest users of information. Students need information about assignments, study materials, homework, and extracurricular activities. Textbooks provide necessary information about the subjects each student is learning. The more information the student has, the more successful he or she will be in studies and other activities.

Farmers.   Farmers are an example of another group of people who need information in order to make good decisions. They need up-to-date information about such things as weather forecasts, the right

Figure 1–1
Enrollments in computing classes have increased greatly in recent years.

amount of fertilizer, the amount of seed to plant per acre, expected crop yields, and future crop prices.

Valuable up-to-date information is made available to farmers by the agricultural departments of state universities and the county extension services. Although many farmers obtain the information they need by writing to or telephoning one of these sources, others use a different method.

John Fuller is a farmer in Irby, South Carolina. Each year he plants 400 acres in corn and feeds 100 head of beef cattle. He uses a small computer to process and obtain information that helps him operate his farm more efficiently. His computer is connected to the county agricultural agent's computer that, in turn, is connected to the large computer at their state university. The university's computer processes and stores valuable farming information. This information is automatically relayed to the county agent's computer and can then be obtained by Fuller on his. Fuller uses this information to make decisions about planting, cultivating, harvesting, and selling his corn and cattle. The Fullers also use their computer for other purposes

Figure 1–2
More and more farmers and ranchers are using computers to manage their farming and ranching businesses more efficiently. Here, a group of midwestern ranchers is checking current beef prices provided by a commodity exchange.

such as keeping accurate farm records, maintaining an up-to-date schedule of loan payments to the bank, preparing the family budget, planning family meals, and storing recipes.

Businesspeople.   Businesspeople are important information consumers. Retailers, for example, need information about the products their business sells, including product descriptions, prices, availability, suppliers, ordering procedures, and discounts. They also need information about their competitors' procedures, with regard to their business locations and products. Equally important to retailers is information about employees, sales, business expenses, profits, and the figures that must be provided to the government such as the amount of sales taxes collected from customers.

Manufacturing companies must have information about the cost and availability of raw materials, production schedules, and shipping. Other important information, such as descriptions of the products being ordered, product prices, and the number of units the customer is ordering, is provided on customer purchase orders.

Keeping accurate records is an important activity of every successful businessperson and business firm. Records are kept on employees, customers, sales, and business expenses and on the many activities in which the business is involved. Frequently, this information will be used to make decisions that will affect the business's future success.

Everyone.   We have learned about some individuals and groups that need information and about how they use information to function more effectively in their jobs and in their daily lives. Although the kind and amount of information needed will vary among individuals and businesses, everyone needs information regularly.

Figure 1–3
For a businessperson, the computer has become an indispensable business tool.

What Information Is . . . and Is Not!

Information is knowledge we use to make sound decisions and to function more effectively in our daily lives. Marilyn Allison used a computer terminal to provide information (knowledge) to the warehouse clerk who filled her order at Service Merchandise. Without the information she provided, it would have been impossible for the clerk to carry out his job or even to know that Marilyn wanted to place an order in the first place. Agricultural information provided by the state university enabled Mr. Fuller to make wise farming decisions. Without this information, Mr. Fuller's decisions would have been the result of mere guesswork.

Data consists of raw, unprocessed facts. When these facts are processed, they become information. Information, then, is based on data—the raw, unprocessed facts that people process in order to create information. Sometimes data and information are one and the same. Take the telephone number 226–5015 as an example. By itself, it is a single piece of data.* And unless you plan to use the number for some purpose, it remains simply data. If it is the telephone number of a friend you plan to call, however, then it is information. In this case, you use this information (telephone number) to function effectively (to call your friend).

Data can be processed into information by hand, by machine, or by computer. Assume, for example, that in a certain subject Luis received the following test grades: 75, 83, 91, 94, and 82. By adding these test grades and dividing the total by 5, Luis can determine that his test average is 85. Knowing this, Luis has processed raw data (test grades) into information (his average) he can use.

DO YOU
REMEMBER

1. . . .Why information is important?

2. . . .Specific groups of people who need and use information.

3. . . .The difference between *information* and *data?*

*Grammatically speaking, data is plural; datum is the singular form. But many computer users prefer to use the term ''data'' as both a singular and a plural noun. In this book, the term data will be used regardless of the amount of data.

Characteristics of Good Information

Information, as well as data, must have certain characteristics in order for it to be useful. It must be complete, concise, accurate, relevant, and timely.

Complete.   Cindy, a college freshman, works on weekends at a local restaurant. Last Friday when she received her paycheck for two weeks' work, she was dismayed to find that it contained all of the usual printed information except the amount of her net pay. Knowing that the bank would not cash a check with incomplete information (net pay), Cindy returned her paycheck to the manager. She was then issued a new check that contained all the necessary information.

   Information is **complete** when all important data is included. Like Cindy's new paycheck, complete information is more valuable to a user.

Concise.   Joel's high school history teacher assigned the class a fifteen hundred-word term paper on the Battle of Gettysburg. The teacher imposed a fifteen hundred word minimum to the paper to encourage students to research the topic carefully and completely. Those students who did, in fact, carefully research the topic had no trouble writing fifteen hundred words. Joel, however, did not research the topic adequately; instead, he inserted unnecessary words, phrases, and sentences in his paper so that it would contain the minimum number of words required. Joel's term paper then was not concise.

   Concise information is more useful because unnecessary words, statements, or figures are omitted. An effective communicator is one who is capable of communicating minimum information without omitting any important information.

Accurate.   Information is **accurate** when it is free of errors. If inaccurate data is used, the results will be wrong. If, in the example of Luis's grade calculation, a "64" were used instead of a "94," then the computed average would be "79," and not "85."

   The above illustration shows that inaccurate information can result from the use of inaccurate data. In the world of computers, the acronym **GIGO** refers to the use of inaccurate data. It stands for **Garbage-In, Garbage-Out.** If incorrect data (garbage) is put into the computer, the information the user gets from the computer will also be incorrect (garbage).

Keying incorrect data into a computer can result in serious problems. A computer cannot correct human mistakes. This is why teachers who use computers in their classes emphasize the importance of accuracy when entering data.

Relevant.   Information is **relevant** when all of it is directly related to the information needed by the user. If after giving a traveler directions to a certain city, you were also to tell him about an event that happened to you while you were there three months earlier, then part of your information would be irrelevant. The experience you had is probably of no value to the traveler who needs only travel directions.

When we ask questions, usually we want only relevant answers. This is particularly true in data processing. If, for example, the plant manager requests an up-to-date list of all employees, he or she does not want, in addition, a list of company creditors or any other information that is not relevant to the request.

When providing information or data, a person should provide only what is requested. Providing additional, unrelated information or data wastes the user's time and energy.

Timely.   Information is **timely** if the user receives the information when he needs it. Assume, for example, that you subscribe to **TV Guide,** a weekly publication. If your copy arrives a week late, it obviously has little or no value to you as information. Timeliness is an essential characteristic of good information.

Methods for Processing Data

We have learned that information is created by processing data. Computers are only one of several methods by which to process data. Data can be processed **manually, mechanically, electromechanically,** and **electronically**. The advantages and disadvantages of each of these four methods should be considered before deciding which to use.

Manually

Originally, all data was processed **manually** (by hand). Even prehistoric cave dwellers kept records by drawing pictures and symbols on cave walls to record such information as the number of animals they

Figure 1–4
The abacus is still used today in some parts of the world.

had killed for food. They recorded special activities and events, such as the birth of a new child into the family, by making special markings on the wall.

Throughout history, people have processed data manually. When small amounts of data are involved, this is often the most efficient method. You are processing data manually when you take notes in class and when you write a check to pay a bill.

Processing data manually will continue to be an important and widely used method. Many people in the world do not have computers or other devices to use, and even when they do, situations in which small amounts of data are to be processed make it impractical to use machines.

For centuries, people lived on earth without keeping written records. But as populations increased and societies became more complex, it became necessary to keep accurate records. By 3500 B.C., the Babylonians were using clay tablets to record information and to improve communications. About the same time, the Egyptians developed papyrus (a crude type of paper) and the calmus (a sharp pen) for use in recording information.

One of the first calculating devices was the **abacus.** This centuries-old device is still used in the Orient by merchants and businessmen to make mathematical calculations. Although the abacus itself can be regarded as mechanical, mathematical calculations are made by manually manipulating the beads on the wires.

Prior to this century, most data processing was done manually. During the Civil War period in the United States, the main tools used to process data were pens, pencils, rulers, journals, and ledgers.

There are both advantages and disadvantages to processing data manually. One advantage is that changes and corrections can be made quickly and easily. Another is that both the data and the information it creates are in a form that is easily read and understood. A disadvantage of this method is that people frequently make errors while doing mathematical calculations, copying data, or recording information. Also, processing data manually can be slow and time-consuming, particularly when there are large amounts of data. In such cases, the cost of processing the data can be quite high, and sometimes even prohibitive.

Mechanically

If you've ever used a manual typewriter, then you've processed data **mechanically** (by machine). The typewriter was first introduced in the early 1900s. This mechanical recording device increased writing speeds and improved legibility.

Blaise Pascal, a Frenchman, led the way in mechanical processing with his development in 1642 of the first mechanical adding machine, called **Pascal's Calculator.** His machine consisted of gears and teeth. The teeth represented the digits 0 to 9. When a gear rotated past the tooth representing the ninth digit, the next gear to the left would be moved by one tooth to reflect the carry.

In the early 1800s Charles Babbage, an English inventor and mathematician, decided to build a machine that could solve mathematical equations. He designed a model of what he called a **Difference Engine** on paper. He could not complete his machine, however, because the existing technology was not advanced enough to manufacture the gears and other parts of his machine to the specifications required.

Despite his setback, Babbage went on to design the **Analytical Engine,** another mechanical machine capable of performing even more complex mathematical calculations. But like his Difference Engine, this device could not be built because of technological limitations.

After Babbage's death, his son built the Analytical Engine from the plans his father had designed. The device contained the major

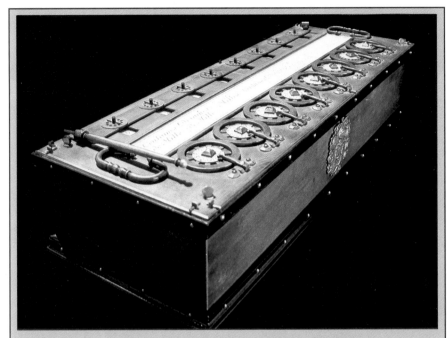

Figure 1–5
Concepts underlying Pascal's Calculator were used in other machines until electronic calculators were introduced in the 1960s.

elements found in modern digital computers: an input device, a processing unit, a control unit, a storage unit, and an output device. Due to these important contributions, Charles Babbage is now recognized as the **"Father of the Computer."**

Devices capable of making calculations and printing the results appeared in the late 1800s. Following World War I, customized accounting machines appeared. Most were designed for specific purposes, such as recording retail sales or calculating a payroll, and they allowed the user to combine processing steps. An example of such a machine is a mechanical cash register capable of summarizing what merchandise is sold each day.

The mechanical method is usually faster and more accurate than the manual method. Machines, however, contain moving parts that can malfunction or break down, and they can require frequent maintenance or repairs.

Figure 1-6
The Analytical Engine contained basic components found in modern computers. For his discoveries, Babbage is recognized as the "Father of the Computer."

Electromechanically

Both mechanical and electronic devices are used to process data **electromechanically.** Unlike a mechanical device, a truly electronic device has no internal moving parts.

Professor Howard Aiken of Harvard University built an electromechanical machine in 1944. This machine, called the **Mark I,** contained both mechanical and electronic parts. Data was stored electronically inside the machine with the use of electromagnetic relays. Mathematical calculations, however, were performed by the machine's internal mechanical counters.

Many modern machines are electromechanical. Most computer printers, for example, contain both mechanical and electronic parts.

Figure 1–7
The Mark I was an automatic calculator, but it was not a computer. It was used by the U.S. Navy until the end of World War II.

Electronically

A computer is an electronic device that contains no internal moving parts. It consists of electronic circuitry carefully designed to allow data to be processed by directing the flow of electricity through the circuitry using tiny "**on**" and "**off**" switches.

Data processed **electronically** is processed quickly and accurately. Consider the electric lighting system in a house. If the wall switch is turned to the "on" position, the circuit is closed, or "on," allowing electricity to flow swiftly through the switch (circuit) along a wire to an overhead light fixture. If the switch is turned to the "off" position, the circuit is opened, or "off," and the light goes out equally as fast. If this procedure were to be repeated thousands of times, the results would be the same each time. A computer, like a wall switch, will do exactly what it is designed to do. This makes a computer a very accurate device for processing data.

The history of electronic data processing is relatively brief. In less than four decades, the computer has revolutionized data processing and has been largely responsible for transforming an industrial and manufacturing society in the United States into one in which the primary end-product is now information.

In 1946, J. Presper Eckert and John W. Mauchly built the first all-electronic computer, called the **ENIAC** (**E**lectronic **N**umerical **I**ntegrator **A**nd **C**alculator). Credit for developing the concept underlying the electronic digital computer, however, belongs to Dr. John Atanasoff, a professor of mathematics and physics at Iowa State College. Earlier, Atanasoff and his assistant, Clifford Berry, built a similar machine called the **ABC** (**A**tanasoff-**B**erry **C**omputer).

In recent years, several technological improvements have resulted in the development of modern digital computers with tremendous capabilities. But many experts believe that the computer age is still in its infancy. We cannot help but wonder what the adult stage will be like.

Figure 1–8
Built by Eckert and Mauchly, the ENIAC was the first general-purpose electronic digital computer. It was used by the U.S. government for a variety of computing tasks.

4. . . .Five characteristics of useful information and the meaning of each?

5. . . .The meaning of the term *GIGO?*

6. . . .Four methods of processing data?

7. . . .The primary historical contributions of Pascal, Babbage, Eckert and Mauchly, and Atanasoff and Berry to data processing?

DO YOU
REMEMBER

The Information Processing Cycle

Regardless of the method used, all information processing follows the same basic **information processing cycle,** shown in Figure 1–9. When using a computer, data must first be **input,** or entered, into the computer where it is then processed into information. After **processing,** the resulting information is obtained via an **output** device, such as a monitor or printer. The information may also be **stored** for future use.

In the following sections, specific activities involved in inputting, processing, and outputting data are explained.

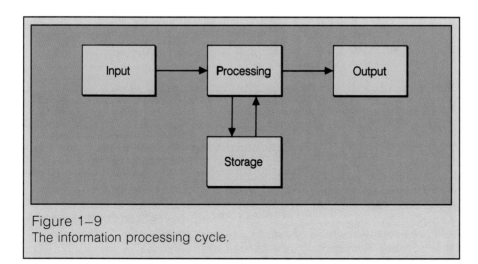

Figure 1–9
The information processing cycle.

Input

Input is data that is entered into the information processing cycle for processing. Inputting data involves three important activities: (1) the data must be collected; (2) its accuracy must be verified; and (3) it must be coded before it is put into the computer.

Sometimes data must be gathered from several sources, as when employee timecards must be collected from various locations in a plant. This assembling of the data at the location where it is put into the computer is called **collecting.**

Data is checked for accuracy and completeness. This is called **verifying** the data. Remember that inaccurate data results in inaccurate information from the computer.

Before data can be entered into the computer, it must be **coded** in a form that can be processed by the computer because a computer cannot understand English. Computers require that instructions and data be in **machine language** form, explained later in Chapter 3.

Processing

After these activities have been completed, the data is put into the computer for processing. The data can then be processed by one or more of the following activities.

Data can be **classified** according to certain characteristics so it will be meaningful to the user. For example, student data can be grouped according to freshman, sophomore, junior, or senior status.

Data is often **sorted** on the basis of some predetermined sequence. For example, student names can be sorted alphabetically to make it easier to locate a particular student name on a class roster.

THE COMPUTER DIDN'T DO IT!

Clara Muse was delighted when she received her paycheck last Wednesday and discovered that her paycheck was for much more than she expected. Rather than the usual amount of $188.25, her paycheck was for $1882.50. When she arrived home from work, she received a telephone call from a clerk in the company's payroll office. Clara was informed that the clerk had made an error while keying payroll data into the computer. She had keyed the decimal point into the wrong position. Clara was told that all employees were being asked to return their paychecks and that new correct paychecks would be distributed after the incorrect ones were returned.

Data can also be manipulated arithmetically and/or logically. This is called **calculating.** Students' grade-point averages can be calculated, for example.

Sometimes users need to put large amounts of data into a more concise and usable form. **Summarizing** eliminates unnecessary data. A sales manager, for example, might need a report of each salesperson's monthly sales total. For this report, daily sales data is eliminated thereby making the report more concise and useful to the sales manager.

Data can be saved or stored for future use on a secondary storage medium as magnetic tape, magnetic disk, or microfilm. The user decides if the data is important enough to **store.**

Output

Output is what is obtained after the data has been processed. The output is made available to the user. Three activities involved in the output phase of the information cycle are retrieving, converting, and communicating.

The computer user can **retrieve** any processed or stored information via an output device. Any one of several output devices may be used, such as a monitor or a printer.

Usually, people cannot use information in the form in which it is stored in a computer. The stored information must first be **converted** into a form that people can understand and use, like alphabetic and numeric English characters.

To be useful, information must be available to the user when it is needed. Otherwise, it could be useless. The information must be **communicated.**

A computer can perform numerous processing activities on the data quickly and accurately. Thus, a computer is a valuable machine for a wide variety of processing applications.

Processing data electronically is rapidly becoming one of the most important and popular methods, largely because of the speed and accuracy with which computers process data. And, too, the declining cost of computers is making them more affordable to more potential users.

During the past three decades, millions of computers have been purchased by individuals, businesses, and institutions. Today, computers are being used in virtually every segment of our society for thousands of different applications. Many of these applications are examined in other parts of this book. One such application is this book itself. The authors used small computers for word processing when they prepared this work because computers are faster and more efficient than typewriters.

Storage

Programs and data are often stored on a secondary storage medium. When needed, the programs and/or data can be entered into the computer for processing. After processing, the programs and new data can be stored in secondary storage. Programs that are purchased from a software vendor, for example, are often contained on a diskette. These programs are loaded into the computer from the diskette by using a disk drive.

This book focuses on the use of computers as an increasingly important means of processing data and on the people who use them. In the broadest sense, everyone is a **computer user,** including people who use only computer output. After studying the contents of this book, you'll agree that computers are changing the ways in which we think and do our work.

DO YOU REMEMBER

8. . . .The main steps in the information processing cycle?

9. . . .Specific activities that can be included in the input phase of the information processing cycle?

10. . . .Specific activities that can be performed in the processing phase of the information processing cycle?

11. . . .Specific activities that can be performed in the output phase of the information processing cycle?

Summary

(This summary provides answers to DO YOU REMEMBER . . . questions in the chapter.)

1. Why is information important?
Information is important because every individual needs infor-

mation to help him or her make wise decisions and to perform daily activities.

2. **What are some specific groups of people who need and use information?**
Specific groups that need information include *students, farmers,* and *businesspeople.* Actually, everyone needs and uses information regularly.

3. **What is the difference between *information* and *data?***
Information is knowledge we use to make decisions and is based on data that has been processed into information. *Data* are merely unprocessed facts. In situations where single pieces of data are useful in decision making, data can actually be information.

4. **What are the five characteristics of useful information, and what is the meaning of each characteristic?**
The five characteristics of useful information are completeness, conciseness, accuracy, timeliness, and relevancy. Information is *complete* when nothing is missing. It is *concise* when unnecessary data, words, and sentences are eliminated. Information is *accurate* when it is free of errors, and *relevant* when all the information is related directly to what is needed by the user. Finally, information is *timely* when the user receives it when it is needed.

5. **What is the meaning of the term *GIGO?***
GIGO is an acronym for Garbage-In, Garbage-Out. This acronym points out that if incorrect data (garbage) is entered into a computer for processing, the output will also be incorrect (garbage).

6. **What are the four methods of processing data?**
Data can be processed *manually, mechanically, electromechanically,* and *electronically.*

7. **What were the primary historical contributions of Pascal, Babbage, Eckert and Mauchly, and Atanasoff and Berry to data processing?**
Pascal developed the first mechanical calculator, called *Pascal's Calculator,* in 1642. In the early 1800s, Babbage designed the *Difference Engine,* a device capable of solving mathematical equations. Later, he designed the *Analytical Engine,* which contained the major elements found in modern digital computers. For his contributions, Babbage is recognized as the *Father of the Computer.* Eckert and Mauchly built the first all-electronic computer, called the *ENIAC* (Electronic Numerical Integrator and Calculator). Atanasoff and Berry are credited with developing the

concept underlying the electronic digital computer in their *ABC* (Atanasoff-Berry Computer).

8. **What are the main steps in the information processing cycle?**
   The main steps in the *information processing cycle* are *input, processing,* and *output.* A fourth step, *storage,* is included in the cycle because users often need to store information for future use.

9. **What specific activities can be included in the input phase of the information processing cycle?**
   Specific activities in the *input* phase are *collecting, verifying,* and *coding* the data for entry into a computer.

10. **What specific activities can be included in the processing phase of the information processing cycle?**
    Activities included in the *processing* phase are *classifying, sorting, calculating, summarizing,* and *storing* data.

DATA PROCESSING CAREER . . . .
SERVICE AND REPAIR TECHNICIAN

CAREER OPPORTUNITY FOR COMPUTER PROFESSIONAL

JOB TITLE:
Service and Repair Technician

JOB DESCRIPTION:
Computer equipment manufacturer is now hiring persons willing to train to service and repair computer equipment, including microcomputers, CRTs, monitors, printers, disk drives, and other computer peripherals. The person hired will work with other trained repair and service personnel at the company's local repair and service center. Some travel required but most work done in-house. Applicants must agree to take a series of examinations to determine aptitude for employment in electronics.

EXPERIENCE REQUIRED:
None

EDUCATION REQUIRED:
A high school diploma or technical school certificate

PERSONAL QUALIFICATIONS:
Applicants must be quality-conscious, dependable, career-minded, and customer-oriented, and must enjoy working with others.

11. **What specific activities can be included in the processing phase of the information processing cycle?**

Activities involved in the *output* phase are *retrieving, converting,* and *communicating* the information to the user.

Key Terms

Abacus	ENIAC
Accurate	GIGO
Howard Aiken	Information
Analytical Engine	Information processing cycle
John Atanasoff	Input
Charles Babbage	Manually
Clifford Berry	Mark I
Calculating	John W. Mauchly
Classifying	Output
Coding	Blaise Pascal
Collecting	Pascal's Calculator
Communicating	Processing
Complete	Relevant
Computer user	Retrieve
Concise	Sorting
Converting	Store
Data	Storing
Difference Engine	Summarizing
J. Presper Eckert	Timely
Electromechanically	Verifying
Electronically	

Test Yourself

1. Information is important because it enables us to make wise _____ and to function more effectively in our everyday lives.

2. _____ are unprocessed facts, whereas _____ is useful to us in decision making.

3. To be useful, information must be _____ ,
_____ , _____ , _____ , and
_____ .

4. Four methods of processing data are _____ ,
_____ , _____ , and _____ .

5. The steps in the information processing cycle are _____ ,
_____ , _____ , and _____ .

6. Activities in the input phase of the information processing
cycle are _____ , _____ , and _____ .

7. Activities in the processing phase of the information processing
cycle are _____ , _____ , _____ ,
_____ , and _____ .

8. Activities in the output phase of the information processing
cycle are _____ , _____ , and _____ .

9. The first mechanical calculator, called _____ , was
built in 1642 by a Frenchman named _____ .

10. _____ is recognized as the "Father of the Computer."

Review Questions

1. Why is information important, and what are some specific groups
that need and use information? (Learning Objective 2)

2. What is the difference between *information* and *data*. Can you
think of situations in which they are the same? (Learning
Objective 3)

3. What are the characteristics of good (useful) information? (Learning Objective 4)

4. Describe the four methods of processing information. Why is the
electronic method so widely used today? (Learning Objective 5)

5. What are the phases in the basic information processing cycle?
(Learning Objective 6)

6. Identify the main activities in each phase of the information processing cycle. (Learning Objective 7)

7. Can you think of any devices today that operate on the same
principle as did Pascal's Calculator? (Learning Objective 8)

Activities

1. Make a list of information you need to function effectively (1) as a student, (2) in your daily activities outside school, and (3) in your work if you have a job. List the information in order of importance.

2. Talk with one, or both, of your parents. Make a list of information they need in their work and how the information is obtained, such as (1) from a computer, (2) by using a calculator, and/or (3) from a manager or another employee.

3. Visit a business in your area that uses a computer to process data. Find out what kinds of information the business receives from the computer. Share the information you learn with others in your class.

4. Find out if there is a store in your area that uses computer terminals to place orders. If there is, describe how the system works, and list the steps in placing an order.

5. In the text, four methods for processing data were explained. Using these four methods as headings, list the data you frequently need to have processed under the method that would probably be the most appropriate to use.

6. Visit a fast food restaurant in your area that uses computer terminals to place orders. How are these terminals different from the one Marilyn Allison used? How are they the same?

CHAPTER 2
History of Information Processing

Learning Objectives

After studying this chapter carefully, you will be able to:

1. Define key terms introduced in this chapter.

2. Identify the primary contribution(s) of John Napier, Gottfried von Liebnitz, and Joseph Jacquard to the field of computing.

3. Identify the primary contribution(s) of Herman Hollerith, Ada Augusta Byron, and George Boole to the field of computing.

4. Explain why John von Neumann's *stored-program concept* became an important contribution to the field of computing.

5. Identify the primary contribution(s) of Grace Hopper to the field of computing.

6. Identify when each of the four computer generations started and ended, and the primary development that began each generation.

7. Identify the primary developments that occurred in each computer generation.

Chapter Outline

EARLY CONTRIBUTIONS TO COMPUTING
John Napier
Gottfried von Liebnitz
Joseph Marie Jacquard
Herman Hollerith
Ada Augusta Byron
George Boole
John von Neumann
Alan Mathison Turing
Grace Murray Hopper

CONTRIBUTIONS OF THE SPACE AGE

COMPUTER GENERATIONS
First Generation (1951–1958)
Second Generation (1959–1964)
Third Generation (1964–1971)
Fourth Generation (1971–Present)

DATA PROCESSING CAREER: Computer Store Manager Trainee

Application

Towards the end of class, Elaine's computer science teacher told the students to read and study the next chapter in the textbook on the history of data processing. When the class ended, Elaine questioned the importance of the assignment. She wanted to learn more about computers and how to use them. So she suggested that class and study time be used for these purposes instead of for learning history.

"Electronic data processing is a relatively new field," responded her teacher. "In the next chapter, you will learn how people have always sought to discover better methods for processing data, and how several of them devoted their lives to making these discoveries. Learning about these discoveries and the people who made them, helps us understand modern computers and their use. A knowledge of the history of computing can also help us see into the future of computing."

Not totally convinced, Elaine departed for her next class. While reading the assignment that afternoon, she began to see how the history of computing was filled with interesting personalities and fascinating discoveries. She also began to understand how and why modern computers came into existence. Now, she could even begin to envision potential future developments and the impact they might have on society.

Summarizing the importance of studying history, someone once said, "How can we know where we're going if we don't know where we've been." This statement certainly applies to the broad field of electronic information processing. Modern computers did not emerge overnight. Instead, these important machines are the result of technological improvements in earlier devices. Learning about these earlier devices and the people who built them will help us understand how modern computers evolved and why we now find ourselves in what is sometimes called the *information age.*

Early Contributions to Computing

Throughout history people have recorded information. Cave dwellers made drawings of animals, other people, and events on their walls. Historians have learned a great deal about earlier civilizations from these drawings.

Figure 2–1
There is evidence that members of earlier societies recorded information by making drawings on walls.

History teaches that innovations and discoveries result from specific human needs. Indeed, as society became more complex and the need for information increased, better devices and methods for recording and processing data were discovered. And in the past several decades the development of computational machines has been extremely rapid. Some of these developments were identified in Chapter 1. This chapter highlights other important discoveries that contributed to the development of modern electronic information processing.

John Napier

Mathematical discoveries played an important part in the history of the computer. In the sixteenth century, a Scottish mathematician named John Napier discovered an easier way to multiply and divide numbers faster and more accurately. He did this by developing a new method for representing numbers, called **logarithms**. He then went on to invent a device consisting of ivory rods on which the logarithms of numbers were placed. This device was known as **Napier's Bones**. By sliding the "bones" up and down, multiplications and divisions could be performed. Later, in 1630, William Oughtred made improvements to Napier's Bones and developed the **slide rule,** a calculating device still in use today. These inventions represent the development of crude but effective manual calculators.

Figure 2–2
Napier's Bones was a device consisting of logarithms placed on sliding ivory rods. By sliding the "bones" up and down, calculations could be made.

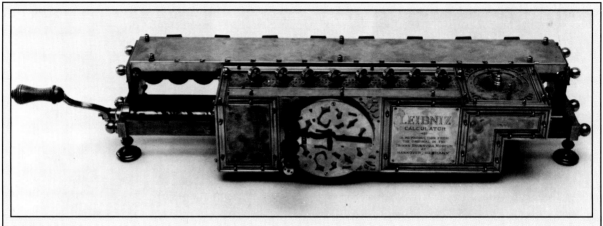

Figure 2–3
Gottfried von Liebnitz's calculator, called the Stepped Reckoner, could multiply, divide, and extract square roots. It proved unreliable, but its underlying concepts were included in later, more reliable machines.

Gottfried von Leibnitz

Gottfried von Leibnitz, a German mathematician, was working in Paris when Pascal's calculating machine (see Chapter 1) caught his interest. From 1671 to 1694, he worked on a machine that was more advanced than Pascal's earlier model. He called his invention the **Stepped Reckoner.** Unlike Pascal's machine that could only count, Liebnitz's Reckoner could also multiply, divide, and extract square roots.

The Stepped Reckoner, however, proved unreliable, and it was not until 1820 that machines capable of adding, subtracting, multiplying, and dividing became commercially available. Many of Liebnitz's ideas were included in these later machines.

Joseph Marie Jacquard

In 1805, the French inventor Joseph Marie Jacquard developed a method for controlling the operation of a weaving loom by using punched cards. With holes punched in specific locations on the cards, a weaving loom could be "programmed" to weave certain patterns in cloth fabric in predetermined colors. His weaving device, called **Jacquard's Loom,** proved to be quite successful. By the early 1900s, the French textile industry had been revolutionized with thousands of these Looms in use. Many of the descendants of the Jacquard Loom are still in use today.

Jacquard's device was one of the first inventions applied directly to industrial production. Previous inventions had been designed primarily to make mathematical calculations easier and faster. For his invention, Jacquard was recognized by Napoleon and given a reward.

The importance of Jacquard's discoveries to computer systems is enormous. His punched card was the forerunner of the modern punched card later developed by Herman Hollerith. Charles Babbage (see Chapter 1) adapted Jacquard's punched-card system for his calculating machine which was the forerunner of the modern computer.

Figure 2–4
Jacquard's Loom used cards with holes punched in them to direct the weaving of fabric with certain patterns and colors.

Herman Hollerith

It has been said that "necessity is the mother of invention." This was certainly the case with **Herman Hollerith** in the late 1800s.

Although Jacquard had used punched cards with his weaving loom, the use of punched cards for processing data went relatively unnoticed until the late 1800s. Prior to the 1890 census, the U.S. Census Bureau manually tabulated census data collected every ten years. Faced with a rapidly growing national population, it became evident that a more efficient method for tabulating the census data would have to be found. The Bureau commissioned Dr. Herman Hollerith, an employee, to devise this more efficient system.

The system he created included the invention of an electromechanical machine, called the **Tabulating Machine,** which was activated by punched cards. Holes punched in the cards represented vital statistics. As the cards were fed through the machine, simple additions

Figure 2–5
Hollerith's Tabulating Machine used punched cards and a special code for punching holes in the cards to tabulate U.S. Census data in the late 1800s.

and sortings could be made and the census tabulations completed. Using Hollerith's system, completion of the census tabulations was reduced from eight years to about two and one-half years. The card he designed became known as the **Hollerith card,** sometimes called the **80-column** card. The code for punching holes in the cards became known as the **Hollerith code.** Both the card and code are still in use today.

Hollerith left the Census Bureau and, in 1911, founded a company called the Tabulating Machine Company. Soon afterwards, this company and two others merged to become International Business Machines Corporation (IBM).

Ada Augusta Byron

Ada Augusta Byron, the Countess of Lovelace and daughter of the poet Lord Byron, was a gifted mathematician. At age twenty-seven, she went to work with Charles Babbage who was working on his Analytical Engine (see Chapter 1).

Figure 2–6
For her work with Charles Babbage on his machines, Lady Ada Augusta Byron has become known as the "world's first programmer."

Although Charles Babbage's Analytical Engine was never built, Lady Byron wrote a demonstration program for it as part of an English translation of a technical paper about the engine. By preparing the instructions needed to carry out computations on the machine, Ada Augusta Byron became the "world's first programmer." A **programmer** is a person who writes a series of step-by-step instructions (a program) for a computer to execute.

Lady Byron's translation, the only one of her papers to be saved, was the best description of the computer to be written in almost a hundred years. Through her writings, an understanding of the Analytical Engine has been preserved into the twentieth century. For her work, the U.S. Department of Defense named a new computer language "Ada" in her honor.

George Boole

One of the most important features of modern computers is their ability to perform complex mathematical calculations. This was made possible by the contributions of George Boole. He developed a system of mathematical logic which eventually led to the design of electronic computers and which is still used in the design of modern computers today.

Figure 2–7
George Boole developed a system of mathematical logic that came to be known as Boolean algebra in his honor.

Boole is not well known outside the computing field. However, his name is a household word among computer scientists and mathematicians.

---

1. . . .Two important contributions of John Napier to the field of computing?

2. . . .The primary contribution of Gottfried von Liebnitz?

3. . . .The developments of Joseph Jacquard that revolutionized the French textile industry?

4. . . .The primary contributions of Herman Hollerith to computing?

5. . . .Why Ada Augusta Byron is recognized as the world's first programmer?

6. . . .George Boole's primary contribution to the development of computers?

John von Neumann

John von Neumann, one of the greatest mathematicians of the twentieth century, was born in Hungary in 1903. His brilliance quickly became apparent when he began reading Greek and Latin at age five, and practicing calculus at age eight. At age twenty-seven, he joined the faculty at Princeton University.

In 1945, he proposed an idea for a computer that could be programmed internally. This idea came too late to be built into the ENIAC (Chapter 1). However, recognizing the importance of **stored-program** capability built into a computer, in 1949 Eckert and Mauchly built another machine, the Electronic Discrete Variable Automatic Computer (the EDVAC), capable of accepting and storing a set of instructions. This meant that computer instructions could be stored in the computer and reused to process different data. The stored program enabled the computer to be ''self-directing,'' thereby requiring no human operator to guide each step in processing the data. Prior to this time, programs were contained externally on wired control panels or punched cards. By having the programs in the computer, instructions could be manipulated and modified by machine commands.

Figure 2-8
John von Neumann and the EDVAC.

Alan Mathison Turing

Alan Turing, born in London in 1912, was one of the most creative of the computer scientists. From his early years, Turing was keenly interested in mathematics and science. By age twenty-three, he had begun work on mathematical logic, an investigation of computable numbers, and a device called the Turing Machine. He spent several years at Princeton University working on his ideas with John von Neumann and other distinguished mathematicians.

Turing spent a major portion of his life trying to determine whether machines could think. Believing that machines do think, in 1947 he designed the **Turing Machine**. It simulated thinking by playing a single move in a chess game, thereby proving that machines can perform deductive analysis by solving mathematical equations and making logical decisions.

Figure 2–9
Alan Turing designed a machine called the Turing Machine which was capable of simulating human thinking.

Grace Murray Hopper

After receiving a doctorate degree from Yale University in 1934, Grace Hopper entered the United States Navy where she learned to program the first large-scale digital computer, the Mark I. In 1949 she joined, as Senior Mathematician, the Eckert-Mauchly Computer Corporation (later to become Sperry Corporation) which was then in the process of building the UNIVAC I, the first commercial large-scale electronic computer.

Hopper was an early pioneer in the field of computer languages. She is credited with writing the first practical compiler program and was a leader in the development of the COBOL programming language. A **compiler** is a set of instructions that translate a computer program into a language that can be executed by a computer. **COBOL,** an acronym for *Common Business-Oriented Language*, is a computer language used by programmers primarily for writing computer programs for business applications. Hopper is sometimes referred to affectionately as ''Grandma COBOL.''

Figure 2–10
Rear Admiral Grace Hopper, now retired, was instrumental in developing the first practical compiler and the COBOL language.

For her many contributions, Grace Hopper is recognized as a leader and major contributor to the field of electronic data processing and was promoted to the rank of Commodore by President Reagan. She recently retired from the Navy with the rank of Rear Admiral. Her insight, wisdom, and expertise in computer software make her a popular lecturer and consultant throughout the world.

Contributions of the Space Age

During his 1960 Inaugural Address, President John F. Kennedy declared that by the end of the decade the United States would put an astronaut on the moon. As a result of that commitment, billions of dollars were immediately poured into technological research and development. Small computers would be needed to monitor activities in the spacecraft and to guide the vehicle to its destination.

Much of the technical knowledge gained from the space program has been used by private companies and individuals to improve computer hardware and software. Some of the more recent developments in the history of computing are overviewed in Table 2–1.

Table 2–1
Summary of Recent Developments in Computing Technology

Year	Development
1958	Jack Kilby, an engineer at Texas Instruments, develops and introduces the integrated circuit (IC).
1958	John McCarthy creates the programming language LISP. He also developed *interactive computing* and coined the term *artificial intelligence*.
1964	John Kemeny and Thomas Kurtz developed the BASIC programming language, an easy-to-learn and easy-to-use language.
1965	The first "minicomputer" is developed by Digital Equipment Corporation.
1967	Professor Seymour Papert of MIT introduces LOGO, a computer language sometimes used by students in learning geometry.
1968	Niklaus Wirth creates Pascal, a highly structured programming language taught at all grade levels.
1971	Ted Hoff of Intel Corporation designs the first "microprocessor."
1974	The Altair 8800, the first microcomputer, is offered for sale (in kit form).
1977	Commodore PET microcomputer is introduced by Jack Tramiel of Commodore International, Ltd.
1977	Steve Jobs and Steve Wozniak form Apple Computer, Inc., and introduce the Apple II microcomputer.
1977	Radio Shack Division of Tandy Corporation releases the TRS-80 microcomputer.
1980	Seymour Cray of Cray Research, Inc., introduces the Cray-1, the world's first supercomputer.
1981	IBM enters the personal computer market with the IBM–PC.
1984	The Seiko DATA 2000, world's first wrist computer, is introduced by Seiko.

THE COMPUTER DIDN'T DO IT!

Confusion abounded last Tuesday among employees at Gates' Building Supply Company as clerks had to visually check each item ordered by a customer to determine if the item was in stock.

Two months ago, Gates' installed a new computerized sales/inventory system to improve service. Using one of the newly installed terminals, a clerk could simply enter a product stock number into his or her terminal. Almost instantly, information about the product would be displayed on the terminal monitor, including product description, price, and the quantity remaining in inventory. However, this was not the case last Tuesday. While updating the computer program the previous evening, a programmer accidentally deleted the current inventory field in each product record stored in the computer.

DO YOU REMEMBER

7. . . .The importance of John von Neumann's stored-program concept to modern computing?

8. . . .Alan Turing's belief and the machine he designed to test the validity of his belief?

9. . . .Grace Hopper's primary contribution to the field of computing?

10. . . .Important discoveries made by the space program during the 1960s and 1970s that contributed greatly to modern computing technology?

Computer Generations

The first part of this chapter dealt with important discoveries that led to the development of modern computers and with the people responsible for them. These discoveries did not occur by accident. They were the result of years of planned research and work by individuals seeking to find better ways to solve problems by processing data more efficiently.

Many advancements have been made in computer technology over the years. These advancements are often classified into four categories or, as they are generally called, **computer generations**.

First Generation (1951–1958)

The first generation of computers began with the introduction of the UNIVAC I in 1951. First generation computers used large numbers of vacuum tubes that required substantial amounts of power and generated tremendous heat. These computers were large and heavy and often required difficult repairs. They were expensive to operate, and only the largest business firms could afford them.

Magnetic drum was used for internal storage. Internal storage capacity was limited. These computers were capable of performing calculations in milliseconds. A **millisecond** is one-thousandth (1/1,000) of a second. To perform one million calculations on these computers cost almost $200.

Second Generation (1959–1964)

The development of solid-state **transistors** ushered in the second generation of computers. Transistors were smaller, faster, and more powerful than vacuum tubes. They required less power, generated less heat, and were only about one-fiftieth the size of the vacuum tubes they replaced.

Magnetic core replaced magnetic drum as the primary internal storage medium. Secondary storage devices and media, such as magnetic tape and magnetic disk, were introduced during the second generation.

Several high-level programming languages, including FORTRAN and COBOL, were developed. With the use of punched cards, batch processing began.

With second generation computers, calculating speeds increased by a thousand times! These speeds were now measured in microseconds. A **microsecond** is one-millionth (1/1,000,000) of a second.

Primary storage capacity increased. The cost per million calculations decreased to about $16.

Third Generation (1964–1971)

The third generation began with the introduction of the IBM 360 series of computers. This generation of computers used integrated circuitry, called ICs, which were smaller, faster, and less expensive than the solid-state transistors of the second generation.

Computer manufacturers began developing and selling software programs with their computers. New companies emerged that specialized in developing and selling software programs to computer owners.

Communications channels were developed providing for remote input/output capabilities. This made it possible to use terminals at remote locations to communicate with the computer.

Calculating speeds were now measured in nanoseconds. A **nanosecond** is a billionth (1,000,000,000) of a second. As a result, calculating costs declined to less than $3 per million calculations.

Fourth Generation (1971–Present)

Most computer professionals agree that we are now in the fourth generation of computers that began in 1971 with the IBM 370 series of computers. Modern computers use large-scale integrated circuitry (LSICs). These LSICs are actually thousands of microscopic transistors densely packed on a silicon chip. As a result, modern computers have more storage capacity, are smaller, faster, and more reliable. Computing speeds are now measured in nanoseconds and, for some computers, picoseconds. A **picosecond** is a trillionth (1,000,000,000,000) of a second.

The development of LSICs made microprocessors and microcomputers possible. A **microprocessor** consists of miniature integrated

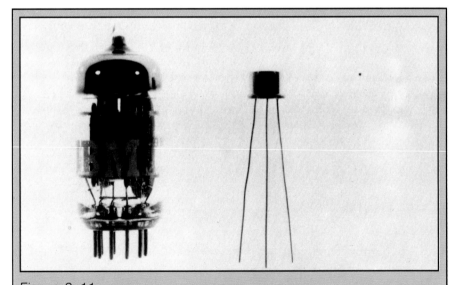

Figure 2–11
(Left) A vacuum tube from a first-generation computer. (center) A transistor from a second-generation computer. (right) A computer chip used in modern computers. Sizes shown are for comparison.

circuits on a silicon chip. A **microcomputer** is a small, highly specialized computer. Its main component is one or more microprocessors that make the design of these small computers possible.

Large modern computers have greatly increased storage capacity to 50 million bytes and more. In computing, the term **byte** means an alphabetic character, a number, or a special character such as a dollar sign ($). Calculating costs have dropped to about ten cents per million calculations. This is quite inexpensive when compared to an estimated cost of about $12,000 to perform one million calculations manually.

During each of the four generations, many important advances were made. Table 2–2 summarizes some of the more significant ones.

Table 2–2
Summary of Advancements in Computer Technology by Generation

	First Generation	Second Generation	Third Generation	Fourth Generation
Hardware	Vacuum tubes	Transistors	Integrated circuits	Large-scale integrated circuitry
	Magnetic drum storage	Core storage	Semiconductor storage	Bubble memory, laser storage, LSIC chips
		Secondary storage (tape and disk)		
Other Technology	Stored programs and machine language	High-level programming languages (FORTRAN and COBOL)	Other high-level languages developed	Microprocessors and microcomputers
Speed	Milliseconds	Microseconds	Nanoseconds	Picoseconds
Calculations Per Second	3,000	12,000	43,000	900,000,000
Cost per Million Calculations	$200	$18	$3	.10

DO YOU
REMEMBER

11. . . .Important developments made during the first generation?

12. . . .Important developments made during the second generation?

13. . . .Important developments made during the third generation?

14. . . .Important developments made during the fourth generation?

Summary

(This summary provides answers to DO YOU REMEMBER . . . questions in the chapter.)

1. **Name two important contributions of John Napier to the field of computing.**

   John Napier's first contribution to the field of computing was his discovery of *logarithms*. This new method made it possible to multiply and divide numbers by simply adding and subtracting representations of the numbers in geometrical series. Napier then placed these logarithms on a set of ivory rods called *Napier's Bones*. Multiplications and divisions could then be done by sliding the rods up and down. Napier's contributions later led to the invention of the slide rule, a device still in use today.

2. **What was the primary contribution of Gottfried von Liebnitz?**

   Gottfried von Liebnitz's main contribution was his *Stepped Reckoner*. Unlike Pascal's Calculator, which could only add, Liebnitz's Stepped Reckoner could also multiply, divide, and extract square roots.

3. **What were Joseph Jacquard's developments that revolutionized the French textile industry?**

   Jacquard designed and built a weaving device called *Jacquard's Loom*, and a method for controlling its operation using punched cards. By punching holes in specific locations on the cards, and "feeding" these cards through his loom, certain patterns could be woven in the cloth in predetermined colors.

4. **What were the primary contributions of Herman Hollerith to computing?**

Herman Hollerith, an employee of the U.S. Census Bureau, developed a *coding method* for storing census data on *punched cards*. To tabulate the census data punched into the cards, he designed and built a *machine* that could "read" data recorded on the cards and process the data. His discoveries greatly reduced the time required to tabulate census data.

5. **Why is Ada Augusta Byron recognized as the world's first programmer?**

   Ada Augusta Byron gained recognition as the world's first programmer through the *instructions* she wrote for Charles Babbage's Analytical Engine. These instructions enabled the machine to perform mathematical calculations.

6. **What was George Boole's primary contribution to the development of computers?**

   George Boole designed a *system of mathematical logic* used in computers today.

7. **What was the importance of John von Neumann's stored-program concept to modern computing?**

   John von Neumann's stored-program concept was incorporated into modern computers which meant that these computers were capable of accepting and storing a set of reusable instructions to process different data without human intervention.

8. **What did Alan Turing believe and what machine did he design to prove the validity of his belief?**

   Alan Turing believed that it was possible to design and build a machine (a computer) that could *think*. He built the *Turing Machine*, a machine that simulated thinking by playing a single move in a chess game.

9. **What was Grace Hopper's primary contribution to the field of computing?**

   Although Rear Admiral Grace Hopper has made several contributions to computing, probably the most important is the first practical *compiler* program she wrote for the COBOL language. She was also instrumental in the development of the *COBOL language* itself.

10. **What were the more important discoveries made by the space program during the 1960s and 1970s that contributed greatly to modern computing technology?**

   During the space program of the 1960s and 1970s, *large-scale integrated circuits* (LSICs) were developed. These led to the development of *microprocessors* and, ultimately, to the development of *microcomputers*.

11. What were some important developments made during the first generation?

During the first generation, computers capable of *storing programs* were developed. *Magnetic drums* were also developed for storage of instructions and data.

12. What were some important developments made during the second generation?

During the second generation, small, powerful *transistors* replaced first-generation vacuum tubes, *magnetic core storage* was developed for internal storage, *magnetic tape* and *magnetic disk* were developed for secondary storage, and the *FORTRAN* and *COBOL* languages were developed.

13. What were some important developments made during the third generation?

During the third generation, *integrated circuits* (ICs) and *semi-*

DATA PROCESSING CAREER. . . . .
COMPUTER STORE MANAGER TRAINEE

CAREER OPPORTUNITY FOR COMPUTER PROFESSIONAL

JOB TITLE:
Computer Store Manager Trainee

JOB DESCRIPTION:
National computer store chain is seeking qualified applicants who are willing to undergo intensive on-the-job training in all aspects of retail computer store management. Training will include sales, product merchandising, record-keeping procedures, ordering, and employee relations and management. Also, employee will receive training in hardware and software technology and usage. Success can lead to a position as store manager at a location determined by the company.

EXPERIENCE REQUIRED:
Experience in sales desirable but not required.

EDUCATION REQUIRED:
Applicant should have a college degree in a computer-related field. Courses in accounting, management, and marketing helpful.

PERSONAL QUALIFICATIONS:
Applicant should be aggressive and career-minded. Good communications skills essential. Applicant should be well-groomed, self-motivated, enthusiastic, and well-organized.

conductor storage were developed. Several other computer languages were developed during this period.

14. **What were some important developments made during the fourth generation?**

The primary developments during the fourth generation included *large-scale integrated circuitry, microprocessors* and *microcomputers, bubble memory,* and *laser storage.*

Key Terms

George Boole
Ada Augusta Byron
byte
COBOL
compiler
computer generation
EDVAC
Herman Hollerith
Hollerith card
Hollerith code
Grace Murray Hopper
integrated circuit (IC)
Joseph Marie Jacquard
Gottfried von Leibnitz
Jacquard's Loom
logarithms
large-scale integrated circuit
    (LSIC)

microsecond
millisecond
nanosecond
John Napier
Napier's Bones
John von Neumann
picosecond
programmer
slide rule
stored-program concept
Stepped Reckoner
Tabulating Machine
transistor
Alan Mathison Turing
Turing Machine

Test Yourself

1. A crude, but effective calculating device in which logarithms were placed on a set of ivory rods was called _____ .

2. An early computer pioneer whose weaving loom revolutionized the textile industry was _____ .

3. In the late 1800s, _____ developed a system for tabulating census data which included a machine, punched cards, and a method for punching holes in the cards.

4. The person who is generally recognized as the world's first programmer is _____ .

5. _____ developed a system of mathematical logic used in modern computers.

6. John von Neumann's major contribution to modern computing was his _____ concept.

7. A machine called the _____ simulated thinking by playing a single chess move in a chess game.

8. Grace Murray Hopper was instrumental in developing the first practical compiler and the _____ language.

9. A computer _____ is a period during which significant improvements were made in technology.

10. First-generation computers used _____ which required large amounts of power and generated tremendous amounts of heat.

11. The FORTRAN and COBOL languages were developed during the _____ computer generation.

12. The second computer generation began with the development and introduction of solid-state _____ .

13. Integrated circuits (ICs) were introduced during the _____ computer generation.

14. _____ -generation computers use LSICs which are thousands of microscopic transistors densely packed on a silicon chip.

15. The development of LSICs made the development of microprocessors and _____ possible.

Review Questions

1. What was the primary contribution of each of the following individuals to the field of computing? (Learning Objectives 2 and 3)

a. John Napier   d. Herman Hollerith
b. Gottfried von Liebnitz   e. Ada Augusta Byron
c. Joseph Marie Jacquard   f. George Boole

2. Explain how Jacquard's method for controlling the operation of his weaving loom revolutionized the French weaving industry. (Learning Objective 2)

3. Discuss the importance of storing instructions internally in a computer. How would a stored program be important to a computer user? (Learning Objective 4)

4. Discuss the primary contributions of Grace Hopper to the field of computing. (Learning Objective 5)

5. On what dates did each of the four computer generations begin and end, and what were the primary developments that occurred in each generation? (Learning Objectives 6 and 7)

Activities

1. Prepare a written report about someone who made an important contribution to the field of computing. Include in your report detailed information about the person and his or her contribution.

2. In addition to those mentioned in the chapter, several other people have made significant contributions to computing. Use your school or community library to prepare a report about one such individual.

3. Important new products are still being introduced in the computer market. Use current magazines or journals to find a newly introduced computer product. Prepare a written report about the product you select and tell why you think this product will prove valuable to computer users.

4. Use the information in the "Early Contributions to Computing" section of this chapter to prepare a written table showing the individual making the contribution, his or her contribution, and the year or approximate time the contribution was made. The table you prepare can be turned in as a project and/or serve as a study reference.

PART II
Computer Hardware: Components and Functions

CHAPTER 3

The Electronic Computer

Learning Objectives

After studying this chapter carefully, you will be able to:

1. Identify the key terms introduced in the chapter.

2. Identify computer classifications.

3. Define what a digital computer is and is not.

4. Identify characteristics of digital computers.

5. Identify the advantages and disadvantages of a digital computer.

6. Identify and define the components of the central processing unit.

7. Identify the types of primary storage.

8. Identify how data is represented in an electronic computer.

9. Identify computer input and output types and processes.

10. Identify the four categories of computer systems.

Chapter Outline

Application

Several years ago, a college president remarked that he didn't understand all the attention that was being paid to computers. He pointed out that he had been president of that college for fourteen years, and that the college's graduates had always found good jobs after graduating. He went on to say that many former students were presently in top-level executive positions in business and government and in other organizations throughout the world. He offered his opinion that computers were just an expensive fad. He expressed his disapproval of spending the college's money to buy computers, and of teaching students how to use them when computers probably wouldn't even be around a few years later. He suggested there were better uses for the college's resources.

Today, computers can be found in almost every office and classroom building on this same college campus. And, yes, there is even one in the office of the president who made those remarks.

Over the years, many decision makers, including college administrators, have changed their minds about computers and their importance. They, like we, now realize that computers have, indeed, changed the ways we do many things, and that they are not a fad. Instead, they are useful tools that can help us in our work, and even improve the quality of our lives.

Computer Classifications

In this chapter, computers will be classified in terms of purpose and use. There are no established industry standards for classifying computers; typically, computers are classified as general purpose and special purpose.

Special-Purpose Computers

Special-purpose computers are designed and built to do one task or a small number of related tasks. The instructions to do these tasks are built into the computer by the manufacturer. After the computer has been built and is operating, what the computer can do cannot be changed.

Embedded computers are the most limited kind of special-purpose computer. They are a part of another device, such as a microwave oven, a television, or a video game. People using these devices press buttons to make their selections known to the computer. With the aid of the permanently installed set of instructions, the computer scans the push buttons on the machine's control panel and causes parts of the machine to carry out the user's instructions.

Analog computers are used for solving specific problems that relate to physical quantities, such as heat or speed and to measuring change in amount. They are used in process control during manufacturing processes in industry and scientific research projects. A good example of an analog computer is a gasoline pump at a service station. As gasoline is pumped from an underground tank, it is measured physically and priced as it moves through the pumping mechanism. The United States military uses a large number of analog computers for solving specific military problems.

General-Purpose Computers

General-purpose computers, sometimes called programmable computers, are designed to solve a wide variety of problems. A specific problem to be solved requires a set of instructions, called a **program.** The program is also called **software,** and can be written by the user or purchased from someone else, such as a **software vendor.** The program can be rewritten or replaced by a new program if it becomes necessary to change the way a computer performs a particular operation. General-purpose computers are limited only by their size and speed.

What a Digital Computer Is . . . and Is Not!

The computer is an amazing machine used by people to solve problems. It is a human tool, just like a hammer used to drive a nail. And like a hammer, computers are our servants, not our masters. A computer cannot think for itself. It has no brain and cannot produce correct answers unless it is fed correct data. A computer, by itself, can do nothing.

A computer can perform many operations at very high speeds. It can add, subtract, multiply, and divide numbers. It can compare numbers, sort long lists of items in any order, store large amounts of data, and communicate with its human users.

A computer solves these problems in a logical manner much like a person does. Figure 3–1 shows five logical steps a person might follow in adding two numbers. Compare these five steps with the five similar steps a computer goes through in adding two numbers.

Characteristics of Digital Computers

Digital computers have unique characteristics that make them very popular and widely used. These characteristics are accuracy, speed, memory, reliability, and versatility.

Accuracy

Modern digital computers are extremely **accurate** when programmed properly. While mechanical and electrical failures are possible and sometimes happen, most of the ''computer mistakes'' we hear about are caused by people and not the computer. Errors in computer programs and incorrect data supplied to the computer are the two main reasons for incorrect computer output. Computers do only as they are instructed and will produce incorrect results when programmed incorrectly or when inaccurate data is fed into them.

After processing begins, a computer requires no human intervention. It has no mechanical parts to wear out or malfunction. Thus, a computer can perform millions of operations every second and run errorless for days at a time. It also has self-checking capabilities enabling it to monitor the accuracy of its internal operations.

If data entering the computer is correct, and if the program of instructions is correct, then the computer can be expected to produce accurate output. Can you recall the term that people who work with computers use for describing incorrect data entry? **GIGO** (*Garbage-In—Garbage-Out.*)

Five Steps a *Person* Goes Through in Adding Two Numbers	Five Similar Steps a *Computer* Goes Through in Adding Two Numbers
Step 1. You collect the information. That is, you either see or hear the numbers to be added.	Step 1. The computer receives the information, or data, from the outside. It changes the data into electronic language, called *input*.
Step 2. You find a method to solve the problem. In this case, you remember how to do addition.	Step 2. The computer has been given a *program* containing instructions for solving the problem. The instructions are found in *storage*.
Step 3. You bring together the information (two numbers) and the method (addition).	Step 3. The computer brings together the data from the input and the instructions from storage. This is done by the computer's *control unit*.
Step 4. You perform the operation of adding the two numbers.	Step 4. The computer follows each instruction to *process* the data.
Step 5. You report the results, by either writing down the answer or speaking it out loud.	Step 5. The computer changes the results from electronic language to human language. It presents the results as *output*.

Figure 3–1
Comparison of two methods used in adding two numbers.

Speed

The **speed** at which data is processed by the computer is increasingly important. This is due to the large amounts of processing done by businesses, some of which must be completed quickly and by a particular time. In a large company with several hundred employees, for example, processing the payroll involves many thousands of math-

THE COMPUTER DIDN'T DO IT!

OVER-VALUED HOME COSTS AREA $7 MILLION

CLEVELAND—Red faced officials admitted recently that someone assessed a $35,000 house at over $500 million—and now Cleveland's budgets are out of whack.

Lost revenues to the city, schools, and county: $7 million.

Cuyahoga County Auditor Tim McCormack speculated that someone punched a "5100" into a computer in front of the real value—coming up with $510,035,000.

"It's so embarrassing to everyone," McCormack said.

ematical calculations. The faster the computer can perform these calculations, the sooner the task of processing the payroll will be completed. Individual employee paychecks must be distributed to employees at a certain time or the company might be confronted with labor problems.

Processing data by computer is extremely fast. In 1985 the fastest computers could add about 2.4 trillion pairs of 5-digit numbers in one minute. Compare this, for example, with the addition of 42,971 + 26,975 = 69,946: using a desk calculator, five similar additions can be done in about one minute. Figure 3–2 shows how many times 5-digit figures can be added up in one minute using different equipment.

Year	Equipment	Number of Times Two Five-Digit Numbers Can Be Added In One Minute
5000 B.C.	Stones	1
500 B.C.	Abacus	12
1900	Desk calculator	12
1950	Digital computer	2,400
1963	Digital computer	2,400,000
1975	Digital computer	2,400,000,000
1985	Digital computer	2,400,000,000,000

Figure 3–2
Processing speeds using different equipment.

Unit of Time	Fractional Part of a Second	Interpretation
Millisecond	$\dfrac{1}{1,000}$	An automobile traveling at 90 miles per hour (mph) would move less than 2 inches in a millisecond.
Microsecond	$\dfrac{1}{1,000,000}$	A rocket traveling at 100,000 miles per hour (mph) would move less than 2 inches in a microsecond.
Nanosecond	$\dfrac{1}{1,000,000,000}$	There are as many nanoseconds in 1 hour as there are hours in 66,000 centuries.
Picosecond	$\dfrac{1}{1,000,000,000,000}$	Electricity travels less than 1/50 of an inch in one picosecond.

Figure 3–3
Internal computer speeds.

Although automobiles and other machines are fast, they are quite slow when compared to computers. The computer can process data as rapidly as electricity can flow through circuits. Electricity travels through circuits at about 186,000 miles per second. But the combined length of the circuitry (wiring) inside a computer is much less than 186,000 miles. Thus, the computer can process data in a mere fraction of a second.

As mentioned in Chapter 2, computer speeds are expressed in fractions of a second—in milliseconds, microseconds, nanoseconds, or picoseconds. Figure 3–3 shows these speeds and an interpretation of each.

Memory

Perhaps the greatest progress to date in computer technology has been in computer memory. **Internal memory** is where data and/or instructions are stored inside a computer's electronic circuitry. Recent improvements in memory have come about with advances in chip technology. It is now possible to put thousands of tiny integrated circuits, called ICs, on a small silicon chip about the size of a fingernail, or even smaller. A small but powerful microcomputer contains many such chips, each serving a special purpose. Thousands of pieces of data and hundreds of program instructions can be stored in the circuits on a single silicon chip. As technology improves, even more circuits will be packed onto smaller chips. The result will be smaller but more powerful computers.

All digital computers are accurate and fast, and have memory. Processing data with computers also offers the user other distinct advantages.

Reliability

Digital computers must be reliable in carrying out the three functions of input, processing, and output. **Reliability** here means that the **hardware,** which is the physical equipment, functions consistently each and every time it is operated. Computers vary in reliability, however, because of the internal makeup of circuitry within the hardware devices. Even though some errors may occur during processing, a digital computer has a very high reliability rating. If the data that is processed by the computer is accurate, then a user can expect the computer to carry out its functions, basically error-free, time after time. Reliability is a characteristic that should be given adequate consideration before acquiring a computer.

Versatility

The digital computer is the most **versatile** of all computers. It can be used for processing both business and scientific applications. A digital computer can be used to process a payroll application, which may be the first job task; meanwhile, the second job task might be an engineering one, entirely different and unrelated to the payroll problem. It can flip-flop between business and scientific applications easily.

1. . . .The two computer classifications?

2. . . .What a digital computer is and is not?

3. . . .The characteristics of digital computers?

DO YOU
REMEMBER

Advantages and Disadvantages of Digital Computers

As mentioned before, computers are self-directing, requiring no human intervention once processing has begun. Processing data with a computer offers many advantages. Some of the more important ones are these:

1. Processing data with a computer is faster than any other method.

2. A wide variety of operations can be performed by a computer because it operates from instructions stored in it.

3. After instructions and data have been entered into the computer, the processing is continuous.

4. Instructions and data can be stored inside the computer indefinitely and retrieved almost instantly.

5. The computer is capable of greater accuracy than any other method of processing data.

There are also disadvantages of using digital computers. When large amounts of data are to be processed, the advantages exceed the disadvantages. But when processing requirements are small, it may not be practical to use a computer. In these situations, it may be best to use a manual or mechanical method. Some of the more important disadvantages of using computers are these:

1. Even though their prices are declining, computers are expensive. Using a computer to process small amounts of data is not cost effective.

2. Writing computer programs can be expensive and time consuming. Thus, it is impractical to write a program to be used once or only a few times. Also, programs purchased from a software vendor can be expensive.

3. It is practical to spend the time required to learn about a particular computer and how to use it efficiently only when the user plans to use it frequently and for a variety of tasks.

Digital computers, then, are not perfect for solving all problems, but they are versatile enough to provide a solution to many.

Central Processing Unit— "Heart of the Computer"

The **central** *processing* ***unit*** (CPU) is the heart of a computer. The basic functions are carried out or directed by the CPU under program control (see Figure 3–4). The CPU is made up of three basic components: the storage unit, the control unit, and the arithmetic/logic

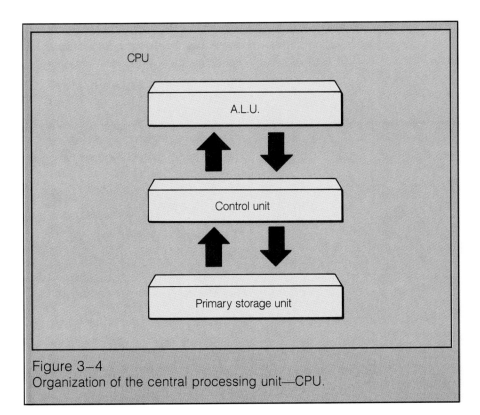

Figure 3–4
Organization of the central processing unit—CPU.

unit (ALU). The following sections explain, in more depth, the three components of the CPU.

Storage Unit

A computer's internal storage unit is sometimes referred to as the **primary storage unit** or primary memory. Primary storage will be discussed in more detail later on in this chapter. Primary memory temporarily holds data and instructions that have been received from an input device. Data is passed to the arithmetic/logic unit one piece at a time from primary storage under supervision of the control unit. Program instructions are called for and are passed to the control unit one instruction at a time. Data and program instructions are not processed in primary memory. Data is processed in the arithmetic/logic unit and instructions in the control unit.

Control Unit

The **control unit** directs all the internal activities of the CPU. It reads program instructions from primary memory one at a time and interprets what operation is to be performed. It manages the activities of all the other units of the computer.

Arithmetic/Logic Unit

The *arithmetic/logic unit* (ALU) directs the arithmetic and logic operations for the computer. The ALU functions under the supervision of the control unit. The control unit manages passing data from primary memory to the arithmetic/logic unit where specific processing operations take place. As stated earlier, the ALU enables the computer to add, subtract, multiply, divide, and make comparisons. The results of the processing in the ALU are passed back to the primary memory unit as intermediate results to be processed again later or as output.

It takes all of the parts above in order for the CPU to process data and instructions. The storage, control, and ALU units are contained on silicon chips that are 1/4-inch square in size or smaller. The chips are wired together on a printed circuit board that carries electrical signals between CPU parts.

Types of Primary Storage

There are basically four types of primary storage: *Random-Access Memory* (RAM), *Read-Only* Memory (ROM), *Programmable Read-Only Memory* (PROM), and *Erasable Programmable Read-Only Memory* (EPROM). Some types provide only temporary, also called (volatile), storage while others allow for permanent (nonvolatile) storage. These types of memories are represented as semiconductor memory. Semiconductor memory is manufactured from silicon crystals that are placed on a chip in layers. Transistors are etched into the semiconductor material; each one represents a bit. The transistors either stop the flow of electricity or allow the flow of electricity, thus allowing a bit to represent either an off (0) or on (1) condition. An actual semiconductor chip is shown in Figure 3–5.

Let us now examine each type of primary storage individually.

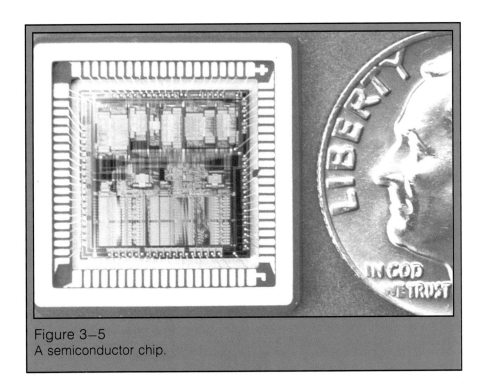

Figure 3–5
A semiconductor chip.

Random-Access Memory (RAM)

Random-Access Memory (RAM) is regular, nonpermanent primary memory, also referred to as read/write memory. It is semiconductor memory that allows data to be stored and retrieved using instructions within a computer program. It allows for data that has been previously written and/or stored to be written into it or read from it. It provides temporary storage for data and program instructions. RAM is physically made up of an **integrated circuit chip** (ICC).

Read-Only Memory (ROM)

Read-Only Memory (ROM) provides for permanent storage of data and program instructions in an integrated circuit chip that cannot be changed. The ROM chip has become known as **firmware,** a combination of hardware and software. Firmware actually has fixed, non-changeable software built into it. The computer has rapid access to ROM/Firmware chip(s). Video game cartridges that plug into video machines contain ROM(s). Data and instructions concerning the game are read from the ROM, but no data or instructions are allowed to be written back to ROM.

Programmable Read-Only Memory (PROM)

Programmable Read-Only Memory (PROM) is similar to ROM with the exception that it can be programmed after manufacturing, but only once, by either the manufacturer or the user. The programs that are placed into the PROM chip are actually burned into place with ultraviolet light. Programs that are stored on PROM chips will be used over and over again, thousands of times, such as, a standardized sorting program that can be used by all programmers in a company for sorting data into a predetermined sequence.

Erasable Programmable Read-Only Memory (EPROM)

Erasable Programmable Read-Only Memory (EPROM) allows the user to erase the contents of the EPROM chip and enter new program instructions. The content of the EPROM chip is changed only by a customer engineer from the chip manufacturer or by a specially trained analyst/engineer because of the special equipment needed to make changes.

RAM, ROM, PROM, and **EPROM** are used in all sizes of computers manufactured today. These types of primary storage are referred to as firmware and they help increase the speed of a computer.

In the primary storage unit, groups of memory chips are placed side by side on printed circuit boards. They are tied together to make up one printed circuit board. Many printed circuit boards are placed into a rack side by side one after the other. If problems occur on a particular board, it can be removed quickly and replaced with a new one.

---

4. . . .The advantages and disadvantages of digital computers?

5. . . .What the central processing unit—the heart of the computer consists of?

6. . . .The types of primary storage?

DO YOU REMEMBER

How Data Is Represented

Data and program instructions are represented in primary storage of an electronic computer in a coded form known as the base-two or binary numbering system. In the binary system, there are two numbers, 0 and 1, that relate to the two states of primary memory locations. A zero (0) state represents an *off* condition, and a one (1) state represents an *on* condition.

Primary memory locations are similar to light switches that can be turned on or off. Locations are storage areas in memory similar to a group of mailboxes positioned side by side. Data can be stored in each storage location or mailbox. The data in a storage location is represented by binary zeros and ones. A string of binary characters (0s and 1s) is assigned values that represent characters of data. These values are used to carry out all arithmetic and logic operations executed by a computer.

Numbering Systems

At this point, the three most commonly used numbering systems—decimal, binary, and binary coded decimal (BCD)—will be discussed in more detail. It is important to understand the basics of numbering systems in order to understand how data is represented inside a computer.

Decimal.   The **decimal numbering system** (base 10) is the one we use most commonly. Money expressed in dollars and cents, such as $250.25, and temperature expressed as 98.6 degrees are examples of how we use the decimal numbering system daily. People, in fact, take the decimal numbering system for granted because of their familiarity with it. Although this system works well for humans, it is not appropriate for computers.

We are aware that the decimal numbering system deals with successive locations, or positions, to the left of the decimal point. These locations or positions are referred to as units, tens, hundreds, thousands, ten thousands, and so on. Each one of these locations represents a specific power of the base (base = 10). Any number (0–9) that is multipled by the base in a specific location/position would give the total value. By arranging numbers in different positions any value can be represented (See Figure 3–6 for a comparison of the decimal and binary numbering systems).

Binary.   Data is represented in a computer by the electrical state of the machine's internal circuitry, (0) off and (1) on. These are the only two possible states or conditions for representing data and instructions.

The **binary system** is known as a two-state system and is referred to as binary representation. The binary system uses two digits, zero (0) and one (1). It is a base-two numbering system. This system was first recommended for representing data in computers by John von Neumann.

Figure 3–7 includes several examples of how the binary system works. As the examples indicate, a binary 0 represents an *off* condition and a binary 1 represents an *on* condition. Electronic switches in the computer's memory are naturally either off (0) or on (1). Each switch in combination with other switches can represent a piece(s) of data electronically.

The binary system can represent the same data that the decimal system can. The binary system, however, is more efficient for computers because it represents data in the same format the computer

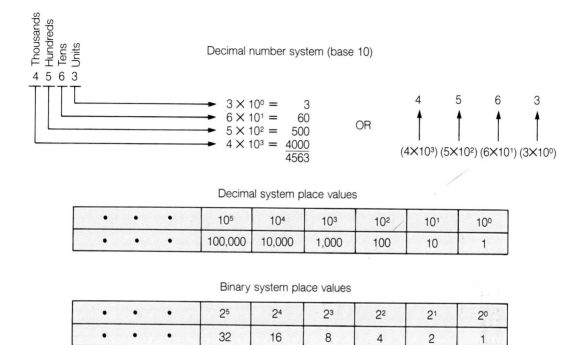

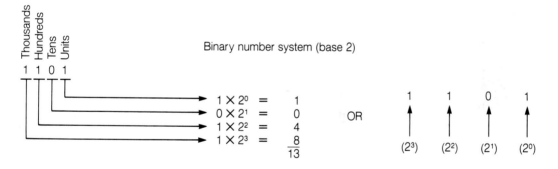

Figure 3–6
Comparison of decimal and binary numbering systems.

operates in. Also, the design of circuitry is simplified, the cost is less, and performance is greater.

Binary Coded Decimal (BCD).   There is more than one coding scheme that can be used to represent data inside a computer. The **binary coded decimal** (BCD) codes are used to represent data in a computer's

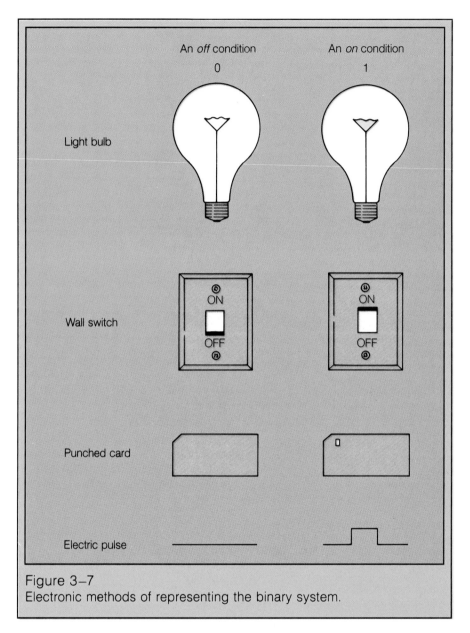

Figure 3–7
Electronic methods of representing the binary system.

primary memory. There are three BCD codes: 4-bit, 6-bit, and 8-bit. Today 8-bit is the most popular. The BCD codes represent data as a binary equivalent according to a predefined format. The 4-bit BCD code represents numeric data (0–9) only with four-position binary

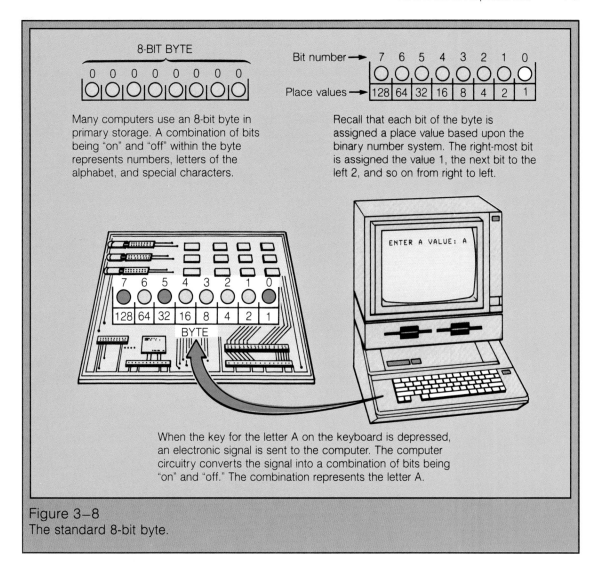

8-BIT BYTE

0 0 0 0 0 0 0 0

Many computers use an 8-bit byte in primary storage. A combination of bits being "on" and "off" within the byte represents numbers, letters of the alphabet, and special characters.

Bit number → 7 6 5 4 3 2 1 0

Place values → 128 | 64 | 32 | 16 | 8 | 4 | 2 | 1

Recall that each bit of the byte is assigned a place value based upon the binary number system. The right-most bit is assigned the value 1, the next bit to the left 2, and so on from right to left.

7 6 5 4 3 2 1 0

128 | 64 | 32 | 16 | 8 | 4 | 2 | 1

BYTE

ENTER A VALUE: A

When the key for the letter A on the keyboard is depressed, an electronic signal is sent to the computer. The computer circuitry converts the signal into a combination of bits being "on" and "off." The combination represents the letter A.

Figure 3–8
The standard 8-bit byte.

format. The 6-bit BCD code represents alphanumeric data (letters A–Z and numeric characters 0–9) and special characters, such as $, @, #, %, ^, &, *, −, + and others, with a six-position binary format. Each format requires a certain number of positions to be turned off and on in a particular sequence to represent a certain character. Each character is represented by a unique combination of zeros and ones defined as a **byte** (see Figure 3–8).

The two popular 8-bit BCD codes are the ***Extended Binary Coded Decimal Interchange Code*** (EBCDIC) and the ***American Standard***

Character	EBCDIC	ASCII–8
A	1100 0001	1010 0001
B	1100 0010	1010 0010
C	1100 0011	1010 0011
D	1100 0100	1010 0100
E	1100 0101	1010 0101
F	1100 0110	1010 0110
G	1100 0111	1010 0111
H	1100 1000	1010 1000
I	1100 1001	1010 1001
J	1101 0001	1010 1010
K	1101 0010	1010 1011
L	1101 0011	1010 1100
M	1101 0100	1010 1101
N	1101 0101	1010 1110
O	1101 0110	1010 1111
P	1101 0111	1011 0000
Q	1101 1000	1011 0001
R	1101 1001	1011 0010
S	1110 0010	1011 0011
T	1110 0011	1011 0100
U	1110 0100	1011 0101
V	1110 0101	1011 0110
W	1110 0110	1011 0111
X	1110 0111	1011 1000
Y	1110 1000	1011 1001
Z	1110 1001	1011 1010
0	1111 0000	0101 0000
1	1111 0001	0101 0001
2	1111 0010	0101 0010
3	1111 0011	0101 0011
4	1111 0100	0101 0100
5	1111 0101	0101 0101
6	1111 0110	0101 0110
7	1111 0111	0101 0111
8	1111 1000	0101 1000
9	1111 1001	0101 1001
$	0101 1011	0010 0100
*	0101 1100	0010 1010
.	0100 1011	0010 1110
,	0110 1011	0010 1100

Figure 3–9
Standard ways of representing data.

Code for *I*nformation *I*nterchange (ASCII). EBCDIC is used basically to represent data and instructions, whereas ASCII is used to represent data and instructions internally and data transmission/communications from one point to another.

Most computer systems can use several coding schemes. The BCD codes are used as a substitute for pure binary representation of data and instructions. Figure 3–9 is a limited comparison of EBCDIC and ASCII coding schemes.

Data Hierarchy

Data is measured in bits, bytes, fields, records, files, and databases. Bits represent the smallest amount of data, whereas a database represents the largest amount of data. The range of data representation is referred to as the **data hierarchy** (see Figure 3–10). The following sections deal specifically with each component of the data hierarchy.

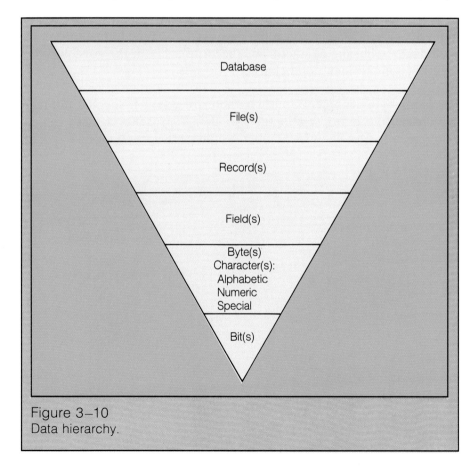

Figure 3–10
Data hierarchy.

Bit.   Each binary position in primary memory is referred to as a **bit** (*Bi*nary Dig*it*). A bit is the smallest unit of data that can be represented in primary memory. Within the circuitry of the computer, a bit is represented as a very small transistor on an integrated circuit chip that is in an off (0) state or an on (1) state.

Byte.   In order to give some meaning to stored data, we must group a specific number of bits together as a unit. This unit is referred to as a **byte.** Generally, a standard byte is a string of 8 bits. In order to represent a character of data (alphabetic, numeric, or special) using the BCD system, with 8 bits equaling a byte (character), we must break down the byte into two parts. These parts are the zone and digit components (see Figure 3–11). It takes 8 bits (one byte) being turned off (0) and on (1) in a specific combination to represent any character of data. In Figure 3–11, the specific combination of bits we see in the table is the binary coded decimal (EBCDIC) representation 1111 0001; this represents the decimal character 1. The zone portion of the byte determines whether a character is to be an alphabetic, numeric, or special character; the digit portion of the byte determines specifically what the character will be. It takes both the zone and the digit portions to make one character of data.

Field.   A byte represents one character of data. A specific number of consecutive bytes (characters) of data represents a **field**. As an example, a 7-digit decimal number would need 7 continuous bytes of

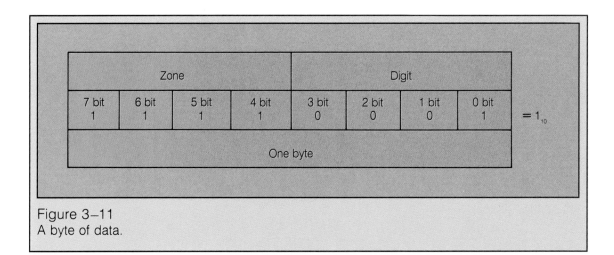

Figure 3–11
A byte of data.

primary storage to be stored. An 18-byte alphabetic name field (alphabetic characters and blanks) would need 18 continuous bytes of primary storage to be stored.

A computer has a specific amount of primary storage, and it is convenient to measure storage capacity in bytes. The computer industry refers to a computer's primary storage size in kilobytes. The alphabetic character <u>K</u> is used as a shortcut notation for kilobyte. A kilobyte is 1,024 bytes in computer mathematics. A computer with 128K of primary memory would have the storage capacity of 131,072 bytes (1,024 × 128 = 131,072). In large computer systems, primary memory is usually expressed in megabytes (MB); 1 megabyte equals a million bytes.

As explained above, a field of data has a specific number of bytes (characters) grouped together. A field of data can be any combination of alphabetic, numeric, alphanumeric, or special characters. A field represents specific data. This can be a person's name, home address, city, state, or zip code. These individual related fields collectively make up a record.

Record.   A **record** is made up of a specific number of related fields of data. A record can be as little as one field or as large as *x* number of fields to represent the data needed for processing. One person's record for a payroll application might include the following fields: employee name, home address, city, state, zip code, social security number, regular hours worked, overtime hours worked, regular rate of pay, and overtime rate of pay. A computer processes one record at a time from a file.

File.   A **file** is a collection of related records. A file can have one or more records in it. Usually, a data file has hundreds or thousands of records in it. A computer program processes a file of data records one record at a time, such as for an employee payroll. Each employee's payroll record contains all the appropriate fields needed for processing.

Database.   A collection of related files is a **database.** Many computer application programs can share the data in a database. Database technology allows for the pooling of data into one source. This concept cuts down on duplicate and redundant data that might be stored in several conventional files. More information on database technology will be provided in Chapter 14.

From the information presented above, we have learned what a bit, byte (character), field, record, file, and database are composed of. Figure 3–10 summarizes the data hierarchy. It is important to have a good understanding of data representation.

DO YOU
REMEMBER

7. . . .How data is represented in a computer?

8. . . .What numbering systems are used to represent data?

9. . . .The data hierarchy and what it represents?

Computer Input

Data entered into the computer for processing into information is called **input.** Many devices can be used to enter data. The input process must occur before any other process can take place in data processing. Input devices will be discussed in greater detail in Chapter 4, but the following sections will introduce the more common devices.

Keyboard

A popular way to input data to the computer is through a **keyboard.** The usual keyboard that is found attached to most video- and printer-type terminals is similar to the keyboard on a typewriter. It is extremely important to input data accurately. Data typed on the keyboard is transmitted to the computer for processing, and then information is returned to the video screen or printer for viewing by the user.

Pressure-Sensitive Keyboard

Another way of inputting data that is gaining in popularity is the **pressure-sensitive keyboard**. This method operates from the pressure created by a person's fingers. When a finger touches a particular key or switch, it makes an electrical connection that sends the character of data represented by that key to the computer for processing. Some keyboards used with game-oriented microcomputers are pressure-sensitive. These keyboards are very quiet because there are no mechanical keys to make noise. Basically, this device is a laminated plastic (membrane) keyboard with all the characters of the alphabet and special characters represented. As a person locates the characters to be entered, he or she presses them with the fingers.

Touch-screen input is another pressure-sensitive concept that is becoming popular. The operator of a video terminal enters a particular function, command, or data by touching the screen.

Voice

Voice response and/or voice recognition is another popular way to input data to the computer for processing. In this method, a human voice speaks into a microphone. Voice waves, which are analog signals, are converted to digital signals that the computer can accept and process. Many banks, insurance companies, and telephone companies use this method of input. There will be more users of this method of input when the equipment prices are reduced and the vocabulary the computer can understand is expanded.

Computer Output

Computer **output** is the end product of processing data. Output is what a user takes to help formulate a decision. The output of a computer can be one of many elements a manager uses to help in decision making and problem solving.

Hardcopy

Many devices are used for outputting information from a computer. Some of these devices create **hardcopy** (paper copy). Hardcopy output is physical, visible, and touchable. The hardware device that is used most often to produce hardcopy is a printer. Hardcopy output still remains the most popular means of computer output. We will study more about output devices in other chapters that follow.

Softcopy

Another popular means of computer output is **softcopy.** Softcopy video output is produced by an output device referred to as a video terminal or **cathode *ray* *tube*** (CRT). The output appears on a screen much like a television screen. Softcopy output is temporary. Once it is created, it stays on the screen only until it is replaced with new output or until the computer is turned off.

Voice Response

Voice-response computer output is beginning to increase in popularity. The hardware device that allows for both voice input and output to and from the computer is referred to as a voice-response unit. The device creates the spoken word, in English, as output. The user can speak to the unit through a microphone, giving it instructions to carry out a task. The voice-response concept is presently being researched and perfected by computer manufacturers. We can expect to see more voice-response input/output devices being used as improvements are made and prices decline.

Computer Systems

There are many different sizes of computer systems in the market-place today. It is difficult to distinguish between computer systems on the basis of physical size, cost, and capabilities alone. For convenience, we might say there are four basic systems that are accepted in the computing industry: supercomputers, mainframe computers, minicomputers, and microcomputers.

Supercomputers

Supercomputers are machines that have the capacity to store vast amounts of data and instructions in main memory. These computers are extremely fast. The newest supercomputers can perform approximately 200 million mathematical calculations per second, and can store approximately 5 million (64-bit) words in main memory.

Supercomputers are capable of executing more than one program instruction simultaneously. The cost of a supercomputer is $10 to $15 million or more, depending on the design of the system. The prediction is that over the next three to five years, approximately two hundred supercomputers will be sold and installed worldwide to meet the needs of certain users that deal in areas where very high speed calculations are required (see Figure 3–12). The oil industry would be one such user, for example. The supercomputer market will not be as large, in number of units sold, as other computer markets.

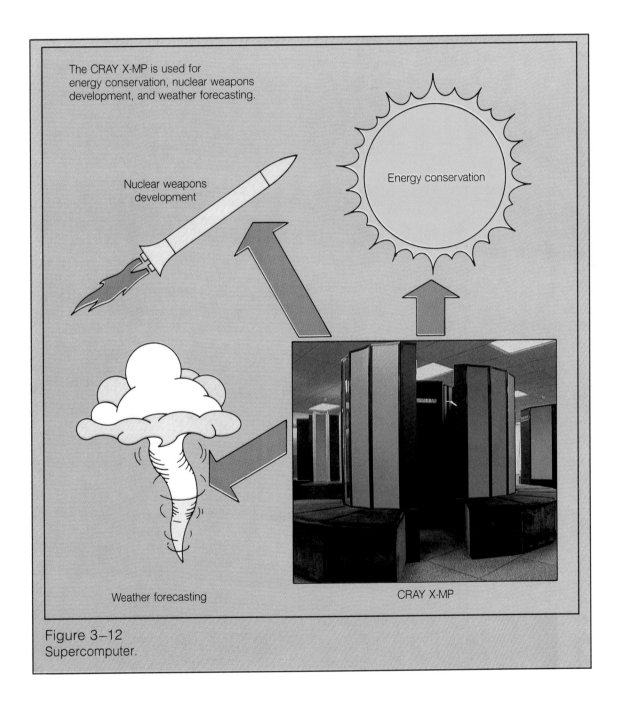

Figure 3–12
Supercomputer.

Mainframe Computers

Mainframe computers have been around for many years. In fact, the first electronic computers available for business use were classified as mainframes. A mainframe is usually thought of as a large computer at a centralized location. This, however, is not an altogether accurate description. Today, mainframe computers are used as workhorses in large decentralized networks. The mainframe is usually the largest computer in a company's network of computers (see Figure 3–13). The exception to this is the supercomputer, which might be used by certain large companies for research and development. The mainframe is normally used to store vast amounts of data and instructions for users at remote sites. It is also used to manage the data communications network and databases.

Mainframes are much faster machines than minicomputers or microcomputers. They handle large amounts of data and instructions very quickly and efficiently. The cost of a mainframe computer ranges from $200 thousand to $1 million or higher, depending on a particular user's need. Main memory size for mainframes usually ranges from a half megabyte to 10 megabytes or more. Mainframes usually require special environmental conditions, such as air conditioning for cooling and for controlling dust and humidity.

Figure 3–13
Mainframe computer.

These machines are not table-top units and are much too large physically for personal use. A special power supply is necessary to provide the appropriate electricity to operate the system. These systems will be around for the foreseeable future because of the need for high capacity and very fast processing speeds.

Minicomputers

Minicomputers were introduced into the marketplace in the late 1960s. They were initially used for specialized purposes in industry and production. In the early 1970s minicomputers were introduced to do business data processing applications, such as payroll and inventory control.

Minicomputers are smaller in physical size than mainframe computers (see Figure 3–14). The processing speed is slower, and the

Figure 3–14
Minicomputer.

main memory storage capacity is much less than for mainframes. Today's minicomputers are used for just about any data processing application. They are capable of monitoring temperature or measuring the flow of liquid through a pipeline. Many small companies use minicomputers because they are less expensive than mainframes. The cost of a minicomputer ranges from $30,000 to $100,000 or higher, depending on the design chosen by the purchaser. Main memory sizes range from 64 kilobytes to 5 megabytes or more. Minicomputers have less storage capacity than mainframes and more storage capacity than microcomputers.

Microcomputers

A **microcomputer** is much smaller in physical size than even a minicomputer (see Figure 3–15). However, its computing capability can be just as great as many low-end minicomputers. A microcomputer can be used for a broad range of tasks, from word processing in the home to developing distributed networks of computers in business and industry. Microcomputers use microprocessors which are contained on silicon chips. The microcomputers of today have many times

Figure 3–15
Microcomputer.

the capability of the mainframe computers of ten years ago, but at a much lower price. The sizes of microcomputers vary from hand-held units to table-top units.

There are many manufacturers of microcomputers. The first microcomputers entered the marketplace in the mid-1970s. They are much slower than most minicomputers and mainframe computers. The primary memory size ranges from 64 kilobytes to 2 megabytes or more. The cost of a microcomputer ranges from $50 to $20,000, depending on the type chosen by the purchaser. Microcomputers do not require any special environmental conditions. The microcomputer market is extremely large. Almost every household and business are potential microcomputer customers. As the average citizen and small business are educated in the uses of microcomputers, more will be sold. We are truly at the beginning of the microcomputer and information age. In fact, microcomputers may eventually replace the minicomputers in use today.

10. . . .How computer input takes place?

11. . . .How computer output takes place?

12. . . .The four categories of computer systems?

DO YOU
REMEMBER

Summary

(This summary provides answers to DO YOU REMEMBER . . . questions in the chapter.)

1. **What are the two computer classifications?**
   The two computer classifications are *special-purpose* computers and *general-purpose* computers.

2. **What is and is not a digital computer?**
   A computer is an electronic machine that can be used to help people solve problems. A computer cannot think for itself because it has no brain.

3. **What are the characteristics of a digital computer?**

The characteristics of a digital computer are *accuracy, speed, memory, reliability,* and *versatility.*

4. What are some of the advantages and disadvantages of digital computers?

Advantages: It is faster and more accurate to process data with a computer than with any other method. *Disadvantages:* Even though their prices are declining, computers are expensive. Writing computer programs can be expensive and time consuming. Thus, it is impractical to write a program that is to be used once or only a few times.

5. What does the central processing unit (CPU)—"Heart of the Computer"—consist of?

The central processing unit is made up of three components: the *storage unit,* the *control unit,* and the *arithmetic/logic unit.*

6. What are the types of primary storage?

The four basic types of primary storage are random-access memory (RAM), read-only memory (ROM), programmable read-only memory (PROM), and erasable programmable read-only memory (EPROM).

7. How is data represented in a computer?

Data is represented in binary notation. Data is broken down into *bits, bytes, fields, records, files,* and *databases* (data hierarchy).

8. What are the numbering systems used to represent data?

The numbering systems used to represent data are 4-bit BCD, 6-bit BCD, and 8-bit BCD (EBCDIC and ASCII).

9. What is the data hierarchy and what does it represent?

The data hierarchy is an inverted pyramid that represents the different levels of data incorporation from the lowest level (bit) to the highest level (database).

10. How does computer input take place?

Computer input is done through a keyboard, a pressure sensitive keyboard or screen, and voice response.

11. How does computer output take place?

Computer output is done through hardcopy, softcopy, and voice response.

12. What are the four categories of computer systems?

The four categories of computer systems are supercomputer, mainframe computer, minicomputer, and microcomputer.

DATA PROCESSING CAREER. . . . .
POINT-OF-SALE CLERK

Figure 3–16
Computer engineer in computer operations.

CAREER OPPORTUNITY FOR COMPUTER PROFESSIONAL

JOB TITLE:
Point-of-Sale Clerk

JOB DESCRIPTION:
New department store offering many lines of general merchandise will open for business in about 30 days. A leader in the industry, our new local store will feature the latest computerized sales technology. Thus, we are recruiting applicants to become top salespersons with access to, and use of, modern point-of-sale cash registers and computer terminals. Complete in-store training will be available to those hired. Specific job duties after training will include direct customer sales requiring use of computerized point-of-sale terminals and cash registers.

EXPERIENCE REQUIRED:
None

EDUCATION REQUIRED:
High school diploma

PERSONAL QUALIFICATIONS:
Applicants must be well-groomed, customer-service-oriented, ambitious, and dependable. Must be public-minded and work well with others.

Key Terms

analog computer	file
analyst	firmware
arithmetic/logic unit	GIGO
ASCII	hardcopy
bit	mainframe computer
byte	main memory
cathode ray tube	memory
central processing unit	microcomputer
compare	minicomputer
computer input	PROM
computer output	RAM
computer program	record
control unit	ROM
database	silicon chip
data hierarchy	softcopy
digital computer	software vendor
EBCDIC	sort
electronic computer	store
engineer	supercomputer
EPROM	voice recognition
field	voice response

Test Yourself

1. Computers may be classified according to _____ and _____ .

2. _____ computers are the kind most widely used in business because of their ability to process alphanumeric data.

3. The three main characteristics of digital computers are _____ , _____, and _____.

4. A _____ is one-billionth of a second.

5. The _____ unit directs all activities within the central processing unit (CPU).

6. The _____ unit is the part of the central processing unit in which all processing of data takes place.

7. _____ memory provides for permanent storage of instructions and data and cannot be changed.

8. The _____ numbering system is a base–2 system that enables data to be stored in a computer as *on* or *off* conditions.

9. A combination of bits form a _____ which represents an alphabetic character, a number, or a special character.

10. A group of related files makes up a _____.

11. Computer output displayed on a video screen (cathode ray tube) is called _____ output.

12. Supercomputers are machines that have a large _____ capacity and are extremely _____.

13. _____ computers are used today as workhorses in large decentralized networks.

14. Minicomputers were introduced to the marketplace in the 1960s and were initially used for specialized purposes in _____ and_____.

15. Microcomputers use _____ which are contained on _____.

Review Questions

1. Distinguish between general-purpose and special-purpose computers. (Learning Objective 2)

2. Why are digital computers more widely used by business than analog computers? (Learning Objective 3)

3. The five main characteristics of digital computers are accuracy, speed, memory, reliability, and versatility. Explain the importance of each. (Learning Objective 4)

4. What are the advantages and disadvantages of using digital computers? (Learning Objective 5)

5. What are the three components of the central processing unit? What purpose is served by each component? (Learning Objective 6)

6. Discuss the differences among RAM, ROM, PROM, and EPROM types of memory? Why is ROM used extensively for video games? (Learning Objective 7)

7. Explain and illustrate the data hierarchy for *electronic data processing* (EDP). How are data and instruction represented in a computer? (Learning Objective 8)

8. Discuss the different types and processes for computer input and output. (Learning Objective 9)

9. Discuss the four categories of computer systems. What are some of the differences between categories? (Learning Objective 10)

Activities

1. Draw the data hierarchy using the inverted pyramid symbol. Place into each level of the pyramid the appropriate information.

2. Take a decimal number, such as 48 and convert it to binary using the 8-bit EBCDIC coding scheme.

3. Go to your school library and look up current articles with pictures and illustrations of the four categories of computer systems. Write a brief three- to five-page research paper comparing the four categories of computer systems. Include pictures and illustrations of each category in your research paper.

4. Visit a microcomputer store near your school or home and examine the different types of input and output devices that can be used on a microcomputer. Write a brief three-page paper about your findings.

CHAPTER 4

Input Devices and Media

Learning Objectives

After studying this chapter carefully, you will be able to:

1. Define key terms introduced in the chapter.

2. Explain the data entry process.

3. Identify the types of input devices.

4. Identify the types of input media.

5. Identify other data entry methods.

Chapter Outline

Application

The **input process** is probably the single most important procedure in data processing. Without accurate input, a computer is worthless to the user. Take the following case, for example.

A small, progressive, young company found itself growing so rapidly that it was virtually impossible to keep up with recordkeeping using a manual approach. The management decided to look into faster and more efficient ways of processing data for their record-keeping. The decision was made to install a microcomputer system with the appropriate data input and output devices and media.

The microcomputer was installed by hardware and software vendors. Immediately after receiving its new computer system, the company realized that it had no data entry operators to handle the process. Thinking that it was just a question of hiring some cheap labor, the company then employed two persons who had never before used a computer, with the hope that they could be given on-the-job training. After several weeks of basic in-house instructions, the two data entry persons became fairly knowledgeable about the computer system and the data entry process (Figure 4-1).

The largest problem the company encountered with its two new employees was in the accuracy with which they entered the data. The two data entry people entered the data accurately only fifty percent of the time. This created a tremendous problem in that it produced large amounts of unusable output from the system. In other words, the reports that were generated from the new computer system were less than half accurate, giving management unreliable information from which to make decisions. This is a good example of the GIGO (Garbage-In—Garbage-Out) principle. Computer systems depend on people performing their duties in a responsible and accurate manner. People are the most important component in any system.

Figure 4–1
Data entry operators in on-the-job training.

The Data Entry Process

Data entry is the most important process in the data processing cycle. If you feed bad data into a computer program, the program has no way of correcting it, so it manipulates the data and produces incorrect results. A payroll application program that produces a payroll check and transaction register, for example, must have accurate data to process, or the output will be inaccurate and useless to the payroll department.

There are certain processes involved in preparing data correctly for input to the computer. And it is important for computer users to have a good working knowledge of these processes.

Inputting Data from Source Documents

Data that is entered into the computer is called **raw data** or **original data.** Raw data can be input directly to the computer as it originates, or it can be recorded first on forms. The forms on which data is recorded are called **source documents.** Payroll time tickets, for example, are the source documents used for data entry in the payroll system. Once a data entry operator has a batch of payroll time tickets, he or she can begin to enter the data into a data file which is created under program control on a video terminal (CRT) or some other data entry device.

Verifying the Data

Once the data has been recorded on punched cards, tape, or disk, it is verified for accuracy. Verification means that the data that has been stored on the medium is checked to make sure it matches what was keyed in from the original source documents. **Verification** is usually done by a person other than the one who originally keyed the data. In this way, an error is less likely to be overlooked.

Taking the time to check the accuracy of the data before it is processed by an application program is important because it eliminates any reprocessing that would have to take place if the data proved incorrect. REMEMBER—GIGO.

Entering the Data

There are many ways data can be fed into a computer from source documents. Sometimes the source document itself can be used to enter data directly. There are several ways to enter data using a keyboard as the input device. Key-to-punched-card, key-to-tape, and key-to-disk are typical ways of placing data onto a medium that can be used by a computer.

After data has been recorded on an appropriate recording medium, it is ready for processing. The medium, such as punched cards, tape,

---

THE COMPUTER DIDN'T DO IT!

Ho ho ho. One December, the Arizona State Finance Center in Phoenix discovered that one of its computer tapes was missing. When it went to get the backup punched cards to reconstruct the data, it discovered the true meaning of Christmas. Two thousand of the cards had been folded, gilded, and used as tree ornaments.

Source: From page 254 of *The Naked Computer.* Copyright © 1983 by Jack B. Rochester and John Gantz. Reprinted by permission of William Morrow and Company.

or disk, must be placed in, or on, the proper hardware device before it can be processed by the computer. After the medium is in, or on, the appropriate device, the unit is turned on and the data is read from the medium by the hardware device and transferred to the computer's CPU for processing.

Entering Data Into the Computer

Several methods can be used for getting data into the computer. Among them are the punched-card, the key-to-tape, and the key-to-disk methods.

Punched-Card Data Entry

The **punched card** has been a popular medium for entering data into a computer since the first generation of computers. Data is keyed to punched cards by using a keypunch machine (see Figure 4–2).

Figure 4–2
IBM–029 keypunch machine.

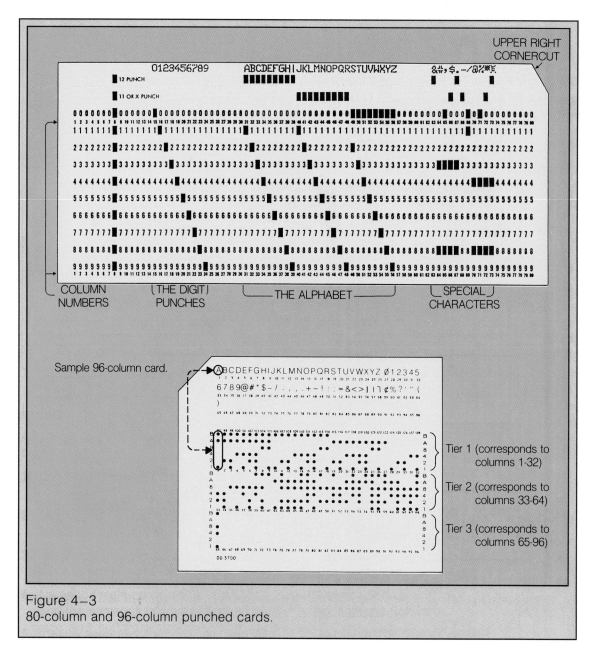

Figure 4–3
80-column and 96-column punched cards.

The two standard punched cards generally accepted by the computing industry are the 80-column and 96-column cards (see Figure 4–3). As mentioned in Chapter 2, the 80-column card was developed by Herman Hollerith, and the 96-column card was developed by the IBM Corporation. Each card has its own unique coding structure.

The punched-card approach to data entry is slower, more costly, and less efficient than other approaches. The punched card has a low data density rate. The low data density rate refers to the amount of data that can be stored on a card. In contrast, tape and disk have high data density rates. The punched card has a triple purpose: it is used to store data, to input data, and to output data. One important advantage of punched cards is that the data is in both a human-readable and a machine-readable format, while tape and disk are only in a machine-readable format.

Punched cards are not as popular today as they once were because of the new, more efficient, and cost-effective methods for data entry. While many data processing departments in business and industry still use some punched cards, cards are quickly being phased out in favor of newer approaches, such as the key-to-disk method.

Key-to-Tape

When data is recorded on magnetic tape through the use of a key-board, this process is referred to as **key-to-tape.** The key-to-tape process is similar to key-to-punched cards (see Figure 4–4).

Magnetic tapes still remain a viable media for storing data. Data can be read from the tapes and written to the tapes. In Chapter 6, a more detailed explanation is given about tape drives and magnetic tape reels, and how they work.

Key-to-Disk

The **key-to-disk** approach to data entry for larger computer systems has become the most popular approach because of the flexibility of magnetic disk. When data is stored on disk, it can be accessed more quickly by the CPU for processing. Data is entered to disk through the use of a keyboard under program control by the computer (see Figure 4–5).

Additional information on disk drives and magnetic disks will be presented in Chapter 6. The magnetic disk is still the most widely used storage medium for all categories of computers today.

1. . . .The data entry process?

2. . . .The basic methods of entering data into the computer?

3. . . .Why verification of data is important?

4. . . .What data density rate is?

DO YOU
REMEMBER

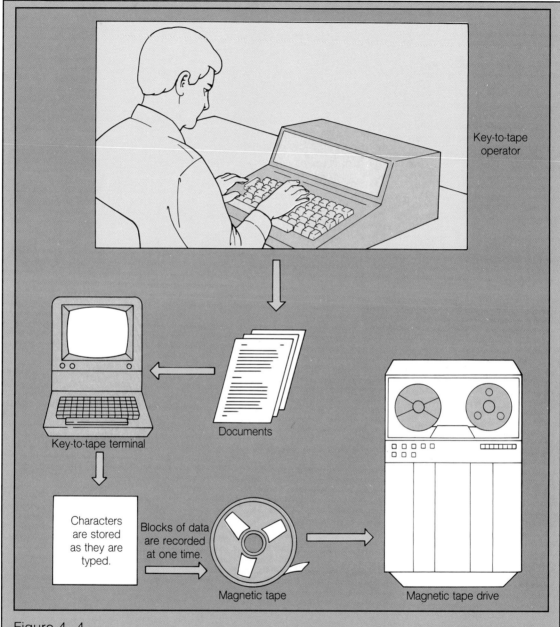

Key-to-tape operator

Documents

Key-to-tape terminal

Characters are stored as they are typed.

Blocks of data are recorded at one time.

Magnetic tape

Magnetic tape drive

Figure 4–4
Key-to-tape operator, tape drive, and magnetic tape reel.

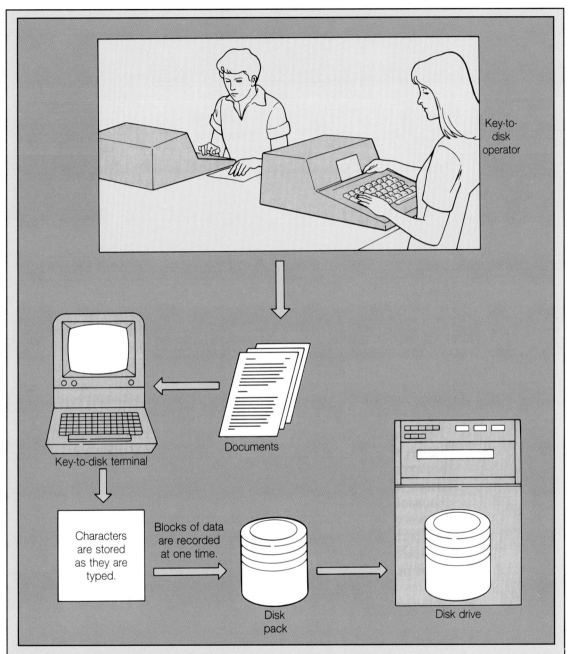

Figure 4–5
Key-to-disk operator, disk drive, and magnetic disk pack.

Other Methods of Data Entry

There are a number of special-purpose data entry methods and devices used in unique environments. It is important to have a general knowledge of these methods and devices.

Optical Scanning Methods and Devices

Optical scanning devices have become a popular method of entering data into a computer. This method of data entry works in a way similar to the way the human eye works. The optical scanner "looks at" a character of data and sends it to the CPU for recognition and translation. There are three optical recognition methods: Optical Character Recognition (OCR), Optical Mark Recognition (OMR), and Optical Bar Code Recognition (OBCR).

The optical scanning process works from a reflective light process. For example, as an optical scan sheet is run through an optical scanner/reader, the graphite pencil marks on the sheet are recognized by the reader head in the scanner. A light beam recognizes the dark graphite pencil mark and causes the light to be reflected back to and recognized by the scanner as a particular character. The optical scan sheet approach to optical scanning is popular for use in objective testing in most schools. This is only one example of optical scanning and how it works.

Optical Character Recognition (OCR).   In the **Optical Character Recognition** (OCR) method of optical scanning data is entered through specially designed characters (see Figure 4–6). There is more than one font (character shape/style) available for OCR. The character set is made up of alphabetic, numeric, and special characters. Oil companies use OCR to enter data from credit cards at service stations into their accounts receivable and billing systems. No special ink is required for imprinting the OCR characters on forms used to collect the data. Unlike some other optical scanners, the OCR reader looks only for the shape of characters to be entered. Some new OCR devices can also read handwritten characters (see Figure 4–7).

Optical Mark Recognition (OMR).   The **Optical Mark Recognition** (OMR) method of optical scanning is frequently used in schools for

ABCDEFGHIJKLMN
OPQRSTUVWXYZ,.
$/*-1234567890

Figure 4–6
OCR character set.

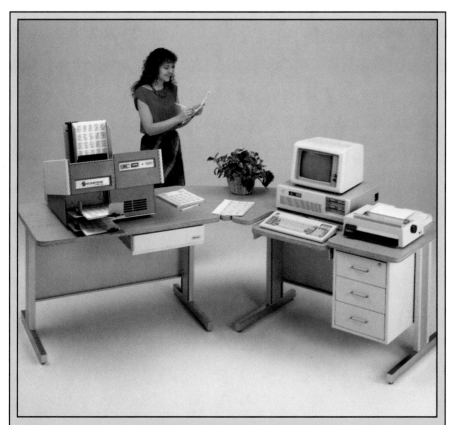

Figure 4–7
OMR reader and operator.

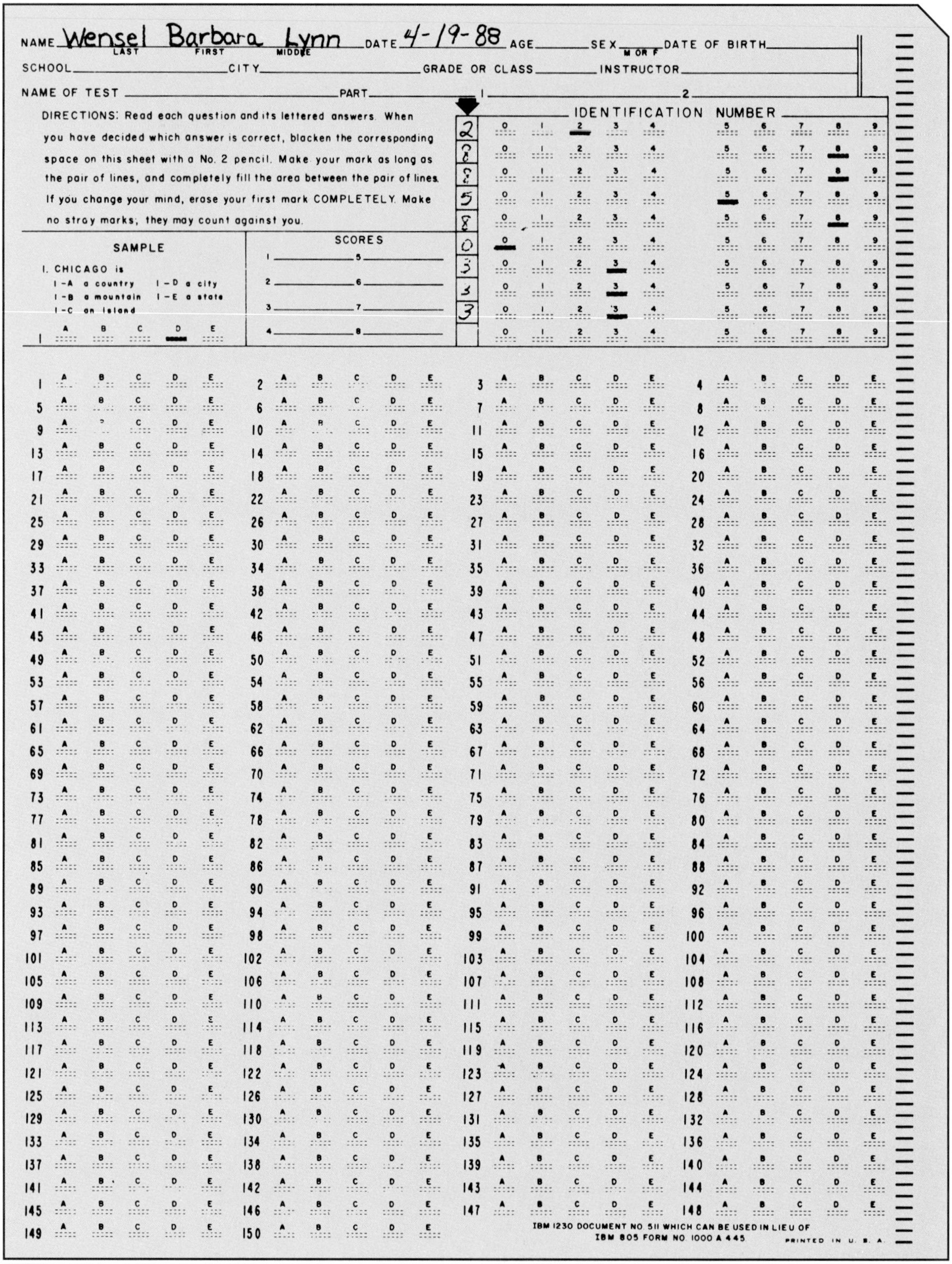

NAME *Wensel Barbara Lynn* DATE *4-19-88* AGE_____ SEX_____ DATE OF BIRTH_____
LAST   FIRST   MIDDLE   M OR F

SCHOOL_____CITY_____GRADE OR CLASS_____INSTRUCTOR_____

NAME OF TEST _____ PART_____ |_____1_____|_____2_____

DIRECTIONS: Read each question and its lettered answers. When you have decided which answer is correct, blacken the corresponding space on this sheet with a No. 2 pencil. Make your mark as long as the pair of lines, and completely fill the area between the pair of lines. If you change your mind, erase your first mark COMPLETELY. Make no stray marks; they may count against you.

IDENTIFICATION NUMBER

	0	1	2	3	4	5	6	7	8	9
2										
8										
8										
5										
8										
0										
3										
3										
3										

SAMPLE

I. CHICAGO is
  I-A a country   I-D a city
  I-B a mountain I-E a state
  I-C an island

   A   B   C   D   E
I

SCORES

1 _____ 5 _____
2 _____ 6 _____
3 _____ 7 _____
4 _____ 8 _____

IBM 1230 DOCUMENT NO. 511 WHICH CAN BE USED IN LIEU OF
IBM 805 FORM NO. 1000 A 445

PRINTED IN U.S.A.

Figure 4-8
Optical scan sheet.

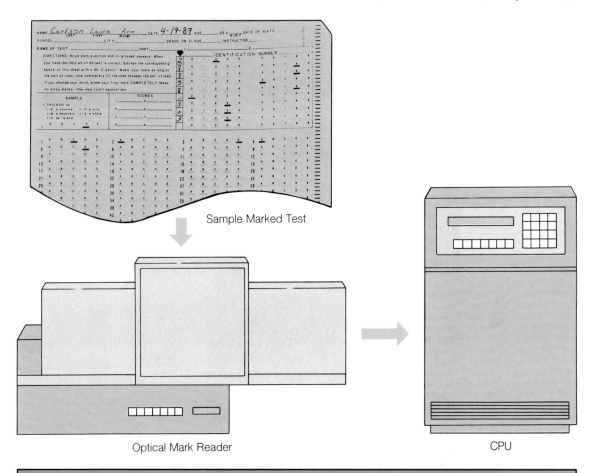

Sample Marked Test

Optical Mark Reader

CPU

Figure 4–9
Optical mark reader.

grading multiple-choice tests. The process relies on graphite pencil marks (usually no. 2 pencil lead) located in specific areas on a special form called an optical scan sheet (see Figure 4–8). The optical mark reader recognizes the location of the marks and reads the data that is transferred to magnetic disk for processing. This is the simplest type of optical recognition (see Figure 4–9).

Optical Bar Code Recognition (OBCR).   **Optical Bar Code Recognition** (OBCR) has become a very popular method for identifying products in the marketplace. Many large department stores, supermarkets, and discount stores use OBCR to help them control inventory and pricing. OBCR is used to collect data at a point-of-sale (POS)

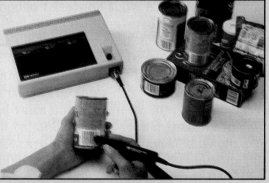

Figure 4–10
Bar code types and bar code reader.

terminal. This is a quick and efficient way to enter data to the inventory control, billing, and pricing systems. The product code is represented by a bar code, which is read by a bar code reader (see Figure 4–10). The bar code represents the manufacturer's code and product code. The industry standard code for the OBCR is called the **Universal Product Code** (UPC). There is currently more than one type of bar code structure. This has caused some concern to users of this method of optical scanning. It is hoped that a true industry standard will be established for OBCR in the near future.

Magnetic Ink Character Recognition (MICR)

Magnetic Ink Character Recognition (MICR) has been used as a data entry method since 1959. The banking industry was the primary force behind the development of MICR. Because billions of checks and deposit slips flow through the banking system each year, a faster and more efficient method for processing these items had to be developed.

The MICR input system involves a character set of fourteen characters. Figure 4–11 shows what an MICR character set looks like. As can be seen in Figure 4–11, the MICR coding structure can only support numeric data (0 thru 9). There are no provisions made in the code to represent alphabetic or special characters, which limits the use of MICR. There are two fonts, or shapes, of characters: OCR-A and OCR-B. The shapes of the characters are unusual and are both machine-readable and human-readable.

Note that the bank check in Figure 4–12 is encoded at the bottom in magnetic ink characters..The characters represent the customer's account number and bank number. The amount of the check cannot be encoded as the checks are being printed at the check manufacturer. After the check is written, an individual or company will cash or deposit the check in a bank. The first bank that receives the check encodes the amount of the check in magnetic ink characters at the bottom of the check. After the check has been fully encoded, it can then be processed by a machine called a MICR reader/sorter (see Figure 4–13).

Most banks have at least one reader/sorter to read the MICR data from a check and transfer it to magnetic tape or disk for processing. This is usually done later that same day. The machine also sorts checks by customer account number and/or bank number. After the checks have been sorted, they are sent to a Federal Reserve bank for further processing. Then they are sent back to the bank of origin where the customer's account is debited (reduced) for the amount of the check. The checks are then photographed by the bank of origin

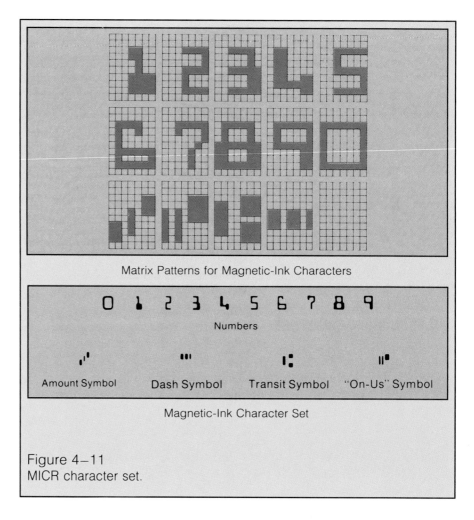

Figure 4–11
MICR character set.

and finally sent back to the customer on a monthly basis. Deposit slips are processed in a similar manner, but are handled exclusively by the bank of origin.

The MICR data input system has revolutionized the processing of checks and deposit slips in the banking industry. Without such a system, it would be very difficult for banks to process the millions of checks and slips written.

Point-of-Sale (POS) Terminals

Point-of-Sale (POS) terminals work in combination with optical bar code recognition. The idea is to collect the original data at its source

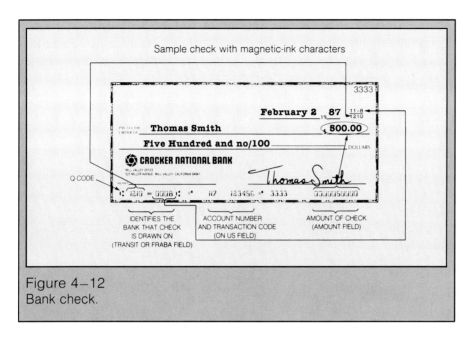

Figure 4–12
Bank check.

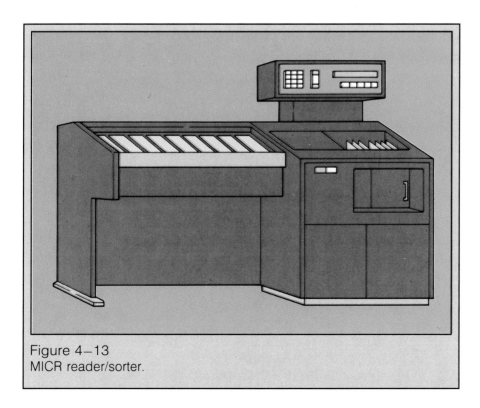

Figure 4–13
MICR reader/sorter.

of origin. The bar code on a product may be scanned using a table-top scanner with a low-level photoelectric laser beam device embedded in it. The bar code is read as the product is pulled over the scanner. The data collected during the scanning process is passed to tape or

Figure 4–14
POS terminal.

disk and then processed when needed. In many cases, after the scanning has been done, the data is passed to the computer for immediate processing. The results are transmitted back to the terminal on which the transaction was initiated (see Figure 4–14).

Many supermarkets, department stores, and discount stores are using this method to process sales transactions. This method for entering data to a computer is fast, efficient, and relatively inexpensive.

Voice Recognition/Response Units

The **voice recognition/response** method of data input and output is gaining in popularity because it is both efficient and economical. This method allows the user to input data by voice through a microphone. After words have been entered, the audio response unit searches for the user's request in its dictionary of terms and words. It then carries out the command. The output is in the form of synthetic spoken words. The hardware synthetically produces the results in English and/or other languages that it has been programmed to recognize. See Figure 4–15. The vocabularly the hardware uses and recognizes is

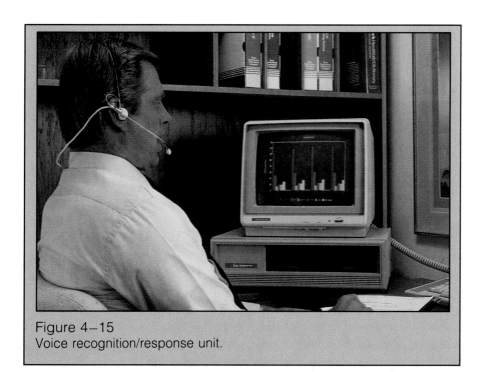

Figure 4–15
Voice recognition/response unit.

Figure 4–16
Video display terminal.

currently limited to approximately two thousand words. Several hardware vendors, including Texas Instruments, Inc., are working on better hardware and software to improve this method of input and output.

Video Terminals

A **video terminal,** sometimes referred to as a cathode ray tube (CRT) is a video display unit similar to a television screen, as illustrated in Figure 4–16. This input/output device presents data and information to and from the computer. The screen displays the data entered by the user so that it can be checked for accuracy before being transmitted to the computer for processing. After processing takes place, the results are transmitted back to the screen for the user. Video terminals are used where input/output is needed at remote sites and where softcopy, rather than hardcopy, is desired. The two basic types of video terminals are alphanumeric and graphics.

Figure 4–17
Alphanumeric video terminal.

Alphanumeric Video Terminal.   An **alphanumeric video terminal** is a device that looks like a television screen with a keyboard that allows the user to input data made up of letters, numbers, and special characters to a computer for processing (see Figure 4–17). The results of processing are displayed on the screen as output. This type of video terminal is widely used. Airline reservation centers use alphanumeric video terminals to display flight information. Any changes the user makes to the data on the screen can be made by the computer instantaneously. The stock exchanges use alphanumeric video terminals for requesting the most current stock quotations and other related information.

Graphics Video Terminal.   A **graphics video terminal** is a video display device with a keyboard. It is similar to an alphanumeric video terminal except that it also has the capability to display graphics in the form of pictorial and animated data on a screen (see Figure 4–18). Some people believe that using graphics for business applications and presentations provides management with more information and more

Figure 4–18
Graphics video terminal.

decision-making capability than using the traditional paper report approach. An engineer might use a graphics video terminal to design a new product and simulate its capability before mass production takes place. This allows changes to be made to the model being simulated, so that the best possible product can be developed and produced. The engineer can make changes to the design on the screen by using a light pen as an input device.

Light Pen Input

Light pen input uses a beam of light that captures data from a graphics video terminal screen and transfers it to the computer for processing. A light pen, as shown in Figure 4–19, is a wand that is held in a person's hand. Engineers use graphics video terminals with light pen input to design new products. The light pen allows the engineer to make changes to the design on the screen until he or she gets the desired new design. This allows the engineer to simulate and experiment with many different possibilities before deciding on a final design. Graphics video terminals with light pen input are widely used in business and industry to help solve a variety of problems.

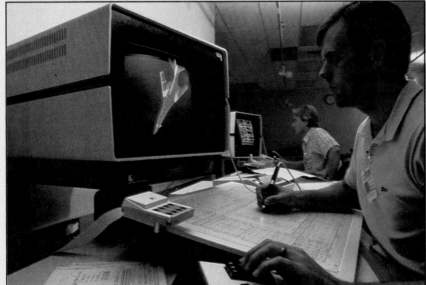

Figure 4–19
Graphics video terminal with light pen input.

5. . . .What the four types of optical scanning are?

6. . . .What magnetic ink character recognition (MICR) is?

7. . . .What a point-of-sale (POS) terminal is?

8. . . .What a voice recognition/response unit is?

9. . . .What the two types of video terminals are?

10. . . .What light pen input is?

Summary

(This summary provides answers to DO YOU REMEMBER . . . questions in the chapter.)

1. **What is the data entry process?**
   The data entry process includes *inputting* from source documents, *verifying*, and *entering* the data.

2. **What are the basic methods of entering data into a computer?**
   The basic methods of entering data into a computer are *punched-card, key-to-tape,* and *key-to-disk* data entry.

3. **Why is verification of data important?**
   Verifying or checking data after it has been keyed helps eliminate input errors.

4. **What is data density rate?**
   Data density rate refers to the amount of data that can be stored in a specific amount of space on a particular storage medium.

5. **What are the three types of optical scanning?**
   The three types of optical scanning are optical character recognition (OCR), optical mark recognition (OMR), and optical bar code recognition (OBCR).

6. **What is magnetic ink character recognition (MICR)?**
   MICR is a method of encoding data with magnetic ink so it can be recognized by an MICR reader for input to a computer.

7. **What is a point-of-sale (POS) terminal?**
   A *point-of-sale terminal* is an input device that allows data to be collected at its source.

8. **What is a voice recognition/response unit?**
   A *voice recognition/response unit* is an input/output device that recognizes voice input of data and responds with voice output of information.

9. **What are the two types of video terminals?**
   The types of video terminals are the *alphanumeric video terminal* and the *graphics video terminal.*

10. **What is light pen input?**
    Light pen input is a method of entering data into a computer by using a hand-held wand device that picks up data from a video terminal screen or graphics table.

DATA PROCESSING CAREER. . . . .
Data Entry Specialist

CAREER OPPORTUNITY FOR COMPUTER PROFESSIONAL

JOB TITLE:
6Data Entry Specialist

JOB DESCRIPTION:
Applicant will be responsible for keying, verifying, and entering data to the computer. Applicant should have experience with various input devices and media.

EXPERIENCE REQUIRED:
One or more years of experience helpful but not mandatory. Employer is willing to train on the job.

EDUCATION REQUIRED:
A high school diploma is required. Additional education a definite plus.

PERSONAL QUALIFICATIONS:
A person must like to work very closely with other people. A pleasing personality and a cooperative attitude are necessary.

Figure 4–20
Data entry specialist.

Key Terms

data entry
font
key-to-tape
key-to-disk
light pen
magnetic ink character recognition (MICR)
MICR character set
optical bar code recognition (OBCR)

optical character recognition (OCR)
optical mark recognition (OMR)
point-of-sale (POS) terminal
punched card
video terminal
voice recognition/response unit

Test Yourself

1. A _____ is a paper record of data collected from its original source.

2. Once the data has been placed into punched cards, tape, or disk, it should be _____ for accuracy.

3. _____ , _____ , and _____ are popular ways of placing data onto a medium that can be used by a computer.

4. The _____ approach is a method of recording data on magnetic tape.

5. Punched cards are used for _____ and _____ , and data can be punched into cards as _____ .

6. _____ is a method of optical scanning that deals with entering data through specially designed characters.

7. An optical scanning method that relies on graphite pencil marks located in specific areas on a special form is called _____ _____ .

8. A _____ terminal is used to collect data at the point of sale.

9. The _____ approach to data entry uses a character set of fourteen characters.

10. _____ works in combination with optical bar code recognition.

11. _____ allows the user to input data through human voice.

12. The two types of video terminals are _____ and _____ .

13. A _____ light beam reads data on a video terminal screen and transfers it to the computer for processing.

Review Questions

1. Explain the data entry process and the steps that make it up. Why is the accuracy of data entry so important in data processing? (Learning Objective 2)

2. What are the differences between the devices for entering data into a computer? (Learning Objective 3)

3. Name the different types of input devices. What are the advantages and disadvantages of each type? (Learning Objective 3)

4. Identify the different types of input media. What are some of the differences? (Learning Objective 4)

5. Why are punched cards being phased out as a data entry medium and replaced by magnetic tape and disk approaches? What is the main difference between the 80-column and 96-column punched cards? (Learning Objective 4)

6. Identify the three optical scanning methods and devices. What is each method best used for? (Learning Objective 5)

7. What is MICR, and how is it used in the banking and industry? (Learning Objective 5)

8. Discuss the point-of-sale (POS) method of data entry. Who uses this method and how? (Learning Objective 5)

9. Explain voice recognition/response and its basic uses. In what situations is this data entry and output method used? (Learning Objective 5)

10. Identify the two basic types of video terminals. What is each type used for? (Learning Objective 5)

Activities

1. Design a source document, to be called a time ticket, for collecting the basic input data for a payroll application.

2. Borrow one of your parents' personal checks and/or deposit slips and examine the MICR characters at the bottom of the document. Identify what each coded area on the document represents.

3. Examine a charge slip from a gasoline purchase. Look carefully at the OCR characters on the document. What does this data represent?

4. While at the check-out counter at a supermarket or discount department store, examine the process being used to collect the data for determining how much you owe for the products you are purchasing. What type of optical scanning method, device, and medium are used?

CHAPTER 5

Output Devices and Media

Learning Objectives

After studying this chapter carefully, you will be able to:

1. Define key terms introduced in the chapter.

2. Identify softcopy output devices and media.

3. Identify hardcopy output devices and media.

Chapter Outline

Application

When the school board recently decided to offer a course in BASIC language programming in the high school business department, Mary West was asked to teach the course. Over the years, the school had purchased several microcomputers, but until now, only one introductory computer course had been offered. In that course students received limited hands-on experience with the computers, and final grades were based on written tests. In a programming class, however, Mary knew the students would need considerable hands-on experience. In addition to tests, students would need to produce output printed on paper. Unfortunately, the school had no printers.

Mary discussed the need for printers with the principal. After agreeing that printers would be needed, the principal questioned Mary about the number, types, and costs. Aware that many types of printers were available in a wide range of prices, Mary asked permission to investigate before making a recommendation.

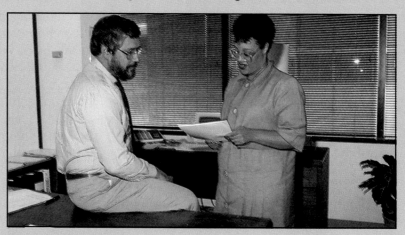

Figure 5–1
Mary West and principal discussing computer needs.

Softcopy Output Devices (CRT)

Softcopy output is produced on a hardware device called a video terminal, cathode ray tube (CRT), or visual display terminal (VDT). These devices are used to display the output of an application program on a screen similar to a television screen. Softcopy terminals display the output in monochrome (black and white, black and green, or black and amber) or in full color. A full-color video terminal is usually more expensive.

Most softcopy output devices are used with all categories and sizes of computer systems. When used with larger systems, these devices are often more advanced with expanded capabilities and versatility.

Alphanumeric Video Terminal

Alphanumeric video terminals are popular output devices used to display alphabetic, numeric, and special characters on a screen. These terminals are most frequently used to display text—that is, sentences and paragraphs (see Figure 5–2). Alphanumeric terminals are used

Figure 5–2
Alphanumeric video terminal.

for programming, word processing, and numerous other purposes. Although they can be used for displaying graphics, a graphics video terminal, explained below, produces higher quality graphics.

Graphics Video Terminal

Graphics video terminals are used to display graphics with alphanumeric headings. The terminal looks similar to an alphanumeric video terminal, but its display capability is greater. Usually, these terminals display the output in full color. The resolution (clarity) of the screen is much better than with other types of video terminals, and the images on the screen are clearer and sharper (see Figure 5–3).

These terminals are used when extensive graphing of data is necessary, especially in business and industry. You will find graphics

Figure 5–3
Graphics video terminal with graphics display.

THE COMPUTER DIDN'T DO IT!

Recently, a common problem occurred in the data processing department within a small business. One of the applications programmers was working with a newly purchased COBOL compiler package for microcomputers. The computer room floor had a thick carpet covering it. As the programmer walked across the floor, static electricity built up on his body. When he reached his microcomputer, he placed the diskette(s) for the COBOL package into the diskette drives and the static electricity that had built up in his body was immediately transferred (grounded) to the microcomputer and diskettes. The static electricity caused the data on the diskettes to be destroyed and, at the same time, the microprocessor chip in the computer was destroyed.

This is a potentially serious problem in any computer center, large or small. The atmospheric conditions must be controlled in the computer room to reduce the presence of static electricity. The computer didn't do it—people did.

video terminals used for engineering applications and in **Computer-Assisted Design** and **Computer-Assisted Manufacturing** (CAD/CAM) systems to help develop new designs for products, such as automobiles and airplanes. In business, graphics video terminals are used to display statistical data in pie charts, bar charts, or line charts.

Video terminals have gained in popularity for use in entering data, through keyboard and light pen, into a computer, and displaying data/information as output from a system. They act as a convenient interface between humans and computers.

Hardcopy Output Devices

Users frequently need output in hardcopy (printed) form to store permanently, to show to someone else, and/or to make reference to later. A sales manager might need to have a hardcopy report of inventory; a geometry teacher might need a transparency illustrating an isosceles triangle. Both the printed report and the transparency are examples of hardcopy output.

Various devices are used to produce hardcopy output. Although printers are the most widely used, there are other devices that are important because of the unique outputs they produce.

Printers

Printers are the most popular and widely used hardcopy output device. There are two principal ways of classifying printers. They are classified either according to how an image is made on the paper, or according to the amount of information they print at a time. There are two ways of making an image on paper: impact and nonimpact. There are also two methods of expressing the amount of data printed: character at a time and line at a time.

Impact printers. **Impact printers**, like typewriters, form images by physically striking the character(s) against a ribbon and paper. Some are capable of printing a single character at a time while others can print an entire line at a time.

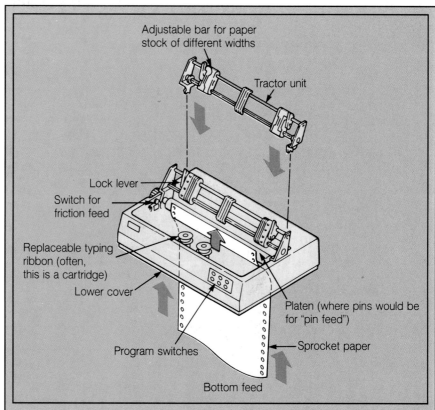

Adjustable bar for paper
stock of different widths

Tractor unit

Lock lever

Switch for
friction feed

Replaceable typing
ribbon (often,
this is a cartridge)

Lower cover

Platen (where pins would be
for "pin feed")

Sprocket paper

Program switches

Bottom feed

Figure 5–4
Character printer. The components of a typical dot-matrix printer.
Tractor-feed printers use a detachable tractor unit to feed continuous-form paper through the printer. *Pin-feed* printers have pins permanently mounted on their platens.

Character printers (also called character-at-a-time or serial printers) print like typewriters, character by character across the paper from one margin to another. Two popular character printers are the dot-matrix printer and the daisy-wheel printer. Both are used with computers of all sizes (see Figure 5–4).

A **dot-matrix printer** uses a print head that is made up of wires. A character of data is shaped by signals received by the print head assembly from the CPU. The wires in the print head are fired against a ribbon and the signals appear on the paper as a particular character of data. Dot-matrix printers also create noise as the pins/wires in the print head fire against the paper. This firing and/or striking action is referred to as *impact printing*. Dot-matrix printers are used to produce draft-quality or near-letter-quality paper output. Draft-quality is printed output in which the dots that make up the character images can be seen. In near-letter-quality printed output, the dots that make up the character images are barely visible to the human eye. Dot-matrix printers operate at speeds of from 50 to 1,000 characters per second (cps). Figure 5–5 shows a dot-matrix printer.

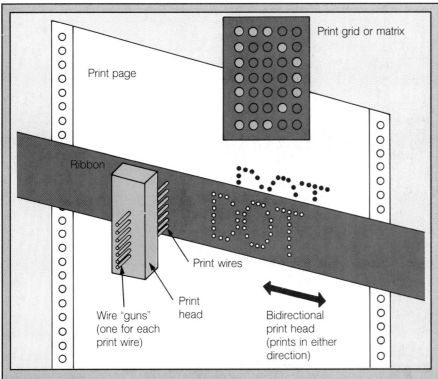

Figure 5–5
Dot-matrix printer. The print head of a dot-matrix printer uses a single column of five or more wires to create a character.

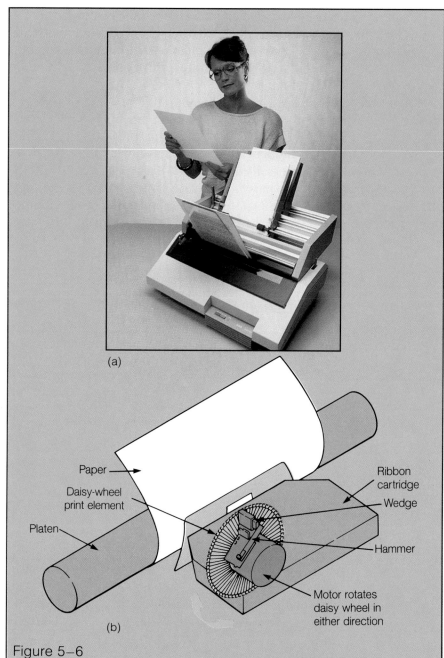

Paper

Daisy-wheel
print element

Platen

Ribbon
cartridge

Wedge

Hammer

Motor rotates
daisy wheel in
either direction

(a)

(b)

Figure 5–6
(a) Xerox Diablo 635 daisy-wheel printer. (b) The daisy-wheel
element is placed on a central spindle which spins until a specific
print character lines up with the print hammer. The hammer strikes
the back side of the character, projecting it into the ribbon and onto
the paper.

A **daisy-wheel printer** uses a print wheel as opposed to a print head to form characters of data on paper. Like a typewriter print element, a print wheel is a plastic or metal element with the character set cast into it. The "petals" on a daisy wheel each have a cast letter or character at the end, and as the print wheel rotates, a hammer strikes the particular petal containing the character to be printed. The image is imprinted on the paper when the hammer causes the petal to strike against a ribbon onto the paper, similar to a typewriter's action. Daisy wheels can be purchased in many different fonts. The daisy wheel can be removed from the printer for storage or for changing to a different daisy wheel. Daisy-wheel printers are used to produce letter-quality paper output. Daisy-wheel printers operate at speeds from 10 to 100 characters per second (cps). Figure 5–6 shows a daisy-wheel printer.

Line printers (also called line-at-a-time printers) assemble all characters to be printed on a line of paper (called a print line), and print all of them simultaneously. Several different line printers are used today, including chain printers, band printers, and drum printers (see Figure 5–7).

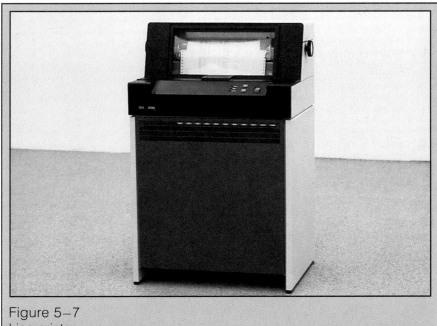

Figure 5–7
Line printer.

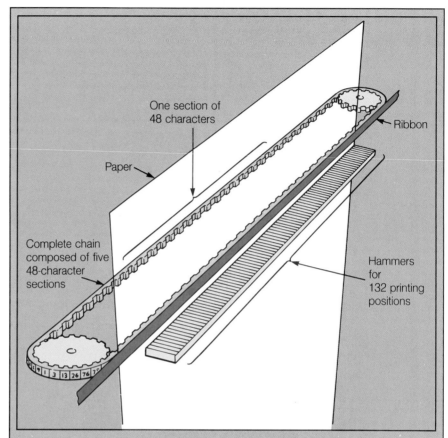

Figure 5–8
Chain printer. The print chain of a chain printer is much like a chain saw with print characters on it. The chain cycles continuously in a loop. Print hammers strike the paper from behind, forcing the paper against an inked ribbon and into the print characters on the chain.

A **chain printer** consists of a chain with links engraved with character printing slugs. Hammers behind the paper and ribbon are aligned with every printing position. As the chain speeds past the printing positions, the hammers strike the appropriate characters against the ribbon and onto the paper. From 200 to over 3,000 lines can be printed per minute depending on the printer used (see Figure 5–8).

A **band printer** operates in a manner similar to a chain printer with about the same speed. Instead of using a chain, a band printer has a steel print band with characters embossed on it. Like chain printers,

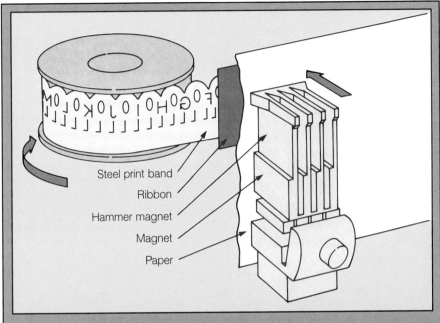

Steel print band
Ribbon
Hammer magnet
Magnet
Paper

Figure 5-9
Band printer. A band printer is much like a chain printer except that the band printer uses a thin steel band instead of a chain for its print characters.

band printers have hammers aligned to strike the ribbon and paper when the proper characters are in position (see Figure 5-9).

The printing mechanism of a **drum printer** is a metal cylinder of bands. Each band contains all the possible characters in a character set. One revolution of the rapidly rotating drum is required to print one line. A fast-activating hammer opposite each band strikes the desired character against a ribbon onto the paper as it passes. With one rotation of the drum an entire line is printed (see Figure 5-10).

There are both advantages and disadvantages to using impact printers instead of nonimpact printers. The major advantage is that they can make multiple copies (carbon copies) of a page or document. Another advantage is price. Some impact printers are relatively inexpensive; thus, they are more affordable for many users.

Generally speaking, many impact printers are slower than some nonimpact printers. Also, impact printers offer a limited choice of fonts. Because this technology requires more moving parts in printing, they tend to be less reliable and more noisy.

Number of bands corresponds
to number of printing positions

Each band consists
of all printing
characters available

Figure 5–10
Drum printer. A drum printer uses 80 or more character sets imprinted
on a cylindrical drum. A separate hammer for each character set
forces the print page into an inked ribbon and the character when the
character aligns at the print position.

DO YOU
REMEMBER

1. . . .The two types of softcopy output devices?

2. . . .The types of hardcopy output devices?

3. . . .How printers are classified?

4. . . .How impact printers print character images on paper?

5. . . .Which impact printers print a character at a time and which
print a line at a time?

Nonimpact Printers.   **Nonimpact printers** do not print characters by
physically striking a ribbon and paper. Instead, a variety of methods
are used.

The printing method used by **xerographic printers** is similar to that
used in common xerographic copy machines. With speeds up to 6,000
lines per minute, xerographic printers are fast and desirable for many

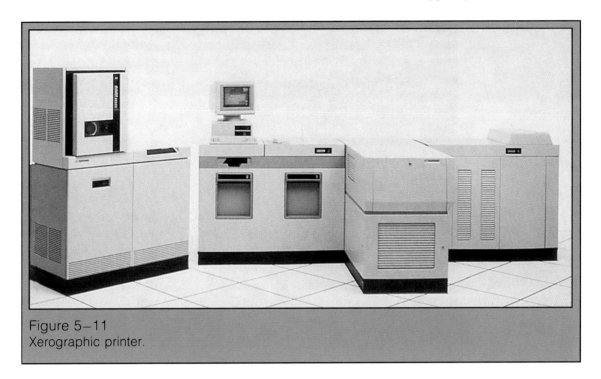

Figure 5–11
Xerographic printer.

heavy volume applications. Xerographic printers are used mostly by large companies that require large volumes of printed output. Customer orders, accounts payable, and accounts receivable systems often require the use of a xerographic printer because of the large volume of printed output generated by these computer-based applications (see Figure 5–11).

Laser printers can be used with computers of every size. Capable of printing up to 28,000 lines per minute, laser printers produce high quality print. Because of the fast speeds and the quality of the print, laser printers are often used to print books and magazines as well as regular hardcopy output for management reports. Thus, laser printers are normally used with larger computer systems. The cost of laser printers is more than any other type of printer because of the technology used in them (see Figure 5–12).

Ink-jet printers are becoming more popular for use with computers of all sizes. Using a tiny spray of ink and templates, a wide variety of fonts are possible. Their print quality is excellent, and ink-jet printers are capable of printing from 100 to 1,000 characters per second (see Figure 5–13).

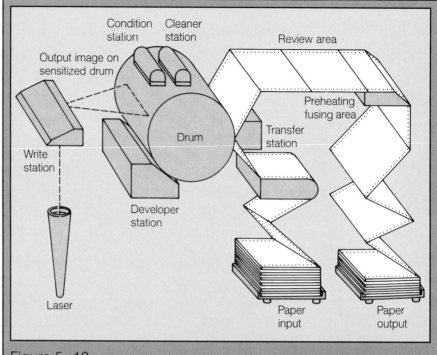

Figure 5–12
Laser printer. A laser printer uses a photosensitive drum that is cleaned and conditioned for each printing cycle. The laser beam creates a print image on the drum, which is then developed and transferred to the print page.

There are advantages and disadvantages to using nonimpact printers. Among the advantages are print quality, speed, reliability, quietness, and versatility. Their versatility lies in the wide range of fonts available for them. The most serious disadvantage is their inability to make carbon copies—a frequent necessity for some applications. As improvements in technology continue to be made, nonimpact printers will become the predominant means of producing hardcopy output.

Special-Purpose Output Devices

Larger computer systems frequently use special-purpose output devices for certain applications. Among them are plotters and graphics display devices.

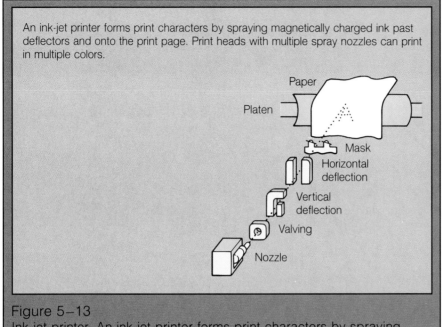

An ink-jet printer forms print characters by spraying magnetically charged ink past deflectors and onto the print page. Print heads with multiple spray nozzles can print in multiple colors.

Paper

Platen

Mask

Horizontal deflection

Vertical deflection

Valving

Nozzle

Figure 5–13
Ink-jet printer. An ink-jet printer forms print characters by spraying magnetically charged ink past deflectors and onto the print page. Print heads with multiple spray nozzles can print in multiple colors.

Plotters. **Plotters** are used regularly in business, institutions, and government. A **plotter** is a hardcopy output device that creates images on a piece of paper by the movement of one or more pens across the surface of the paper, or by the movement of the paper under the tip of the pens. There are three types of plotters: flatbed, drum, and electrostatic. Plotters initially were used for architectural, automotive, and aircraft designs, but now they are used extensively for business graphics applications to create bar, pie, and line charts. A drum pen plotter and a flatbed plotter are illustrated in Figure 5–14.

Digitizers are used as input devices in connection with plotters. A digitizer transforms points, lines, and curves from a sketch, photograph, or drawing to digital signals and sends them to the computer for processing. They are used by engineers to design new products, such as automobiles and televisions. Engineers draw graphic designs of their products on a digitizer tablet or a graphics display monitor with light pen. They then produce the design as hardcopy output on a plotter. This process is called **Computer-Assisted Design** (CAD).

Figure 5–14
Drum plotters are used by businesses to prepare commercial-grade output.

Computer-generated art is produced through the use of a digitizer and plotter. Figure 5–15 shows a person using a digitizer. And Figure 5–16 illustrates an example of digitized art.

Music Synthesizer.   With the use of a **music synthesizer**, computers can be used to compose music and to play and refine existing musical works. A music synthesizer is a specialized output device that converts electronic signals into sounds. Synthesizers can produce a wide variety of musical sounds and can imitate the sounds of many musical instruments, including electronic organ sounds, with high quality. This

Figure 5–15
Digitizer.

output device has become a tool in the music industry (see Figure 5–17).

Graphics Display Devices.   When a newly designed product is approved for manufacturing, exact design specifications are followed in manufacturing the product. When a computer is used to monitor the manufacturing process itself, this process is referred to as **Computer-Assisted Manufacturing** (CAM). When both CAD and CAM are used in industry for designing and manufacturing products, such as automobiles and airplanes, the processes are collectively called CAD/CAM. CAD is used to design the various parts that make up a product, and CAM is used to monitor the manufacturing process to be sure all parts are assembled correctly into a complete unit. A graphics display monitor with CAD/CAM capabilities is illustrated in Figure 5–18.

Computer Output Microfilm (COM).   Printed paper output requires storage space and is often cumbersome to store, use, and find. In situations where large volumes of output are to be stored and used

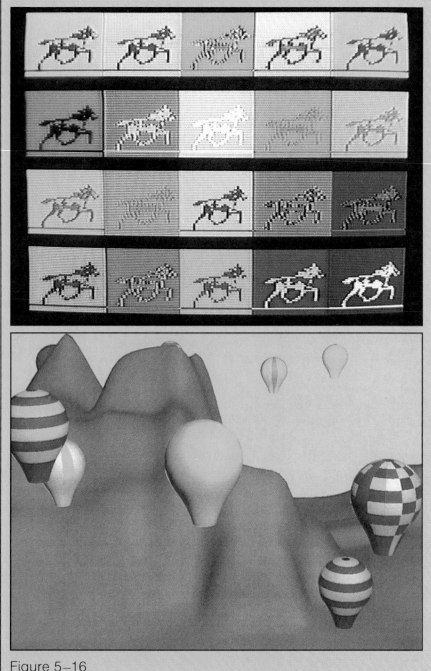

Figure 5–16
Digitized art.

(a)

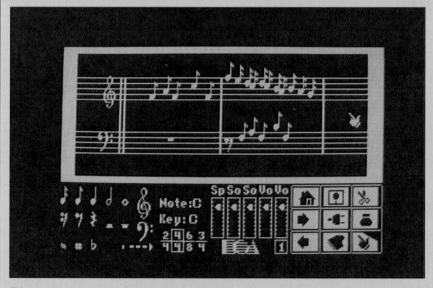

(b)

Figure 5–17
Music synthesizer. (a) Experimental computer music center at MIT.
(b) Music construction set allows user to compose melodies for the
computer to play. With the aid of a joystick, the user moves music
symbols from the area at bottom onto the music staff.

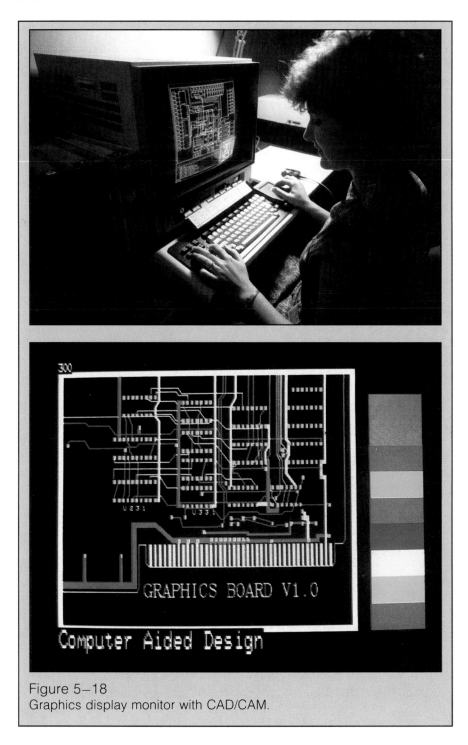

Figure 5–18
Graphics display monitor with CAD/CAM.

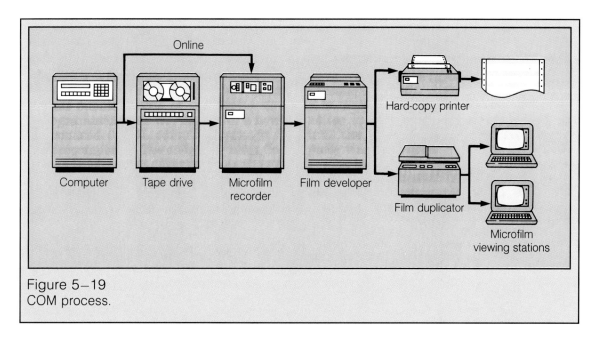

Figure 5–19
COM process.

for future reference, computer output microfilm (COM) can be used to record computer output as microscopic images on film. With this method, the computer produces miniature photographic images. The output can first be recorded on magnetic tape and then transferred to 35-mm rolls or 4 × 6-inch microfiche. Microfiche is a special type of plastic card used to store photographic images. Figure 5–19 shows a diagram of the COM process.

Graphics, as well as characters and records, can be stored with the COM system at speeds of up to fifty times as fast as regular printing. An additional advantage is that extra copies can be made at little added cost. A microfilm reader that magnifies the microscopic images from microfilm so that they can be read by the human eye is shown in Figure 5–20.

6. . . .How nonimpact printers print character images on paper?

7. . . .The types of nonimpact printers and their advantages over impact printers?

8. . . .The special-purpose output devices and their uses?

9. . . .The process of computer-output-microfilm (COM)?

DO YOU
REMEMBER

Figure 5-20
Computer output microfilm (COM) reader.

Summary

(This summary provides answers to DO YOU REMEMBER . . . questions in the chapter.)

1. What are the two types of softcopy output devices?

The two types of softcopy output devices are the alphanumeric video terminal and the graphics video terminal. Each of these video terminals is used for specific purposes. The *alphanumeric video terminal* is used to display alphabetic, numeric, and special character data on a screen called a *c*athode *r*ay *t*ube (CRT). The *graph-*

ics video terminal is used to display graphics data, such as a bar chart, pie chart, or line chart.

2. What are the types of hardcopy output devices?
Several devices are used to produce hardcopy output including *printers* and *special-purpose output devices.*

3. How are printers classified?
Printers are classified according to the ways they make an image on the paper and according to the amount of information they print at a time.

4. How do impact printers print character images on paper?
Impact printers form images by physically *striking* the character against a ribbon and paper.

5. Which impact printers print a character at a time and which print a line at a time?
Some impact printers that print a character at a time are dot-matrix printers and daisy-wheel printers. Chain printers, band printers, and drum printers print a line at a time.

6. How do nonimpact printers print character images on paper?
Nonimpact printers form images by electrostatic, xerographic, and laser transfer of data to paper. There is very little, if any, noise during the transfer process.

7. What are the types of nonimpact printers and their advantage over impact printers?
Nonimpact printers include xerographic printers, laser printers, and ink-jet printers. They are faster, more reliable, and more versatile than impact printers.

8. What are the special-purpose output devices and what are they used for?
The special-purpose output devices include *plotters, digitizers, music synthesizers,* and *graphics display devices.* These devices are used for numerous applications including computer-*a*ssisted-*d*esign (CAD) and computer-*a*ssisted-*m*anufacturing (CAM).

9. What is the process of computer-output-microfilm (COM)?
Computer-output-microfilm (COM) uses special technology to reduce large amounts of output to microscopic size for permanent and efficient storage. The output is recorded on magnetic tape and then transferred to microfiche. Graphics, in addition to text and records, can be produced using this special-purpose output technology.

DATA PROCESSING CAREER. . . . .
Input/Output Control Specialist

CAREER OPPORTUNITY FOR COMPUTER PROFESSIONAL

JOB TITLE:
Input/Output Control Specialist

JOB DESCRIPTION:
Applicant will be responsible for processing user input/output requests from the various departments within the company.

EXPERIENCE REQUIRED:
One year of experience desired but not required. Employer is willing to provide on-the-job training for new employee.

EDUCATION REQUIRED:
A high school diploma is required. Additional schooling/training is a plus.

PERSONAL QUALIFICATIONS:
Applicant must possess good basic communication skills. A pleasing personality and good work habits are essential.

Figure 5–21
Input/output control specialist.

Key Terms

alphanumeric video terminal
band printer
chain printer
computer-assisted design
   (CAD)
computer-assisted manufacturing (CAM)
computer output microfilm
   (COM)
daisy-wheel printer
digitizer

dot-matrix printer
graphics video terminal
impact printer
ink-jet printer
laser printer
light pen input
music synthesizer
nonimpact printer
plotter
resolution

Test Yourself

1. The two types of softcopy output devices (CRTs) are _____
   and _____ .

2. The two classifications of printers are _____ and
   _____ .

3. _____ , _____ , and _____ are used by
   engineers as special-purpose output devices to design new products, such as automobiles and televisions.

4. _____ is used to record
   computer output as microscopic images on film.

5. A _____ is capable of printing up to
   28,000 lines per minute.

6. Using a tiny spray of ink and templates, a wide variety of fonts
   are possible using a(n) _____ .

7. _____ and _____ are used to print graphics
   output.

Review Questions

1. Identify the two types of video terminals used to display softcopy
   output. What is each best used for? (Learning Objective 2)

2. What are the two main categories of printers and their subcategories? What are the differences between the two main categories of printers? (Learning Objective 3)

3. Explain the uses of, and compare, the following special-purpose output devices: plotters, digitizers, and graphics display monitors. (Learning Objectives 2 and 3)

4. Explain COM. What is it used for? How is it used in business and industry? (Learning Objective 3)

5. Identify the basic differences between hardcopy output and softcopy output. (Learning Objectives 2 and 3)

Activities

1. Make arrangements to visit your local microcomputer store and examine the different computer output devices.

2. Visit your school's computer lab. Make a list of the available output devices and how they are used in a laboratory environment.

3. Plan a visit to your school's library to determine how COM is being used. Write a brief paper describing your findings and experiences.

CHAPTER 6

Secondary Storage

Learning Objectives

After studying this chapter carefully, you will be able to:

1. Define key terms introduced in this chapter.

2. Explain the importance of secondary storage.

3. Explain how the storage hierarchy can be used to select the most appropriate type of storage.

4. Describe the two main types of secondary storage used with microcomputers.

5. Identify some other types of secondary storage.

Chapter Outline

STORAGE HIERARCHY

MAGNETIC TAPE
Magnetic Tape for Large Computers
Magnetic Tape for Microcomputers

MAGNETIC DISK
Magnetic Disk for Large Computers
Magnetic Disk for Microcomputers

OTHER TYPES OF SECONDARY STORAGE
Tape Cartridge Mass Storage
Optical (Laser) Disk Storage

DATA PROCESSING CAREER: Librarian

Application

It was Friday afternoon when Chou Tran arrived at the airport to make arrangements to fly to London, England, for a two-week visit with her parents. She had not seen her parents in several months and was looking forward to her reunion with them.

At the airport, Chou went to the Apollo Airlines reservations counter where she inquired about flights to London. The agent immediately used her computer terminal to inquire about the airline's flight schedule. On the screen appeared a complete schedule of information for all flights to London, including departure and arrival times, ticket prices, and in-flight meals. Chou reserved a seat on flight #946 and paid for her ticket. After receiving payment, the agent checked in Chou's luggage.

The airline's on-line secondary storage system made it possible for the agent to obtain flight information needed to make Chou's reservation. This information had been stored in the computer's secondary storage system which was connected to the computer. Because the agent's terminal was connected to the computer, the agent had immediate access to the needed information.

Most airlines now use on-line secondary storage to provide passengers with information quickly. Depending on their particular needs, other computer users may use different kinds of secondary storage. Various types of secondary storage media and devices are explained in this chapter.

Storage Hierarchy

Computer users sometimes need more storage than the limited amount of primary storage available in the CPU. To overcome this limitation, primary storage can be supplemented with secondary storage. **Secondary storage,** also called auxiliary storage, consists of all computer storage that is not part of the CPU. Secondary storage may be either on-line or off-line. An **on-line** secondary storage device is one that is connected to the computer, such as a disk drive. When the device is on-line, information stored on the medium is immediately available to the computer user. An **off-line** storage device is one that is not connected to the computer. When information is not needed immediately, it is often stored in an off-line medium. When it is needed, the device can be connected to the computer, putting the device on-line and making the information available.

Computer users often use a **storage hierarchy** to determine which type of storage is best for their particular needs. Figure 6–1 illustrates and explains the storage hierarchy.

Three important criteria should be considered when selecting the type of storage to be used: speed, storage capacity, and cost of storage. By applying each criterion to the storage hierarchy, a computer user should be able to determine the most appropriate storage for a particular application.

Let's look now at the meaning of each of the three criteria.

1. **Speed** refers to the amount of time required to retrieve stored data. In many applications, the speed at which data can be stored and/or retrieved is important.

2. **Storage capacity** refers to the amount of data that can be stored on the particular storage medium and device. Having sufficient storage capacity is essential.

3. The **cost of storage** is the cost per byte of stored data. The cost varies according to the particular storage device and medium.

By applying these three criteria (speed, storage capacity, and cost of storage) to the storage hierarchy in Figure 6–1, a computer user should be able to select the most appropriate type of storage. Notice

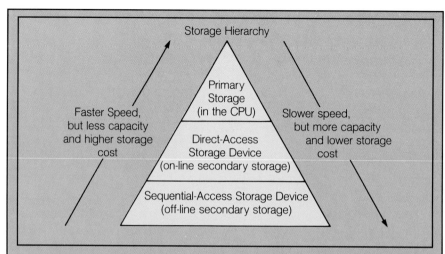

Figure 6–1
Primary storage is part of the CPU. Secondary storage is all storage that is not part of the CPU and is needed to supplement primary storage to provide permanent storage of instructions and data. The pyramid shows the relationship between primary storage, direct-access secondary storage, and sequential-access storage. Faster storage and access can be achieved by moving up the pyramid; however, storage cost increases. Increased storage capacity and lower cost are achieved by moving down the pyramid.

that there are "tradeoffs" when moving up and down the pyramid. As shown by the upward arrow, the top level of the hierarchy pyramid illustrates that data stored in primary storage can be retrieved more quickly than data stored on tape or disk. However, primary storage in the CPU is the most limited and expensive type of storage. At the bottom of the pyramid, sequential-access storage, explained in the

DO YOU
REMEMBER

1. . . .The three types of storage shown on the storage hierarchy pyramid?

2. . . .The three criteria for selecting the type of storage to be used for a particular computer application?

3. . . .The "tradeoffs" resulting from upward and downward movement on the pyramid?

4. . . .The difference between on-line and off-line secondary storage?

next section, provides the slowest retrieval speed but the largest amount of storage at the lowest cost per byte. Recall that primary storage was explained in Chapter 3. The following sections explain some of the more popular and widely used secondary storage devices and media.

Magnetic Tape

Magnetic tape is a sequential-access secondary storage medium consisting of a long, narrow strip of plastic material upon which particles are magnetized to represent data. As a storage medium, it is suitable for many computer applications. For computer applications requiring the periodic processing of several to even hundreds of individual records, computer users often use magnetic tape as the storage medium.

The processing of a company's payroll is an example of this. Individual employee records containing payroll data are stored on the tape in a sequence, or order, determined by the company as shown in Figure 6–2. Individual records may be stored on the tape alphabetically by employee last name, numerically by employee number, or in another manner determined by the company.

Notice that the individual records are separated by blank spaces called interrecord gaps (IRGs). An **interrecord gap** (IRG) is a blank space between two records which allows a single record to be processed individually, if desired.

Each employee record can easily be retrieved by the computer that processes the data for each employee according to instructions stored in the computer. Following the processing of each record, individual paychecks can be printed using an output device.

Magnetic tape can be used with both large and small computer systems. While the tape for large and small computers is similar, there are minor differences. The tape used with large computers is called standard tape. That used with smaller computers is microcomputer tape.

Magnetic Tape for Large Computers

Magnetic tape is a thin film of plastic similar to the sound tape used with a reel-to-reel tape recorder. The tape is coated with a thin substance containing microscopic particles that can be magnetized to represent data, as shown in Figure 6–3.

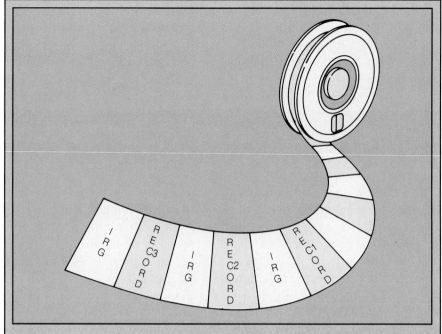

Figure 6–2
Individual employee records are stored sequentially (in order) on the tape. Individual records are separated by interrecord gaps (IRGs).

The tape itself is contained on a supply reel. A typical reel holds about 2,400 feet of ½–inch wide tape. The supply reel is loaded (installed) onto a machine called a **tape drive** (Figure 6–4) which must be connected to the computer before data can be written to, or read from, the tape. Because a particular supply reel is loaded only when needed, magnetic tape storage is often referred to as *off-line storage*. While not in use, a tape reel is stored for safekeeping in a tape library.

To load a reel of magnetic tape, the leading end of the tape from the supply reel is threaded through the tape drive's **read/write head assembly** and connected to a take-up reel. Data is written to, or read from, the tape as the tape passes the read/write heads that are housed in the read/write head assembly. This procedure is similar to that of a reel-to-reel tape recorder/player. As a person speaks into the microphone of a reel-to-reel sound recorder, sound is recorded on the tape as the tape passes the write (recording) head. When the tape is played back, the person's recorded voice can be heard as the tape passes the read (playback) head.

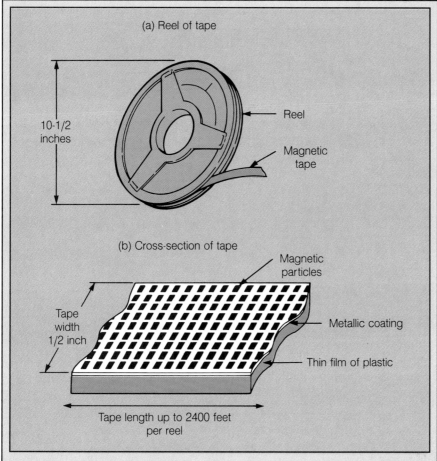

(a) Reel of tape

10-1/2 inches

Reel

Magnetic tape

(b) Cross-section of tape

Magnetic particles

Tape width 1/2 inch

Metallic coating

Thin film of plastic

Tape length up to 2400 feet per reel

Figure 6–3
A typical magnetic tape reel can hold up to 2,400 feet of ½-inch-side tape. The tape is made of thin plastic, and coated with a substance containing particles that can be magnetized to represent data.

An important characteristic of magnetic tape is that data must be written to, and read from, the tape sequentially (in order), as with a sound tape recorder/player. When using a sound recorder/player, the first word spoken is recorded first, then the second, and so on until all words have been recorded. When the tape is replayed (after re-winding), the words are heard in the same order in which they were recorded. This same sequential-access concept applies to computer tape, making magnetic tape an excellent sequential-access storage medium for many applications.

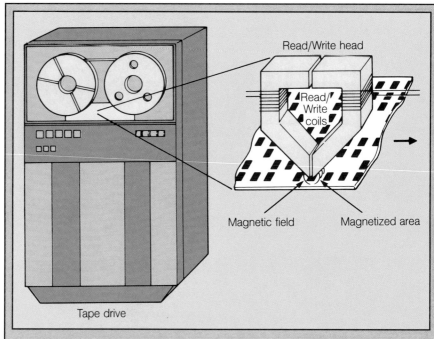

Figure 6–4
During processing, the tape moves past a read/write head that can
store (write) data on the tape by magnetizing particles on the tape, or
retrieve (read) data already stored on the tape.

How Data Is Stored on Tape. The magnetic particles on the tape
surface may be magnetized to represent alphabetic, numeric, and
special characters. As the tape passes the read/write heads, combinations of these particles (bytes) are magnetized in a systematic
manner.

To accomplish this, the tape is divided into horizontal rows, called
tracks. Each track extends the full length of the tape. Tape may contain
any number of tracks, but nine-track tape is the most popular. The tape
drive is designed to store data on tape according to the EBCDIC coding
scheme. This scheme coded on tape is illustrated in Figure 6–5. Notice
that eight tracks are used for recording data. One track, called a **parity
track,** is used to ensure that the number of individual magnetized particles (bits) is the correct number.

Notice how data is recorded on the tape. The letter *I* is recorded
by magnetizing a single particle vertically in each of the tracks 0, 3,
6, and 7. The character *A* is recorded by magnetizing a single particle

in each of the tracks 0, 6, 7, and 8. Notice how other characters are recorded using the EBCDIC code.

An input device, such as a keyboard, enables the user to record data on the tape automatically. By pressing the 5 key, for example, the number 5 is automatically stored on the tape.

Magnetic tape is an excellent medium for storing large amounts of data sequentially. The actual amount that can be stored depends upon

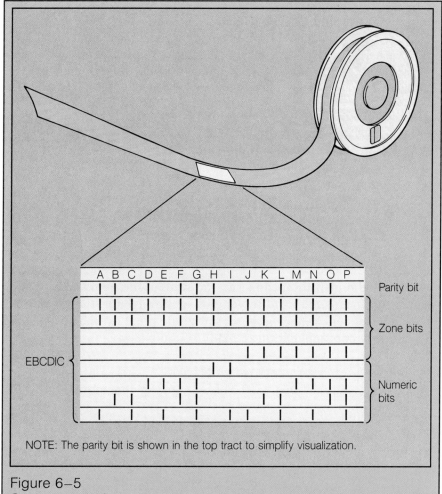

NOTE: The parity bit is shown in the top tract to simplify visualization.

Figure 6–5
On the tape surface, magnetic particles are arranged vertically and magnetized to represent data according to the EBCDIC code. Magnetized particles (shown) represent 1s. Non-magnetized particles (not shown) represent 0s.

the **density of the tape** (number of bytes per inch of tape). Tape is available in single, double, and triple form. Triple-density tape contains about three times as many bytes per inch as single-density tape; it is also more expensive. While densities of 1,600 bytes per inch are common, some tapes can hold 6,250, or more, bytes.

Speed of Magnetic Tape.   Magnetic tape moves through a tape drive at speeds ranging from 25 to 200 inches per second. The speed of the drive and density of the tape determine the speed at which data can be written to, or read from, the tape by the CPU. The following formula can be used to calculate the speed at which data can be written to, or read from, the tape:

$$\begin{array}{c} \text{Bytes per inch} \\ \text{(BPI) of tape} \end{array} \times \begin{array}{c} \text{Speed of} \\ \text{tape drive} \end{array} = \begin{array}{c} \text{Speed of} \\ \text{writing/reading} \end{array}$$

Consider the following example. If the tape density is 1,600 bytes per inch (BPI) and the speed of the tape drive is 50 inches per second, the speed at which data can be written or read is 80,000 bytes per second (1,600 × 50 = 80,000).

Illustration of Magnetic Tape Use.   We have seen that information is stored on tape in units called records. Individual records can consist of any number of fields such as student name, address, grade level, courses completed, course grades, and grade point average. All student records, collectively, make up a student file. Using a computer, the school administration can store the student file on magnetic tape. At certain times, such as at the end of each semester, the file can be updated to reflect changes in grades or grade point average. Actually, this is a common application in many schools today.

Advantages and Disadvantages of Magnetic Tape.   Magnetic tape offers several advantages to the user. Among the more important advantages are these:

1. Large amounts of data can be stored on tape.

2. Magnetic tape can be erased and reused.

3. Errors can be corrected easily and information updated quickly.

4. Magnetic tape is relatively inexpensive.

5. Magnetic tape is an excellent sequential-
access storage medium.

There are, however, disadvantages to using magnetic tape. These
are among the more important:

1. Because data is stored sequentially, the data
cannot be accessed directly. This can be a
disadvantage when the stored data is needed
immediately.

2. Data stored on magnetic tape can be accidentally erased or altered.

3. Tape and reel containers must be labeled
properly for identification because the stored
data is not in human-readable form.

4. The data stored on tape can be affected by
environmental hazards such as dust and
static electricity.

---

5. . . .The physical characteristics of magnetic tape for large computers?

6. . . .How data is recorded on magnetic tape?

**7. . . .How to calculate the speed at which data can be written to, or
read from, tape?**

8. . . .The advantages and disadvantages of using magnetic tape?

DO YOU
REMEMBER

Magnetic Tape for Microcomputers

Many earlier microcomputers used magnetic tape for secondary storage. However, relatively few are still in use today. In recent years,
magnetic tape has been replaced by magnetic disks, which will be
explained later, as the dominant type of secondary storage for
microcomputers.

Magnetic tape for these microcomputers is contained in a durable
plastic cassette. The tape is $\frac{1}{4}$-inch wide and ranges between 150 and

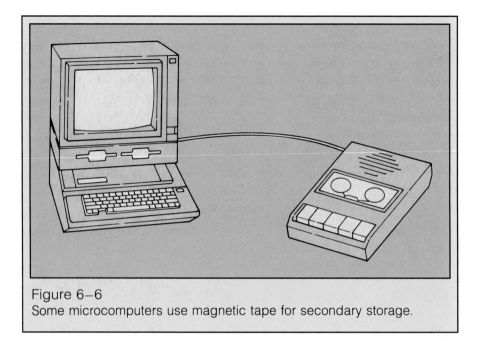

Figure 6-6
Some microcomputers use magnetic tape for secondary storage.

300 feet in length. Inside the cassette is a supply reel and a take-up reel.

A small tape recorder/player serves as a tape drive for writing data onto, and retrieving data from, the tape. When needed, the tape cassette is inserted into the player/recorder that is connected to the computer, as illustrated in Figure 6-6.

When the recorder/player is plugged into the microcomputer and turned on, data stored on the tape is available to the computer. Unlike the nine-track tape used with large computers, microcomputer tape has only one track. A major reason for a single track is that a small tape recorder/player has only one read/write head. Data is recorded on the tape horizontally as magnetized bits, as shown in Figure 6-7. Because data is represented horizontally, the amount of data that can be stored on a single tape cassette is limited—a disadvantage for some applications.

DO YOU
REMEMBER

9. . . .The physical characteristics of magnetic tape for micro-computers?

10. . . .Why microcomputer tape has only one track for recording data?

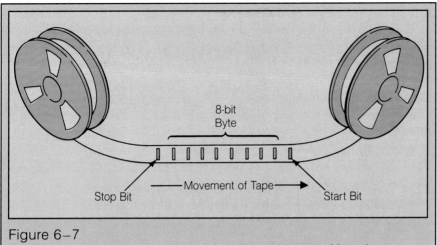

Figure 6–7
A byte of data is represented horizontally on the tape. Note the two extra bits that indicate the beginning and end of the byte.

Magnetic Disk

Magnetic disk is the most widely used type of **on-line** secondary storage and is used with computers of all sizes. Later in this chapter, disk storage for microcomputers will be explained. First, let's look at magnetic disk usage and characteristics for large computers. A magnetic disk for a large computer is often referred to as a standard magnetic disk.

Magnetic Disk for Large Computers

A **standard magnetic disk** is a thin metal disk with two usable sides. Like magnetic tape, the disk is coated with a thin layer of plastic-like material containing magnetizable particles.

Several disks are housed in a **disk pack** resembling a cake platter. Inside, individual disks are arranged vertically resembling layers of a cake. A small space between each disk allows read/write heads to move in and out between the disks.

When the disk pack is loaded into a **disk drive** and the cover removed, an **access mechanism** consisting of access arms and read/write heads writes data to, and reads data from, the disks. The access mechanism is designed so that read/write heads quickly move in and out between the disks, as shown in Figure 6–8. There is one read/write head for each usable disk surface.

How Data Is Stored on Disk.   Data is stored as magnetized spots, representing 0s and 1s, in concentric circles (rings) called **tracks** on the disk surface. Usually, there are 200 tracks on each disk surface numbered 000 to 199 (see Figure 6–9). All tracks hold the same amount of data.

To understand how data is written to, or read from, a magnetic disk, imagine a record player. The arm holding the needle can be positioned in the outermost groove. As the needle moves inward on grooves, songs are played in sequence. Any particular song can be played by positioning the needle at the beginning of that song.

A magnetic disk, however, contains tracks and not grooves. Data is stored on the individual tracks as shown in Figure 6–10.

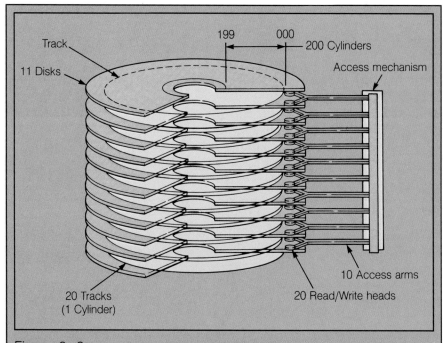

Figure 6–8
When mounted in a disk drive, read/write heads move inward and outward between the disks to store and/or retrieve data.

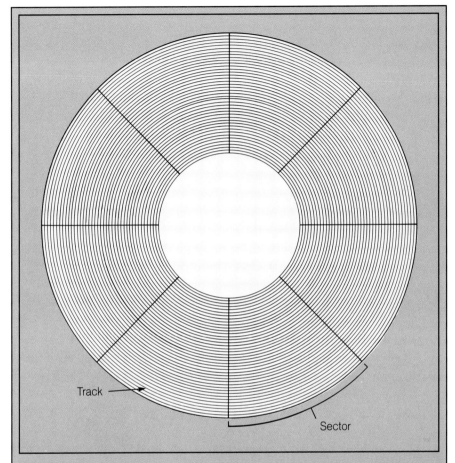

Track

Sector

Figure 6–9
Tracks and sectors on the surface of a magnetic disk. Tracks are invisible concentric circles along which data is stored. Data is also stored according to sector. Sectors are defined by special codes recorded on the tracks.

It is not necessary for a read/write head to touch the disk to write or read data. The head merely "floats" slightly above the surface of the rapidly spinning disk but does not touch the surface. If the read/write head accidentally touches the disk, the data could be destroyed and the disk damaged. This is known as a **head crash.**

Because of the rapid rotation of the disks and the speed at which the read/write heads move across the disks' surfaces, any stored data

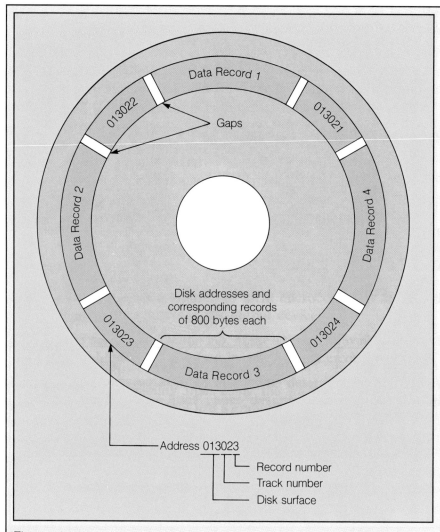

Figure 6–10
Records are stored according to disk surface number, track number, and record number. An address can be used to locate a particular record.

can be read (accessed) very fast. Thus, magnetic disk provides **direct-access** storage for the user. This means that data or information can be written to, or read from, the disk randomly (in any order) by the user.

Manufacturers know that users often need to store more data than can be stored on a single track, and have designed standard disks to meet this need. Recall from Figure 6–8 that disks are arranged vertically in a disk pack similar to the arrangement of phonograph records on a turntable. Thus, track #000 on each disk is aligned vertically with track #000 on each of the other disks, and track #199 on each disk is aligned vertically with track #199 on all other disks. These vertical alignments are called **cylinders.** There are the same number of cylinders in a disk pack as there are tracks on a single disk. Cylinders are important in data storage because when the amount of data being stored exceeds the capacity of a particular track, the remaining data is often stored in the next track in the same cylinder.

Like magnetic tape, the storage capacity of a disk pack is referred to as **data density.** Disks are available in single, double, and triple densities.

Standard disk packs may be either removable or nonremovable. A removable disk pack can be loaded into a disk drive when needed, and removed and stored when it is no longer needed. A nonremovable disk pack is permanently installed in the disk drive with stationary read/write heads that allow data to be written to, or read from, the disk much faster.

Speed of Magnetic Disk.   When data is accessed (retrieved) from a magnetic disk, the data goes to primary storage in the CPU. The speed at which this is accomplished is determined by the density (bytes per inch) of the stored data and the rotational speed of the disk. With standard disk packs, the speed at which data is transferred from disk to primary storage ranges from 400,000 and 2,000,000 bytes per second.

Illustration of Magnetic Disk Use.   The story at the beginning of this chapter illustrates an important use of magnetic disk for secondary storage. Recall that Chou Tran needed information about flights to London in order to make a reservation. The reservations agent obtained the needed information via a computer terminal. The terminal was connected to a large computer that, in turn, was connected to a magnetic disk storage system. Complete information about all flights was stored on the disks. This **on-line** storage system enabled the agent to retrieve needed flight information almost immediately.

A computer program allowed the agent to retrieve information about all flights to London simply by typing the keyword *London* on the terminal keyboard. Almost instantly, the information was displayed on the terminal screen. Using this information, Chou could decide which flight she wanted to take.

All major airlines use on-line magnetic disk storage in order to provide customers with fast and complete flight information. When a reservation is made, the particular flight record is updated. Among other things, the update shows that one less seat is available to prospective passengers.

Advantages and Disadvantages of Magnetic Disk.   Although magnetic disk storage is a popular and widely used type of secondary storage, it is not suited for all applications. The user must decide which type of storage is best for a particular application because magnetic disk storage offers both advantages and disadvantages. When compared to magnetic tape, disks have the following advantages:

1. Records can be stored for direct-access processing, or they can be stored and processed sequentially, like records on magnetic tape.

2. On-line disk records can be accessed and processed almost immediately (in a few milliseconds).

3. On-line disk records and files can be updated simultaneously with a single input transaction.

Compared to magnetic tape, disks have some disadvantages. Among the more important disadvantages are these:

1. When magnetic disks are used for sequential processing, this medium is often slower, less efficient, and more expensive than magnetic tape.

2. An amount of disk storage space comparable to the amount of space on a reel of tape is several times more expensive. On a cost-per-byte basis, disk storage is more expensive than tape.

3. Using remote terminals, it is easier to gain access to on-line disk files than to gain access to off-line tape files. There have been many cases in which intruders have altered or destroyed information stored on on-line disks.

11. . . .How data is stored on magnetic disk?

12. . . .How the speed of magnetic disk is determined?

13. . . .The advantages and disadvantages of magnetic disk storage?

Magnetic Disk for Microcomputers

The most popular type of direct-access storage for microcomputers is magnetic disk. Because of its small size and low volume of processing, a microcomputer requires a small disk. Two commonly used types of disks for microcomputers are floppy disks (also called diskettes) and hard disks.

Floppy Disk.   A **floppy disk** (also called a **diskette**) is a thin, flexible plastic disk coated with magnetic material. Floppy disks are available in sizes ranging from 3 inches to 8 inches in diameter, the most popular size being $5\frac{1}{4}$ inches. The disk is housed in a protective jacket. An oval opening, called a **read/write notch,** exposes the tracks on the disk (see Figure 6–11).

Data is stored on a floppy disk surface by track and by sector as illustrated in Figure 6–12. A **sector** is a portion of a track on a disk. Sectors on a floppy disk resemble a cake that has been cut into several slices. Each sector (slice) can hold a small amount of data. For example, a single floppy disk track for an IBM PC holds 4,608 characters (bytes) of data. Each of the ten sectors holds 512 characters. Dividing a disk into sectors increases the speed at which data can be recorded and retrieved. For example, suppose you store on this disk a brief letter that you've written to your friend Mary. Your entire letter can be stored in one sector of one track, making your letter easy to store and retrieve.

When inserted into a disk drive, a read/write head positioned on the disk surface through the read/write notch can record data onto, or read data from, the disk (see Figure 6–13). To record or retrieve data, the disk drive must be connected to the CPU by means of a cable.

A floppy disk rotates at about 350 revolutions per minute which is much slower than the speed of standard disks. The CPU can retrieve data from the disk at speeds ranging from 30,000 to 150,000 bytes per second.

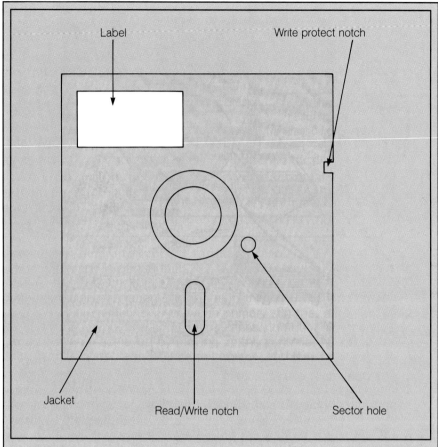

Label   Write protect notch

Jacket   Read/Write notch   Sector hole

Figure 6–11
A floppy disk. Tracks are exposed through an opening (called a read/write notch) in the protective jacket.

Hard Disk.   In addition to floppy disk secondary storage, hard disk storage for microcomputers is also available and becoming more popular. A **hard disk** gets its name from the fact that the disk is made of rigid material. Hard disks for microcomputers are similar to, but smaller than, standard disks used with large computers. When a hard disk is permanently housed in a disk drive, it is sometimes referred to as a **fixed disk.**

Hard disks for microcomputers range in size from 3 to 8 inches in diameter. Depending on the size and density of the disk, millions of bytes of data can be stored on a single disk. More and more microcomputer users are now using hard disk systems for storing programs and large amounts of data.

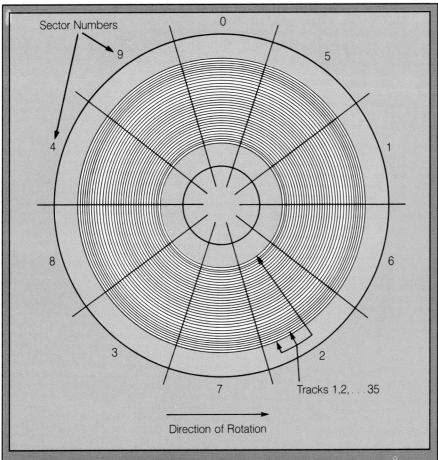

Sector Numbers

0

9

5

4

1

8

6

3

2

7

Tracks 1,2,...35

Direction of Rotation

Figure 6–12
Data is stored on and/or read from a floppy disk by track and sector.
Notice the arrangement of tracks and sectors.

Other Types of Secondary Storage

Although magnetic tape and magnetic disk are the most widely used
kinds of secondary storage, other kinds are available. When huge
(mass) amounts of data need to be stored and retrieved, special kinds
of secondary storage can be used. Two such kinds are tape cartridge
and optical disk storage.

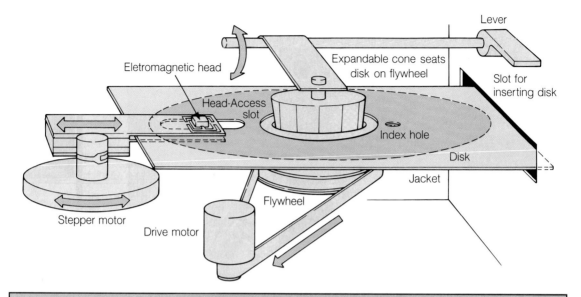

Figure 6–13
A floppy disk drive can store huge quantities of data on a floppy disk. The disk rotates at approximately 300 revolutions per minute. Data is written to, and/or read from, the floppy disk by a read/write head that touches the floppy disk through the opening in the disk jacket.

THE COMPUTER DIDN'T DO IT!

BELLEPLAIN, N.J.—A family here recently learned just how expensive it could be when a computer gets a wrong number.

Several weeks ago, the Atlantic City Electric Company sent Mrs. Samuel Heaton her monthly computer-generated electric bill. However, when she opened the bill and scanned the amount due column, she discovered that she did not owe the usual $45, but was asked to pay $613,051.

Shocked by the inflated amount and thinking the bill some sort of joke, Heaton called the electric company for an explanation. After some fast DP sleuthing, utility officials there discovered the root of the error. Part of Heaton's telephone number was input to the firm's twin UNIVAC 70/45 processors as the amount owed for electric service.

A relieved Mrs. Heaton was just happy to have the whole misunderstanding cleared up. Originally, "an Atlantic Electric secretary told me not to worry. She said I could pay a little off each month."

Source: Reprinted from *Computerworld* (June 9, 1980), p. 11. Copyright © 1980 by CW Communications, Inc., Framingham, MA 01701.

Tape Cartridge Mass Storage

Several devices and media are available that allow huge (mass) amounts of data to be stored and retrieved. One such system is a **tape cartridge mass storage system.** This works somewhat like a jukebox. After depositing a coin, a song is selected by pressing a certain button. Pressing the button causes an access arm in the jukebox to move across a stack of available records, pull out the one selected, and place it on the turntable to be played.

The mass storage system, shown in Figure 6–14, works in a way similar to a jukebox, but it selects tape cartridges rather than songs.

Figure 6–14
This system can be used by large organizations whenever large amounts of data must be stored and retrieved. For example, the U.S. Internal Revenue Service uses this system for storing income-tax data.

Each cartridge contains magnetic tape capable of holding 50 million bytes of data. Cartridges are stored in honeycomb-shaped storage compartments.

When a certain file is needed, the cartridge containing that file is automatically retrieved by a mechanical arm and mounted onto the read/write mechanism. The cartridge is then opened and the contents of the tape are transferred electronically to a standard disk pack. This process is called **staging.** After processing has been completed, only the new data is written back to the tape in the cartridge. The cartridge is then returned to its compartment.

Mass storage systems can accommodate between 35 and 472 billion bytes of data. This is roughly equivalent to the amount of data that can be stored on 47,175 reels of standard magnetic tape. It should be obvious that mass storage provides an excellent alternative to standard magnetic tape when huge amounts of data need to be stored.

Optical (Laser) Disk Storage

One of the newest and most exciting types of secondary storage for computers of all sizes is **optical (laser) disk storage.** The storage medium is actually a disk. You're probably aware that similar disks are now being used by electronics companies to record movies, music videos, sporting events, and other audio/visual presentations for playback on television sets.

Data is permanently stored on the disk in the form of microscopic holes "burned" into the disk surface by means of a powerful laser beam (see Figure 6–15). The presence of a hole represents a *1* while the absence of a hole represents a *0*. To read data from the disk, a less powerful laser beam senses the presence or absence of the holes.

Laser disks provide random-access storage. Most types cannot be erased or reused. Storage capacities begin at about one billion bytes per disk for large computers and twenty million bytes for microcomputers. Even a small disk has as much storage capacity as twenty reels of magnetic tape.

DO YOU
REMEMBER

14. . . .The physical characteristics of a floppy disk?

15. . . .How data is stored on a floppy disk?

16. . . .Two types of mass storage for data?

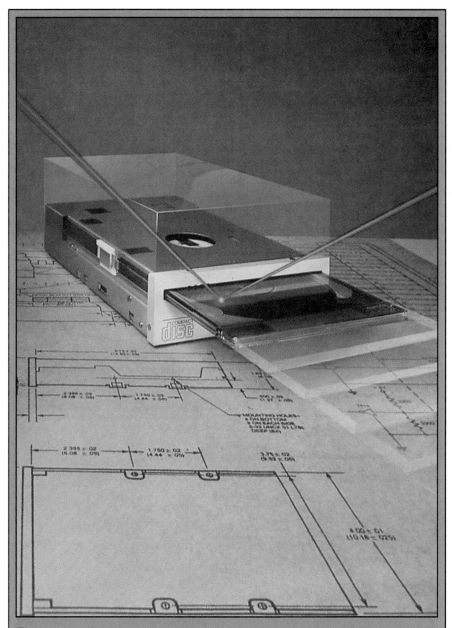

Figure 6–15
Optical (laser) disk storage. A laser beam burns microscopic holes, approximately 1 micron in diameter, into the surface of an optical disk to store data. A laser beam is also used to read the stored data. Huge amounts of data can be stored on a single disk.

Summary

(This summary provides answers to DO YOU REMEMBER . . . questions in the chapter.)

1. **What are the three types of storage shown on the storage hierarchy pyramid?**
   The three types of storage shown on the storage hierarchy pyramid are *primary storage, direct-access (on-line) storage,* and *sequential-access (off-line) storage.*

2. **What are the three criteria for selecting the type of storage to be used for a particular application?**
   The three criteria for selecting the type of storage to be used for a particular computer application are *speed, storage capacity,* and *cost of storage.*

3. **What "tradeoffs" result from upward and downward movement on the pyramid?**
   The "tradeoffs" resulting from upward and downward movement on the storage hierarchy pyramid are as follows: moving upward shows that the user is gaining speed but is sacrificing storage capacity at a higher cost of storage. Moving downward, the user sacrifices speed but gains more storage capacity at a lower storage cost.

4. **What is the difference between on-line and off-line secondary storage?**
   The difference between on-line and off-line storage is that an on-line device is in direct communication with the computer, whereas an off-line device is not.

5. **What are the physical characteristics of magnetic tape for large computers?**
   The tape is a $\frac{1}{2}$-inch-wide strip of thin plastic material coated with a thin film of magnetic material. Approximately 2,400 feet of tape are wound onto a supply reel which must be labeled for identification.

6. **How is data recorded on magnetic tape?**
   Data is recorded on magnetic tape along tracks extending the full length of the tape. Magnetizable particles are magnetized to represent data using the EBCDIC coding scheme.

7. **How is the speed at which data can be written to, or read from, magnetic tape calculated?**

The speed at which data can be written to, and read from, magnetic tape can be calculated by multiplying the number of bytes per inch of tape by the speed of the tape drive.

8. **What are the advantages and disadvantages of using magnetic tape?**

The advantages of using magnetic tape include the following: the storage capacity is large, tape can be erased and reused, errors can be corrected easily and information updated quickly, tape is inexpensive, and tape is an excellent sequential-access storage medium. The disadvantages include the following: stored data cannot be accessed immediately, stored data can be accidentally erased or altered, tape containers must be labeled, and tape can be damaged by dust, humidity, and static electricity.

9. **What are the physical characteristics of magnetic tape for microcomputers?**

The physical characteristics of microcomputer tape are basically the same as those of the tape used with large computers. The main differences are that the microcomputer tape is narrower and shorter than the other tape and the microcomputer tape is contained in a cassette or cartridge.

10. **Why does microcomputer tape have only one track for recording data?**

Microcomputer tape has only one track because standard cassette recorder/players used with microcomputers have only one read/write head.

11. **How is data stored on magnetic disk?**

Data is stored on magnetic disk on *tracks* by *sector* and *cylinder*.

12. **How is the speed of magnetic disk determined?**

The speed of magnetic disk is determined by the *density* of the stored data and the *rotational speed* of the disk.

13. **What are the advantages and disadvantages of magnetic disk storage?**

The advantages of magnetic disk storage are that it provides both direct-access and sequential-access storage, data can be accessed and processed very quickly, and records and files can be updated with a single input transaction. The disadvantages are that tape is better suited for sequential processing, disk is more expensive than tape, and it is easier for unauthorized persons to gain access to data stored on disk than to data stored on tape.

14. What are the physical characteristics of a floppy disk?

A floppy disk is a thin, flexible plastic disk coated with magnetic material. The disk is contained in a protective jacket that has a read/write notch to expose the tracks on the disk.

15. How is data stored on a floppy disk?

Data is stored on a floppy disk on tracks by sector. The read/write notch in the protective jacket allows a read/write head in the tape recorder/player to write data to, and/or read data from, the disk.

16. What are two types of mass storage for data?

Two types of mass storage for data are *tape cartridge mass storage* and *optical (laser) disk storage*.

DATA PROCESSING CAREER. . . . .
LIBRARIAN

CAREER OPPORTUNITY FOR COMPUTER PROFESSIONAL

JOB TITLE:
Computer Media Librarian

JOB DESCRIPTION:
Applicant will work with other skilled computer professionals in the operations area of the computer center. Specific duties include controlling, maintaining, and dispensing storage media including disks and tape along with program documentation; implementing rigid control procedures; and periodically inspecting and cleaning all storage media housed in the library.

EXPERIENCE REQUIRED:
None

EDUCATION REQUIRED:
A high school diploma

PERSONAL QUALIFICATIONS:
Applicant must be well-groomed, possess good communication skills, be well-organized, enjoy working with others as a team, and enjoy a challenging work environment.

Key Terms

access mechanism
cylinder
data density
direct-access
disk drive
disk pack
floppy disk
hard disk
head crash
interrecord gap (IRG)
librarian
magnetic disk
magnetic tape
nonremovable disk pack
off-line

on-line
optical (laser) disk storage
parity track
read/write head
read/write notch
removable disk pack
secondary storage
sector
sequential-access
staging
storage hierarchy
tape cartridge mass storage
tape cassette
tape drive
track

Test Yourself

1. For many applications, secondary storage is needed because there is not enough _____ storage in the computer.

2. Computer users often use a storage _____ to determine the type of secondary storage needed for particular applications.

3. Two main types of secondary storage are magnetic tape and magnetic _____ .

4. Data is stored on tape as magnetized particles in _____ .

5. A popular direct-access secondary storage medium is _____ .

6. Data is written to, and/or read from, magnetic disks by _____ that are housed in a read/write mechanism in a disk drive.

7. The most widely used type of secondary storage for microcomputers is _____ .

8. With _____ storage, microscopic holes are "burned" into the surface of a disk.

Review Questions

1. Explain why secondary storage is necessary for many computer applications. (Learning Objective 2)

2. How can a storage hierarchy pyramid be used to determine the most appropriate type of secondary storage for a particular application? (Learning Objective 3)

3. Describe two main types of secondary storage for microcomputers, including the physical characteristics of each and how data is stored on each. (Learning Objective 4)

4. Identify two types of storage, other than standard magnetic tape and magnetic disk, that can be used to store huge amounts of data. (Learning Objective 5)

Activities

1. Visit a business in your area that uses a computer. Find out which type(s) of secondary storage the business uses for storing data and the kinds of data stored. Record, on paper, the information you acquire.

2. If your school uses a computer and secondary storage to store information, make a list of the various kinds of information stored on secondary storage media and devices.

3. Visit a computer store in your area and ask a salesperson to demonstrate the various types of secondary storage available for microcomputers. Make notes of the procedures for storing and retrieving data with each type.

PART III

Microcomputers

CHAPTER 7

A Microcomputer System

Learning Objectives

After studying this chapter carefully, you will be able to:

1. Define key terms introduced in this chapter.

2. Distinguish between personal and professional microcomputers.

3. Identify different types of microcomputer input devices.

4. Name the main components of a CPU and the primary functions of each.

5. Identify several output devices used with microcomputers.

6. Identify three main types of secondary storage used with microcomputers.

7. Explain the difference between applications software and systems software.

Chapter Outline

TYPES OF MICROCOMPUTERS
Personal Microcomputers
Professional Microcomputers

MICROCOMPUTER HARDWARE
Input Devices and Media
The Central Processing Unit (CPU)
Output Devices and Media
Secondary Storage

MICROCOMPUTER SOFTWARE
Systems Software
Applications Software

DATA PROCESSING CAREER:
  Microcomputer Educational
  Representative

Application

For several weeks the Adams family discussed buying a micro-computer for their home. Finally, it was decided that Mr. and Mrs. Adams would visit computer stores in the area, talk with salespeople, and compare brands and prices. Afterwards, they would purchase a microcomputer, which they did. Their purchase included a processor, a keyboard, and a video display monitor.

When Mr. and Mrs. Adams returned home with the new micro-computer their daughter, Nell, questioned why her parents had not bought a printer for word processing. Their son, Joel, quickly noticed that neither joysticks nor computer games were included in the purchase. Their parents learned that they had made the same mistake hundreds of microcomputer shoppers make every day: they had purchased a microcomputer before determining how it was to be used. This is as serious a mistake as purchasing an automobile before first determining how it will most often be used. A prospective buyer would ask many questions that would influence his decision. For instance, if the vehicle is to be used primarily on the farm, perhaps a pick-up truck would be best, or if the entire family will be traveling together regularly, maybe a station wagon would be best.

Similar questions should be asked before purchasing a micro-computer system. In other words, will it be used for playing games, for word processing, for home management, for education, or perhaps for a combination of applications?

Figure 7–1
A salesperson explains the features of a microcomputer system to Mr. and Mrs. Adams.

Types of Microcomputers

The scientific creation of microprocessors in the 1960s led to the development of microcomputers in the 1970s. As the name implies, a **microprocessor** is a tiny central processing unit (CPU) about the size of a thumbnail. It contains, on a silicon chip, all of the electronic circuitry needed to perform the CPU's functions. Microprocessors can be thought of as the brains of the microcomputer, and they are sometimes classified by function or size. Typical sizes are 4-bit, 8-bit, 16-bit, and 32-bit. Generally speaking, the greater the number of bits, the faster and more powerful the microprocessor. Video game devices, for example, frequently contain 4-bit microprocessors while personal microcomputers typically contain either 8-bit or 16-bit microprocessors. With some microcomputers, additional microprocessors can be installed that provide the user with more advanced mathematical processing capabilities. Microprocessors are also found in other devices such as stereos, microwave ovens, refrigerators, and automobiles.

Figure 7–2
A microcomputer system. Software is an essential part of a microcomputer system.

There is no industry-wide standard for classifying microcomputers. In addition to size, usage is another way by which microcomputers can be classified. While some are used primarily for playing games, others are used for applications such as balancing checkbooks, billing customers, and keeping track of inventories. The intended use for a microcomputer should influence the buyer's decision about the particular microcomputer to buy.

Microcomputers are **general-purpose** computers just like large mainframe computers. Although smaller in size, many microcomputers are capable of performing most applications. To perform these applications, however, the user must have a computer system. A **computer system** includes all the hardware and software necessary for a user to complete the desired computing tasks. Computer stores sometimes advertise "starter systems," which might include a central processing unit (CPU), a keyboard, a monitor, and a disk drive. Such a system is adequate for some, but not all, applications. While a beginning, or inexperienced, user might find such a basic system adequate, an experienced user will probably want to expand the system so that both a greater variety of applications and more advanced applications can be performed.

Personal Microcomputers

Personal computer is the name given to a microcomputer used by an individual for a variety of personal tasks such as word processing and preparing individual income tax returns. Examples include the Apple IIe, and the Commodore 64. Compared to professional microcomputers, personal microcomputers usually execute programs more slowly, have less internal storage, and are less expensive. Because of their limited internal storage capacity, they cannot handle some of the more complex software programs. Some complex programs, for example, require a minimum of 256K of internal storage; however, several personal microcomputer brands have 128K or less, so they are incapable of handling these complex programs.

Personal microcomputers, however, represent the fastest growing sector of the computer industry. Sales of personal microcomputers are expected to increase 40 to 60 percent each year during the present decade. According to some predictions, one out of every two homes will have some kind of computer by 1990.

When first introduced in the 1970s, no one could have accurately predicted the growth in popularity of microcomputers or the technological improvements to them that would be made by the mid-1980s.

Figure 7–3
An Apple IIGS microcomputer.

But today, millions of microcomputers are being purchased each year. Newspapers and magazines are filled with sales ads for personal microcomputers, also called personal computers, home computers, or desk-top computers. These ads are aimed at prospective customers with little, or no, computer training or experience. To make their products more appealing to inexperienced customers, computer manufacturers and software companies are making their products more **user-friendly** (easier to use).

Professional Microcomputers

Today, computers are no longer confined inside the walls of data processing departments of large corporations. The development of microcomputers, the advances in microcomputer technology, and the vigorous marketing campaigns waged by manufacturers have resulted in the proliferation of professional microcomputers throughout the business world. A **professional microcomputer** is similar in appearance to a personal computer, but it usually has more internal storage, can handle more complex applications, and can execute programs faster. For example, professional microcomputers often have 256K or more of internal storage. They are used, for example, by large and small businesses, institutions, government offices, physicians, lawyers, accountants, and insurance agents. The kinds of applications they can handle are virtually endless. For many businesses, applications can be implemented faster and more economically with microcomputers than with large computers. Most traditional business functions such as accounting, word processing, financial analysis, payroll processing, and inventory control can now be done on microcomputers. The more than 4 million small businesses in the United States offer a potentially huge market for microcomputer hardware and software manufacturers. Several microcomputer brands may be classified as *professional*, including the AT&T 6300 Plus, Apple Macintosh, and IBM-PC AT. These are relatively small, yet powerful microcomputers capable of performing most of the tasks in a small or medium-size business.

Figure 7–4
A microcomputer system can be useful in our work.

1. . . .What led to the development of microcomputers?

2. . . .Two ways to classify microcomputers?

3. . . .The primary differences between personal microcomputers and professional microcomputers?

Microcomputer Hardware

A computer system, as stated earlier, includes all of the physical equipment (hardware) and programs (software) needed by the user. Included in the system are input and output devices and secondary storage for storing programs and information. Sometimes additional devices are needed for specialized tasks.

Input Devices and Media

Several input devices are now available for use with microcomputers, and new ones are appearing in the marketplace almost daily. Each year, billions of dollars are spent on research, development, and marketing of microcomputer input devices and media. The resulting new and improved input devices are making microcomputing easier and more exciting. Traditional types of input devices, however, still remain popular with users, who regard them as essential components of a microcomputer system.

Keyboard.   The most popular input device is the keyboard, and almost all microcomputers use one. As stated in Chapter 4, a **keyboard** consists of alphabetic, numeric, and special keys that send data to the computer each time a key is struck. A **standard keyboard**, similar to that of a typewriter, is the most common type; its keys are activated by pressing them downward (see Figure 7–5). Some microcomputers have a **membrane keyboard**, which has a flat surface. On this keyboard, the keys are activated by touching them, like touching the numbers on a microwave oven.

On some keyboards, the keys are grouped in special arrangements. Regardless of arrangement, almost all keyboards include keys rep-

Figure 7–5
A typical keyboard used for entering instructions and data into a microcomputer. Some keyboards have special function keys.

resenting letters, numbers, and symbols. Some have special-function
keys such as **TAB, RETURN**, and **ERASE** keys that instruct the
computer to do specialized tasks, such as erasing information from
primary memory.

Some microcomputers have a keyboard that is built into the computer cabinet, while others have a separate keyboard that must be
plugged into the cabinet. The quality and ''feel'' of a particular keyboard is usually more important to the user than whether it is a built-
in or plug-in type.

For computer users, learning and developing good keyboarding
skills can be a valuable asset. More and more occupational fields are
now using computers and require employees to enter data via a keyboard. Some future employees might discover their inadequate keyboarding skills to be a serious disadvantage.

THE COMPUTER DIDN'T DO IT!

Roger Ainsley, a union employee at
Melodrex Manufacturing Company, was
shocked when he opened his pay envelope
and found a notice that he had been given
a two-week termination notice by his employer. According to the union's contract
with the company, any layoffs would be
based on seniority. Ainsley first went to
work at Melodrex in 1964. An investigation revealed that an office employee had
incorrectly entered Ainsley's initial employment date as 1984, instead of 1964.
Much to Ainsley's satisfaction, he was retained by the company.

Figure 7–6
Voice recognition is helping this young person use a computer.

Voice Input.   Research is under way to develop equipment that will allow users to "talk" to computers. The general term describing this technology is voice recognition system. A **voice recognition system** is designed to accept and translate spoken commands into coded impulses that can be understood by the computer (see Figure 7–6). Some equipment is already available, making it possible for a computer to accept thousands of unique words. More research is needed to perfect this technology.

The once-popular television show *Knight Rider* suggested the possibilities for people who can converse with computers. In the show, Michael Knight's indestructible car, KIT, is controlled by a marvelous computer intelligent enough to comprehend Michael's every command, and with enough memory to store virtually all information Michael might need. The show is televised fiction. Those astounding **voice input** and **voice output** features aren't available yet—but eventually they will be, and perhaps sooner than we might think.

With the huge expenditures being invested by companies to perfect this kind of input technology, some companies might well achieve success by the end of this decade. When perfected, users will be able to input instructions and data simply by speaking instead of by typing, or even by pushing buttons. Computers, then, will become more user-friendly and their use even more widespread.

Figure 7–7
Joysticks are popular devices. The lever allows a user to move objects about on the monitor screen.

Magnetic Disk and Tape Drives and Media.   Later in this chapter, the importance of magnetic disk and tape drives for secondary storage is explained. Here, it should be emphasized that these devices and media are also important input devices and media. Much of the software used for computing applications is entered into primary storage directly from disks or tapes. Without magnetic disks or tapes, almost all computer programs would have to be entered via a keyboard or another input device each time they are used.

Special-Purpose Input Devices.   In addition to standard input devices, special input devices are available for microcomputers. Most are designed for particular applications.

The **joystick** is a popular gadget dear to the hearts of video game users. Actually, a joystick is a small box with a lever that moves in all directions, allowing the user to move the cursor on the computer screen (see Figure 7–7). By moving the lever, figures on the screen can be moved around. Some joysticks have one or more buttons that are used for purposes such as making the game appear to fire weapons.

Figure 7–8
This person is using a light pen to enter data. A light pen may also be used to scan data displayed on a monitor.

Joysticks also have other uses. The lever can be used to move the cursor to a particular location in order to select a menu item, to identify a group of data, or to highlight a block of text. Using a joystick is easier and faster than typing various key combinations to move the cursor.

A **light pen** is another popular input device used with microcomputers. Frequently used by drafters and engineers, this device is about the size of a standard writing pen. One end of the light pen is connected to the computer via a wire; the other end contains a tiny light-sensing cell. When pointed toward the screen, the light-sensitive cell senses a bright point of light projected to the surface of the monitor by the computer. As the user moves the pen, lines are created on the monitor screen. These combinations of lines, or drawings, can then be printed or stored on magnetic storage medium. A light pen enables users to enter, change, or erase data. Figure 7–8 shows a person using a light pen to enter data into a microcomputer.

A light pen allows the user to draw pictures or images, called **graphics**, on the screen. The drawings can be changed or erased in a manner similar to that for drawings made with pencil and paper.

Like a light pen, a **graphics tablet** allows the user to make drawings on the monitor screen. But with a graphics tablet, the user draws images on the tablet rather than on the screen. The image is immediately displayed on the monitor screen.

The popularity of graphics tablets is increasing. One of the more popular brands has a pressure-sensitive surface. Images can be drawn using a stylus or finger. Available software enables the user to make menu selections such as coloring the drawn image and saving a drawing on a diskette. The versatility of graphics tablets makes them popular among students for preparing color drawings in art, music, and drafting, for example.

A **mouse**, like its living namesake, has a body and a tail. The tail is a wire cable that connects the mouse's body to the microcomputer. The body has one or more push buttons. A small ball is housed underneath the body. As the mouse is moved about, the ball rotates, causing the cursor (usually an arrow) on the monitor to move in the same direction. The action taken depends on the particular computer program being used at the time. For example, one computer program

Figure 7–9
This microcomputer graphics tablet allows the user to enter data by writing on the tablet. The data is then displayed on the monitor screen.

Figure 7-10
Moving a mouse around on a desktop positions a cursor on the computer screen and allows a user to select an item from a menu.

allows several possible actions. In this program, moving the mouse to a certain position points the cursor (pointer) at the word "file." One press of the button loads the file into primary storage. Frequently, selections can be made from several available options.

4. . . .What a computer system consists of?

5. . . .The most popular device for entering instructions and data into a computer?

6. . . .Four special-purpose input devices explained in the chapter?

7. . . .What a joystick is and what happens when the lever is moved around in different directions?

The Central Processing Unit (CPU)

The main part of every digital computer, as explained in Chapter 3, is the **central processing unit (CPU)**. Every microcomputer system must have a CPU, sometimes called a **microprocessor**.

As mentioned earlier in this chapter, the microcomputer is built around a microprocessor that contains all the electronic circuitry needed to perform the CPU's functions on a silicon chip. Thus, the microprocessor may be thought of as the **heart** of a microcomputer.

Built into the CPU are the arithmetic/logic unit, the control unit, and the primary storage unit. The circuitry can be contained on one, or several, microprocessor chips, but regardless of the number of chips, every microcomputer must contain all three units. Although each was explained in Chapter 3, the purpose of each, as it relates to microcomputers, is summarized briefly in the following sections.

Arithmetic/Logic Unit. The **arithmetic/logic unit (ALU)** performs the arithmetic operations of addition, subtraction, multiplication, and division. It can also make comparisons and perform logical operations. It can, for example, compare two values such as A and B, to determine if the value of one is equal to, greater than, or less than the other. The results of such comparisons can then be sent to the control unit to determine which program instruction will be executed next.

Another important function of the ALU is to examine the logic of individual program instructions. Assume, for example, that the user wants to run a payroll program to compute an employee's net pay. The ALU determines that an instruction for computing the employee's gross pay must precede an instruction for computing the employee's net pay because the amount of gross pay must be used in computing net pay. Otherwise, the instructions are not in logical sequence and cannot be executed correctly by the computer.

Control Unit. To understand how the **control unit** works, imagine a traffic officer directing traffic at a busy intersection. All the motorists follow the officer's instructions. Similarly, the control unit directs activities within the computer.

The control unit retrieves instructions and data from primary storage and sends them to the arithmetic/logic unit for processing. Because instructions and data are stored in primary storage in binary code, the control unit decodes each instruction and data item, and then sends appropriate signals to the arithmetic/logic unit that processes the data according to the instructions. After processing, the control unit sends the results back to primary storage. When instructed to do so, the control unit directs the processed information to an output device, such as a printer.

Primary Storage Unit. In microcomputers, **primary storage** is divided into a large number of individual storage (memory) locations, each capable of holding a certain amount of data. These storage locations are called **registers**. Each register has an **address** that is used by the central processor to identify which register data is to be stored in or retrieved from.

One difference between large and small microcomputers is in the number of registers they have. A large mainframe computer, for instance, has more registers than a microcomputer. Another difference is in the size of individual registers, called word size. **Word size** refers to the number of bits (0s and 1s) an individual register can hold to represent a byte. Usually, microcomputers have smaller, and fewer registers than large computers. Large computers have registers that are capable of handling 64 bits, while registers in microcomputers are often limited to 8, 16, or 32 bits.

Primary storage can be thought of as an array (columns and rows) of mail boxes in a post office, each box having its own address and capable of holding a limited amount of mail. After reading the address on the piece of mail, the clerk deposits the mail in the correct box. The quantity of mail that can be placed into an individual box is limited by the size of the mail box and the size of the pieces of mail. A register in computer memory is limited **to one byte of limited size**.

Data can be stored in, or accessed from, memory in a fraction of a second. Recall that the types of internal primary storage were explained in an earlier chapter. Here, only the two main types used in microcomputers—RAM and ROM—will be summarized briefly.

Recall that **RAM** storage allows the user to store or retrieve data from primary storage locations quickly and in any order. RAM is **volatile**, meaning that its contents are lost when the computer is turned off. Thus, RAM is temporary storage that can be used again and again.

Many microcomputers also contain **ROM** memory, which is **nonvolatile**. Turning the computer off does not erase ROM memory. Also, ROM memory cannot be changed. A program can read from a ROM but cannot store data in it. With a ROM as part of internal storage, instructions and data can be installed permanently in the computer.

Figure 7–11
Inside view of an Apple IIe microcomputer. Note the chips and the slots for installing circuit boards that allow peripherals (such as a monitor and printer) to be connected to the microcomputer.

An application such as word processing or a language such as BASIC can be permanently installed in ROM. Because ROM is permanent, these programs can be used over and over.

Output Devices and Media

Microcomputer users receive output through a variety of output devices and media. Some are standard and can be used with computers of all sizes. Others are nonstandard, meaning that they are used almost exclusively with microcomputers.

Video Display Monitor.   A **video display monitor** resembles a television set in that it displays output on a screen. Most monitors use picture tubes similar to those used in television sets. These are cathode ray tubes, called CRTs. Thus, a monitor itself is frequently called a CRT. Sometimes, a television set is used as a monitor.

Monitors can be inexpensive or can cost up to several hundred dollars. Usually, more expensive monitors offer extra features, such as color and clearer images.

Some monitors display text only, whereas others can display graphics and drawings. Depending on the kind of monitor being used, the output can be displayed in black and white, green and white, or amber and black. Some can display in attractive colors like a color television. For certain applications, as in graphics or computer games, a color monitor might be preferable. In such cases, color quality and image clarity, called **resolution**, can be important. Figure 7–12 shows a high-resolution color monitor capable of producing clear and attractive images on the screen.

Printer.   Much of the output from microcomputers is printed on paper. Recall that printed output (hardcopy) can be retained permanently but softcopy output cannot. Printers are the most popular hardcopy output devices for microcomputers. Both **impact** and **nonimpact** printers can be used with microcomputers. In fact, most of the printers explained earlier in Chapter 5 can be used with microcomputers.

Voice Output.   One of the newer and more fascinating forms of microcomputer output is **voice output**, whereby a computer speaks to the user. In fact, a computer has probably already "talked" to you several times. For instance, when you try to call a telephone number that has been changed, you might hear: "**The number you have called has been changed. The new number is 2–5–8–5–0–5–1.**" The message, in whole or in part, was given by the computer's **voice response unit**.

Voice response works by keeping a "dictionary" of words stored in secondary storage. A computer program locates the words to be spoken in the dictionary. The dictionary shows how the word is to be pronounced, and the computer then sends codes representing each sound to the voice response unit that, in turn, produces the sound.

Extensive research is under way to improve speech quality and to increase the number of words that can be spoken. Improvements in this technology are appearing in the marketplace almost daily. The result is lower prices making voice response capability affordable to more microcomputer users.

Special-Purpose Output Devices.   The microcomputer market is expanding rapidly. So are the ways microcomputers are being used. New uses have created a need for devices capable of producing spe-

Figure 7–12
A video display monitor is the most popular softcopy output device.

cialized output. Industry has responded to this need by producing special-purpose output devices such as plotters and graphics display monitors.

Plotter. A **plotter** allows a computer to produce a hardcopy of drawings seen on a screen. Almost any drawing can be produced

Figure 7–13
A plotter produces hardcopy of output displayed on a monitor.

including graphs, maps, and detailed engineering drawings. Patterns from which integrated circuits are manufactured are often drawn by plotters.

Graphics Display Monitor. While a plotter produces hardcopy, a **graphics display monitor** produces softcopy output on the screen. With a color graphics monitor, drawings can be produced in attractive color. This is an appealing feature for users wanting to identify each part of a drawing by a particular color.

The use of plotters and graphics monitors is becoming widespread. In highly technical fields, such as the automobile industry, engineers use them to design new products. The person in Figure 7–14 is an engineer who is using a graphics display monitor.

Figure 7–14
Using a graphics display monitor and other appropriate hardware and software makes it possible for engineers to speed up their work and reduce costs.

8. . . .Three main components of a CPU and the primary function of each?

9. . . .The kind of output produced by a video display monitor and by a printer?

10. . . .Two special-purpose output devices and the kind of output produced by each?

DO YOU
REMEMBER

Secondary Storage

We've already learned that users often need to store programs and information permanently and to retrieve them when needed. With microcomputers, just as with large computers, this is accomplished by using secondary storage.

Almost all microcomputer secondary storage devices use **removable storage media**. Thus, it is possible for the storage medium (tape or diskette) to be removed from the storage device and stored separately. This feature makes the capacity of secondary storage seem virtually unlimited.

Although several types of secondary storage are available, the most common are magnetic tape, diskette, and hard disk storage, all of which were explained in Chapter 6. Because of their importance as secondary storage devices for microcomputers, they are briefly reviewed here.

Magnetic Tape.   Have you ever used a portable tape player/recorder? If so, then you've used magnetic tape similar to that used with microcomputers. The main computing use of magnetic tape is to store programs and information. This is similar to the use of a tape for recording sound on a tape player/recorder. Recall that magnetic tape is a **sequential-access** storage medium. This means that information is stored sequentially (in order) and must be retrieved in the same order it was stored. When you use a tape player/recorder for playing and/or recording music, items (songs) were recorded sequentially (one after another) on the tape. To play a song located on the first part of the tape and a second song located near the end of the tape, you have to speed up the tape (fast forward) to get to the song near the end of the tape.

For microcomputers, the magnetic tape medium is contained in a protective cassette or cartridge. Tape cassettes are often used with a standard **tape player/recorder** attached to the computer.

Magnetic Disk.   The most popular secondary storage medium for microcomputers is **magnetic disk**, commonly called **diskette** or **floppy disk**. Diskettes of various sizes are available, but the most popular size is 5 1/4 inches in diameter. Other sizes include 3 inches, 3 1/4 inches, 3 1/2 inches, and 8 inches. Information is stored on the diskette in the same way it is stored on disks used with large computers. The main differences are in size, in the speed at which information is stored or retrieved, and in the amount of information that can be stored. Compared with magnetic tape, the main advantage of the diskette is the speed at which information can be retrieved. The device that houses the diskette is called a **disk drive**. Together they provide inexpensive direct-access storage.

Before data can be stored on a diskette, the diskette must be formatted, or prepared for use. The computer's operating system contains instructions for formatting a disk. The user's manual provides

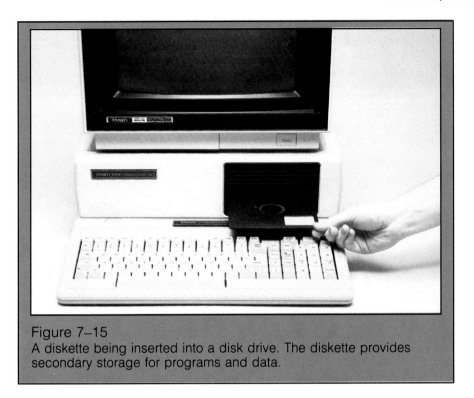

Figure 7–15
A diskette being inserted into a disk drive. The diskette provides
secondary storage for programs and data.

information about formatting a diskette. Usually, all a user needs to
do is to enter a few simple keystrokes.

All magnetic storage media, including magnetic tape and disks,
should be handled carefully and protected from potential environmental hazards because data stored on a magnetic medium can easily
be altered or destroyed. When a diskette is not being used, it should
be stored in its protective jacket in a safe place such as a plastic file
cabinet away from excessive moisture, dust, and smoke. Some brands
contain instructions on each diskette jacket for the proper care and
handling of the diskette. A diskette should not be bent, exposed to
any magnetic device, or exposed to extreme heat or cold. In addition,
a user should not touch any part of the surface of a diskette. When
labeling a diskette, a soft (or felt) tip pen should be used. Any physical
abuse to a diskette can alter or destroy data and shorten the life of
the diskette.

Hard Disk.   Several companies manufacture hard disks, another secondary storage medium for microcomputers. Originally developed by
IBM, hard-disk technology consists of one or more hard (rigid) disks

encased in a sealed disk drive. Hard-disk drives are expensive, but can store 5 to 140 megabytes of data. Hard disks are many times faster than floppy disks. And they are more reliable because they are sealed against contamination by outside air and human hands.

Optical (laser) disk technology is now available whereby a laser beam can actually "burn" holes in the disk surface. The disk is usable only once, but a disk can hold 10 billion holes (bits) or more, or the equivalent of about 834 books. In the future, optical disk storage will likely become more important as a permanent secondary storage medium.

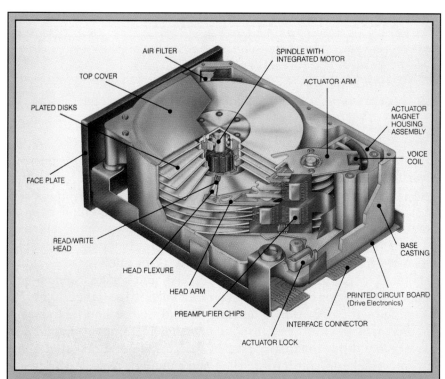

Figure 7-16
Hard disk storage vastly increases the amount of data that can be stored and speed at which the data can be retrieved. Because of their declining cost, many more people are now using hard disks for storing and retrieving programs and data.

Microcomputer Software

As explained in Chapter 3, all digital computers, including microcomputers, require two kinds of software. These are systems software and applications software. Without software, a microcomputer is useless.

Systems Software

Systems software consists of sets of programs that enables the computer to manage its own operations. The programs are in two groups called the **operating system** and **translating software**.

Operating System. An **operating system** consists of programs that control the operations of the computer system. Each program enables the computer to perform specific operations. Many microcomputers use operating systems that include an input/output control system (IOCS), a database management system (DBMS), a data communications system, and utilities software.

An **input/output control system (IOCS)** allows the computer to accept instructions and data from an input device and to send processed information to an output device. Without an IOCS, nothing could get into, or out of, the computer.

Some, but not all, operating systems include a **database management system (DBMS)**. For those that do, a DBMS allows the user to build and maintain a common database containing information that can be reused. The information can be updated or changed easily and quickly. Records can also be added to, or deleted from, the file when needed. An easy-to-use **query language**, especially written for a particular database, is often used to retrieve information from the data base.

The ability of a microcomputer user to communicate with another, perhaps larger, computer requires a **data communications system**. People who use electronic information services such as *SOURCE, Dow Jones*, and *Compuserve*, need a data communications system to obtain information from these services.

Special computer tasks are made possible by **utilities software**. For example, special utilities programs enable the user to sort data, copy from one disk to another, or prepare a blank disk for use. The kinds and number of tasks vary from one operating system to another.

Usually, the manual included with the operating system will specify the different utilities programs contained within the operating system. For most microcomputers, the operating system is contained on floppy disk. Because the operating system directs all internal activities, it must be "loaded," or entered into the computer before loading an application program.

Translating Software.   As the name suggests, **translating software** is a set of computer programs that translates a user's program instructions and data into machine language for processing by the computer. Recall that a computer understands only machine language. Thus, translating software (a compiler or interpreter) converts a computer program written in a language such as BASIC or Pascal into machine language for execution. After execution, the output is translated back from machine language into an English-like form that can be understood by the user.

Actually, translating software does essentially the same thing as an interpreter at the United Nations. Suppose the United States and Japanese ambassadors wish to communicate with each other, but neither understands the language of the other. An English/Japanese interpreter makes communication between the two persons possible. Translating software allows communication between a user and a computer.

Applications Software

An **application program** is a user-written or purchased computer program that allows the user to do a specific task. These programs are written using a particular computer language such as BASIC or Pascal.

The specific application can be a business, mathematical, word processing, or other application. After determining the application to be performed, the user loads the appropriate computer program containing the instructions the computer will follow to perform the task.

DO YOU REMEMBER

11. . . .The most popular type of secondary storage for micro-computers?

12. . . .The primary difference between systems software and applications software?

13. . . .The purpose of translating software?

Summary

(This summary provides answers to DO YOU REMEMBER . . . questions in the chapter.)

1. **What led to the development of microcomputers?**
   Space age technologies developed during the 1960s and 1970s, including microprocessors, led to the development of microcomputers.

2. **What are two way to classify microcomputers?**
   Two ways of classifying microcomputers are (1) by *size* and (2) by *usage*.

3. **What are the primary differences between a personal microcomputer and a professional microcomputer?**
   Usually a personal microcomputer has less primary storage, executes programs more slowly, and has less capability than a professional microcomputer. A professional microcomputer can also handle more complex applications programs.

4. **What does a computer system consist of?**
   A computer system consists of all the physical equipment (hardware) and programs (software) needed by the user.

5. **What is the most popular device for entering instructions and data into a microcomputer?**
   The most popular device used to enter instructions and data into a microcomputer is a *keyboard*.

6. **Identify the four special-purpose input devices.**
   The four special-purpose input devices identified in this chapter are a *joystick*, a *light pen*, a *graphics tablet*, and a *mouse*.

7. **What is a joystick, and what happens when the lever is moved around in different directions?**
   A *joystick* is an input device consisting of a small box that contains electronic circuitry, a lever, and one or more buttons. Moving the lever in different directions moves the cursor on the screen in the same direction.

8. **Name the three main components of a CPU and the primary function of each.**
   The three main components of the CPU are the arithmetic/logic unit, the control unit, and the primary storage unit. The *arith-*

metic/logic unit performs arithmetic and logical operations. The *control unit* controls all activity inside a computer. It retrieves instructions and data from primary storage and sends them to the *arithmetic/logic unit* for processing. After processing, the control unit is responsible for sending the results back to primary storage. The *primary storage unit* is the part of the CPU where instructions and data are stored.

9. **What kind of output is produced by a video display monitor and by a printer?**

A *video display monitor,* like a television, is used to display output on a screen. A *printer* is used to produce output on paper.

10. **What are two special-purpose output devices, and what kind of output is produced by each?**

Two special-purpose output devices are plotters and graphics display monitors. A *plotter* allows a computer to produce drawings seen on a screen in hardcopy form. A *graphics display monitor* produces softcopy output on a screen.

11. **What is the most popular type of secondary storage for microcomputers?**

Magnetic disk, called a diskette or floppy disk, is the most popular type of secondary storage for microcomputers.

12. **What is the primary difference between systems software and applications software?**

Systems software consists of sets of programs that enable a computer to manage its own operations. *Applications software* consists of user-written or purchased computer programs that allow a user to do a particular task such as word processing.

13. **What is the purpose of translating software?**

Translating software is needed to convert a user's program instructions and data into machine language for processing and then to reconvert the output into human-readable form for the user.

DATA PROCESSING CAREER. . . . .
Microcomputer Educational Representative

CAREER OPPORTUNITY FOR COMPUTER PROFESSIONAL

JOB TITLE:
Microcomputer Educational
Representative

JOB DESCRIPTION:
Well-established computer, peripheral, and software manufacturer is seeking qualified applicants to market products to schools and institutions. Selected applicants work as customer consultants assisting clients in the selection, acquisition, and implementation of educational hardware and software. All selected applicants will undergo intensive training relative to company products, customer assistance, and product installation and maintenance. Following training, applicant will receive on-the-job experience under direct supervision of experienced company representatives. An applicant must be willing to travel.

EXPERIENCE REQUIRED:
Prior sales experience desirable but not required.

EDUCATION REQUIRED:
Minimum education—high school graduate. One or more courses in computer hardware, software, and usage desirable.

PERSONAL QUALIFICATIONS:
Applicant must be enthusiastic, self-motivated, and career-oriented. Good communication skills essential. Must have a desire to serve customer needs, and a desire to assist in the solution of customer problems.

Key Terms

address
applications software
arithmetic/logic unit
computer system
control unit
database management system
  (DBMS)
data communications system
disk drive
diskette (floppy disk)
graphics display monitor
graphics tablet
hard disk
input/output control system
  (IOCS)
joystick
keyboard
light pen
membrane keyboard
microcomputer
microprocessor
mouse

operating system
personal microcomputer
plotter
primary storage
printer
professional microcomputer
query language
RAM
register
ROM
secondary storage
standard keyboard
systems software
translating software
utilities software
video display monitor
voice input
voice output
voice recognition system
word size

Test Yourself

1. Two broad classifications of microcomputers are _____ microcomputers and _____ microcomputers.

2. _____ is the name given to a microcomputer used by an individual for a variety of tasks including word processing.

3. A computer _____ includes all the hardware and software needed by a computer user.

4. The most common and frequently used microcomputer input device is a _____ .

5. Special-purpose input devices include a joystick, light pen, graphics tablet, and _____ .

6. The main part of every digital computer is the _____ .

7. The three main components of a CPU are the _____ unit, the _____ unit, and the _____ unit.

8. The _____ unit of the CPU performs arithmetic and/or logical operations.

9. An output device used to display softcopy output on a screen is a _____ .

10. A popular hardcopy output device that produces output on paper is a _____ .

11. Two special-purpose output devices are _____ and _____ .

12. Two main types of primary storage are _____ and _____ .

13. A _____ , that resembles a TV, is used to display softcopy computer output on a screen.

14. The most popular hardcopy output device is a _____ .

15. Two types of software are _____ software and _____ software.

16. _____ serves a function similar to that of an interpreter at the United Nations.

Review Questions

1. What are the two broad classifications of microcomputers, and what is the primary difference between them? (Learning Objective 2)

2. Explain the meaning of the term *computer system*. What is needed in order to have a computer system? (Learning Objective 1)

3. Identify each of the input devices presented in the chapter. Which is the most widely used? Why? (Learning Objective 3)

4. What are the three components of a central processing unit? What is the primary function of each component? (Learning Objective 4)

5. What are the two most popular and widely used output devices for microcomputers? What kind of output is produced by each? (Learning Objective 5)

6. What is the most widely used type of secondary storage used with microcomputers? (Learning Objective 6)

7. Distinguish between systems software and applications software. (Learning Objective 7)

8. Why is translating software important to a computer user? In what way is translating software similar to an interpreter at the United Nations? (Learning Objective 7)

Activities

1. Prepare a list of input devices used at your school (in your computer lab and in administrative offices). For each input device, prepare a written summary of the types of data entered into the computer by each input device.

2. If your school has a computer that uses a mouse as an input device, prepare a written explanation of how data is entered using the mouse. If your school does not use mouse input devices, visit a computer store in your area and ask a salesperson to demonstrate its use. Write a summary of the demonstration.

3. Using books, magazines, and periodicals in your school library, find an article about a new computer output device (one you have not used). Explain to your class the kind of output produced by the device.

4. From information in this book and from other sources you select, explain to your class how images are produced on paper by a dot-matrix printer. Your demonstration can be made using a chalkboard.

5. Prepare a drawing of a diskette (floppy disk) showing how data is recorded on the disk. Explain why data stored on a diskette can be altered or destroyed by touching the diskette surface or by exposing it to moisture, dust, smoke particles, and other potential environmental hazards.

CHAPTER 8

Using a Microcomputer System

Learning Objectives

After studying this chapter carefully, you will be able to:

1. Define key terms introduced in this chapter.

2. Describe the main steps in setting up a microcomputer system.

3. Identify three activities that must be performed when starting up a microcomputer system.

4. Identify two ways an operating system may be loaded into a microcomputer.

5. Explain the basic difference between the two main types of applications programs a user might select.

6. Tell why some vendor-written software is copy-protected.

7. Tell why a user might want to make a backup copy of important programs and data.

8. Identify briefly the main steps in shutting down a microcomputer system.

Chapter Outline

Application

For the past two years Ernesto Rivera has worked as an accounts receivable clerk at Hemmingway Distributors, Incorporated, a large wholesale company in the Southwest. His work consists mainly of using a microcomputer in his office to record payments made by customers to his company. Each day, Ernesto records individual customer payments by entering the customer's individual account number, name, invoice number, and amount of payment into the main computer via the keyboard of the microcomputer in his office.

Aside from using them in his work, however, Ernesto had little knowledge of microcomputers. Unfortunately, his lack of knowledge proved costly when he recently purchased and began assembling a new microcomputer system.

Arriving home with his newly purchased system, Ernesto immediately began setting up his new system without following the instructions in the manual. His problem occurred when he connected the disk drive cable to the controller card in the computer. When he turned his computer on, he first noticed a curl of smoke coming from the disk drive. Moments later, he heard a loud bang, and then more smoke poured from the drive. He quickly turned the computer off and disconnected all the components.

A technician at a local computer store where Ernesto took his system for repair explained the problem. While making the connection, Ernesto had failed to align the connector pins properly. As a result, the controller card had been damaged beyond repair.

Ernesto had learned an expensive lesson, for a new card cost him $95. Next time, he would read the manual and follow the instructions carefully.

Because of differences in computer hardware and software, learning about computers is an endless process. For the inexperienced user, it is important to learn how to use a microcomputer properly. By learning and following the procedures explained in the following sections, the user should be able to assemble and begin operating a microcomputer in minimum time and with fewer problems.

Setting Up the System

Assume that you have just returned home after purchasing a new microcomputer system, and that you are now ready to set up (assemble) the components of your system. The first thing you should do is locate your purchase invoice and make certain that you have everything you purchased. As each box is opened, visually compare the contents to the items listed on your invoice. If any part of your purchase is missing, contact the seller immediately.

After removing the individual components from the cartons, record the name, description, and serial number of each component. This can later prove to be valuable information in case of fire or theft. Store your records in a safe place such as a safe deposit box.

Fill out the warranty cards included with the computer system and mail them to the manufacturer. The **warranty card** registers you as

Figure 8–1
Microcomputer system components should be removed from their cartons carefully to avoid damaging the component.

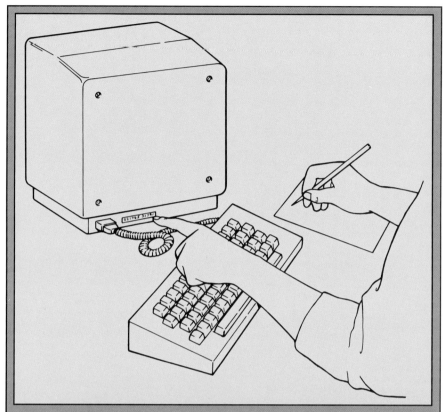

Figure 8–2
The purchaser of a new microcomputer system should record the serial number of each component for safekeeping. This information could prove to be valuable if a component is defective or in the event of fire or theft.

the owner and enables the manufacturer to notify you of important changes in its products.

Next, locate and assemble all the manuals included with your new microcomputer. Manuals are usually included in the boxes along with the components. A special manual, generally titled **owner's manual**, provides detailed instructions for assembling (putting together) computer hardware components such as CPU, monitor, and disk drives. This manual also provides instructions for installing peripheral cards if necessary.

Peripheral cards make it possible to connect peripheral devices such as printers, disk drives, and video monitors to the microcomputer,

Figure 8–3
Manuals that accompany a microcomputer, peripherals, and software programs contain valuable information frequently needed by the user.

and for the microcomputer to communicate with these devices. Without a disk drive peripheral card, for example, a disk drive cannot be connected to the microcomputer. These detailed instructions should be followed precisely while assembling the microcomputer system. Failure to do so can result in damage to the microcomputer. Figure 8–4 shows a person installing a peripheral card.

Start-Up Procedures

After setting up the microcomputer system, the user is ready to begin **start-up procedures**. Activities include turning on the computer and all components, loading the operating system, and loading the translating software. Each activity is explained in more detail in the next sections.

Figure 8–4
Installing peripheral cards (circuit boards) inside a microcomputer
makes it possible to connect peripheral devices, such as a monitor
and printer, to the microcomputer.

Turning It On

After all hardware components have been connected with the appropriate cables, the microcomputer system is ready to be **turned on**. Each component has its own switch for turning it *on* or *off* and an **indicator light** to let the user know when the component is ready for use.

The procedure for turning a microcomputer system on varies among different brands of microcomputers. Some microcomputers (such as the Apple IIe) require that the operating system, usually on a diskette, be inserted in a disk drive before turning the computer on. Others (such as the IBM-PC) allow the microcomputer to be turned on before inserting the operating system disk. Thus, it is imperative that the owner read, and follow precisely, the instructions found in the user's manual.

A microcomputer peripheral device might also have an on-off switch and an indicator light to show whether the device is on or off. Before using the device, the switch should be turned on. The device indicator light will tell whether or not the device is ready for use.

Loading the Operating System

Recall that an **operating system** is a set of computer programs, and that each program consists of instructions that tell a computer what to do and how to do it. Each brand of microcomputer requires a particular operating system, and the user should be aware of the particular operating system required by his or her computer. The diskette containing the operating system can be labeled as DOS 3.3, MS-DOS 2.1, or something similar. DOS 3.3 means Disk Operating System, version 3.3. MS-DOS 2.1 means MicroSoft-Disk Operating System, version 2.1. With some microcomputers, different versions of an operating system can be used, such as MS-DOS 2.0, 2.1, and 3.0. Regardless of the particular operating system included with your microcomputer, it can be located easily. See Figure 8–5 for an illustration of the way a disk program should be loaded in a disk drive.

The user's manual contains instructions for installing, or *booting*, the operating system. Usually, the first step in booting the operating

Figure 8–5
Loading DOS (or any disk program) in a disk drive is a four-step process. (a) Lift the door, or lever, on the front of the disk drive. (b) Remove the disk from the protective envelope, being careful not to touch the surface of the disk. (c) Gently insert the disk into the slot, or read/write opening, being careful not to bend the disk. (d) Gently close the drive door until it clicks shut.

```
                     APPLE II

            DOS VERSION 3.3 SYSTEM MASTER

                  JANUARY 1, 1983

            COPYRIGHT APPLE COMPUTER, INC.
                    1980, 1982

              BE SURE CAPS LOCK IS DOWN
```

Figure 8–6
After DOS (the Disk Operating System) has been loaded into primary storage, a message will appear on the monitor screen informing the user. The message will vary according to the particular version of DOS being used.

system is to insert the operating system diskette into the disk drive. Generally speaking, the operating system can be loaded in one of two ways, depending on the brand of microcomputer being used. Some microcomputers allow the user to simply insert the diskette in the disk drive and then turn the CPU on. Other brands require the computer to be turned on first. Then, the diskette is inserted in the disk drive. Finally, a few keystrokes causes the operating system to be loaded into primary memory. The message on the screen display in Figure 8–6 informs the user that DOS has been loaded into primary storage.

It should be noted that some computers allow tasks to be accomplished without loading the operating system. Some word processing software packages, for example, contain their own version of an operating system along with actual word processing capabilities. The user should always read the instructions with a software package to learn if a separate operating system is required.

Loading the Translating Software

In addition to an operating system, many vendor-written and user-written software programs require **translating software**. Recall that translating software is used to convert computer programs written in a high-level language, such as BASIC, into machine language. Thus, before high-level language programs can be executed by the computer, translating software for that particular language must be loaded into the computer.

The user's manual contains instructions for loading translating software. Usually, this can be accomplished by pressing a few keys after inserting the translating software diskette in the disk drive. After the translating software has been loaded, the user is ready to input a new program or execute a prewritten program.

1. . . .The main steps in setting up a microcomputer system?

2. . . .The main steps included in start-up procedures?

3. . . .Two ways to load an operating system, depending on the particular microcomputer?

4. . . .Why translating software must be loaded before executing a program?

DO YOU REMEMBER

Instructing the Computer

To accomplish a particular task, the user must enter the required **program** into the computer. The program can be either a vendor-written program or one written by the user. The following sections explain these two types and include steps that can be followed in loading and running each. The actual procedure, however, for loading and running both vendor-written and user-written programs will probably vary from one situation to another and between different computers. The individual user, therefore, should study the manuals and carefully follow the instructions for loading and running a particular program.

Vendor-Written Program

A **vendor-written program** is a set of computer instructions written and sold by a software vendor. These are sometimes called **pre-packaged** or **canned** programs. Included along with a program disk is a manual explaining the program and how to use it. Each program has been written for a specific application such as a program that checks the spelling of a document. Vendor-written programs can be purchased from various sources such as a computer store or mail-order house, or directly from the software company.

A back-up copy of the program disk can also be included with a vendor-written program. Some vendor-written program packages do not contain a back-up copy of the program disk. Instead, the manual provides instructions for making a back-up copy or information on how to obtain a back-up copy from the supplier. Some vendor-written programs are **copy-protected**, which prevents the purchaser, or someone else, from making unauthorized copies of the program. In cases where programs are copy-protected, vendors frequently provide a back-up copy or offer legitimate original purchasers an option to purchase a back-up copy for a small fee.

Figure 8–7
Popular vendor-written software packages are usually well written and documented.

The software manual provides details for loading the program. In general, the following steps will enable the user to load and use a vendor-supplied program:

1. Locate the manual and diskette containing the program.

2. Following the instructions in the manual for your particular computer, either load the operating system and turn the computer on, or turn the computer on and load the operating system.

3. If instructed to do so in the manual, make a back-up copy of the original program on a separate disk. To make a back-up copy, follow the instructions provided in the manual.

4. Load the translating software, if required for the program.

5. If a vendor-written program is to be executed, load the program according to instructions in the manual.

6. Execute the program.

User-Written Program

Recall that a **user-written program** is one that is written by the user to solve a specific problem. Usually, it is written in a high-level computer language such as BASIC or COBOL. Although plain paper can be used, programmers generally prefer to use specialized program *coding forms* to minimize errors while writing a program and entering it into the computer. Coding forms are arranged into rows and columns as shown in Figure 8–8. Note that the 80 columns on the sheet correspond to the 80 columns of a typical monitor display. One line of the program is entered from each line of the coding form. Information from each of the numbered columns on the coding form should be entered into the corresponding column of the monitor display.

The process involved in developing a program to solve a particular problem and implementing it using a computer is explained in the next chapter. And writing a program in the BASIC language is explained in Module B.

COBOL CODING FORM

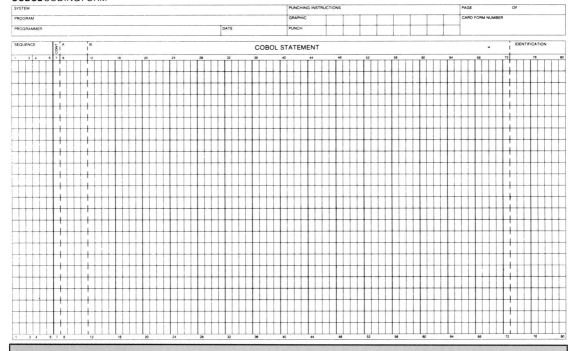

Figure 8–8
A sample COBOL coding form.

THE COMPUTER DIDN'T DO IT!

George Wittmeier of Kirkland, Washington, has a right to be mad at a computer. Somehow, he underpaid his income tax by one penny; the computer added interest and fines totaling $159.58 and sent him a dunning letter. An IRS spokesman said characteristically, "Obviously, the computer has gone beserk." George was less caustic; said he, "If the computer could prove all taxpayers underpaid by one cent each, we could pay off the national debt just like that, without a tax increase."

Source: From pages 25–26 of *The Naked Computer.* Copyright © 1983 by Jack B. Rochester and John Gantz. Reprinted by permission of William Morrow and Company.

After the program has been written, the following general steps can be followed to enter the program into the computer.

1. Load the operating system into the computer.

2. Insert a blank, formatted diskette in the disk drive (generally, drive #1) for storing important data. (Recall from Chapter 7 that formatting means that the user prepares a blank disk for use. A user's operating system manual specifies the procedure for formatting disks.)

3. Load the translating software, such as a BASIC interpreter, into the computer.

4. Using the keyboard, input the program—one instruction at a time until the entire program is in the computer.

5. Save the program on the diskette used for storage.

6. Execute the program.

Getting the Output

After an application program has been executed (run) successfully, the output can be obtained in softcopy or hardcopy, or both. Some microcomputers automatically display output on the screen. To obtain hardcopy output, the user must learn the specific procedure by reading the manual or by getting help from another person. Usually, a few keystrokes will send the output to an output device such as a printer, as shown in Figure 8–9.

The procedure for obtaining output on other output devices, such as a plotter, can be more complex. For this reason, when purchasing such a device, one should be sure to obtain clear instructions on its use from the seller.

Saving or Erasing a Program

A computer user can **save** a program or data on a magnetic storage medium for future use, or **erase** an existing program or data from the

Figure 8–9
A printer is the most popular microcomputer hardcopy output device.
Printers are available for nearly every printing need.

medium if it is no longer needed. Valuable programs are likely to be
saved for future use. Again, the manual provides information for
saving or erasing programs, and generally only a few keystrokes are
involved.

A program can be saved as either a **source program** (in a high-level
language such as BASIC) or as an **object program** (in machine language). Many users prefer to save a program as an object program
because it is stored more efficiently on a diskette. Another advantage
of an object program is that it does not have to be translated each
time it is used, and time is saved when the program is executed.

Shut-Down Procedures

Recall that programs and information stored on a magnetic medium
can be accidentally erased, lost, or damaged. Because of these potential dangers, experienced users often make a back-up copy of the

program and/or data before turning the computer off. By having a back-up copy, the user can avoid the frustration and expense of buying another copy of the program or rewriting the program.

Shutting down a microcomputer system involves (1) removing the secondary storage medium (diskette or tape), (2) storing it for safe-keeping, (3) turning off the computer and components, and (4) placing protective coverings over all hardware components. Although the importance of each step might be apparent, the first two steps deserve additional explanation.

Removal and Storage of Medium

Recall that a secondary storage medium (tape or diskette) is on-line when the medium is in the device and the device is connected to the computer. For most microcomputer secondary storage devices, the storage medium can be removed and stored for future use. The medium should be appropriately labeled and properly stored so it can

Figure 8–10
When not being used, diskettes should be stored in a container for safekeeping, and to protect them from dust, moisture, and other potential hazards.

be easily located when needed. The medium should be stored in a safe container to minimize exposure to potential hazards such as dust, moisture, and static electricity.

Safety Procedure

After back-up copies of important programs and data have been made and safely stored, all computer components should be turned off. For additional safety, many users also disconnect the components from the power source to avoid potential damage that can result from lightning or a power surge.

It should be remembered that all procedures for using a microcomputer system have been described in general terms. Actual procedures vary according to the particular brand of microcomputer and the user. A user should always carefully study the manuals to learn details for using a particular microcomputer system.

5. . . .Two main types of applications programs and the primary difference between the two types?

6. . . .Why some vendor-supplied programs are copy-protected?

7. . . .Why manuals are important to a computer user?

8. . . .Two types of output that can be obtained from a computer system?

9. . . .The main procedures for shutting down a microcomputer system.

Summary

(This summary provides answers to DO YOU REMEMBER . . . questions in the chapter.)

1. **What are the main steps in setting up a microcomputer system?**
   After opening each box, locate the invoice and make certain that all parts of the system are included. If any parts are missing,

contact the seller immediately. Remove all components from the containers and record the name, description, and serial number of each. Save this document for future reference if needed. Locate and fill out the *warranty cards* and mail them to the manufacturer. Locate all manuals included with the system. Follow directions in the manuals for assembling components of the system.

2. **What are the main steps included in the start-up procedure?**
Start-up procedures vary according to the particular brand of microcomputer. Although not necessarily in this order, steps include (1) turning on the computer and other system components, (2) loading the operating system, and (3) loading the translating software.

3. **Depending on the particular microcomputer brand, what are two ways to load an operating system?**
One way is simply to insert the disk containing the operating system and then turn the computer on. Another way is to turn the microcomputer on, insert the disk operating system in a drive, and press certain keys specified in the manual.

4. **Why must translating software be loaded into the computer before executing a program?**
Translating software (a compiler or interpreter) is needed to convert (translate) a program written in a high-level programming language, such as BASIC, into machine language for execution. After processing, the translating software converts the instructions and output into human-readable form.

5. **What are two main types of applications programs, and what is the primary difference between them?**
Two main types of application programs are vendor-written and user-written programs. *Vendor-written programs* are prepared by private companies or individuals for sale to users. Included with these programs are manuals instructing the purchaser on how to use the programs. *User-written programs* are prepared by individuals, businesses, or organizations for their own use, and are not for sale to others.

6. **Why are some vendor-written programs copy-protected?**
Vendors sometimes *copy-protect* the software they sell to prevent people from making *unauthorized* copies of the programs. Some vendors argue that duplicating and distributing unauthorized copies of programs deprives the vendor of revenues they would otherwise gain from additional sales of a program.

7. **Why are manuals important to a computer user?**

   Manuals provide valuable information about hardware and software products, their use, and additional information a user might need to know about the product.

8. **What are two types of output that can be obtained from a computer system?**

   Two types of output are softcopy and hardcopy. *Softcopy* output is displayed on a computer monitor. *Hardcopy* is tangible output on paper or another medium such as overhead transparency plastic.

9. **What are the main procedures in shutting down a microcomputer system?**

   Before turning off the computer, the user should make a *back-up copy* of all important information processed. Secondary storage media should then be removed and stored in a safe place. Next, the computer and components should be turned off. Finally, protective coverings should be placed over the computer and components.

DATA PROCESSING CAREER . . . .
Microcomputer Consultant

CAREER OPPORTUNITY FOR COMPUTER PROFESSIONAL

JOB TITLE:
Microcomputer Consultant

JOB DESCRIPTION:
Following an extensive training period during which the applicant will receive instruction on all of the company's hardware and software products and applications, the applicant will be assigned an area serving both established and new customer base. Specific duties include providing customers with information about new products, installing microcomputer systems and networks, establishing network communications, and providing technical support. Instructional seminars may be scheduled for customer support.

EXPERIENCE REQUIRED:
Three years with established firm.

EDUCATION REQUIRED:
Prefer four-year college degree with substantial coursework in data processing or related field.

PERSONAL QUALIFICATIONS:
Applicant should be self-starter and energetic. Ability to establish and meet demanding schedules essential. Applicant must possess good communication and problem-solving skills.

Key Terms

back-up copy
booting
copy-protection
erase
object program
operating system
owner's manual
peripheral card
peripheral device
program

program disk
save
shut-down procedures
source program
start-up procedures
translating software
user's manual
user-written program
vendor-written program
warranty card

Test Yourself

1. When checking components of a newly purchased microcomputer system against the invoice, if any part or component of the system is missing the _____ should be notified immediately.

2. After removing individual components from the cartons, the purchaser should record the name, description, and _____ of each component.

3. The _____ registers you as the owner and enables the manufacturer to notify you of important changes in its products.

4. _____ installed in a microcomputer make it possible to connect a wide variety of additional equipment to the computer.

5. When setting up or using a computer, the accompanying _____ should be read and studied because it contains valuable information for the purchaser or user.

6. An _____ , usually contained on a diskette, is a set of programs that tell a computer what to do and how to do it.

7. Most programs require that _____ software be loaded into the computer before loading or entering a particular program to convert the program from human-readable form to machine language.

8. Two kinds or groups of programs are _____ programs and user-written programs.

9. A _____ program is one in which the vendor attempts to prevent people from making unauthorized copies of the program.

10. Two kinds of microcomputer output are _____ and _____ .

Review Questions

1. What are the main steps in setting up a microcomputer system? (Learning Objective 2)

2. Name three activities that must be performed when starting up a microcomputer system. (Learning Objective 3)

3. Identify two ways an operating system can be loaded into a microcomputer. (Learning Objective 4)

4. Explain the basic difference between the two main types of applications software a user might select. (Learning Objective 5)

5. Why do some softcopy vendors copy-protect the software they sell? (Learning Objective 6)

6. Why is it sometimes important for a user to make a back-up copy of a valuable program and/or information? (Learning Objective 7)

7. What are the main steps in shutting down a microcomputer system? (Learning Objective 8)

Activities

1. Under close supervision of your teacher, remove the cover from one of the microcomputers in your computer lab. Make a drawing of the inside of the computer. Then, include on your drawing all cables and the peripheral to which each cable is connected. Next, add to your drawing each peripheral device connected to the computer by cable.

On a separate page, write an essay explaining how the computer and peripheral devices are connected (for example, the disk drive is connected by cable to a peripheral card in slot 6). This activity should help you learn how the components of a microcomputer system are assembled.

2. Visit a computer store in your area. Make a list of translating software and operating systems displayed for sale in the store. For each software package, make notes on (1) the amount of memory required by each particular software program, (2) the kind of computer for which the software was prepared, (3) whether the software is copy-protected, and (4) the price. Identify all software programs that could be used with a microcomputer at your school.

3. Write a brief essay describing the procedure for loading the operating system and translating software into a microcomputer at your school.

4. Using a microcomputer in your school's computer lab, load the operating system into the computer. After loading the operating system, use the CATALOG or DIRECTORY command to display a list of programs (files) to the monitor screen. Explain what each program does.

PART IV

Software and Applications

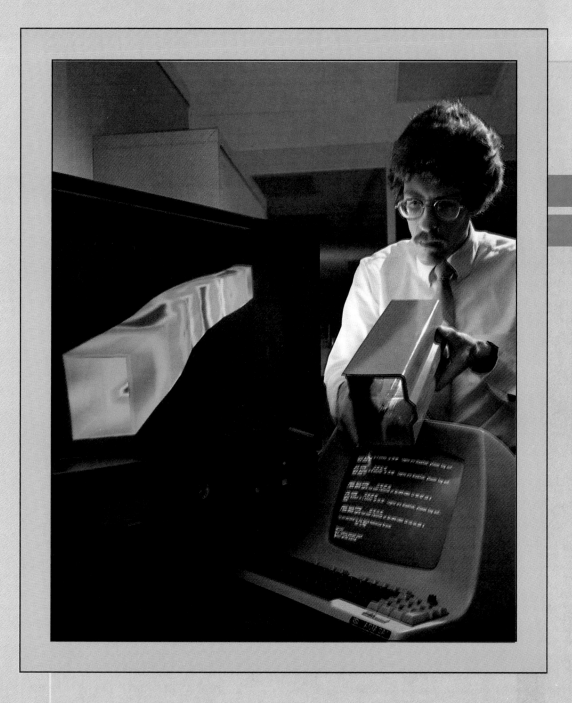

CHAPTER 9

Solving Problems with Computers

Learning Objectives

After studying this chapter carefully, you will be able to:

1. Define key terms introduced in this chapter.

2. Explain why programming is important.

3. Identify steps that should be followed in writing a useful and efficient program.

4. Identify two important programming aids used by programmers to design problem solutions.

5. Identify basic flowchart symbols and the meaning of each.

6. Name four basic logic patterns used to write computer programs.

Chapter Outline

WHY PROGRAMMING IS IMPORTANT

THE PROGRAMMING PROCESS
Defining the Problem
Planning the Solution
Coding the Program
Checking, Debugging, and Testing the Program
Documenting the Program
Maintaining the Program

SYSTEMS ANALYSIS AND DESIGN

DATA PROCESSING CAREER: Applications Programmer

Application

Following their recent retirement, Bill and Agnes Blalock opened a florist shop in the same town where they have lived and worked for thirty-three years. Bill, a former bank officer, was experienced in customer service and in keeping accurate, up-to-date records. Agnes, a former computer programmer at the same bank, was experienced in record preparation, filing, and customer service. Bill and Agnes were confident that their business knowledge, training, and experience would prove valuable in their new business.

But soon after opening their new shop, Bill and Agnes learned that managing a florist business is quite different from banking. Unlike banking, with its steady business volume, the florist business is seasonal. Most customer purchases are for special occasions such as Christmas and Mother's Day. Also, unlike money, flowers are perishable. Agnes soon learned the importance of maintaining a larger inventory of flowers for these special occasions, and a smaller inventory when sales would be lower.

Maintaining an adequate inventory of flowers was only one of many problems the Blalocks faced in their new business. Others included keeping up-to-date records of customers, suppliers, and expenses. Realizing how difficult all this would be without a computer, they began making plans to computerize their new business. They decided that Agnes, with her computing experience, would select and purchase a computer system for their business including both hardware and software. For some applications for which software was unavailable, Agnes would write the needed programs.

During the following weeks, Agnes spent much of her time writing computer programs. Although their computer system could not be used to solve all their problems, Bill and Agnes soon learned just how valuable a computer system can be in operating a business. "Having a good computer system is like having several extra employees," Bill was overheard telling a customer.

More and more people like Bill and Agnes are learning that a computer can be an almost indispensable problem-solving tool. They are also learning that a computer, like any other tool, can be more valuable when the user knows how to use it effectively. A computer's potential uses are virtually unlimited; and the more knowledgeable a user is about computing, the more productive he or she can become.

Figure 9–1
Using a computer in a florist shop.

Why Programming Is Important

The flow of data through a computer system is always under the control of the program being used. Although thousands of vendor-written programs are available for purchase, computer users often find that they either need, or want, to write their own programs. Knowing how to write computer programs to solve specific problems can prove to be quite valuable to a computer user.

Every computer program ever used was written by someone. Although computers are fascinating machines, they are just machines. A computer is not capable of doing anything without instructions (a program) provided by a human being. The responsibility for solving problems belongs to the user, or the programmer, and not the computer.

A computer is very accurate, but "accuracy" may not mean what you think. The results generated by computers are highly predictable. If, for example, you tell a computer to add 4 and 5, it will always give you 9. If you really didn't mean for the computer to add 4 and

5, however, it will still give you 9; the wrong instructions will produce the wrong answer with "perfect accuracy."

A computer is programmed in a computer **programming language.** There are more than 150 computer languages in existence today. Anyone can learn to write instructions in a particular programming language—it's just a matter of practice. Programming, however, does not begin with writing instructions. Before a program can be written to solve a problem, there must be a problem solution. To develop a problem solution, good programmers use a methodical, **structured approach,** also called a **top-down approach.** Most ot the remainder of this chapter explains the steps involved in structured programming.

A word of caution: as you begin to learn more about programming, you will be tempted to skip planning and careful preparation, and immediately begin writing program instructions. Don't give in to this temptation. As your skill in programming increases, you will find yourself attempting more difficult problems, so the need for careful planning never disappears.

The Programming Process

Programming is a process involving a number of procedural steps, all of which should be performed. The process itself is complete only when all steps, or procedures, have been completed. Individual steps in the programming process are listed below in Figure 9–2. Notice

1. Define the problem.
2. Plan the solution.
3. Code the program.
4. Test the program.
5. Document the program.
6. Maintain the program.

Figure 9–2
Steps in the programming process.

step 5, Document the program. As you will learn, documentation begins at the start of the problem-solving process and continues through program maintenance.

With the exception of documentation, each of these steps should be followed in sequence, each being a logical progression from the previous one. As each step in the programming process is accomplished, the solution to the problem should become clearer. After the preliminary steps (steps 1 and 2) have been completed, the actual coding, or writing, of the program (step 3) becomes nothing more than converting the solution into exact and accurate program instructions.

Defining the Problem

The task of defining the problem is simply the task of determining **what is to be done.** While many problems are difficult to define, others are often quite simple. How a problem is defined is often influenced by the training and experience of the person attempting to solve the problem. Assume, for example, that the basic problem is to compute the average of three test grades. If you are a mathematician, your basic definition might be:

$$\text{Average} = \frac{\text{Sum of the three test grades}}{3}$$

If you are not a mathematician, the above definition might not be useful to you. Instead, you might define the problem using the following two English language steps:

1. Add the three test grades.

2. Divide the sum by 3.

The result, in either case, will be an arithmetic average (or mean). And, in either case, you will have just defined an **algorithm,** which is a set of rules that will lead to a correct problem solution if followed precisely. An algorithm can be stated in any form including language, mathematical formulas, and diagrams. Any form is correct and can be used.

After the problem has been clearly defined—after the question **What do I want to do?** has been answered—it is time to answer the question **How do I do it?** Careful planning can help answer this question.

Planning the Solution

Recall that a problem is defined in terms of an algorithm, a series of logical steps that must be followed in order to solve the problem. Suppose you want to solve the "average" problem above using a pocket calculator. With some calculators, your algorithm requires the following steps:

1. Clear the calculator display.

2. Enter a test grade.

3. Press the add (+) button, then the equal (=) button. (Note: on some calculators, it is not necessary to press the (=) button.)

4. Repeat steps 2 and 3 until all grades are entered.

5. Press the division (÷) button, followed by the number 3, and then the equal (=) button to obtain the average.

   Imagine that you have a special machine capable of automatically pushing the right buttons in the right sequence. With such a machine, computing an average could be done without human intervention. All of the steps would, of course, have to be carefully thought out and "programmed" in advance, but the program could be reused any time you wish to compute an average. This machine would be a *computer.*

   Actually, a computer is capable of executing a very limited set of instructions. Computers can do the following things:

1. Add numbers

2. Subtract numbers

3. Multiply numbers

4. Divide numbers

5. Raise numbers to a power

6. Compare numbers and data

7. Copy data from one primary storage location to another, from primary storage to secondary storage, or from secondary storage to primary storage

8. Perform simple yes/no logic

9. Request and receive input of data

10. Request the output of data

With an understanding of what computers can do, it is possible for a human being (a programmer) to write a program, consisting of the above logical functions, and to place the program in the computer's main memory. The computer is then capable of following the instructions without human intervention.

We have seen how an average is computed using a pocket calculator. Now, let's see how problem solutions, that can serve as useful aids for writing programs, are developed using pencil and paper. Two popular ways to represent the solution are pseudocode and flowcharting.

Pseudocode.   A **pseudocode** is a set of English-like sentences appearing in the same order as the actual program instructions will appear in the program. Preparing a pseudocode is analogous to preparing an outline for writing an essay. *Pseudo* means false; a pseudocode is a false code because pseudocode statements cannot be executed directly by the computer. The value of a pseudocode lies in its usefulness as a *programming aid*. It may be thought of as a list of things you want the computer to do. The items on the list should be in a logical order with each brief statement identifying a particular task. An example of the pseudocode for computing an average is shown in Figure 9–3.

```
Start
     Read Three Test Grades
     Sum The Three Test Grades
     Divide The Sum by 3
     Print "Average="; A
Stop
```

Figure 9–3
Pseudocode for computing an average.

A pseudocode can be a valuable programming aid. When writing the actual computer program, reference to the above pseudocode will remind the programmer that instructions must be included telling the computer to read each test grade and add that grade to the total.

Flowchart.   A flowchart is another useful programming aid. Frequently, both pseudocode and flowcharts are used to develop problem solutions.

Like pseudocode, a flowchart is a skeleton of the real thing, the actual computer program. A **flowchart** is a symbolic diagram of the necessary steps in a problem solution rather than English-like statements used in pseudocode. An accurate flowchart is a good visible record of the computer program and how the program was designed. It is a diagram form of algorithm.

Most programmers use special symbols developed by the American National Standards Institute (ANSI). Each symbol has a special meaning. One familiar with ANSI symbols knows their meaning and can quickly recognize each symbol. Some commonly used symbols are shown in Figure 9–4.

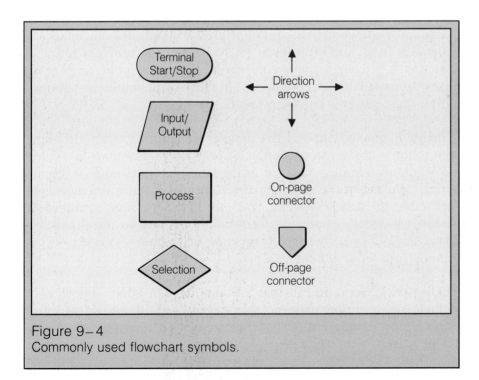

Figure 9–4
Commonly used flowchart symbols.

The flowchart in Figure 9–5 shows the logical development of a solution to the problem of computing an average, illustrated earlier with pseudocode in Figure 9–3. Notice that the solution flows from the top of the flowchart to the bottom. Top-down flowcharting is strongly recommended by professional programmers and required by many employers.

In this flowchart, the *top-down* flow represents the logical sequence of steps followed to compute the average. Notice that after reading the three test grades, the three grades are added, giving the sum of the three grades. Next, the sum is divided by 3, giving the average. Finally, the expression **Average =** is printed, followed by the numerical average (A).

DO YOU
REMEMBER

1. . . . Why programming is important?

2. . . . What an *algorithm* is, and in what form it can be expressed?

3. . . . What pseudocode and flowcharts are?

Basic Logic Patterns.   Four basic **logic patterns** used to develop flow-charts and write computer programs are (1) **simple-sequence,** (2) **selection,** (3) **loop,** and (4) **branch.** Regardless of the problem solution being developed, the completed program will contain one or more of these patterns, but not necessarily all. In more complex programs, all four logic patterns can be present.

Simple-Sequence Pattern. In a simple-sequence pattern, one statement follows another in sequence, or order. The flowchart in Figure 9–6 contains simple-sequence statements. It illustrates a hypothetical solution to the problem of getting to school in the morning. Notice that the first statement, Wake up in the morning, is followed in sequence by the statement Get out of bed, and so on. Programs almost always contain simple-sequence instructions that are to be executed one after another.

Selection Pattern. Recall that a computer can apply simple yes/no logic. A selection pattern (also called a **decision-logic pattern**) enables the computer to choose between two alternatives. A selection pattern that might be used by a motorist at an intersection is shown in Figure 9–7. Notice that the motorist must determine if the traffic light is green—the decision. If the light is green, the motorist proceeds through the intersection; if not, the motorist stops the car.

Notice the similarity between this selection pattern and the one in the flowchart in Figure 9–8 that shows how the average of three test grades might be computed. Remember that with all selection patterns, only one of the two alternatives is possible. The computer will do either one thing or the other, but **not both.**

Notice also the question in the diamond symbol in the flowchart, Have all three test grades been read? The computer is capable of applying yes/no logic in this situation. If all three grades have been read, the computer will then compute the average. If not, the computer will continue reading grades until all three have been read.

Loop Pattern. The advantage of having the computer repeat steps, like reading test grades, is essential in programming. If each step were to be executed only once, it might be easier to do the calculation by hand or by pocket calculator rather than by writing a program to do it. Many programs written for a computer involve repetition, called looping. A **loop,** also illustrated in Figure 9–8, is simply a series of instructions in a program that is executed repeatedly.

Before the computer can begin executing the steps in a loop, there usually is a selection statement, which is a logical expression that must be evaluated. Usually, the statement evaluates a numerical value such as Have all three test grades been read? If more grades are to be read, the computer will continue processing the steps within the loop. After the computer has read the last test grade, the loop will end.

The sequence of instructions in the loop will be executed three times, or until all test grades have been read and the calculations done by the computer. Remember that a loop can be executed as many times as the programmer wishes, providing the program is written correctly.

Branch Pattern. During the execution of a program, the computer analyzes each instruction and takes the action ordered by the programmer. The programmer, however, can order the computer to change the order in which it executes instructions in the program. The programmer can do this by inserting one or more instructions called **control statements** in the program. These control statements cause

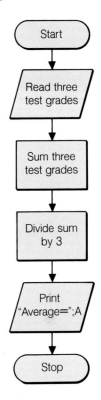

Figure 9–5
Flowchart for computing an average.

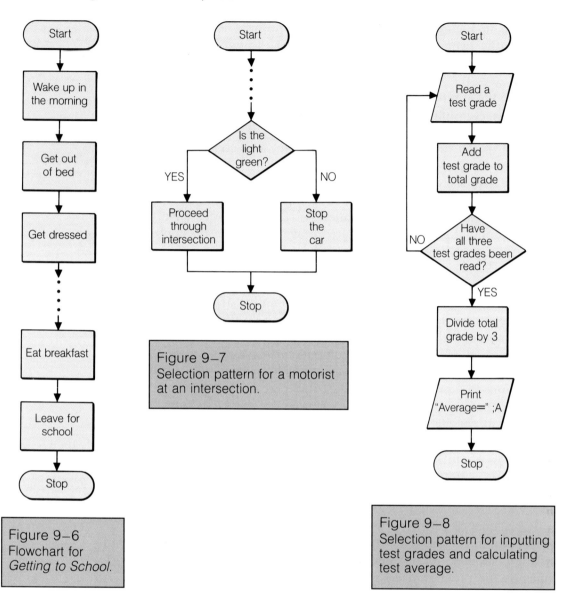

Figure 9–6
Flowchart for
Getting to School.

Figure 9–7
Selection pattern for a motorist
at an intersection.

Figure 9–8
Selection pattern for inputting
test grades and calculating
test average.

program logic to **branch,** taking different paths of execution, rather than proceeding through the instructions in order. After the computer finishes executing the instructions it branched to, the program may return the logic to the next instruction after the one that caused it to branch, or it may go back to the beginning of the program, or it may continue along some other path, depending upon the particular instructions in the program.

The concept of branching is best illustrated with the use of program statements. For this reason, further explanation and illustration of this important concept are included in Module B, which covers the BASIC programming language.

Structured Techniques in Programming.   Programs should be easy to read, easy to modify, and easy to maintain. To achieve these goals, experienced programmers stress the importance of using structured programming techniques. Applying these techniques will result in programs that are (1) easier to understand, (2) more accurate, (3) more efficient, and (4) easier to maintain.

Top-down programming and modularization are among the more important structured programming techniques. Both encourage well-thought-out logic and the use of the simple-sequence, selection, and loop patterns.

The **top-down programming technique** requires that the programmer begin the program with the most general program module and then divide it into more specific modules. Instructions for upper-level modules are written first, followed by instructions for lower-level modules.

The purpose of top-down programming is to direct program control (flow) from the beginning to the end of the program. Some high-level languages, such as structured COBOL, require this technique to be applied in program preparation.

Modularization takes the top-down concept a step further by dividing the program into modules that are totally self-contained. A **module** is a series of instructions that performs a single function, such as calculating the total amount of an employee's deductions in a payroll program. These statements are collectively referred to by the module name, a one-sentence description of the module's function.

---

4. . . .Four basic logic patterns that can be used in writing computer programs?

5. . . .Four advantages of using structured programming techniques?

6. . . .The main purpose of top-down programming?

DO YOU
REMEMBER

Coding the Program

Coding is an important step in the programming process, but it is only one of several important steps. Recall that the problem must be clearly defined and the solution carefully planned **before** the program is actually written.

Coding means translating the program solution (design) into a particular programming language. There are many high-level programming languages that can be used to code a program. Selecting the appropriate programming language that will be used is the responsibility of the programmer.

To solve problems, computers require very specific instructions. Before writing the instructions, a programmer develops an algorithm that combines human logic and computer logic. Using human language and graphic symbols to describe the solution to the problem, one or more flowcharts are developed from which the actual computer instructions are written.

A **computer program** can be defined as a set of well-ordered instructions directing the computer to perform certain operations. Instructions are expressed by letters, numbers, and symbols according to a well-defined set of rules. The character set (letters, numbers, and symbols), together with the grammatical rules of the language, forms the **syntax** of the language. Every programming language has its own unique character set and syntax that must be learned before that language can be used.

Figure 9–9 shows a program that computes an average. Before studying the program, review the pseudocode in Figure 9–3 and the

```
10   READ T1,T2,T3
20   LET S = T1 + T2 + T3
30   LET A = S/3
40   PRINT "AVERAGE=";A
50   END
60   DATA 70,80,90

OK
RUN
AVERAGE= 80
```

Figure 9–9
Sample program that calculates an average.

THE COMPUTER DIDN'T DO IT!

William W. Harmon's relief was obvious when he received a telephone call from the Water & Sewer Department of Boone, NC, informing him that the water and sewer bill he would receive in the mail that day was incorrect, and that before paying his monthly bill, he should wait for a new one.

Fortunately for Harmon, the error was detected early. According to the monthly bill, Harmon had used 9,987,000 gallons of water for which he was charged $18,304.93.

When asked about the incident, Harmon quipped, "I'm sure glad they called me before I got home and opened the bill."

Source: William W. Harmon

flowchart in Figure 9–5, both of which were used as programming aids to write the program in Figure 9–9. Notice the similarities among the pseudocode, flowchart, and program.

In the program in Figure 9–9, line 10 instructs the computer to READ three test grades from the DATA statement (line 60). Line 20 instructs the computer to add the three test grades. Line 30 instructs the computer to calculate the average (A) by dividing the sum of the three test grades (S) by 3. Line 40 directs the computer to print (output) the expression **AVERAGE =** followed by the mathematical average (A). Line 50 was inserted by the programmer to identify the end of the program. By entering the command **RUN,** the computer begins program execution. Following execution, the results of processing, **AVERAGE = 80,** is displayed on the monitor screen or sent to another output device, if desired.

Checking, Debugging, and Testing the Program

Only programs that are free of syntax errors can be executed by the computer. This means that a single syntax error in a program will result in the computer's not being able to **run** (execute) the program. Because of this, computers are said to be unforgiving. Your English teacher may forgive you for incorrect punctuation in your term paper, but a computer will not forgive you for a syntax error in your computer program. You will have to correct the error before the program will execute properly.

Logic errors in a program, however, will not necessarily prevent the computer from executing the program. When a program contains errors in program logic, the program can frequently be executed, but

Figure 9-10
A programmer desk-checking a program. Desk-checking can be helpful in finding mistakes with program language and logic.

the output will likely be incorrect. A programmer should make every effort to avoid both syntax and logic errors while programming.

One way to avoid errors in program development is by desk-checking the program before putting the program into the computer. When **desk-checking** (desk-debugging), the programmer "pretends" to be the computer by reading each instruction and "picturing" in his or her mind how the computer will process the instruction. The few minutes spent desk-checking can save many hours that otherwise might be spent searching for and correcting errors.

The errors might be the result of incorrect language syntax, such as an incorrect variable name or an incorrect character used in an instruction. Or they might be run-time errors. A **run-time error** occurs when the programmer tells the computer to do something it *cannot do*. For example, if the programmer tells the computer to add eight student test grades but gave it only seven, a run-time error occurs when the computer tries to read the eighth test grade that is not there.

Logic errors are the worst kind of errors to have in a program. This is because they produce no error messages alerting the programmer that something is wrong. Executing as though there were no errors, programs with logic errors produce inaccurate output.

Every computer program should be thoroughly **tested** until the programmer is confident that it works properly and produces the right output. To test the program, programmers often run the program several times using data similar to data that will be used in a real application. The purpose is to see how the program works—that is, to test the validity and reliability of the program. A **valid program** does exactly what it is **supposed to do.** A **reliable program** does it **every time.** Thus, a program is complete if it is both valid and reliable.

Documenting the Program

Preparing well-written computer programs can be time consuming and expensive. Moreover, few programs are intended for one-time use. Most are used over and over again for solving recurring problems. Weeks or months might pass before the program is used again. For these reasons, programs should be well documented. Many computer professionals argue that documenting the program is the most important phase in the programming process.

Documenting a program means that written records must be kept that clearly describe the program; explain its purpose; define the amount, types, and sources of input data required to run the program; trace the logic the program follows; and contain an accurate listing of the program itself. Complete, accurate, and current documentation is essential if the program is to be used to its maximum advantage and/or modified in the future.

Maintaining the Program

A final phase in the programming process which could actually be thought of as a part of the documentation phase is that of program **maintenance.** Frequently, after a program has been written and has been in use for some time, it becomes necessary for the programmer to make some minor modifications to it. These modifications can be made much more easily if the documentation for the original program is accurate and complete.

7. . . .Why syntax and logic are essential ingredients in writing a computer program?

8. . . .What *desk-checking* means, and why it is important to desk-check a program before attempting to run it?

9. . . .Why a programmer should always document every program?

10. . . .Why program maintenance is important?

DO YOU REMEMBER

Systems Analysis and Design

Large businesses and organizations employ many people whose jobs and responsibilities vary significantly. Included are such diverse groups as accountants, clerks, production workers, and engineers. In their jobs, individuals and groups have unique problems and information requirements.

A large organization typically views itself as a system made up of subsystems, including accounting, manufacturing, marketing, and shipping. Each area has its own information needs. Providing needed information for each subsystem (department) increases the effectiveness of the overall system (the organization).

Data processing departments are established to assist users (individuals, departments, and management) in solving problems and obtaining information needed to function effectively. Specially trained, experienced professionals called **systems analysts** work closely with

Figure 9–11
A systems analyst with a user.

users, including management, to solve the organization's information problems.

The primary role of a systems analyst is to create and design an information processing system. Within this role, the analyst performs specific duties to assist users in obtaining needed information, including the following:

1. Determine the output (information) required by the user and the input (data) needed to obtain the output.

2. Determine the required resources, including programmers, hardware, and software.

3. Supervise the design of the problem solution and programming.

Systems analysis and design is a continuing process because there are always information problems to be solved. Solving problems is a high priority for any successful business or organization.

Summary

(This summary provides answers to DO YOU REMEMBER . . . questions in the chapter.)

1. **Why is programming important?**
   Programming is important because without a program to follow a computer would be useless.

2. **What is an algorithm and in what forms can it be expressed?**
   An *algorithm* is a set of rules that, if followed precisely, will lead to a correct problem solution. An algorithm can be expressed in any form such as language, a mathematical formula, or a diagram.

3. **What are pseudocode and flowcharts?**
   Pseudocode is a set of English-like statements appearing in the same order the program instructions will appear in the program. A *flowchart* is a symbolic diagram of the necessary steps in a problem solution. Pseudocode and flowcharts are useful programming aids.

4. What are the four basic patterns that can be used in writing computer programs?

Four basic logic patterns are *simple-sequence, selection, loop,* and *branch.*

5. What are four advantages of using structured programming techniques?

Using structured programming techniques will result in programs that are (1) easier to understand, (2) more accurate, (3) more efficient, and (4) easier to maintain.

6. What is the primary purpose of top-down programming?

The primary purpose is to direct program control (flow) from the beginning of a program to the end.

7. Why are syntax and logic essential ingredients in writing a computer program?

A programmer must *know the syntax* (rules) of the language she or he is using to write the program, and must *be able to apply logic* in the development of a problem solution.

8. What is desk-checking, and why is it important for a programmer to desk-check a program before running it?

Desk-checking is the process of mentally (logically) simulating how each instruction will be executed by the computer. This process allows the programmer to detect any logic and syntax errors that might be present in the program.

9. Why should a programmer always document every program?

Generally speaking, programs are intended to be used many times to solve recurring problems. Occasionally, a program needs to be modified or altered which is more difficult to do without adequate documentation.

10. Why is program maintenance important?

Program maintenance is necessary because changing conditions sometimes require changes in the program. Rewriting every program completely can be costly and time consuming.

DATA PROCESSING CAREER. . . . .
Applications Programmer

CAREER OPPORTUNITY FOR COMPUTER PROFESSIONAL

JOB TITLE:
Applications Programmer

JOB DESCRIPTION:
Individual seeking this position must be able to apply the programming process in the solution of well-defined business problems. Applicant should be trained and experienced in structured programming techniques, programming aids, documentation, and program maintenance. Languages include COBOL, Fortran, and Assembly.

EXPERIENCE REQUIRED:
Previous experience helpful but not essential.

EDUCATION REQUIRED:
Four-year college or technical degree in computer science or related area.

PERSONAL QUALIFICATIONS:
Applicant should have good work habits, enjoy working with users, and have the ability to pay close attention to detail. Should enjoy working in a problem-solving and challenging environment. In addition, applicant will be expected to assist and instruct users, and to consult with management on computer-related issues and technology.

Key Terms

algorithm
applications programmer
branch pattern
coding
computer program
control statement
debug
decision-logic pattern
desk-checking
documentation
flowchart
flowchart symbols
logic error

loop pattern
modularization
module
program maintenance
pseudocode
reliable program
run-time error
simple-sequence pattern
structured programming
syntax
syntax error
top-down programming
valid program

Test Yourself

1. Before a program can be written to solve a problem, there must be a(n) _____ .

2. A set of rules which, if followed precisely, will lead to a correct problem solution is a(n) _____ .

3. A set of English-like sentences appearing in the same order as will actual program instructions in a program is known as _____ .

4. A(n) _____ is a diagram of the necessary steps in a problem solution.

5. Four basic logic patterns used in computer programs are _____ , _____ , _____ , and _____ .

6. Two programming techniques recommended by professional programmers are _____ and _____ .

7. Translating a problem solution (design) into a particular programming language is called _____ .

8. One way to detect errors in program development is by _____ .

9. Three kinds of program errors are run-time errors, syntax errors, and _____ errors.

10. Program _____ refers to the updating and/or modifying of the computer program at a future time.

11. A(n) _____ is a person who applies the programming process in solving well-defined problems with the computer.

Review Questions

1. The chapter began with Bill and Agnes Blalock starting a new florist business after retiring from their former jobs at a bank. What are some of the ways they can use a computer to help them in their new business venture?

2. Why is programming important? What advantages does learning to write computer programs offer computer users? (Learning Objective 2)

3. What steps should a programmer follow in order to write useful and efficient programs? (Learning Objective 3)

4. Identify two programming aids widely used by programmers to design problem solutions. (Learning Objective 4)

5. What does each of the following symbols represent in a flowchart? (Learning Objective 5)

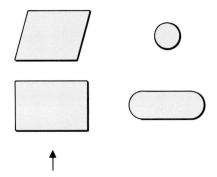

6. Name four basic logic patterns that can be used in writing computer programs. (Learning Objective 6)

Activities

1. Using appropriate symbols, prepare a flowchart showing all decisions you made and actions you took from the time you awoke until you arrived at school today. Make your flowchart detailed and complete.

2. Draw as many flowcharting symbols as you can remember on paper and explain the meaning of each.

3. Using one of the three forms explained in the chapter (English-like form, mathematical form, or diagram form), write an algorithm for starting the engine of an automobile from the time you unlock the door of the automobile.

4. Using what you learned about problem solving from this chapter, write an essay explaining why some professional programmers suggest that writing a computer program requires "common sense."

CHAPTER 10

Computer Software

Learning Objectives

After studying this chapter carefully, you will be able to:

1. Define key terms used in the chapter.
2. Identify the two types of computer software.
3. Identify the parts of operating systems software.
4. Identify the types of applications software.

Chapter Outline

SOFTWARE OVERVIEW

SYSTEMS SOFTWARE
Operating System Software
Translating Software

APPLICATIONS SOFTWARE
Vendor-Supplied Applications Software
User-Written Applications Software

DATA PROCESSING CAREER: Software
   Consultant

Application

During a recent visit to a software company to discuss a new software package, the first question I asked was, "What type of manuals or other documentation exist for this package?" The manager told me that he had nothing at the time, but that he was "working on it."

Though not a typical situation at present, it demonstrates that the problems of software documentation are getting worse, not better. Two of the most persistent problems are poor writing style and inefficient manual development.

In explaining data-processing terms, some writing is so brief that it reads like a glossary. Some manuals are so full of coding and flowcharts that users cannot get through them without professional help.

Some software houses go to the other extreme. They want to sell their software to everyone, so they set the reading level too low and use the writing style of a comic book.

Inefficient procedures present more serious problems for manual development. The documentation specialist is often the last person to learn about new applications software. He or she is at the end of the production line—just before the loading dock—and is expected to do his job as quickly as the packaging is done in the warehouse.

Most companies want their documentation specialists to spend as much time as possible on their word processors. They should only need to assign a liaison person to provide the necessary technical information required to document a new software product.

In small companies, the documentation specialist must often be his or her own editor, technical illustrator, and production manager, responsible for formatting pages and selecting type styles.

As computers become more widely used, documentation of applications software will have to be written as professionally as the programs it is describing.

Software Overview

A computer without software would be similar to a cart without a horse: **computer software** makes the hardware operate.

Many users buy computer software that is already developed to solve a particular problem. Other users write their own software in-house to customize a specific solution to a particular problem. Most businesses today use a combination of these two ways of acquiring software. The programmer/analyst in Figure 10–1 is developing software for a user.

Software development is a major part of what an **electronic data processing** (EDP) organization does. Referred to as programmers or analysts, the people who work for an EDP company develop software solutions to complex problems. This chapter deals with the different types of computer software. You will learn, for example, what software could be necessary to produce output that a manager might use.

There are two main types of computer software: systems software and applications software. Systems software is the "brains" of the computer, whereas applications software deals with the solution to a

Figure 10–1
Programmer/analyst developing software for user.

user's problem—preparing the company's payroll, for example. A good grasp of computer software is necessary for understanding how a computer works.

Systems Software

Systems software consists of programs that direct the operation of the hardware. These programs are divided into two groups: operating system software and translating software.

Operating System Software

The **Operating System** (OS) in a computer actually supervises all the activities of the computer. It carries out its task in a way similar to the way a traffic officer does. In the computer system, the operating system might be thought of as the "brains." It consists of software, or programs, that carry out specific functions that cause the hardware to do something. It tells the hardware what to do and how and when to do it.

The operating system in a computer is made up of the following components: an Input/Output Control System (IOCS), the translating software, the Database Management System (DBMS), a Data Communications System (DCS), and utility software. These components direct the hardware system to carry out specific duties, such as reading data and program instructions from a magnetic disk or printing data. Figure 10–2 shows how the operating system interfaces with other components of a computer system.

There are many different types of operating systems for computers. MS-DOS, PC-DOS, CPM, and p-System are some of the more popular operating systems used with microcomputers. One of the most popular operating systems, fast becoming an industry standard for all sizes of computers, is AT&T's UNIX. Most hardware vendors have their own unique operating system that runs only on their specific hardware. This has caused an incompatability problem within the computing industry because what runs on one vendor's hardware might not run on another's. UNIX has closed some of the gap between incompatability and compatability in operating systems software.

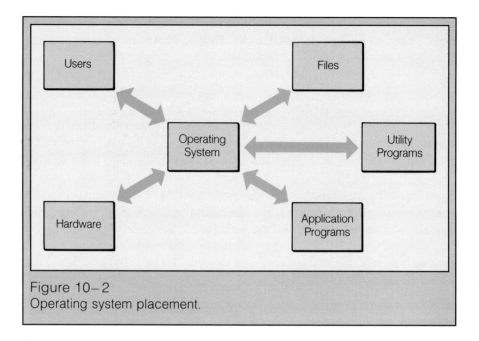

Figure 10-2
Operating system placement.

Before any tasks can be done by the CPU, the operating system must be electronically loaded into primary storage. This is called **booting** or **IPLing** (Initial Program Load) the system. The operating system software is usually stored on a magnetic disk, except in some large computers where part of the operating system software is stored in primary storage.

Translating Software

Translating software converts a computer language that people use, such as BASIC, to machine language the computer uses to execute programs. This is necessary because the computer must have the program represented in its own machine language before it can determine what to do with it.

Translating software (assembler, compiler, generator, or interpreter) does basically the same thing that a human interpreter at the United Nations does when he or she works with delegates who do not speak one another's language. For these delegates to communicate successfully, there must be an interpreter to translate from one language to the other. Figure 10-3 illustrates the steps involved in translating a program.

A programmer usually writes the computer's instructions, called a *source program,* in a high-level human-oriented language such as

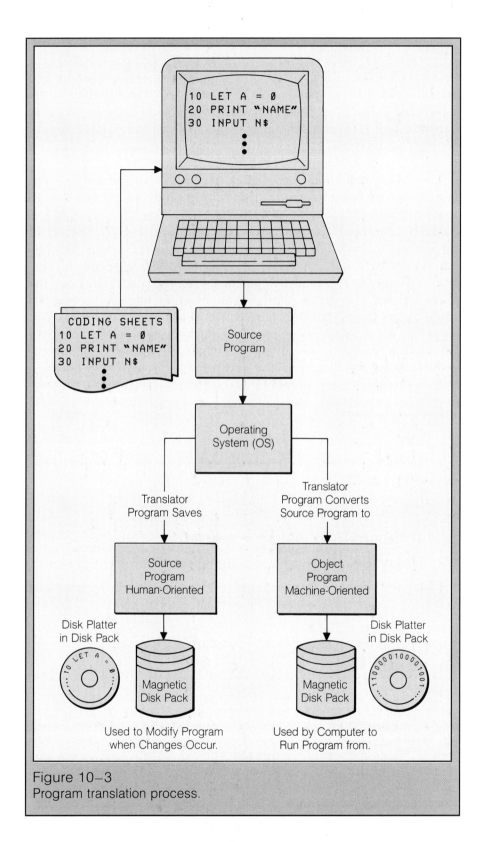

Figure 10–3
Program translation process.

BASIC, COBOL, PL/1, or RPG. These languages are used by programmers to express the logic/steps it takes to solve a problem using a computer. The translating software then converts these programs into machine language, or *object programs,* because the computer does not understand these human-oriented, high-level languages. Recall that machine language is expressed in binary 0s and 1s.

Translating software is most often loaded into the primary storage of a computer from magnetic disk. These modules of software are actually part of the operating system.

Many computers use an interpreter as opposed to a compiler for translating the BASIC language to machine language. One of the basic differences between a compiler and an interpreter is speed of translation. An interpreter is slower in translating the source program that the programmer writes in BASIC to the machine-language object program. Also, the compiler generates an object program, in machine language, all at one time and loads it into primary memory for execution. An interpreter however, sends one line of machine language code to the CPU at a time for execution. A compiled program in object program format normally executes considerably faster than a program that has been translated using an interpreter.

DO YOU
REMEMBER

1. . . . .The two types of computer software?

2. . . . .The components of an operating system (OS)?

3. . . . .What translating software is used for?

4. . . . .The difference between a source program and an object program?

THE COMPUTER DIDN'T DO IT!

A hotel in New York City sent a form letter to past guests thanking them for their business and informing them of the hotel's new services. Unfortunately, the marketing department requested the wrong mailing list. Because of this mistake, hundreds of New York housewives opened letters thanking their husbands for staying at the hotel. After this, the hotel received hundreds of calls from irate husbands requesting that letters of explanation and apology be sent to their wives, who were extremely upset and threatening separation.

Applications Software

Applications software includes both vendor-supplied and user-written software. Vendor-supplied applications software is developed by a software vendor, often a major software company. User-written applications software is developed by a particular user to meet a specific need.

Vendor-Supplied Applications Software

A software vendor can provide certain off-the-shelf or prepackaged solutions to a user's software problems. Some of the time, these prepackaged, generalized solutions must be customized (modified) to meet a particular need. Basically, there are six categories of vendor-supplied software packages. The following section deals with these categories.

Word Processing Packages.   **Word processing software** is one of the most popular and widely sold vendor-supplied packages. These packages are in plentiful supply for all computer systems. They allow the user to develop and edit text made up of sentences and paragraphs. The text that you are reading, for example, was developed by using a word processing package called MultiMate. Other popular word processing packages are WordStar, AppleWriter, PFS Write, Word Perfect, PC Write, and EasyWriter-II. Many businesses are now using microcomputers as word processing tools to process their daily correspondence, memorandums, and other written documents (see Figure 10–4).

Word processing systems have revolutionized administrative secretarial work in business offices. With word processing systems, the tasks of making corrections and modifications to a document is much easier than the same job would be using typewriters. Words, sentences, and paragraphs can be easily manipulated using a word processing system, and the speed of all these operations is increased.

Business Analysis Packages.   The most popular business analysis package in the marketplace today is the **electronic spreadsheet.** This software package allows the user to process financial and statistical data, and to display the results on the video screen (CRT) with title, row, column, detail, and total lines representing the report. Any report that appears on the CRT can also be printed on the printer. See

Figure 10–4
A typical word processing system configuration.

Figure 10–5
Example of an electronic spreadsheet.

Figure 10–5 for examples of what spreadsheets look like and how they can be used.

Business analysis packages are used by many professionals in their everyday business transactions. These business professionals include lawyers, doctors, stock brokers, bankers, teachers, florists, and others who have a need for manipulating data electronically in order to create financial and statistical reports to be used in decision making. Some of the popular spreadsheet packages are Lotus 1-2-3, VisiCalc, SuperCalc, and Multiplan.

263

1988
CORPORATE BUDGET

	1987	1988 Actual	1989 Proj.
Salaries	$525,500.00	$550,000.00	$600,000.00
Telephone	5,250.00	5,525.00	6,525.00
Printing	3,350.00	3,925.00	4,500.00
Travel	10,250.50	12,350.25	15,525.75
Memberships	1,000.00	1,200.00	1,500.00
Energy	12,000.00	14,000.00	16,000.00
Repairs	5,254.25	6,125.45	8,000.00
Miscellaneous	4,000.00	5,000.00	6,000.00
Total	$566,604.75	$598,125.70	$658,050.75

WORKSHEET

THIS SPREADSHEET REPRESENTS
THE MONTHLY SALES
OF UNITS SOLD
1988

	A	B	C	D	E	F	G	H	I	J	K	L	M	N
001		JAN	FEB	MAR	APR	MAY	JUN	JUL	AUG	SEP	OCT	NOV	DEC	TOT
002	Ut X	5	2	3	7	6	9	11	4	1	14	20	22	104
003	Ut Y	4	1	2	6	5	8	10	3	5	13	19	21	97
004	Ut Z	6	3	4	8	7	10	12	5	2	15	21	23	116
005														
006	Total	15	6	9	21	18	27	33	12	8	42	60	66	317

Mathematical and Graphics Packages.   These packages are very popular for manipulating numeric data and displaying it in a graphics format. The graphics display might be in the form of a line chart, bar chart, pie chart, or some other type. If the user has a color monitor (CRT), the display of the chart is more effective and easier to interpret. The graphics display that appears on the video screen can also be printed by certain printers and plotters. PFS Graph is a popular graphics package developed by Software Publishing Corporation. Other frequently used mathematical and graphics packages are PC Graph and MacPaint. Figure 10–6 illustrates a graph produced by a graphics package.

Educational Packages.   These packages are used by educators to help maintain school records of all types throughout the entire school system. Many teachers will use only a specific feature of a package, such as the grade book program which allows for the calculation and posting of grades.

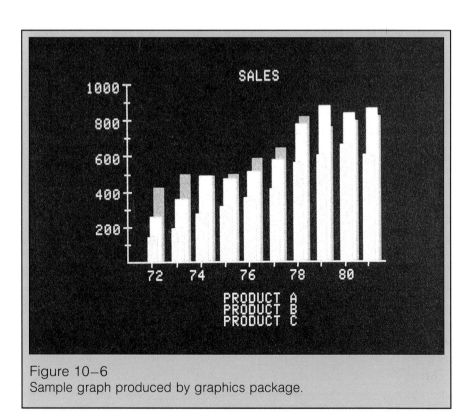

Figure 10–6
Sample graph produced by graphics package.

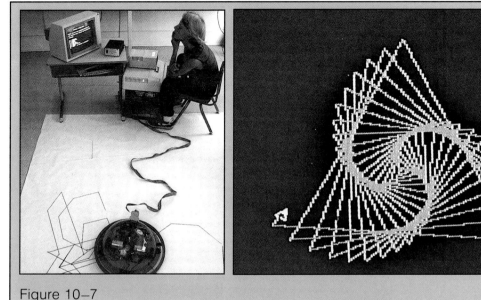

Figure 10–7
Example of an educational software package.

Another type of popular educational software package deals with Computer-Assisted Instruction (CAI). CAI provides an alternate approach to teaching. With this method, the student interacts with a computer by responding to objective questions about a particular topic or subject. This technique is sometimes referred to as *drill and practice*. The CAI package keeps track of all the statistics of the interactive session between it and the student and provides a grade/score for each particular session. CAI packages can be used as tools to help students learn objective material more effectively. The person in Figure 10–7 is engaged in CAI.

Entertainment Packages.   There are many entertainment software packages for home use. The quality of these home game packages varies among games and vendors. It seems like everyone, including high school students, is writing game software for entertainment purposes. This area represents a large portion of the software package business.

Many of the game packages include both audio and video capability making the game more interesting to play. Star Wars, Centipede, and Z-Bat are only a few of the popular video games which can be run

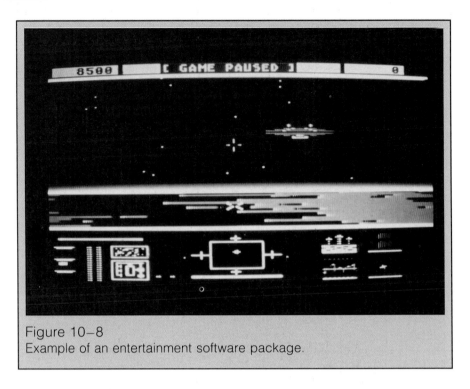

Figure 10–8
Example of an entertainment software package.

on a computer. Figure 10–8 is an example of an entertainment software package.

Integrated Packages.   These packages are becoming extremely popular because of their flexibility. With integrated software, a user can record data once in a database and share this data across many different applications that use word processing, spreadsheets, and graphics concepts. The idea here is to be able to create the data, store it, process it, and pass it, for example, from a spreadsheet to a graphics application for further processing and displaying in graphics format.

Most software vendors develop many of their software packages so that word processing, spreadsheeting, graphics, and database processing programs can interact with each other as an integrated package. This segment of the software market has experienced tremendous growth because of user demand for such software products. Some of the more popular integrated software packages are DataEase, PFS series, Visi-on, MultiPlan, and Lotus 1-2-3. See Figure 10–9 for an example of an integrated software package and a report created from it.

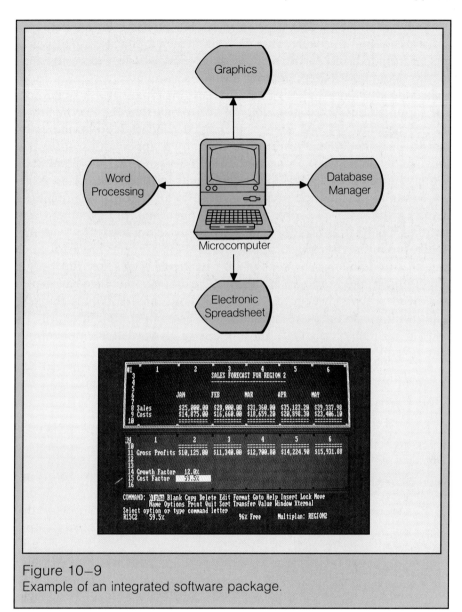

Figure 10–9
Example of an integrated software package.

User-Written Applications Software

Although prepackaged applications software can be exactly what a user needs to solve a problem, many times a specific user's problem cannot be solved without some modifications to the prepackaged software. When prepackaged software does not meet the user's need, it is often practical for the user to write his or her own applications software. When the user writes his or her own applications software, it is referred to as **user-written applications software** (see Figure 10–10).

Most companies large enough to have a computer system of moderate size will have a staff of applications programmers to write specific applications software. (This is not to say that these companies do not periodically buy some specialized prepackaged applications software, too.) When users write their own applications software, they get exactly what is needed to solve a specific problem. It is usually more costly to develop specific user-written applications software than to buy already prepackaged software, the greatest expense being in the cost of people's time. Applications programmers and systems analysts are paid very well to develop software systems. When buying prepackaged applications software, the buyer doesn't pay all the development cost of that particular package, but only a set price for the software package. The development costs of prepackaged software is spread over the thousands of copies that are sold. Still, most companies and personal users of computers normally end up writing a considerable amount of user-written applications software to meet specific needs.

Figure 10–10
Computer programmer writing program code.

5. . . .The two types of applications software?

6. . . .The six major categories of vendor-supplied applications software?

7. . . .When user-written applications software is required?

Summary

(This summary provides answers to DO YOU REMEMBER . . . questions in the chapter.)

1. What are the two types of computer software?
The two types of computer software are systems software and applications software. *Systems software* is the "brains" of the computer that tells the computer hardware what to do and how to do it. *Applications software* is used to solve the user's particular problem, such as preparing a payroll. Both types of software are needed when using a computer.

2. What are the components of an operating system (OS)?
The components of an operating system (OS) are an input/output control system (IOCS), the translating software (assembler, compiler, generator, or interpreter), a database management system (DBMS), a data communications system (DCS), and utility software.

3. What is translating software used for?
Translating software is used to translate a high-level programming language that people use to machine language that the computer uses.

3. What is the difference between a source program and an object program?
A *source program* is written by a person in a high-level language to express the logic it will take to solve a particular problem; an *object program* is the translated binary machine language program the computer uses to execute the program.

5. What are the two types of applications software?
The two types of applications software are *user-written* and *vendor-supplied*.

6. **What are the six major categories of vendor-supplied applications software?**

The six major categories of vendor-supplied applications software are *word processing, business analysis, electronic spreadsheet, educational, entertainment,* and *integrated* software packages. Each category includes hundreds of individual software packages that are commercially available.

7. **When is user-written applications software required?**

User-written applications software is software (programs) written by a user to solve a particular problem. When the software that is needed is *not available* from vendors, a user frequently writes his or her own program(s).

DATA PROCESSING CAREER. . . . .
SOFTWARE CONSULTANT

CAREER OPPORTUNITY FOR COMPUTER PROFESSIONAL

JOB TITLE:
Software Consultant

JOB DESCRIPTION:
Applicant will be responsible for advising clients on the selection of vendor-supplied applications software packages. Also, applicant will be responsible for overseeing the installation of purchased software packages.

EXPERIENCE REQUIRED:
A minimum of three years of actual consulting and advising is required.

EDUCATION REQUIRED:
A two-year associate degree in data processing or related business area required. A four-year bachelor's degree with a major in information systems desired.

PERSONAL QUALIFICATIONS:
Candidate should like working with other people to help them determine solutions to problems. Self-motivation, good work habits, and a pleasing personality are a must.

Figure 10–11
Software consultant at work.

Key Terms

applications software
business analysis package
educational package
entertainment package
integrated package
mathematical and graphics
   package
operating system software

programmer/analyst
translating software
user-written applications
   software
vendor-supplied applications
   software
word processing package
word processing system

Test Yourself

1. The two types of computer software are _____ and
   _____.

2. The _____ consists of programs that direct the hardware system to carry out specific duties.

3. A computer must be _____ before any operations or
   functions can take place inside the _____ .

4. A _____ translates a computer language
   people know into a language the computer can use.

5. The _____ is the software the programmer writes, and the _____ is the program used by the computer.

6. The two types of applications software are _____ and
   _____ .

7. A _____ allows a user to develop and
   edit text.

8. A _____ allows a user to process financial and statistical data.

9. A person that works with a potential software purchaser is
   called a _____ .

10. _____ instruction can be used as a tool to help stu-
    dents learn objective classroom materials more effectively.

Review Questions

1. Identify the differences between the two types of computer software. (Learning Objective 2)

2. Identify the components of an operating system (OS). (Learning Objective 3)

3. What do the terms *boot* and *IPL* mean, and when should this process be performed? (Learning Objective 3)

4. Explain the idea that operating systems software is the "brains" of the computer. What does an operating system do? (Learning Objective 3)

5. Identify the differences between the two types of applications software. (Learning Objective 4)

6. Discuss the integrated software package concept. What advantages does it have over other software packages? (Learning Objective 4)

Activities

1. Visit your school's computer lab and take an inventory of the types of systems software and applications software used. Make a list of this software and what computers they run on. Use this for class discussion.

2. Use your school's vendor-supplied word processing package to write a letter to a friend.

3. Use one of your school's vendor-supplied computer-assisted instruction (CAI) software packages to review material for a course(s) you are taking this term.

CHAPTER 11

Programming Languages

Learning Objectives

After studying this chapter carefully, you will be able to:

1. Define key terms introduced in this chapter.

2. Explain the difference between a machine-dependent and a machine-independent language, as well as the difference between a general-purpose and a special-purpose language.

3. Explain why programs written in machine language execute faster than programs written in other languages.

4. Name three popular languages for personal, home, and education applications.

5. Name three languages that were developed for business applications.

6. Name two languages used primarily for mathematical, scientific, and engineering applications.

7. Name two languages used with artificial intelligence and expert systems.

Chapter Outline

Application

Melanie Crawford's first course in data processing at Waldon High School was one of her favorite courses. She was curious about computers and wanted to learn more about them. In the course she learned about a computer's capabilities and functions, and how to use it.

Melanie, however, was somewhat disappointed because her teacher devoted little class time to teaching a computer language. She wanted to learn a programming language that would allow her to write programs.

Melanie expressed this concern to her teacher who agreed to loan Melanie a BASIC language software tutorial. With the interactive diskette tutorial, a manual, and assistance from her teacher, Melanie began learning BASIC during her spare time in the school's computer lab. In a short time, she was writing programs in BASIC and running them on the computer. Following Melanie's recommendation, several of her friends and classmates are now learning various programming languages with the aid of interactive tutorials.

Figure 11–1
Using a microcomputer in class.

Overview of Programming Languages

There are over 200 different programming languages now in existence. Of these, only about a dozen are being widely used. Some of the languages are machine-dependent, while others are machine-independent. Programs written in **machine-dependent** languages can be run only on the particular machine for which the programs were written. On the other hand, **machine-independent** programs can be executed on virtually any computer.

A computer language can be either a general-purpose or a special-purpose language. A **general-purpose** language can be used to write programs for many different applications, but a **special-purpose** language is limited to one, or a few, applications.

Programming languages can be classified in several ways. One convenient and meaningful way is to classify them according to their primary use or purpose. While some languages can be used for several programming applications, such as business, scientific, and education applications, most programming languages were developed for a specific type of application. In this chapter, programming languages are classified according to the specific applications for which they were originally developed.

Machine Language

Earlier computers were programmed in **machine language** whereby instructions and data were written in binary code that could be directly understood by the computer. You've already learned (in Chapter 3) that data is represented in the computer as binary numbers (0s and 1s). In digital computers, only instructions expressed as binary numbers are understood by the CPU (processor).

Machine-language instructions are written as strings or specific series of binary numbers. For this reason, writing a computer program in machine language is difficult and time-consuming.

Since computers immediately understand machine-language instructions, these programs will execute (run) quickly. Therefore, some programs that require fast execution are written in machine language. Computer games, for example, are written in machine language.

There are both advantages and disadvantages to using machine language. The main advantages are these: (1) machine language stores data efficiently; and (2) programs written in machine language execute quickly.

Two important disadvantages are as follows: (1) writing a machine-language program is difficult and time-consuming; and (2) machine language is machine-dependent, meaning that a program written for a particular computer will not execute on other computers.

Assembly Language

Assembly language was developed in the 1950s to lessen the difficulties of using machine language. Unlike machine language which uses binary code, assembly language uses convenient abbreviations, called **mnemonics.** Thus, a programmer can express instructions in abbreviated terms, making assembly instructions somewhat easier to write. For example, the assembly instruction ADD AX, VALUE instructs the computer to add the contents of the primary storage location named VALUE to the contents of the AX register.

Assembly language programmers have to be very familiar with the computer they are using. Assembly language programs can be used only on the machine for which they are written. Translating software used for programs written in assembly language is called an **assembler.**

Assembly language offers several advantages to the programmer: (1) it allows storage locations to be referred to by name, the programmer only has to specify the first storage location used, and the assembler assigns the others; (2) program errors are more easily correctable; and (3) like machine language, assembly programs execute quickly.

Two important disadvantages are these: (1) assembly programs are lengthy and difficult to write; and (2) assembly programs are not transportable (can't be executed on a different computer), one reason why programmers often prefer to use other languages.

DO YOU
REMEMBER

1. . . .Why a program written in machine language can be directly understood by the computer?

2. . . .The primary features of assembly language, and why assembly programs are easier to write and understand than programs written in machine language?

Languages for Personal, Home, and Education Applications

While several computer languages are suitable for personal, home, and educational applications, three languages have emerged as the most popular. They are LOGO, BASIC, and Pascal. It appears that these languages will remain popular because they are easy to learn and use.

FD 100
RT 90

Starting position

FD 100
RT 90

FD 100
RT 90

FD 100

Figure 11–2
Drawing a square with LOGO.

LOGO

If you hear teachers or programmers using the word "turtle" in conversation, chances are they're talking about **LOGO**, a language developed at MIT in the early 1960s by Seymour Papert. The language LOGO, whose name is derived from the Greek word for "reason," has a syntax that even young children can easily understand and use.

LOGO uses a special kind of cursor, called a *turtle*. The turtle is a triangular pointer that can be moved around on the screen by simple commands such as FORWARD and RIGHT. With these commands, graphic drawings can be created on the screen. This way, students can learn programming, mathematics, music, art, and other subjects. Figure 11–2 illustrates how a square can be drawn with LOGO. The instructions in each diagram are the exact instructions the programmer types on the keyboard.

LOGO is easy to learn and use, and is an excellent language for beginners to develop problem-solving skills. After gaining experience with LOGO, the user's imagination becomes the only limiting factor. Perhaps LOGO's main disadvantage is that it is slower than most other languages.

Several versions of LOGO are available. While there are differences among them, the differences are minor.

A variety of LOGO software is available for users of all ages, and for different applications and equipment. Special devices, such as KoalaPad, incorporate LOGO software features and applications.

Figure 11–3 shows a sample LOGO program and the output it produces. Notice the simplicity of each instruction.

BASIC

The developers of the BASIC language, John Kemeny and Thomas Kurtz, designed their language to simplify programming for students.

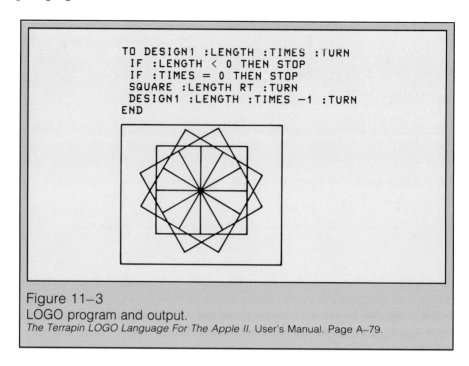

```
TO DESIGN1 :LENGTH :TIMES :TURN
   IF :LENGTH < 0 THEN STOP
   IF :TIMES = 0 THEN STOP
   SQUARE :LENGTH RT :TURN
   DESIGN1 :LENGTH :TIMES -1 :TURN
END
```

Figure 11-3
LOGO program and output.
The Terrapin LOGO Language For The Apple II. User's Manual. Page A–79.

They wanted to make it easy for students to write complex mathematical programs with little instruction.

BASIC (an acronym for <u>B</u>eginners <u>A</u>ll-purpose <u>S</u>ymbolic <u>I</u>nstruction <u>C</u>ode) is a flexible language that allows computer users to write programs in almost any area. Most versions of BASIC are **interactive,** which allows changes and corrections to be made easily because the programmer is immediately informed of errors. Some versions instruct the programmer what to do next, such as when to input data.

When microcomputers appeared in the mid-1970s, several manufacturers offered BASIC with their models. Today, most microcomputer software for personal, home, school, and even business use is written in BASIC.

More and more, businesses are using microcomputers and BASIC for such applications as maintaining customer records, keeping track of inventory, and processing payrolls. Figure 11–4 shows a sample payroll program written in BASIC.

In the program in Figure 11–4, all instructions are numbered in order. The computer will execute the instructions in numerical order. Instruction 80 tells the computer that the user will input the employee identification number (I) and the hours worked (H) for each employee. Instructions 90 through 110 tell the computer how to compute the employee's gross pay, withholding tax, and net pay. Instruction 130

```
10     REM - PAYROLL PROGRAM
20     REM - VARIABLES USED IN THIS PROGRAM
30     REM        I = EMPLOYEE IDENTIFICATION NUMBER
40     REM        H = NUMBER OF HOURS THE EMPLOYEE WORKED
50     REM        G = EMPLOYEE GROSS PAY
60     REM        W = TAX WITHHELD FROM EMPLOYEE
70     REM        P = EMPLOYEE NET PAY
80     INPUT I,H
90         LET G = 6.50 * H
100        LET W =  .18 * G
110        LET P =   G - W
120        PRINT
130        PRINT "PAYROLL DATA FOR EMPLOYEE"; I
140        PRINT
150        PRINT "   GROSS PAY"; G
160        PRINT "   TAX"; W
170        PRINT "   NET PAY"; P
180        PRINT
190    GOTO 80
200    END
RUN

?
234,32

PAYROLL DATA FOR EMPLOYEE      234

     GROSS PAY   208.00
     TAX          37.44
     NET PAY     170.56
```

Figure 11-4
Sample BASIC payroll program.

and instructions 150 through 170 give instructions on the output to be received from the computer. When the computer reaches the command RUN, a question mark prompt (?) is displayed, notifying the user to input the next employee's identification number (234) and hours worked (32). The computer then makes the calculations and displays the output as illustrated.

Pascal

The **Pascal** programming language was named for Blaise Pascal, the inventor of the first mechanical calculator. It was introduced in 1971 by Niklaus Wirth, a Swiss computer scientist. Like BASIC, Pascal

```
(* Program To Calculate Net Pay *)
PROGRAM NETPAY(INPUT,OUTPUT);
VAR TIME, RATE, RDEDUC, GROSS, DEDUC, PAY,:REAL:
BEGIN
READ(TIME, RATE, RDEDUC):
GROSS := TIME * RATE:
DEDUC :=GROSS * RDEDUC:
PAY : GROSS - DEDUC:
WRITELN('1', '         ', 'THE NET PAY FOR THIS EMPLOYEE IS $;
PAY : 9 : :2)
END
```

Figure 11–5
Sample Pascal payroll program.

was developed to teach students programming concepts. Already widely used in education, Pascal is becoming more popular for business and scientific applications. Although its programming rules make Pascal more difficult to learn than BASIC, many programmers agree that Pascal is easier to learn than many other languages.

In recent years, Pascal has found increasing acceptance for business and scientific applications. Because it is available on microcomputers, its popularity is likely to continue, and even increase. Figure 11–5 illustrates a sample Pascal program that calculates net pay.

There are both similarities and differences in the BASIC program illustrated in Figure 11–4 and the Pascal program shown in Figure 11–5. Unlike BASIC, Pascal instructions are not numbered, but like BASIC, they are executed in the order in which they are entered into the computer. In both programs, instructions are included for calculating an employee's gross pay, deductions, and net pay. You will notice that WRITELN, an abbreviation for WRITE LiNe, is an output instruction for the computer to follow. Output instructions were also provided for in the BASIC program.

The main advantages of Pascal are these: (1) it encourages good programming techniques, (2) it allows flexibility in using data, and (3) it is relatively standard.

The main disadvantages of Pascal are as follows: (1) it is more difficult to learn than BASIC, (2) it is weak in handling nonnumeric character strings, and (3) it is a compiled, rather than an interpreted language, which means that finding and correcting errors is more difficult than with BASIC.

3. ...The primary features of LOGO, and its advantages and disadvantages?

4. ...The primary features of BASIC, and its advantages and disadvantages?

5. ...The primary features of Pascal, and its advantages and disadvantages?

Languages for Business Applications

Many of the languages that are widely used today were developed primarily for business applications. In addition to the already established and well-known languages are other good business languages that are beginning to appear. COBOL has been in existence for many years. Ada and C languages are rapidly becoming more popular, and their use in programming is likely to become more extensive.

COBOL

COBOL (COmmon Business-Oriented Language) was the first language developed for business applications. It remains today one of the most widely used languages, especially with large computers. Its development resulted from a need for a machine-independent language—one that could be used on any computer.

One of the advantages of COBOL is that it can handle large amounts of data stored on secondary storage. Also, its English-like sentences make COBOL programs easier for both programmers and non-programmers to understand. This feature also makes a COBOL program easier to maintain and modify than a program written using certain other languages.

COBOL also has several disadvantages. COBOL compilers (translating software) take up more primary storage in the CPU than those for some other languages. Because its structure requires detailed data descriptions and consists of long sentences and divisions, a COBOL program is usually long and takes up considerable primary storage. Thus, COBOL cannot be used with some small computer systems that have very limited primary storage. COBOL is harder to learn than other languages, such as BASIC and Pascal. COBOL also has limited computational capabilities; for applications requiring complex computational capabilities, other languages can be more useful.

For business applications, however, COBOL's advantages outweigh the disadvantages. Compare the sample COBOL payroll program in Figure 11–6 to the previous payroll programs in BASIC and Pascal. Although this program (like the previous programs in BASIC and Pascal) calculates an employee's net pay, notice that this one in COBOL requires many more instructions. It is typical of COBOL programs to require more instructions than similar programs written in other languages.

Ada

One of the world's largest users of computer software is the U.S. Department of Defense. According to some estimates, the Department of Defense spent $25 billion on a "hodgepodge" of computer software, including languages. The Department of Defense needed a powerful language capable of processing many kinds of applications, both scientific and business-related. To meet its language requirements, the department adopted a language called **Ada,** named in honor of Lady Ada Augusta Byron for her work as the world's first programmer.

Originally intended to be a standard language for weapons systems, Ada has also been adopted by other government agencies and business firms. Introduced in 1980, Ada is endorsed and supported by several large computer manufacturers. Ada is now being used on some microcomputers. Some experts believe that Ada is too complex, while others say that it is easy to learn and can increase programming productivity. Some even believe that Ada is superior to established languages such as COBOL and FORTRAN. The Department of Defense has obtained a trademark for Ada in order to maintain control over its use.

One of Ada's advantages is that it is suitable for large and complex applications. Another is that all Ada compilers (translating software) are compatible, allowing Ada to be used on all large computers.

Figure 11–6
Sample COBOL payroll program.

```
IDENTIFICATION DIVISION.
PROGRAM-ID. SAMPLE.
*
ENVIRONMENT DIVISION.
INPUT-OUTPUT SECTION.
FILE-CONTROL. SELECT EMPLOYEE-FILE ASSIGN TO TAPE-1.
              SELECT PAYROLL-REPORT ASSIGN TO PRINTER.


*
DATA DIVISION.
FILE SECTION.
FD  EMPLOYEE-FILE LABEL RECORDS ARE STANDARD.
01  EMPLOYEE-RECORD.
      05   EMPLOYEE-NAME        PICTURE A(20).
      05   HOURS-WORKED         PICTURE 9(2).
      05   HOURLY-RATE          PICTURE 9V99.
FD  PAYROLL-REPORT LABEL RECORDS ARE OMITTED.
01  PAYROLL-RECORD.
      05   FILLER               PICTURE X(5).
      05   NAME-OUT             PICTURE A(20).
      05   FILLER               PICTURE A(5).
      05   HOURS-OUT            PICTURE 9(2).
      05   FILLER               PICTURE (5).
      05   RATE-OUT             PICTURE 9.99.
      05   FILLER               PICTURE (5).
      05   NET-PAY              PICTURE 999.99.
      05   FILLER               PICTURE (81).
WORKING-STORAGE SECTION.
01  EOF                         PICTURE 9         VALUE 0.
*
PROCEDURE DIVISION.
    OPEN INPUT EMPLOYEE-FILE
         OUTPUT PAYROLL-REPORT.
    MOVE SPACES TO PAYROLL-RECORD.
    READ EMPLOYEE-FILE AT END MOVE 1 TO EOF.
    PERFORM WAGE-ROUTINE UNTIL EOF = 1.
    CLOSE EMPLOYEE-FILE
          PAYROLL-REPORT.
    STOP RUN.
WAGE-ROUTINE.
    MOVE EMPLOYEE-NAME TO NAME-OUT.
    MOVE HOURS-WORKED TO HOURS-OUT.
    MOVE HOURLY-RATE TO RATE-OUT.
    MULTIPLY HOURS-WORKED BY HOURLY-RATE GIVING NET-PAY.
    WRITE PAYROLL-RECORD AFTER ADVANCING 2 LINES.
    READ EMPLOYEE-FILE AT END MOVE 1 TO EOF.
```

	- OUTPUT -		
(Employee Name)	(HOURS)	(RATE)	(NET-PAY)
FLOYD FULLER	40	3.35	134.00
PETER MARSHALL	50	4.00	200.00
STAN WILKINSON	30	4.75	142.50

Ada's main disadvantages are its size and complexity that require a painful adjustment on the part of most programmers. Despite these disadvantages, however, it is a reasonably safe prediction that Ada will become an important language in the 1990s because of the support it receives from the government.

C Language

When AT&T decided to start manufacturing computers, its engineers and programmers at Bell Laboratories concluded that system programming, including the development of operating systems, was too time-consuming and difficult. To overcome this problem, the company developed a new language. The result was C language (following versions A and B), a language that was developed in conjunction with its operating system UNIX. UNIX is the operating system developed by AT&T for computers it manufacturers.

With **C language,** operating systems and applications programs can be written faster than with most other languages. Several operating systems and applications programs for computers of all sizes are now prepared using the C language. Some large software vendors now use C to prepare vendor-written software packages.

The advantages of the C language are that it is machine-independent and, therefore, can be used on a variety of computers. Also, it is an efficient language and easy to use. Another important advantage is

---

THE COMPUTER DIDN'T DO IT!

OLYMPIA, WASH. (UPI)—A modern-day Robin Hood used his computer programming skills to route bogus welfare payments to those he deemed needy—including himself.

"I used my own money until it ran out," said Stanley V. Slyngstad . . . "Then I used the state's—an unlimited supply. . . ."

The former $30,000-a-year programmer for the Division of Vocational Rehabilitation in Olympia, Wash., pleaded guilty Wednesday to first-degree theft charges in passing $17,000 in bogus checks through his own personal welfare system.

Slyngstad programmed the division's computer to manage millions of dollars. Then he modified the program in 1982 to make payments to a "Stanley Lyngstad."

Slyngstad said he thought if he dropped the first letter from his name, no one would notice, and he would tell bank tellers when he cashed the checks that "the dumb computer misspelled my name."

"They believed me," he said. "They don't like computers."

Source: *The Lincoln Star* (April 30, 1983), p. 2. Reprinted with permission of *The Lincoln Star.*

that programs written with C execute quickly and require little primary storage. Special effects in several films, including *Star Trek* were developed using C.

On the other hand, the C language is a difficult language to learn. Also, preparing a program in C is difficult, and, once prepared, the program is hard for others to read.

6. . . .Three programming languages used primarily for business applications?

7. . . .The primary advantages of each language?

8. . . .The primary disadvantages of each language?

DO YOU REMEMBER

Languages for Scientific and Mathematical Applications

Some of the earliest users of computers were mathematicians, scientists, and engineers. Today, these professionals still rank among the more active users, and, as you might expect, many attempts have been made over the past two decades to develop computer languages to satisfy their computing needs. During that time, several languages were developed. Two that have gained widespread acceptance are FORTRAN and Forth.

FORTRAN

Many versions of **FORTRAN** (FORmula TRANslator) have been developed over the years, several of which contained errors and inefficiencies. Compounding the difficulties, some computer manufacturers offered their own versions of FORTRAN that could be used only with their brand of computer.

There have been attempts to standardize the language, but, as yet, no widely accepted standard version has been developed. Computer manufacturers continue to offer their own versions, and the lack of compatibility among computers remains a serious problem.

Nearly all versions of FORTRAN have desirable features. FORTRAN has exceptional mathematical capabilities, and programs written in FORTRAN require little primary storage and execute quickly.

Most versions of FORTRAN are difficult to learn and program preparation is time-consuming. This is primarily due to the fact that the rules of the language require that FORTRAN instructions be written in highly symbolic (less English-like) code. Another undesirable feature of FORTRAN is its limited file-handling and editing features, making it poorly suited to business applications. Compared to programs written with COBOL, FORTRAN programs are often poorly documented, making them difficult to read and maintain.

Forth

Forth was designed as a new *fourth-generation language* for microcomputers. The name was shortened from "fourth" to "forth" because the computer on which it was designed limited file names to five characters.

In its basic form, Forth has a limited number of functions but allows a programmer to add new ones that become a part of the language, similar to adding words to a dictionary. For example, a user can add a function that causes a computer to send commands to a heating system that automatically turn the system on and off at specific times. This feature gives a programmer more control over the computer and allows the programmer to use program code written for previous projects and applications. The same on/off function, for example, can be used for other machines.

A typical Forth program runs much faster and uses less primary storage than a comparable program written in BASIC. For these reasons, Forth is a good language for microcomputers.

Forth is well-suited for use in controlling many industrial processes such as blast furnace temperatures and cooling and welding systems. Thus, it has become a popular and widely used language around the world in manufacturing and research.

Languages for Artificial Intelligence (AI) and the Future

Many computer professionals believe we are now on the threshold of a new era in computing. Computer use is no longer limited to just data processing. New computers are being designed and programs are being written that enable computers to intelligently process knowledge rather than simply process data. Several of these programs, called **expert systems,** are already in use. Using this new technology, doctors can diagnose illnesses, lawyers can plan legal strategies, and scientists can simulate environmental conditions. For example, some engineers use this technology to select the correct type and size of rivet to use in a newly designed aircraft. By inputting known data such as the speed of the aircraft, wind resistance, weight supported by the aircraft part, and material from which the parts are constructed, the computer automatically selects the correct types and sizes of rivets for connecting parts of the aircraft.

Research is already under way in a field known as **artificial intelligence** to develop technologies that will make it possible for computer systems to "learn" from their own "experiences." Two languages, PROLOG and LISP, deserve attention because of their uniqueness and future potential.

PROLOG

PROLOG (PROgramming LOGic) is gaining recognition in the academic community as an important language. Its potential as an artificial intelligence language has caught the attention of the Japanese. The Japanese government and several private Japanese companies have embarked on a joint venture that, if successful, will make Japan the world leader in the development of artificial intelligence systems. In choosing PROLOG for this project, the Japanese hope to build computers capable of simulating, or imitating, human logic and intelligence. If the project succeeds, it's possible that PROLOG will become the dominant computer language by 1995.

LISP

LISP (LISt Processor) is a programming language developed by Professor John McCarthy at Stanford University in 1960. It has become more popular in recent years. McCarthy designed his language to manipulate nonnumeric data. The language itself provides an easy way to represent sentences, formulas, and data elements.

In LISP, a "list" is a group of elements in a particular order. Lists are useful for representing many kinds of things, from a class roll, or a list of fifty random numbers, to a group of English sentences. By using lists of elements, LISP is a powerful language for applications such as simulating human problem-solving processes. For this reason, LISP is especially suitable for artificial intelligence applications.

9. . . .Two programming languages well-suited for mathematical, scientific, and engineering applications?

10. . . .Two programming languages suitable for artificial intelligence research and expert systems?

Summary

(This summary provides answers to DO YOU REMEMBER . . . questions in the chapter.)

1. Why can a program written in machine language be directly understood by the computer?
Programs written in *machine language* can be directly understood by the computer because they are written in binary code (0s and 1s) which does not require translating software.

2. What are the primary features of assembly language, and why are assembly programs easier to write and understand than programs written in machine language?
The main features of assembly language are these: (1) instructions and data are written in symbol form rather than in binary codes, (2) storage locations are referred to by name, (3) programming errors are easier to correct, and (4) programs run quickly. Assembly programs are easier to write and understand than machine-language programs because they are more English-like.

3. What are the primary features of LOGO, and what are its advantages and disadvantages?
LOGO uses a "turtle" cursor to produce images on the screen. A few simple commands allow graphic drawings to be created. The primary advantages of LOGO are these: (1) it is easy to learn and use, (2) programmed procedures can be reused, and (3) it is an excellent language for beginners to use to develop logic and problem-solving skills. The main disadvantages are these: (1)

LOGO is not standardized—several versions are available, and (2) it executes more slowly than most other languages.

4. **What are the primary features of the BASIC language, and what are its advantages and disadvantages?**

The BASIC language is easy to learn, and BASIC programs are easy to write for most applications. It is a versatile language with versions available for most computers. BASIC's main advantages are that (1) it is easy to learn and use, (2) its programming errors are easily corrected (largely because it is interactive), (3) it is flexible enough for inexperienced users, and (4) it is available for almost all computers. Its main disadvantages are its unstructured design and somewhat limited applications.

5. **What are the primary features of Pascal, and what are its advantages and disadvantages?**

Like BASIC, Pascal was developed to teach programming concepts to students. It is suitable for personal, home, business, and educational applications. Pascal's main advantages are that (1) it encourages good programming techniques, (2) it allows flexibility in using data, and, (3) it is a relatively "standard" language. Its main disadvantages are that (1) it is weak in its ability to handle nonnumeric character strings, and (2) it is a compiled language rather than an interpreted language, thereby making error detection and correction more difficult.

6. **What are three programming languages used primarily for business applications?**

Three programming languages used mainly for business applications are *COBOL, Ada,* and *C* language.

7. **What are the primary advantages of each language?**

The advantages of COBOL are (1) its ability to handle large amounts of data; (2) its English-like sentences which make programs easy to understand, correct, and modify; and (3) its ability to render programs that will run on almost any computer. Ada's main advantages are (1) its usefulness for both business and scientific applications, (2) its ability to handle large and complex applications, and (3) its ability to increase programmer productivity. C language's main advantages are (1) that it is easy to use and efficient, (2) that programs execute quickly, and, (3) that very little primary storage is required.

8. **What are the primary disadvantages of each language?**

COBOL's main disadvantages are that (1) its programs are wordy and long; (2) it is compiled, making error detection and correction difficult; and, (3) it requires a lot of primary storage. Two important disadvantages of Ada are (1) its size and (2) its complexity. As for C language, (1) it is difficult to learn, (2) program preparation is difficult, and (3) once prepared, programs are hard for others to read.

9. What are two languages that are well-suited for mathematical, scientific, and engineering applications?

Two languages well-suited for mathematical, scientific, and engineering applications are *FORTRAN* and *Forth*.

10. What are two programming languages suitable for artificial intelligence research and expert systems?

Two languages suitable for artificial intelligence research and expert systems are *PROLOG* and *LISP*.

DATA PROCESSING CAREER. . . . .
CRT Clerk Typist

CAREER OPPORTUNITY FOR COMPUTER PROFESSIONAL

JOB TITLE:
CRT Clerk Typist

JOB DESCRIPTION:
Regional newspaper is seeking someone with excellent clerical skills to rekey copy into the CRT and type dictation over the phone. Applicants must type at least 50 wpm, and have excellent spelling and grammar skills. They must work well with others and under pressure, and must be able to deal effectively with the public over the telephone. The hours are 9 A.M. to 6 P.M. Monday through Friday.

EXPERIENCE REQUIRED:
None

EDUCATION REQUIRED:
A high school diploma

PERSONAL QUALIFICATIONS:
Applicants must be neat, possess good verbal and written communications skills, and be career-minded.

Key Terms

Ada
assembler
assembly language
BASIC
C language
COBOL
compiler
Forth
FORTRAN
general-purpose language

interpreter
LISP
LOGO
machine-dependent language
machine-independent language
machine language
Pascal
PROLOG
special-purpose language

Test Yourself

1. A programming language that can be used to write computer programs for several different applications is a _____ language.

2. A language for writing programs that can be directly understood by the computer is _____ language.

3. Assembly language is somewhat similar to machine language but uses _____ instead of binary code for instructions and data names.

4. The first language learned by most programmers is usually _____ .

5. In addition to BASIC language, _____ is a popular language for personal, home, and education applications.

6. The most widely used language for business applications is _____ because of its ability to handle large amounts of data on secondary storage.

7. A language developed by Bell Laboratories that is gaining popularity is _____ .

8. In existence for several years, _____ remains perhaps the most widely used language for mathematical and scientific applications.

9. _____ was designed as a fourth-generation language which "dropped" a character from its original name because it was developed on a computer that allowed only five-character file names.

10. Two programming languages important to artificial intelligence research and expert systems are PROLOG and _____.

Review Questions

1. Explain the primary difference between machine-dependent and machine-independent languages, and between general-purpose and special-purpose languages. (Learning Objective 2)

2. Why is machine language difficult to learn and use? (Learning Objective 3)

3. Why are BASIC and Pascal popular languages for personal, home, and educational applications? (Learning Objective 4)

4. Give reasons why COBOL is a widely used language for business applications. (Learning Objective 5)

5. Name two languages used primarily for mathematical and scientific applications. (Learning Objective 6)

Activities

1. With help from your teachers, school administrators, and other school personnel, prepare a list of different applications performed on your school's computer(s). Beside each application on your list, write the programming language used for that application.

2. Visit two or three businesses in your area. Make a list of each business's computer applications and the programming language used for each.

3. Visit a computer store in your area. Obtain permission from the owner or manager to browse through software packages displayed in the store and prepare a list of software package titles and the language used to prepare the software. (Note: The particular language used for each package is usually printed on the package.)

CHAPTER 12

Computer Applications

Learning Objectives

After studying this chapter carefully, you will be able to:

1. Define key terms introduced in the chapter.

2. Identify ways computers are used in homes by family members and by self-employed professionals.

3. Identify administrative and educational computer applications in schools.

4. Identify computer applications in science and medicine.

5. Identify computer applications in business.

6. Identify computer use in industrial research and development, and engineering.

7. Identify ways computers are used in government.

8. Identify other application software packages and concepts.

Chapter Outline

Application

Until the tenth grade, Greg Sanders showed little interest in his classes. Although his aptitude scores and other standardized tests indicated clearly that Greg possessed exceptional potential for achievement, he lacked motivation.

Fortunately, things changed when Greg arrived for registration at the beginning of his junior year. A counselor suggested to Greg that he enroll in a microcomputer course that was being offered for the first time. He was hesitant, but finally agreed because he was curious about computers. Greg's former microcomputer teacher recalls that Greg became fascinated with microcomputers; occasionally, he spent hours writing and running programs (see Figure 12-1).

Similar situations occur almost every day in public and private schools. Many students are being "turned on" by the exciting challenges made possible by computers and computer instruction. And speaking of Greg, where is he now and what is he doing? After making the honor roll in both his junior and senior years and earning a college degree in data processing, Greg is now a senior vice-president of business information systems for a large corporation at the ripe old age of twenty-six.

Figure 12–1
Greg runs a program on one of the school's microcomputers.

Embedded Computers in Products We Use

Embedded computers, by-products of space-age technology, are used to improve the performance of many of the products we use. These tiny "computers on chips" can be found in a wide variety of products, including home appliances and automobiles.

A stroll through your home will bring you into contact with products containing embedded computers—the microwave oven and the television, for example. The embedded computer in your microwave oven lets you specify when the food will begin cooking and for how long. The one in your washer lets you specify how long your clothes will be washed and the temperature of the water.

If your family owns a new luxury automobile, the instrument panel may contain hidden embedded computers that make your car run better and increase your driving convenience (see Figure 12–2). Several of the more expensive models have embedded computers that

Figure 12–2
A control panel in a new car.

provide driver information such as speed, fuel level, and average mileage per gallon. When used with a speech-synthesizer, a driver of one of these cars might be advised by messages such as "Please fasten your seat belt" or "Please slow down."

Many homes now have devices that regulate energy usage. Built into these devices are tiny computers that control the thermostat in each room and automatically turn outside lights on at any predetermined time. These devices can monitor energy usage of individual appliances, keep track of the amount of electricity used to heat the home, and even detect electrical malfunctions of appliances that cause energy to be wasted.

Perhaps someday embedded computers will remind you to study, to take out the trash, to telephone a friend, or that your wallet is empty. Ridiculous, you might think! A co-author of this book remembers saying "impossible" to a friend upon hearing that a company had made a machine called the "UNIVAC I," that could follow human-written instructions to perform mathematical calculations without human intervention. This author hasn't said "impossible" since!

Computers in Homes

A personal computer is the single most popular device in thousands of homes around the world, and this popularity is increasing every year. Over the past several years, sales of personal computers have been increasing at an amazing rate. Recent research indicates that the sale of personal computers will triple between 1984 and 1990.

Most computers today are personal computers. Although some are used by businesses, most are used in homes by family members for different purposes. Still others are used by family members in their jobs or profession.

For family members, the number of potential computer applications is almost unlimited. While computer games still provide many families with an important source of entertainment, the importance of other applications is increasing rapidly. Recordkeeping and word processing are popular computer applications for family members.

Recordkeeping

An important application for personal computers is keeping household records such as records of insurance policies, savings accounts, shopping lists, names and addresses, and inventories of household goods (such as furniture, appliances, and jewelry). While some people might argue that it is more convenient to use conventional methods like a card file, others argue that updating records on a personal computer is faster and more efficient.

Special software programs allow the user to design special forms for storing information such as names and addresses, financial information, and inventories. After customizing the form, information can be placed on the form, and both the form and information can be stored on tape or diskette for future reference. Records created with this package can be sorted alphabetically or numerically, making it convenient for the user to quickly locate a particular record. The diagram in Figure 12–3 shows how names and addresses can be kept using a compucard system.

Word Processing

Word processing, the electronic manipulation of text data, has become one of the most popular home computer applications. Each year, more people are using word processing in their personal lives, their studies, and their work. Many students, authors, business people, and professionals have bought personal computers primarily for word processing capabilities.

Word processing allows words to be manipulated in such a way that sentences, paragraphs, and entire pages of text can be developed for letters, term papers, or even a textbook like the one you are presently reading. Typewriters are still used to produce letters and other communication documents; however, microcomputers are rapidly replacing typewriters for manipulating and storing written text.

Word processing software allows the user to prepare, edit, print, store, and retrieve various documents needed in personal life and work. All kinds of documents can be produced in a variety of formats.

Word processing software makes the computer operate much like a typewriter, but more efficiently. Many good word processing programs allow the user to begin typing immediately after the program has been loaded into the computer. When typing a document, the user doesn't have to worry about reaching the end of a line or the bottom of a page. When the typed text reaches the end of a line, or margin, the program automatically moves it to the next line. This feature is called **word-wrap.** With adequate computer storage, the user will likely finish the document before using all of the available storage.

Editing takes place on a video screen instead of a typewritten page. Mistakes can be easily corrected by simply backspacing and retyping

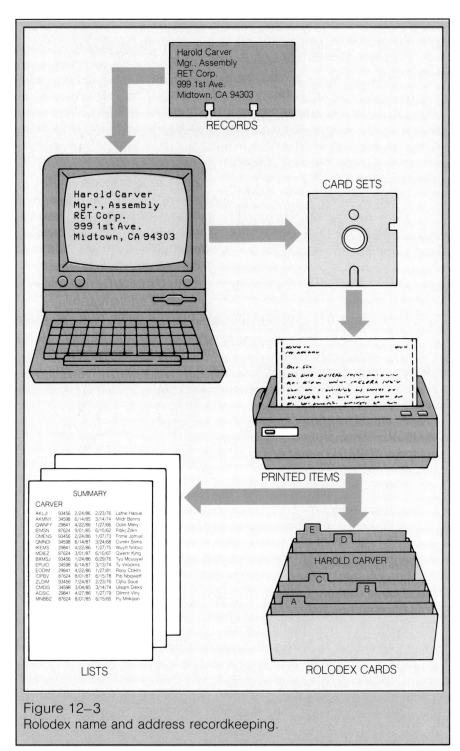

Figure 12–3
Rolodex name and address recordkeeping.

the text. Even beginning users often find that they can produce error-free documents in less time than they could with a typewriter. The following paragraphs briefly explain some of the functions of this important computer application.

Many word processing programs, like the one explained below, are **menu-driven** programs, which means that lists of functions are displayed on the computer screen to assist the user. When the program is loaded into the computer, the program's **MAIN MENU** is immediately displayed on the screen. The main menu lists the major functions of the program, and the user can choose any function listed by typing the identifying number of that function. After one of the functions from the main menu is selected, one or more additional menus (submenus) showing user options for that particular function may appear on the screen. Figure 12–4 shows what a main menu display for word processing looks like on a video screen.

Several popular word processing programs contain built-in user "aids" or "help screens" to assist the user with on-screen explanations of functions. An accompanying *user manual* contains information on how to access and use these aids or help screens, as well as complete instructions for using the word processing program. To get the full benefits of a word processing program, the user should study the manual and learn how to use all of the program's features.

Computers in Schools

In many homes, *education* has become the main justification for owning a personal computer. In recent years, thousands of software programs have appeared that allow users to learn almost any subject including English, math, typewriting, science, and social studies. Many of these software programs are interactive tutorial programs that encourage student involvement by "testing" a student's knowledge after the information has been presented. Many users enjoy this method of learning. Some teachers and students believe that the personal computer, together with good educational software programs, can improve a student's understanding and retention of the information.

While some might object to the word "revolution" to describe the impact computers are having on the American education system, computers are bringing about significant changes in education. School

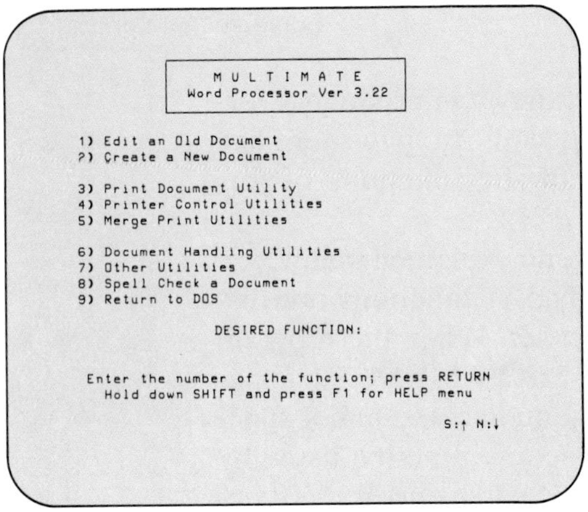

```
            M U L T I M A T E
           Word Processor Ver 3.22

      1) Edit an Old Document
      2) Create a New Document

      3) Print Document Utility
      4) Printer Control Utilities
      5) Merge Print Utilities

      6) Document Handling Utilities
      7) Other Utilities
      8) Spell Check a Document
      9) Return to DOS

             DESIRED FUNCTION:


      Enter the number of the function; press RETURN
      Hold down SHIFT and press F1 for HELP menu

                                  S:↑ N:↓
```

MultiMate Main Menu. User selects one of the nine options by choosing the appropriate function by number. The selected number is keyed in at the Desired Function: prompt. All nine functions can be executed without exiting MultiMate.

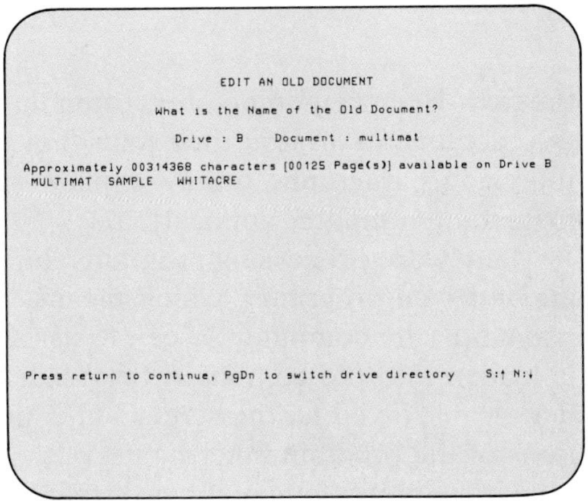

```
                 EDIT AN OLD DOCUMENT

          What is the Name of the Old Document?

            Drive : B    Document : multimat

  Approximately 00314368 characters [00125 Page(s)] available on Drive B
  MULTIMAT   SAMPLE    WHITACRE





  Press return to continue, PgDn to switch drive directory    S:↑ N:↓
```

Selecting Option 1 from the main menu will give a user the "Edit an Old Document" screen. A listing of all the document files on a user's data disk will appear in the top half of the screen along with the amount of space left on the user's data disk. The user is asked to give the name of the document file to be edited, in this case the name is "MULTIMAT". Only the first eight characters in the document name is recognized by MultiMate.

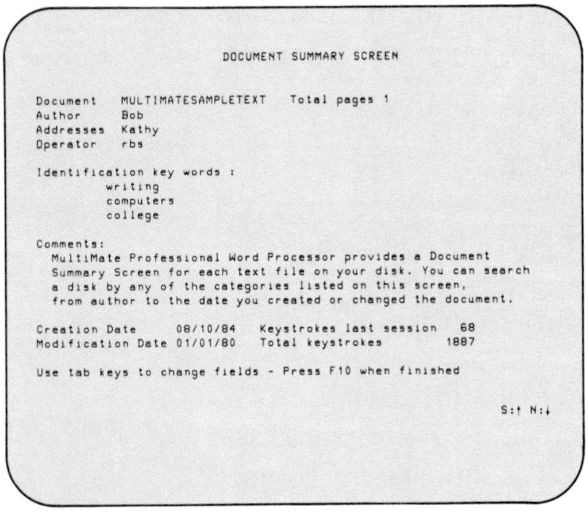

```
                 DOCUMENT SUMMARY SCREEN

  Document   MULTIMATESAMPLETEXT   Total pages 1
  Author     Bob
  Addresses  Kathy
  Operator   rbs

  Identification key words :
              writing
              computers
              college

  Comments:
     MultiMate Professional Word Processor provides a Document
     Summary Screen for each text file on your disk. You can search
     a disk by any of the categories listed on this screen,
     from author to the date you created or changed the document.

  Creation Date   08/10/84  Keystrokes last session    68
  Modification Date 01/01/80  Total keystrokes          1887

  Use tab keys to change fields - Press F10 when finished

                                              S:↑ N:↓
```

After the user presses the return key, the document file to be edited is loaded into memory, and the Document Summary Screen with the name of the user's document appears at the top. The date is entered automatically from the operating system. This screen gives the user basic pre-established information about the document to be edited.

```
  DOCUMENT: MULTIMATESAMPLETEXT  PAGE:   1 LINE:   1 COL:   4
  [1...»........»............»...............»...........»
           «This is the first page of a sample document created
      with the MultiMate Professional Work Processor. The top
      line above (the Status Line) tells you the document title,
      the page you are writing, and the number of the line and
      column (space) the cursor is on. The corners of the top and
      bottom line are used for special messages like "DELETE
      WHAT?" when you press the "delete" key.«
    «
        »The second line is the Format Line. The "1" means this
      document will be printed single-spaced. The character "»
      indicates a tab setting. Format lines can be changed,
      copied and moved to any point in the document if you want
      to change tabs or margins.«

                                              S:↑ N:↓
```

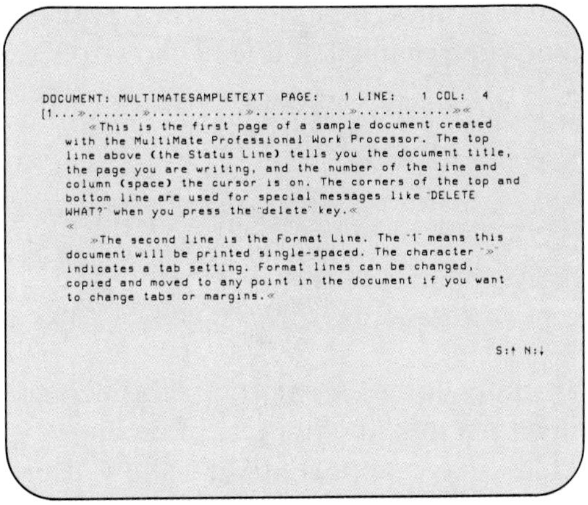

When a user presses the F10 function key it takes him or her from the Document Summary Screen to the document to be edited. This screen is a sample MultiMate document that explains what is actually appearing on the screen. The top line on the screen is called the status line that displays the document title, the page being written, and the number of the line and column (position) the cursor is on.

Figure 12–4
Main menu display for word processing.

officials are quick to identify significant administrative and educational advantages of using computers. In addition to their instructional value, school officials are discovering that computers can relieve them of many tedious and time-consuming tasks.

Administrative Applications

School officials, such as the one shown in Figure 12–5, have discovered many computer applications that make their work easier and enable them and their staffs to be more productive. With computers, they can process school records and reports quickly, efficiently, and more economically than ever before. Routine tasks such as calculating student grade point averages, keeping attendance records, preparing school budgets, scheduling buses, and monitoring energy usage have become easier.

Computers are helping schools develop future plans by preparing **simulation models,** a technique often used by business. This technique enables officials to predict the effect of potential changes. Suppose,

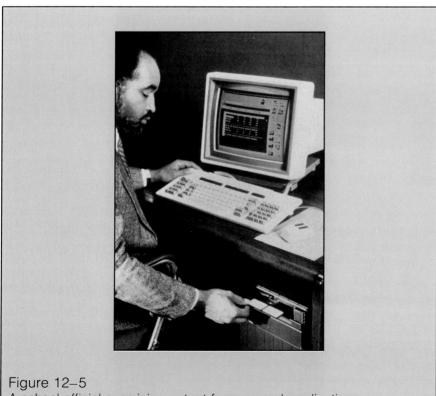

Figure 12–5
A school official examining output from several applications.

for example, that enrollment at a particular school is expected to increase by 25 percent in five years. By including this increase in the model, a computer can determine the number of additional teachers that will be needed, as well as counselors, classrooms, desks, and supplies. These and other important applications have made computers a welcome addition to many overworked administrative staffs.

Instructional Applications

Many educators believe that every student should be "computer literate," meaning that students should learn what computers are and how to use them, and acquire an understanding of their impact on society. The importance of computer literacy courses cannot be overstated because students need this education, particularly those students who will not receive further computer education.

Learning about computers enhances students' education. Programming classes enable students to develop valuable problem-solving skills, and courses in which specific computer applications such as word processing and computer graphics are taught can equip students with potentially valuable job skills (see Figure 12–6).

Figure 12–6
A teacher instructing a student in computer-generated business graphics.

Microcomputers have become more accessible to schools, and many schools have implemented innovative applications. A sampling of schools revealed that, in several schools, students are using software programs to improve their keyboarding skills and to generate correspondence and reports. In other schools, students are using word processing software to prepare applications and data sheets for summer jobs.

Students have developed several even more creative applications. At a high school in California, two industrial arts teachers wrote a program that allows students to prepare cost estimates for construction jobs, and students at another school wrote a computer program to design floor plans.

Computers in Science and Medicine

Perhaps nowhere have the advances made possible by computers been more widely felt than in science and medicine. A brief tour of any large modern research laboratory or hospital will convince the visitor of the important role computers play in scientific and medical research and technology. Computers are now making it possible for scientists to perform many tasks believed impossible only a few years ago.

Figure 12–7
Computer modeling.

There are times when it is impractical, unethical, or too costly to experiment with the lives or welfare of people. In such cases, a computer program can be written that enables a scientist or engineer to build a **model** of the system and to measure the effects of changes upon the system. A model of an airplane system, for example, can be prepared using a computer as shown in Figure 12-7. Changes in weather conditions, air speed, and altitude can be introduced into the model, and the effects of these changes upon the airplane can be seen. It might be observed that an air speed above 500 miles per hour results in damage to the airplane's wings causing a crash. This information might lead to a redesigning of the airplane.

The number of scientific and medical applications is increasing daily. While all these applications are important, a few widely used ones are summarized briefly in the following sections.

Computer-Assisted Diagnosis and Patient Monitoring

The computer can serve as a diagnostic tool that saves doctors' time; this time, in turn, can be spent with patients. Nurses or trained technicians use computer equipment in performing **computer-assisted diagnosis** which means that computers are used to evaluate medical data. Doctors then use the data to diagnose illness and to prescribe treatment. The patient shown in Figure 12–8 is receiving various types of computerized scans to aid in diagnosis.

Two types of computer-assisted diagnosis used in hospitals and clinics are **multiphasic screening** and **computerized axial tomography,** known as **CAT scan. Multiphasic screening** is a computer-assisted testing plan that compiles data on patients and their test results, which are compared with norms or means to aid a medical doctor in making a diagnosis. **Computerized axial tomography (CAT)** is a computer-controlled x-ray technique that shows a picture of a view through the body at a given depth. The computer is used to bring out the details of this picture, recording x-rays passing through the body in changing directions, and generating an image of the body's structure. Both types, although expensive, represent important advancements in medical computer-assisted diagnosis.

Computers can monitor the physical condition of critically ill patients in intensive care units and coronary care units of hospitals. A patient's vital signs (temperature, blood pressure, and heart rate) can be carefully monitored by a computer which will alert a nurse, such as the one shown in Figure 12–9, of any change that might occur in a patient's physical condition. The computer can also monitor a patient's fluid input and output. For example, the amount of chemo-

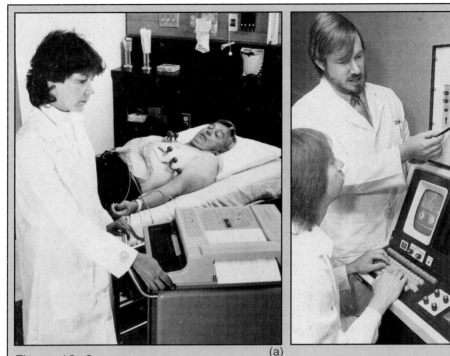

Figure 12–8
Two types of computer-aided diagnosis: (a) patient receiving computer cardiograph analysis; (b) computer-aided diagnosis of disorders and diseases by generating three-dimensional "slices" of organs.

theraphy solution a cancer patient is receiving can be monitored by a computer.

A major advantage of computerized monitoring is that the nurse is freed from constantly watching over critically ill patients. If any abnormality occurs, the computer immediately alerts the nurse, allowing the nurse to react promptly. Separate video monitors located at the nurse's station makes it possible for several patients to be monitored simultaneously.

Medical Research

In recent years, computers have assisted doctors, biologists, and biochemists in research. Computers allow elaborate mathematical models to be developed that describe the behavior of biological systems. Error-free models can predict the effects of various stimuli upon the biological system.

Figure 12–9
Nurse monitoring patients from central location.

In medical research, computers make it possible to retrieve information faster. The **Medical Library Based Literature Retrieval System,** called MEDLARS, is located at the National Library of Medicine in Bethesda, Maryland. The system, which has access to over 3 million references to health articles and books, is available to universities, medical schools, hospitals, and government agencies. Similar information retrieval systems are becoming available in several other fields. The era in which literature searches had to be performed manually is rapidly coming to a close.

DO YOU
REMEMBER

1. . . .The purposes and uses of embedded computers?

2. . . .The applications of microcomputers in homes?

3. . . .The applications of computers in schools?

4. . . .The applications of computers in science and medicine?

Computers in Business

A business operates from information that comes from two sources—internal (inside) and external (outside). **Internal information** is generated inside the company through the nine function systems which make up the business. **External information** is generated from outside the company and is used internally as needed. Some external information, such as social security numbers and zip codes, are required to be used internally. A company uses both social security numbers and zip codes in their payroll and personnel systems. As we have already learned, without appropriate information, a company cannot operate successfully.

A business might be defined as a system of systems (purchasing, receiving, inventory, production, sales, distribution, billing, collection, and paying) which make up the business. Employees of a company require the outputs of these systems (information) to help them make decisions in order to do their jobs. Information is a company resource that must be managed and available to all employees.

Office automation is a combination of information processing tools and techniques used to produce timely, accurate, and concise information. Company employees and management use this information in order to make decisions. The basic components of an electronic office automation environment are word processing, electronic mail, teleconferencing, videotex, professional computing, and spreadsheets. All six components are computer-based. Electronic mail and electronic spreadsheet analysis will be examined in the following sections.

Electronic Mail

Electronic mail is being used by many companies to transfer information from one location within a company to another. This allows entire documents to be sent electronically from one site to another site without any paperwork. Electronic mail depends heavily on a good reliable data communications link to and from participating users.

The central control center for an electronic mail system would probably be where the mainframe computer is located. The mainframe computer would be similar to a post office where messages (electronic mail) are received, stored, and routed to the appropriate location. Electronic mail can be sent directly from one computer to another. A portion of the central computer's memory would be reserved to store

Figure 12–10
Electronic mail.

messages in storage locations similar to a mailbox. Each person on the system would have his or her own electronic mailbox in memory. Messages can be sent to a particular mailbox and messages can be taken out of a mailbox similar to the way the U.S. Postal Service handles regular mail. The difference, of course, is that these are electronic messages and not physical letters as shown in Figure 12-10.

Electronic mail works well, saves time, saves money, and cuts down on the flow of physical paperwork within a company. This component of office automation is becoming more popular; it will continue to be a viable way to communicate information efficiently within an organization.

Electronic Spreadsheet Analysis

Electronic spreadsheet analysis deals with using a software package, such as Multiplan or Lotus 1-2-3, to help solve accounting and financial problems. One of the main reasons professional microcomputers have become so popular in business is that they are able to use electronic spreadsheet applications. Spreadsheeting has been used to help make financial decisions in most companies for years. Tables of data were generated by hand before microcomputers became available.

An **electronic spreadsheet** is a table constructed of rows and columns which are used to store and manipulate any kind of numeric data. The size of a spreadsheet varies, but a generally accepted size is 254 rows by 64 columns. The entire spreadsheet cannot be displayed on the video screen at once because of the limited amount of display area on the screen. Thus, vertical and horizontal scrolling is used in order to position certain portions of a spreadsheet on the screen at a time.

The specific position in a spreadsheet where a row and column meet is called a **cell.** A cell is a unique position within the spreadsheet where a piece of data is stored. If a spreadsheet is 254 rows by 64 columns, there will be 16,256 cells. Specific formulas can be entered into a cell to carry out a particular mathematical function, such as addition, subtraction, multiplication, division, or exponentiation. Some spreadsheet software packages allow for the use of predefined math functions that can be placed into a cell, such as sum and average.

Many spreadsheets have a **status area** at the top and a **command area** at the bottom. The status area indicates the location of the cursor and shows what was entered into a specific cell. The command area shows the commands available to the user.

In Figure 12–11, Screen A is the initial screen of the VisiCalc electronic spreadsheet. The letters horizontally across the screen represent the columns A–H and the numbers running vertically down the screen represent the rows 1–21. The upper-left-hand corner of the screen represents the current cell position. Screen B demonstrates how a spreadsheet can be used to calculate a monthly home budget. Labels are entered in columns A and B. Cell B8 sums the value contained in

THE COMPUTER DIDN'T DO IT!

Mr. and Mrs. Emmanuel Kops received a bank statement that showed a deposit of $20,200,071.49. Although they reported the deposit as erroneous, the Union Bank of West Los Angeles denied an error had been made. Their computer, said bank officials, couldn't handle figures that high. Despite a computer system that couldn't handle numbers as high as $20,200,071.49, the Union Bank of West Los Angeles adjusted the bank account of Mr. and Mrs. Emmaneul Kops manually.

Source: From page 254 of *The Naked Computer.* Copyright © 1983 by Jack B. Rochester and John Gantz. Reprinted by permission of William Morrow and Company.

A

```
A1                                          C
(C) 1979,1982 Software Arts, Inc.          201

       A    B    C    D    E    F    G    H
   1
   2
   3
   4
   5
   6
   7
   8
   9
  10
  11
  12
  13
  14
  15
  16
  17
  18
  19
  20
  21
```

This screen represents the first screen of the VisiCalc Electronic Spreadsheet for the IBM PC from Software Arts, Inc. The columns (A-H) which run horizontally across the screen are represented by alphabetic letters, whereas the rows (1-21) which run vertically down the screen are represented by numbers. The upper left corner of the screen identifies the present cell position.

B

```
B8 /F$ (V) @SUM(B3...B6)                    C
                                           201

          A       B    C    D    E    F    G    H
   1  EXPENSES
   2  --------
   3  RENT      200.00
   4  FOOD      120.00
   5  UTILITIES  75.00
   6  AUTO      150.00
   7  --------
   8  TOTAL     545.00
   9
  10
  11
  12
  13
  14
  15
  16
  17
  18
  19
  20
  21
```

This screen represents how an electronic spreadsheet can be used to calculate a monthly personal budget. Both column and row headings/labels are placed into cells A1-A8. Numeric data are placed into cells B3-B6. Cell B8 holds a formula to sum the values contained in cells B3-B6, which is the total.

C

```
B3 /F$ (V) 250                              C
                                           201

          A       B    C    D    E    F    G    H
   1  EXPENSES
   2  --------
   3  RENT      200.00
   4  FOOD      125.00
   5  UTILITIES  75.00
   6  AUTO      150.00
   7  --------
   8  TOTAL     550.00
   9
  10
  11
  12
  13
  14
  15
  16
  17
  18
  19
  20
  21
```

To modify any cell position in the budget Spreadsheet, a cursor can be positioned to that cell and new data can be placed into it. For example, the cursor can be placed at cell B4 and the value for FOOD changed from 120.00 to 125.00. Once the new FOOD value is entered, the TOTAL is recalculated automatically to reflect the change.

Figure 12–11
Electronic spreadsheet analysis.

cells B3 through B6. Screen C demonstrates how the user can alter the budget by positioning the cursor at cell B4 and changing value of FOOD to 125.00. Once the new FOOD value is entered, the TOTAL is recalculated to represent the change.

Computers in Industrial Research and Development, and Engineering

Research and development, and engineering use computers continually to help generate appropriate information necessary to make decisions about new product lines. Much of the information concerns new designs, testing, experimenting with new ideas, and determining what the competition down the street is doing. Let's examine in more detail product research, design, development, modeling and simulation, and mathematical analysis and modeling.

Product research, engineering, design, and development are the life line to the continuing success of a company in the marketplace. Research is a continuous process within a company because a company must always be thinking about bringing new products to the marketplace, and about making current products better. Small and large companies allocate millions of dollars each year toward ''R&D'' (research and development). Many ideas for new products are generated in research and development facilities using trial-and-error analysis. This approach to generating new ideas and solutions to problems is a valid method for determining what will work and what will not work under a given set of circumstances. Engineers, like the one in Figure 12–12, use computers to design and pretest products by modeling and simulating them before actual production takes place. This approach saves a company thousands of people-hours and thousands of R&D dollars.

The **management science** techniques of modeling and simulation are used by many different types of employees within a large production-oriented company. Some of the most commonly used techniques are **CPM** (Critical Path Method) techniques including **PERT** (Program Evaluation and Review Technique), **linear programming, queuing method, mathematical modeling,** and **Monte Carlo method.** Each technique is used to help solve a specific problem. As an example of a management science technique, let's examine simulation. In **simulation,** a model is developed and used to study the workings of an actual system.

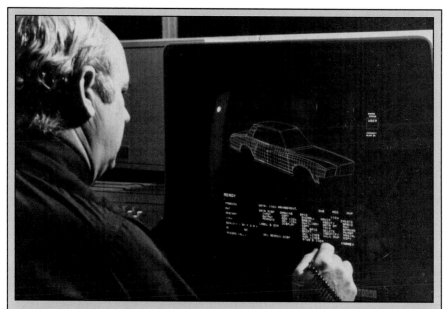

Figure 12–12
Engineer designing a new product using a CAD.

The developed model must resemble the real-world system as closely as possible. There are three forms of simulation: *what if analysis, sensitivity analysis, and goal seeking. What if* analysis allows a manager to interactively work through several decision alternatives, examining their possible outcomes extremely quickly. Many independent variables within the model can be changed to see what will result when a particular change is made. Figure 12–13 shows a *what if* simulation model for a company's advertising budget. All three forms of simulation are used to enhance a management's decision-making processes. These techniques are used to support management problem solving and decision making. They are not intended to make the decision itself. The decision is made by management.

DO YOU
REMEMBER

5. . . .Computer applications in business?

6. . . .Computer applications in industrial research and development, and engineering?

```
? MODEL ADSALES
READY FOR EDIT, LAST LINE IS 50
? WHAT IF
MODEL ADSALES VERSION OF 07/28/84 10:53 - 1 COLUMNS 4 VARIABLES
WHAT IF CASE 1
ENTER STATEMENTS
? BUDGETED EXPENDITURES = 80000000
? SOLVE
ENTER SOLVE OPTIONS
? GENREPORT RPSALES


***** WHAT IF CASE 1 *****
1 WHAT IF STATEMENT PROCESSED
```

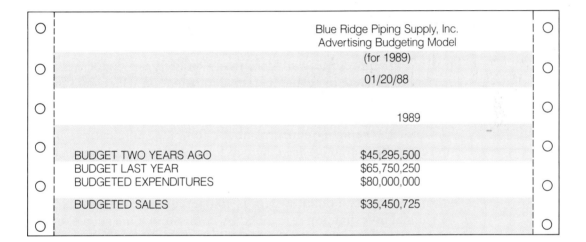

Blue Ridge Piping Supply, Inc.	
Advertising Budgeting Model	
(for 1989)	
01/20/88	
	1989
BUDGET TWO YEARS AGO	$45,295,500
BUDGET LAST YEAR	$65,750,250
BUDGETED EXPENDITURES	$80,000,000
BUDGETED SALES	$35,450,725

Figure 12–13
What if analysis simulation example.

Computers in Government

In the following sections, we will look at some of the ways government is using computers to solve problems. Most government applications deal with solving business-oriented problems, such as payroll, accounting, inventory, and human resource allocation. Also, personal data about individuals is collected and used for decision making by governments. There are laws that protect the individual citizen against invasion of privacy and disclosure of personal information. Computers are used to increase the productivity of people, and are essential for efficiency and economy of operating a government. The quality of American life depends on government bodies using computer technology to provide efficient and cost-effective services to its citizens.

Since governments at all levels are made up of citizens, it is necessary for each individual to have a basic understanding of how their government uses computers.

Law Enforcement

Computer use in law enforcement has been a controversial subject for years. Taxpayers question whether or not computers are cost-effective in enforcing laws. Also, many citizens are concerned with the right of privacy to certain personal information. Once data on law offenders is stored in a computer file, many persons wonder how safe and secure the data is and who has access to it.

Even with the many concerns about computer applications in law enforcement, computers have helped to solve many problems. Hopefully, we as citizens can trust our elected officials to keep the information stored in computer files accessible only to the appropriate authorities. No computer system is 100 percent secure, however.

Criminal investigations are aided by computers. One such example is the FBI's Organized Crime Information System (see Figure 12–14). Computer data files can be used to help keep track of the operation and behavior of known criminals, of nicknames and aliases, of fingerprints, and of any reports made by law enforcement officers concerning illegal activity. In law enforcement laboratories throughout the country, many experiments are carried out with the aid of a computer on confiscated materials collected at the scene of a crime. Investigators assigned to a particular case use the computer as a source of information to support their investigations. They inquire into databases that contain large amounts of information about known criminals. This information can give an investigator clues about the possible involvement of a particular criminal in a specific case. The computer is being used successfully in managing and controlling law enforcement activities at all levels.

Providing adequate police protection for all citizens is an awesome responsibility. Taxpayers expect to have the best protection possible provided to them. In order to provide this protection, computers are being used to speed up police service.

Figure 12–14
FBI's Organized Crime Information System (OCIS) database shown on line.

Inquiry response is a very helpful technique for a law enforcement agency (see Figure 12–15), but only if the data in the databases is correct and up to date. This has become a big problem within certain agencies. It is embarrassing to police officials if they make decisions about a violator on the basis of outdated data and information. Outdated and incorrect police reports have even led to injuries and the deaths of innocent citizens. The databases for inquiry response systems must be kept current and up to date; otherwise, serious harm might occur.

Military

As computers have found their way into business and industry, public and private school systems, they have also been used for many years by the United States Department of Defense. They have been employed as tools for modeling and simulation, accounting and inventory

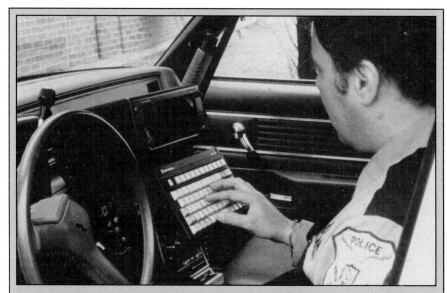

Figure 12–15
Computer technology has become an important tool for police work.

control, and launch control of missiles and satellites. The U.S. military is one of biggest users of computers. New computer-based educational programs for military training are being used today to train military personnel in many aspects of defense operations (see Figure 12–16).

Computers are used in new military weapons to help control the functions and operations that the weapons were designed for. Computers allow for greater accuracy in guiding and directing the operation of a specific weapon. The launching of a missile from a submarine, aircraft, or tank, for instance, is controlled by on-board computers inside the launching device. The computers, because of greater accuracy in calculating necessary data, cause the target to be hit more often than is the case when people do the same thing manually. So, people use computers as tools to help them control and manage military weaponry.

In military aircraft, which can range from a conventional cargo jet to missiles and rockets, computers are being used to guide, direct, control, and manage operations. Using computers to make detailed calculations very quickly and accurately improves the reliability of information used for a successful mission. The space shuttle Columbia has many computers on board to provide the astronauts and Mission

Figure 12–16
Military "OJT" (on-the-job training).

Control with information necessary to control and manage the aircraft. The use of computers in military and civilian aircraft will continue to grow at a rapid rate.

Social Services

Social services are services provided to the general public that are totally, or in part, supported by taxes. These services must be managed and controlled by people. To speed up the processing of application request forms, computers can be used to help collect the initial data, process the raw data, and convert it to meaningful and useful information that helps determine a requester's service status. There are many administrative and accounting applications that can be handled more effectively and efficiently by a computer.

The Social Security and Retirement systems in the United States deal with millions of applications for benefits each year. This work is of such a large volume that doing things by hand is inefficient and ineffective. As an example, just processing by hand the thousands of benefit checks sent out each month became a serious problem because of the time it took. Computers are now used to speed up the processing of benefit checks, and to cut down on errors in the overall process of handling checks. If computers were taken out of the Social Security and Retirement Systems Administration, it would not be long before these systems would collapse.

Medicare and Medicaid are two health care systems that help fund the expenses of retired persons, or persons who are unable to pay health care expenses. These systems are federally sponsored and administered by each state. Thousands of applications are processed each year, and millions of dollars in benefits are paid out. Without computers, it would be next to impossible to process all the requests for benefits on a timely basis.

Another example of effective government use of computers is the postal service. The U.S. Postal Service handles millions of pieces of mail each month. The timely movement of the mail from one location to another must be efficient and effective in order to provide first-class service to the public. Computers have been used for years by the postal service. Optical scanning equipment connected to computers is used in combination with sorting equipment to route pieces of mail to a particular bin to be bagged for shipment to a certain point (see Figure 12–17). Computers are used in many post offices to control and monitor room temperatures and fire and smoke detectors, and to locate empty equipment throughout the more than thirty thousand post offices in the U.S. Without computers the postal service could not function successfully today.

Other Applications Software

Other applications software that can be used in all the areas mentioned—homes, schools, science and medicine, industrial research and development, and engineering, and government—are graphics and integrated software packages. A brief overview of these software concepts is presented in the following sections.

Graphics Software

A **graphics software package** is designed and developed to allow the user to display images on a video terminal and/or print images on paper. Images that can be displayed range from different types of charts, such as a pie chart or graph, to the extremely detailed designs of an object that an engineer might develop.

Figure 12–17
U.S. Postal Service operations.

The use of a graphics package is as simple as selecting options from a main menu of functions (see Figure 12–18), or as complex as controlling the individual dots, called **pixels,** to develop images on the screen. All screens have a certain number of pixels that are used to make up a certain image on the screen. The user can develop any image, with the detail desired, by controlling the pixels. Graphics can help the user see in pictorial format the solution to a particular problem more clearly.

The applications for graphics packages range from business uses to artistic and drafting uses. In business they are used to create graphs and charts that are used by management to summarize data for presentations. The graphs and charts created can be displayed on a video terminal or printed out. The printed output from graphics packages can be used to make transparencies or slides for a presentation.

```
              PFS:GRAPH MENU


       1 GET/EDIT DATA    4 SAVE CHART

       2 DISPLAY CHART    5 GET/REMOVE CHART

       3 DEFINE CHART     6 PRINT/PLOT



               SELECTION NUMBER: ■


       (C) 1984 Software Publishing Corporation
```

This screen illustrates the main menu for Software Publishing Corporation's PFS:GRAPH graphics package. After a graph has been created it can be saved and used as many times as needed. If a user chooses SELECTION NUMBER:5 from the functions menu it allows the user to GET/REMOVE a chart that has been saved on disk.

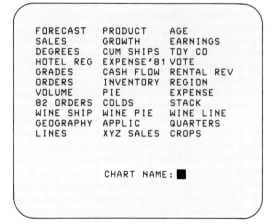

This screen displays all the graphs available in PFS:GRAPH. The user is prompted by CHART NAME: line. From a diskette of sample graphs that Software Publishing supplies to purchasers of PFS:GRAPH, we have chosen FORECAST to demonstrate. The CHART NAME: FORECAST is entered followed by the CONTROL-C key.

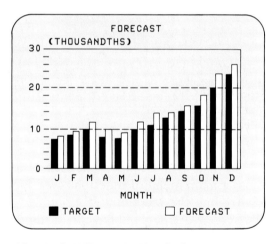

After the CHART NAME: FORECAST is chosen, the graph appears on the screen.

Figure 12–18
Examples of graphics application software packages.

Graphics packages are being used by production-oriented companies to design complete objects or parts. As an example, computer-assisted design uses a graphics package to allow an engineer to design a new product as complex as an airplane.

Some artists are now using graphics packages to help develop, or "paint", pictures or images on the video terminal. An advantage to this is that if the pictures created are not exactly what the artist desires, he or she can make instant changes to the existing picture to make it more acceptable.

Video game developers use graphics packages to create pictures and images. These pictures and images are then stored and recalled as the video game runs. This area of graphics has become one of the fastest growing and most popular uses of graphics software.

Integrated Software

Integrated software allows one or more data files to be passed between more than one application software package. For example, a data file can be created by using a word processing package. This data file could not only be used by the word processing package, but could also be passed to a spreadsheet, graphics, or data management package. The spreadsheet package might manipulate the data mathematically for displaying in table format (rows and columns), and the data file created from the spreadsheet manipulation could be passed to the graphics package for graphing as a line, bar, or pie chart. Different data files created by the various applications software packages can be passed back and forth between the integrated packages.

The concept of sharing data files between integrated packages saves a large amount of time required to re-enter data for separate applications software packages. When purchasing application software packages, the purchaser should consider what his or her needs are, and, if more than one package is needed, integrated software might be the best solution to meet those needs.

A **windowing software package** allows more than one application software package to run concurrently. Windows are presently found mostly on microcomputers, and are considered to be on the leading edge of computing technology.

With windowing software packages, the user can see through a number of windows at packages that are currently being used or available to be used. As an addition to the normal operating environment, windows have some significant advantages over regular applications software packages. Some of these advantages are a more user-friendly environment, a generally consistent command structure across

(a)

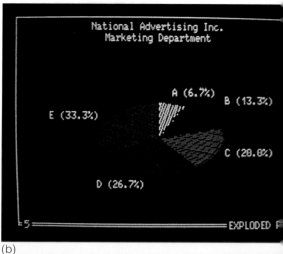

(b)

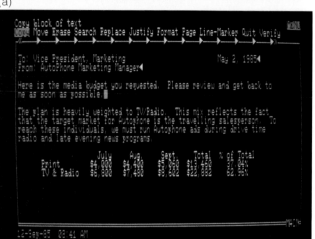

(c)

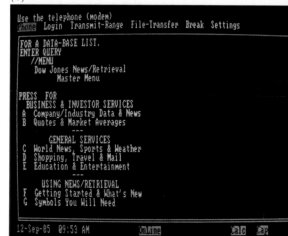

(d)

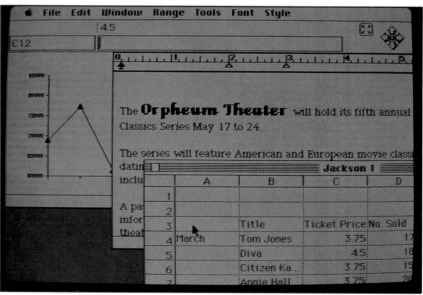

(e)

Figure 12–19
Example of integrated software package and windowing. Integrated Software by Lotus Development Corporation (Symphony). (a) Electronic Spreadsheet Module. (b) Graphics Module. (c) Word Processing Module. (d) Database Communications Module. (e) Jazz by Lotus Development Corporation. An example of three different application windows opened simultaneously.

application packages, the ability to transfer data between applications, and the use of a mouse or other positioning device. Windows will be used to a greater extent in the near future because of their ability to simplify and enhance the environment in which computer users perform their work. Figure 12–19 shows a sample of a windowing software package.

DO YOU REMEMBER

7. . . .Computer applications in government?

8. . . .The other applications software, and how are they used?

Summary

(This summary provides answers to DO YOU REMEMBER . . . questions in the chapter.)

1. What are some purposes and uses of embedded computers?
Embedded computers are used to improve the performance of many products we use. These tiny "computers on chips" can be found in a wide variety of products we use including *home appliances* and *automobiles*.

2. What are the applications of microcomputers in homes?
Family applications, recordkeeping, planning and budgeting, education, and word processing are some of the applications for microcomputers in homes.

3. What are the applications of computers in schools?
Personnel and *payroll accounting* are administrative applications. *Computer-assisted instruction* (CAI) is an example of a classroom application.

4. What are the applications of computers in science and medicine?
Computer-assisted diagnosis, computerized patient monitoring, and *medical research* are a few of the applications for computers in science and medicine.

5. What are some computer applications in business?
Electronic mail, electronic spreadsheet analysis, and *word processing* are some of the applications for computers in business.

6. **What are some computer applications in industrial research and development, and engineering?**

Product research, engineering, design, development, and *management science techniques* for problem solving are a few of the applications for computers in industrial research and development, and engineering.

7. **What are some computer applications in government?**

Law enforcement, military training, and *social services administration* are some of the applications for computers in government.

8. **What are the other applications software, and how are they used?**

Graphics software and integrated software are the other applications software. *Graphics software* is used by design engineers and business people to create designs for new products and charts and graphs for analysis. *Integrated software* is used by business and industry to bring together major data processing functions, such as word processing, database processing, spreadsheet processing, graphics processing, and electronic mail processing. One integrated software package may have all five functions built into it so they can share from one or two sources of data.

DATA PROCESSING CAREER. . . . .
Data Processing Teacher

CAREER OPPORTUNITY FOR COMPUTER PROFESSIONAL

JOB TITLE:
Data Processing Teacher

JOB DESCRIPTION:
Applicant will be responsible for preparing teaching materials to be used in the classroom, and will also be involved in student advising and counseling. Applicant will serve on school committees, attend PTA meetings, and attend and participate in sports activities when necessary. Good classroom teaching skills are absolutely mandatory and a number one priority.

EXPERIENCE REQUIRED:
Experience required varies depending on the position and school need.

EDUCATION REQUIRED:
A B.S., M.A., or Ph.D. degree, depending on the school system and teaching level. In high school a B.S. and/or M.A. in business education, in a community college an M.A. in business education information systems, and at the university level an M.A./Ph.D. in business education systems would be necessary.

PERSONAL QUALIFICATIONS:
Applicant must like to work with other people in order to help them learn. Patience, understanding, caring about the welfare of other people, and a pleasing personality are necessary qualifications.

Key Terms

CAD (computer-assisted design)

CAI (computer-assisted instruction)

CAM (computer-assisted manufacturing)

CAT (computerized axial tomography)

computer graphics

data processing teacher

electronic mail

electronic spreadsheet analysis

graphics software package

integrated software package

model

multiphasic screening

office automation

windowing software package

word processing

Test Yourself

1. A computer application that allows a student to learn subject material by using a computer is known as _____ _____ .

2. Computers make it possible for a scientist or decision maker to build a _____ of the system and to test the effects of changes on the system.

3. A technique known as _____ is used by airplane and other manufacturers in designing products. This technique saves time and money.

4. A medical technique involving the use of computers by nurses, trained technicians, and doctors to evaluate medical data to show variations from the normal is known as _____ .

5. Two types of computer-assisted diagnosis are _____ and _____ .

6. All persons at all levels within a company's organizational structure require _____ to perform and carry out the duties of their jobs.

7. A business operates from information that comes from two sources which are _____ and _____ to the company.

8. _____ is a relatively new concept that allows people to communicate with each other at different locations through appropriate electronic communications links.

9. _____ allows a user to electronically process text data.

10. _____ are constructed using rows and columns of numbers to help solve accounting and financial problems.

11. The largest user of computers is the _____.

12. No computer is 100 percent _____ because of the part people play in computing.

13. Computers are being used successfully in _____ and _____ law enforcement activities at all levels of government.

14. Databases for inquiry response systems must be keep _____ and _____ ; otherwise, serious harm might befall both a police officer and a citizen.

15. A(n) _____ software package is designed and developed to allow the user to display images on a video terminal and/or print images using a printer.

16. _____ software allows one or more files to be passed between more than one application software package.

17. A _____ software package allows more than one application software package to run _____ .

Review Questions

1. Identify ways computers are used in homes by family members and by self-employed professionals. (Learning Objective 2)

2. Identify and explain some of the administrative and educational applications for computers in schools. (Learning Objective 3)

3. Identify important computer applications in science and medicine. (Learning Objective 4)

4. One major advantage of word processing on a microcomputer is that it increases human productivity. Discuss this statement. (Learning Objective 5)

5. Explain electronic spreadsheet analysis and how it is used to help solve accounting and financial problems. (Learning Objective 5)

6. Discuss CAD/CAM. What is each used for in a production-oriented environment? (Learning Objective 6)

7. Discuss the purposes and uses of computers in government at all levels. (Learning Objective 7)

8. Explain other application software packages, such as graphics software and integrated software. (Learning Objective 8)

Activities

1. Make a list of the possible uses of a microcomputer in your home.

2. Take a tour of your school to determine how computers are being used in areas of administration and instruction. Discuss your findings in your data processing class.

3. Visit the local hospital in your community to see how computers affect health care. Write a brief paper describing your experience.

4. Choose a business close to where you live that you can visit to examine the use of computers in office automation.

5. Select a production-oriented company to visit for the purpose of seeing how computers are being used in the manufacturing and production processes. Share your experiences with your data processing class.

6. Make arrangements with a government agency in your community to tour and examine how computers are being used as a tool to enhance decision making. Present an oral report to your data processing class on your findings.

7. Create a design for an object or part using the available graphics application software package(s) your school owns. Display the image on the video terminal, and also print the final design.

8. Using the integrated software your school owns, create a data file using the word processing package or data management package. After editing this file for errors, pass it to the graphics package to display the results in graph or chart format. Display the final results on the video terminal, and also print the graphs and/or charts.

PART V

Information Processing Systems

CHAPTER 13

Communications and Remote Data Processing

Learning Objectives

After studying this chapter carefully, you will be able to:

1. Define key terms introduced in the chapter.

2. Name the basic hardware components of a data communications system and the primary purpose of each.

3. Name three grades of communications channels and give an example of each grade.

4. Identify three methods for transmitting data.

5. Distinguish between a single CPU system and a multiple CPU system.

6. Distinguish between a star network and a ring network.

7. Explain the purpose of a multiplexor and a concentrator.

Chapter Outline

While shopping for a birthday gift for her mother, Joan Mathews learned that computers can communicate with other computers. Although this technology is not new, Joan only recently became aware of this important capability.

After selecting her mother's gift, the salesperson recorded Joan's purchase using a cash register. This information—the price and item identification number—was instantly sent to the store's main computer in another city. At Joan's request, the salesperson explained that this system allows the company to keep track of each store's sales and inventory. The cash register serves as a small computer capable of communicating with the company's main computer.

Many businesses, including retail stores, banks, hotels, and airlines, use computers for similar purposes. As individuals, we can use personal computers to conduct banking transactions, obtain many kinds of information, and even communicate with each other.

Data Communications

Communication means the exchange of information. Until a little over a hundred years ago, information was communicated face to face, by messenger, or by mail. Communications methods began their dramatic change in 1876 when Alexander Graham Bell spoke the famous words, "Mr. Watson, come here, I want you," over the first telephone. This ability to transmit both voice and data over communication lines has led to the development of complex communication systems allowing individuals, companies, and even computers to communicate around the world.

Using computers to communicate data over communications lines is called **data communications.** The task of communicating data from one computer to another is accomplished by connecting the computers by standard communications channels such as telephone lines. A data communications system requires special communications equipment and programs. The technology required for such a system is complex, but, once installed, communications systems are relatively easy to learn and use. The following sections examine this rapidly growing and specialized data processing field.

Components of a Data Communications System

Computers of all sizes can communicate with each other and with remote terminals. Personal computers can communicate with a large central (or host) computer, large computers can communicate with each other, and personal computers can communicate with other personal computers.

Data communications is a "system" made up of hardware, software, and people. In the following sections, the basic hardware components of a data communications system that allows personal computers, or terminals, to communicate with a large host computer will be examined. Use of this type of system is becoming widespread as more users want to obtain information about such areas as stock market quotations, shopping services, and travel information.

The basic components of a data communications system in which personal computers can communicate with a central (host) computer are listed below and illustrated in Figure 13–1.

1. A **personal computer** or **terminal** located at a remote site from the host computer with which it communicates.

2. A **modem,** a device that converts data from digital form (bits) to analog form (sound) for transmission over a communication channel (such as a telephone line).

3. A **communication channel** that transmits data to, and from, the host computer. The channel can be a telephone line or another channel such as a microwave or satellite link.

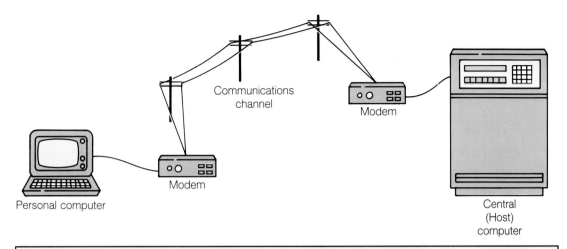

Figure 13–1
Hardware components of a data communications system. To send and receive data electronically, essential components are needed. Note the combination of technologies (computing and communications), and the basic components used to communicate data.

4. Another **modem** at the other end of the communication channel that converts data from analog form to digital form.

5. A **central,** or **host,** computer with which communication takes place.

Assume that you wish to use the personal computer in Figure 13–1 to obtain information from the host computer. You can do so by first entering an appropriate command via the personal computer keyboard; this links (connects) your computer to the host computer. The command you enter is in digital form (remember, you are using a "digital" computer), and in order for your digital signal to travel across a telephone line, it must be converted to a sound signal, called **analog.** The reason for this is that most telephone lines are designed to handle only analog, or sound, signals. Figure 13–2 illustrates digital and analog signals.

The purpose of the two modems in Figure 13–1 is to resolve the problem of the different signals. First, the command you enter into your personal computer goes from your computer to the modem. When your command (in digital form) reaches the modem, the modem automatically converts your digital signal to an analog signal, allowing your command to pass along the telephone line. When your command

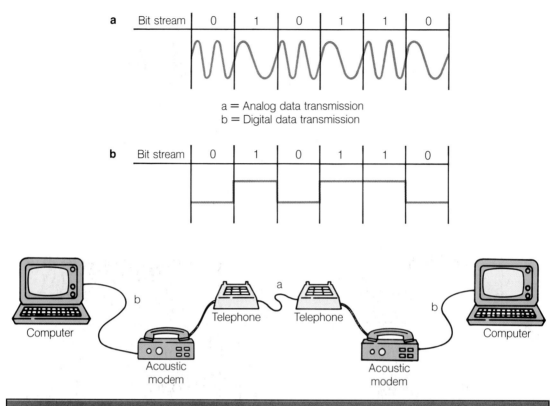

a Bit stream | 0 | 1 | 0 | 1 | 1 | 0

a = Analog data transmission
b = Digital data transmission

b Bit stream | 0 | 1 | 0 | 1 | 1 | 0

Computer   b   Telephone   a   Telephone   b   Computer

Acoustic modem   Acoustic modem

Figure 13–2
Digital and analog signals. To send and receive data via a communication channel such as a telephone line, data often must be converted from digital form to analog form and vice versa.

(now in analog form) reaches the host computer, it must first pass through another modem, which converts your command from analog to digital so that the host computer can understand your command. This process of conversion and reconversion is called modulation-demodulation. **Modulation** is the conversion from digital form to analog form. **Demodulation** is the conversion from analog form to digital form. The term *modem* is an acronym for *mo*dulator-*dem*odulator because it modulates (converts from digital to analog) and/or demodulates (converts from analog to digital) communications messages, such as your command.

Figure 13–3 shows the components of a communications system, and the type of signal produced by each component. Each component in Figure 13–3 can have many forms and configurations, although the functions are the same as those explained above. Figure 13–3 should

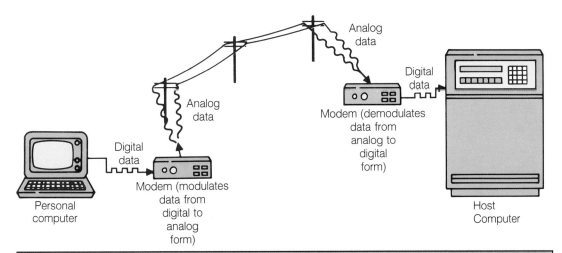

Figure 13–3
Basic hardware components of a data communications system and the type of signal produced by each. Data sent from a microcomputer or terminal to another computer is converted to analog by a modem and reconverted by another modem before the data enters the receiving computer. This process is reversed when data is returned to the microcomputer.

be kept in mind as each component is explained in more detail in the following sections.

Personal Computer or Computer Terminal

The **personal computer** or **terminal** can be of almost any brand or model that has the necessary hardware and software. To be used for communications, a personal computer must contain a communications adapter and serial interface board. Both are often included on one board.

Some personal computers come with a communications adapter already internally installed, but most do not. Unless one has already been installed, the user can purchase and install a communications adapter board in a slot provided by the manufacturer for this purpose.

Recall from Chapter 3 that data moves around inside a computer in parallel form—that is, a *byte* at a time. But when data is sent from a computer across a communication channel, such as a telephone line, it must be sent in serial form, or one *bit* at a time. Thus, the data must be converted from parallel form to serial form for transmission. This conversion can be achieved by installing a circuit board inside the microcomputer. This board also allows the microcomputer to communicate with other serial devices such as a printer.

When a personal computer is used for communications, special communications software is needed. **Communications software** enables a user to perform such communications tasks as making contact with the host computer, directing the transmission of data across communications channels, and accepting data from the host computer.

Different types of communications software packages are available. Some merely allow the user to establish contact with the host computer, and to transmit and receive data. Other, more sophisticated software packages also allow the user to transfer large amounts of data from the host computer to the personal computer for storage in a process called **downloading,** and to transfer data files from the personal computer to the host computer for storage in a process called **uploading.** Because of differences in communications software packages, users should carefully review their communications needs before obtaining a software package so that the software package they choose will meet their communications requirements.

Modem

The purpose of a **modem,** as explained earlier, is to change data from digital form to analog form at the sending end of the communications system, and to change analog data to digital data at the receiving end. A variety of modems is available for personal computers. These include (1) internal modems, (2) external direct-connect modems, and (3) acoustic couplers.

An **internal modem** is an electronic circuit board installed inside the personal computer in a slot designated by the computer manufacturer. It is relatively inexpensive, and most are designed to fit a particular computer.

An **external direct-connect modem** is connected to the computer by cable. Because it is contained in a small case or cabinet, it can be placed near the computer. The modem can be plugged into a standard telephone jack to allow communication over telephone lines.

An **acoustic coupler modem** (see Figure 13–4) is attached to a personal computer or terminal by a cable. The modem contains rubber cups into which a standard telephone headset can be inserted. When in use, the modem converts digital signals from the computer into analog, or sound, signals that are picked up by the mouthpiece in the headset in a manner similar to the way they are picked up when a person speaks into the mouthpiece. The sound signals are transmitted across telephone lines to the host computer. Some acoustic couplers

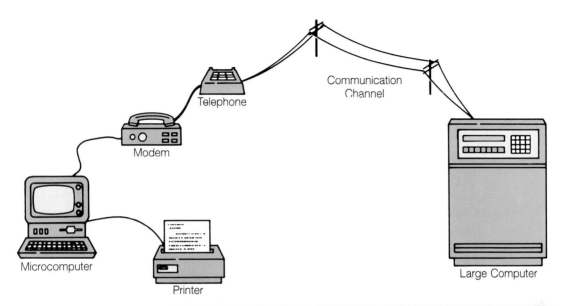

Figure 13–4
Acoustic coupler modem. An acoustic coupler modem allows a user to send data via a standard telephone by converting a computer's digital signal to analog.

are portable, allowing them to be used with small portable computers. One disadvantage of the acoustic coupler modem is that, because it accepts sounds, it can pick up and transmit external noises, thereby making it somewhat less reliable than other types of modems.

An important factor to be considered when selecting a modem is the speed at which it can send data. This speed, called the **baud rate,** is actually the number of bits that can be sent per second. These speeds usually range from 300 to 1,200 bits per second. Thus, if a modem has a baud rate of 1,200, it means that it can send 1,200 1s and 0s per second. A baud rate of 300 is a common transmission speed for personal computers. However, when large amounts of data are to be sent, a baud rate of 1,200, or more, might be preferred.

Communications Channels

The third component of a data communications system is the communications channel. A **communications channel** is a communications medium that allows a personal computer or terminal to communicate with another input/output device or another computer.

Data communications is not new. Pony Express riders carried messages until they were replaced by telegraph lines, and the telegraph enjoyed a monopoly on data communications until Alexander Graham Bell demonstrated that electrical signals could be used to transmit voice messages along telephone lines. In the last century, a complex network of telecommunications systems has been established in an effort to increase the speed and efficiency of data communications. The word **telecommunications** refers to the sending of data along a communications channel such as a telephone or telegraph line.

It was not until the 1950s, however, that the computing/communications linkage began in earnest. In the late 1950s and the early 1960s, American Airlines and IBM jointly developed a computerized airline passenger reservation system, one of the first large-scale telecommunications systems. Hundreds of computer terminals at airports throughout the country were linked to computers in the airline's central processing center.

Since that time, communications usage has grown steadily. Today most large computer systems are able to communicate with outlying personal computers and terminals. A variety of communications channels is now being used including telegraph lines, telephone lines, coaxial cables, microwave links, and satellites. More recently, fiber optic cable and laser transmission have been developed, allowing data to be communicated as light impulses at approximately 186,000 miles per second.

The grade of a communication channel (called **bandwidth**) determines the speed at which data can be transmitted along the channel. Channels are classified into narrowband, voiceband, and broadband categories. The wider the bandwidth of a channel, the more data it can transmit in a given period of time. **Narrowband channels,** such as telegraph lines, have a slow transmission speed ranging from about 45 bytes to 90 bytes (characters) per second. Although this speed is adequate to accept data being keyed into a personal computer or terminal, the use of narrowband channels has declined as other faster and more efficient channels have become more popular.

Voiceband channels, such as telephone lines, have a wider bandwidth with transmission speeds ranging from about 100 characters per second to over 1,000 characters per second (cps). These channels are often selected because they are economical and readily available to most users.

When data is to be transmitted on an irregular basis, a personal computer or terminal user might simply use a regular dial-up telephone, dial the number of the computer location, and enter the data. However, when large volumes of data are to be transmitted on a regular basis, it is often more economical to acquire a **leased** or **dedicated line** which can be used for both voice and data communications.

Broadband channels, such as coaxial cables, microwaves, and satellites, are more suitable for applications requiring high-speed transmission of large volumes of data. Depending on the channel selected, transmission speeds of 100,000 cps or more are possible. A **coaxial cable** is a group of insulated wires capable of carrying data at very high speeds. A **microwave system** transmits data through space in the form of high-frequency radio signals. When microwaves are used, data can be transferred along a ground route between microwave towers about 20 miles apart. Each microwave tower along the route picks up the signal, amplifies it, and relays the amplified signal to the next tower.

Data can also be transmitted by means of a communications satellite. A **communications satellite** acts as a reflector by receiving signals from a particular location on earth and transmitting the signals to another location on earth. The satellite is positioned 22,300 miles above the equator and orbits the earth at exactly the same speed as that of the earth's rotation. Several satellites are now orbiting the earth to handle domestic and international data, video, and voice communications around the world.

The communications channels just described are widely used. When data is to be sent over long distances, several different channels are often used together, as shown in Figure 13–5. Large companies with branch offices in foreign countries, for example, often use a combination of channels to send data between locations.

Fiber optic cables and **lasers** represent two emerging technologies that permit huge amounts of data to be routinely transmitted at virtually the speed of light through tiny threads of glass. Because of their lower cost, smaller size, and greater efficiency, fiber optic cables such as the one shown in Figure 13–6 are beginning to replace conventional copper cables. A fiber optic cable weighing slightly more than 1 pound can transmit more data than 20 pounds of copper wire.

Data is sent through the tiny glass strands as light pulses (signals) by a laser device that sends amplified light beams through individual glass strands. For long distance transmission, laser devices can be positioned at intervals to strengthen weakened light signals (data).

Central (Host) Computer

The fifth component of a communications system which allows a personal computer or terminal to communicate with another computer

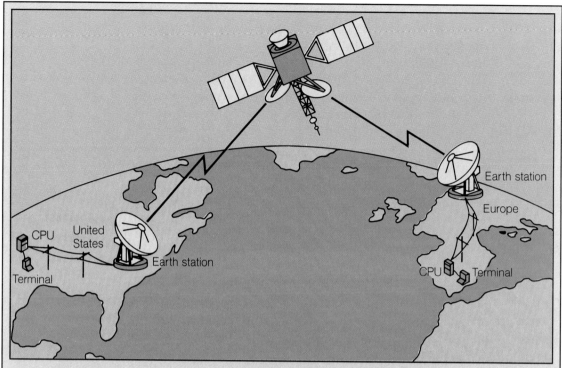

Figure 13–5
Communications channels. Note the two communications channels used for data transmission. Data can be transmitted around the world if the appropriate equipment is available.

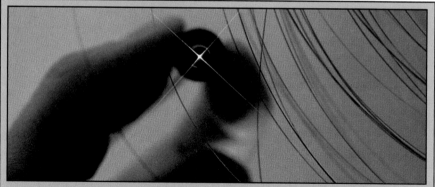

Figure 13–6
Fiber optic cable. This relatively new technology allows data to be transmitted in digital form using a laser beam to send light impulses through tiny glass fibers that are about one-half the diameter of a human hair.

is the host computer itself. The **host computer** may actually be a computer of virtually any size, ranging from another personal computer to a powerful supercomputer. Typically, however, the host computer will be one larger than the personal computer communicating with it.

It should be remembered that when communications occur over telephone lines or other communications channels where an analog signal is used, a modem is needed at the receiving end as well as the sending end. The modem at the receiving end converts the analog signal to digital form before the data enters the host computer.

1. . . .The primary hardware components of a data communications system?

2. . . .The purpose of a modem?

3. . . .What a communications channel is, and what some examples of communications channels are?

4. . . .What the term *baud rate* means?

5. . . .Three grades of communications channels?

DO YOU REMEMBER

Methods for Transmitting Data

Communications channels can be classified according to the method used to transmit data. There are three basic ways that channels are used to transmit data. These are the simplex method, the half-duplex method, and the full-duplex method.

Simplex Method

The **simplex method** allows a one-way transmission of data. For example, a public announcement system at an athletic contest is simplex because the announcer can make announcements to the audience but cannot receive announcements from the audience. Similarly, a personal computer or terminal that transmits data via a simplex channel

Figure 13–7
Simplex method of transmission. A simplex method can send or receive data, but it cannot do both.

can either send or receive data, but it cannot do both (see Figure 13–7). Because it is often necessary to both send and receive data, simplex channels are seldom used by businesses for data communications applications.

Half-duplex Method

The **half-duplex method** allows data to be sent from, or received by, a computer or terminal, but not at the same time. If you've used a two-way radio system or a walkie-talkie system (see Figure 13–8), you've used half-duplex. Recall that you could send and receive information, but you could not send and receive at the same time.

Half-duplex channels are often used when a personal computer or terminal is communicating with a host computer. This is because data is first sent by the user to the host computer, followed by a response from the host computer to the personal computer user. The elapsed time between sending and receiving data is called **turnaround time.** Few applications require data to be transmitted in both directions at the same time.

Full-duplex Method

A **full-duplex** communications channel allows data to be transmitted in both directions at the same time. For example, during a telephone

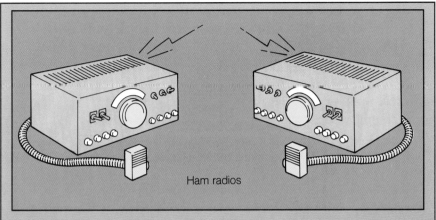

Figure 13–8
Half-duplex method of transmission. When a half-duplex method is
used, data can be sent or received, but not at the same time.

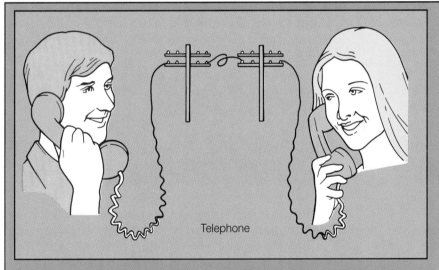

Figure 13–9
Full-duplex method of transmission. When a full-duplex method is
used, data can be sent and received at the same time.

conversation, it is possible for both parties to talk at the same time
(see Figure 13–9). There is no loss of time due to *turnaround*, which
can be an important advantage when large amounts of data are transmitted between large computers. A full-duplex channel is most likely,
though, to be used when large amounts of data or information are to
be transmitted between two or more large computers.

Communications Networks

You learned in Chapter 3 that a computer system includes hardware, software, and people, and that it is used for information processing. Some computer systems have a single computer, or CPU. Others have more than one CPU. Some computer systems use several CPUs to handle the large volume of processing required by large businesses and organizations.

Single CPU Systems

A **single CPU system** has only one CPU, but it can be used by one or more users. In the home, for example, family members can use a microcomputer for word processing, accounting, or any number of applications. When a computer system is located in a particular place, and all users come to the same location to use it, the computer system is sometimes referred to as a **local system.** Local systems are used by many small businesses.

Other single CPU systems can serve any number of users. An airline reservation system, for example, must be able to handle reservation requests from thousands of travel agents in different cities. A computer system that allows users at remote locations to use the system is a **remote system.** With special equipment, a reservation agent in Dallas, Texas, can use a computer located in Chicago, Illinois; or a salesperson in St. Louis, Missouri, can place an order using the computer at the home office in Syracuse, New York.

A **time-sharing system** makes it possible for several users to use the same computer at the same time. In a time-sharing system, several input devices (usually terminals) can communicate via communications channels with the same computer; the different terminals share the central processor's time. The terminals can be located near the central processing unit and connected to the CPU by cable, or they can be located far away in another city or country. The users can be doing either the same tasks or different tasks with the computer. Some schools have time-sharing systems that allow school officials, teachers, and students to use the computer at the same time. These are usually large computers capable of processing several computer programs concurrently. The processing of several (multiple) programs concurrently, using a computer system with this capability, is called **multiprogramming.**

Multiple CPU Systems

When computers were first used in business, the computer and related equipment were typically centralized at one location. These early computers were large, expensive, and difficult to operate and service. These factors made it more effective for the business to have computer professionals, including users and technicians, located near the computer and related equipment.

As smaller and less expensive computer systems became available, large businesses and organizations sometimes found it more efficient for individual departments to have their own computers. Today, many companies have a **multiple CPU system** with two or more CPUs linked together in a network that enables the computers to communicate with each other. A **network** is a collection of CPUs and terminals that are linked together via communications channels such as telephone lines and/or coaxial cables. Networking computers together allows information to be transferred to them and/or to a host computer. One disadvantage of a multiple CPU system is that it is not always efficient since it is unlikely that every CPU and its related equipment will be needed, or used, 100 percent of the time.

6. . . .Three methods for transmitting data?

7. . . .What a time-sharing system is?

8. . . .Why a full-duplex channel would probably be used when large amounts of data are to be transmitted between two or more large computers?

DO YOU
REMEMBER

Types of Multiple CPU Networks

Multiple computer networks can be individually tailored to meet the needs of users. The most common types of networks are the star network, ring network, and area network.

Star Network

A **star network,** as shown in Figure 13–10, consists of one or more smaller computers linked to a larger host computer. All transactions

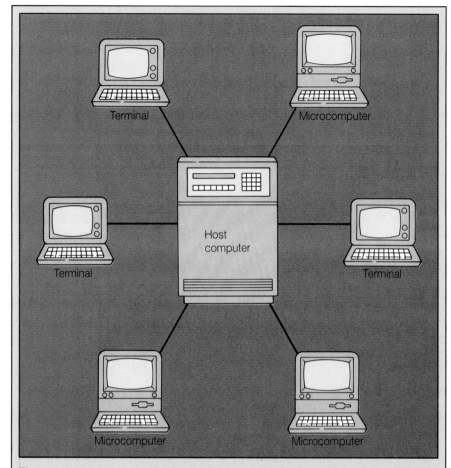

Figure 13–10
A star network. A star network may be designed with several small computers, such as minicomputers or microcomputers, connected to a larger central or host computer. Data can be shared between the central computer and each of the smaller computers.

must go through the host computer before being routed to the appropriate network computer. The host computer keeps track of all transactions and can distribute the work load among other computers in the network when necessary.

A star network is suited for an organization such as a bank. A large host computer located at the bank's main office can be connected to the smaller computers located in each of the bank's geographically dispersed branch offices. Many newspaper offices use star networks for sending information to, and receiving it from, a large host computer.

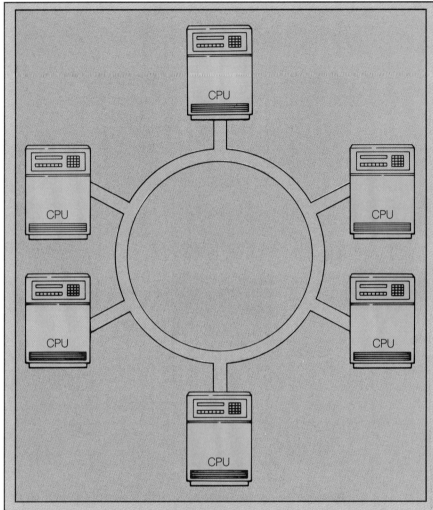

Figure 13–11
A ring network. A ring network can be designed with several computers connected to each other by a communications channel. Unlike a star network, there is no host computer. Information can be sent to, or received from, any computer in the network.

Problems can occur if the host computer malfunctions. Information cannot be passed to other computers since all messages are routed by the host computer.

Ring Network

A **ring network,** like the one illustrated in Figure 13–11, is a ring of computers at local sites connected to each other by a communications channel. Unlike the star network, there is no host computer. Decentralized organizations frequently use a ring network to pass communications between computers, but not on a regular basis.

Some law enforcement agencies use a ring network, enabling them to occasionally pass information to each other. Unlike a star network, if one of the computers in the network malfunctions, the others can still pass information between them.

Area Networks

A data communications network can be established for a specific geographic area, such as a city or a university campus, that allows data to be transmitted to locations within the area. This type of network is called a **local area network** (or **LAN**). For example, a city might use a LAN to allow government offices to transfer data back and forth and to send messages to various offices within the network. A local area network can increase the efficiency of offices and departments within the network and reduce the necessity and expense of transmitting information by other means.

A **private area network (PAN)** is a configuration of CPUs similar to that of a LAN, but it is privately owned and controlled. It is usually confined to a small area, such as the main offices of a company. An insurance company with departments and offices located in a large office building, for example, can link together microcomputers or terminals in all offices by coaxial cable. This enables the employees and managers throughout the building to communicate easily and quickly with each other, and to have access to information stored in the company's main computer system. More and more companies and institutions are using this capability to improve communications throughout the organization.

THE COMPUTER DIDN'T DO IT!

Calvin Quils, the owner of Quil's Hardware Company, was upset when the truck driver began unloading his order of hardware supplies. The shipment included three times the amount he had ordered.

An investigation revealed that Quil's order had been entered into the supplier's computer by three different order clerks, one clerk on each shift. The two extra orders were returned to the supplier.

"I appreciate their giving my order prompt attention," commented Quils, "but on this order they overdid it a little."

Special Communications Equipment

Input/output (I/O) devices operate much more slowly (100 to 150 bits per second) than communications channels such as a telephone channel (300 to 9,600 bits per second). Therefore, a channel is not used to its full capacity by a single I/O device. By installing special communications equipment, such as multiplexors and concentrators, the number of I/O devices that can use a communications channel can be increased. This can improve the overall efficiency of a computer system.

A **multiplexor,** such as the one shown in Figure 13–12, is a hardware device that increases the efficiency of a communications channel.

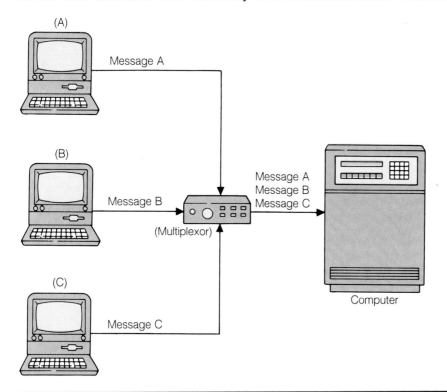

Figure 13–12
A multiplexor. A multiplexor can receive data from several microcomputers or terminals at one time and send all the data to another computer at the same time over a single communications channel. This eliminates the need for a separate channel for each microcomputer or terminal.

When installed between terminals and the computer, it can receive data from several terminals; then it combines the data into a single data input stream that can then be sent to the computer over a single channel. When the computer has completed processing, the output is then sent back to the multiplexor that routes the output to the appropriate computer terminal or to another output device, such as a printer. The use of a multiplexor reduces the number of channels that would otherwise be needed.

Because multiplexors allow data to be sent and/or received by several terminals at the same time, they are often used by large banks. They enable several tellers to have immediate access to customer records via a single communications channel.

A **concentrator** (see Figure 13–13) allows data to be transmitted from only one terminal at a time over a communication channel. A

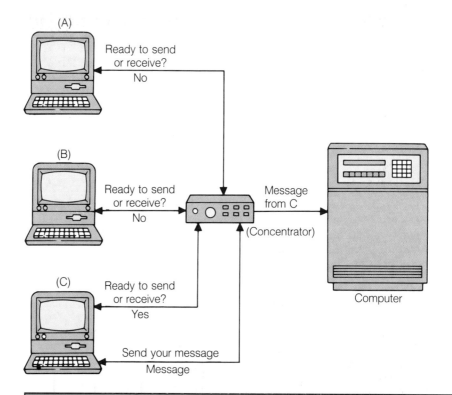

Figure 13–13
A concentrator. Using a "polling" procedure, a concentrator "concentrates" on the next terminal that is ready to either send or receive data. After either accepting input from it or sending data to it, the next terminal is polled.

basic assumption is that not all terminals will be ready to send or receive data at the same time. A concentrator therefore "polls" the terminals one at a time to see if they have data to send. The first terminal ready to send or receive data will get control of the channel for as long as it is needed. The concentrator then searches out another terminal waiting to use the channel.

Concentrators are used when speed is not a priority, and when there are few users. For example, schools sometimes use concentrators to allow students to use terminals in a computer laboratory to communicate with a central computer. In such cases, a concentrator can usually handle the limited number of terminals at speeds appropriate for student needs.

DO YOU REMEMBER

9. . . .Two types of multiple CPU systems explained in the chapter?

10. . . .The primary purpose of a local area network (LAN)?

11. . . .The basic difference between a multiplexor and a concentrator?

Summary

(This summary provides answers to DO YOU REMEMBER . . . questions in the chapter.)

1. **What are the primary hardware components of a data communications system?**
   The primary hardware components are (1) one or more personal computers, terminals, or computers; (2) a modem connected to each personal computer, terminal, or large computer; (3) one or more communications channels; (4) a modem connected to the host computer; and (5) the host computer, or another personal computer or large computer.

2. **What is the purpose of a modem?**
   A *modem* is an electronic device that converts a computer's digital signal into analog form so that the signal can be transmitted across a communications channel, and then reconverts the signal from analog form to digital form when it reaches another computer or terminal.

3. **What is a communications channel, and what are some examples of communications channels?**

A *communications channel* is a communications medium that allows a personal computer, terminal, or other input/output device to communicate with another computer. Communications channels include *telegraph lines, telephone lines, coaxial cables, microwave links, satellites,* and *fiber optic cables.*

4. **What does the term *baud rate* mean?**

The term *baud rate* refers to the speed, measured in bits per second at which data is transmitted.

5. **What are the three grades of communications channels?**

Three grades of communications channels are *narrowband, voiceband,* and *broadband.*

6. **What are the three methods for transmitting data?**

Three methods for transmitting data are the *simplex,* the *half-duplex,* and the *full-duplex methods.*

7. **What is a time-sharing system?**

A *time-sharing system* is a data communications system that allows concurrent use of the same computer by several users.

8. **Why would a full-duplex channel probably be used when large amounts of data are to be transmitted between two or more large computers?**

A full-duplex channel would probably be used because it allows large amounts of data to be transmitted in both directions at the same time.

9. **What are the two types of multiple CPU systems?**

The two types of multiple CPU systems are the *star network* and the *ring network.*

10. **What is the primary purpose of a local area network (LAN)?**

The primary purpose of a local area network (LAN) is to allow data to be transmitted between locations within a certain geographic area. For example, a city government might use a LAN for transmitting data between various city government offices and departments.

11. **What is the basic difference between a multiplexor and a concentrator?**

A *multiplexor* can receive data from several personal computers or terminals and simultaneously transmit all data to a central computer over a communications channel. A *concentrator* "polls" several personal computers or terminals to determine which one is ready to send or receive data. The microcomputer or terminal ready to send or receive data will gain immediate access to the communication channel.

DATA PROCESSING CAREER. . . . .
Word Processor

CAREER OPPORTUNITY FOR COMPUTER PROFESSIONAL

JOB TITLE:
Word Processor

JOB DESCRIPTION:
Insurance company is seeking someone with good clerical skills to do word processing. Duties include using a microcomputer and word processing software to prepare all types of business letters, memos, reports, and other business documents. Applicant must be able to take dictation and type at least 50 wpm. Proofreading skills are a necessity. Person hired will undergo training and must be willing to share work assignments with others.

EXPERIENCE REQUIRED:
None

EDUCATION REQUIRED:
A high school diploma

PERSONAL QUALIFICATIONS:
Applicant must be neat, possess good verbal and written communications skills, and be career-minded. The ability to work closely with others is essential.

Key Terms

acoustic coupler modem
analog signal
baud rate
central (host) computer
communication
communications channel
concentrator
data communications
demodulation
digital signal
full-duplex method
half-duplex method
local area network (LAN)

modem
modulation
multiplexor
multiprogramming
network
parallel transmission
private area network (PAN)
ring network
serial transmission
simplex method
star network
time-sharing system

Test Yourself

1. A ＿＿＿＿＿＿＿ system consists of hardware and software components that allow one or more personal computers or terminals to communicate with another computer over communications channels such as telephone lines.

2. A(n) ＿＿＿＿＿＿＿ is an electronic device used for modulation and demodulation.

3. The three types of modems are the internal, the external, and the ＿＿＿＿＿＿＿ modem.

4. The ＿＿＿＿＿＿＿ is the speed at which data can be sent from a modem.

5. The speed at which data can be transmitted along a communications channel is determined by the ＿＿＿＿＿＿＿ of the channel.

6. Three grades of communications channels are ＿＿＿＿＿＿＿ , ＿＿＿＿＿＿＿ , and ＿＿＿＿＿＿＿ .

7. ＿＿＿＿＿＿＿ cables and laser technology represent the newest types of communication channel.

8. Personal computers use ＿＿＿＿＿＿＿ transmission, meaning that one character at a time is transmitted, to communicate with a host computer.

9. The three basic methods for transmitting data are the ＿＿＿＿＿＿＿ method, the ＿＿＿＿＿＿＿ method, and the ＿＿＿＿＿＿＿ method.

10. A method for transmitting data that allows data to be sent in both directions at the same time is the ＿＿＿＿＿＿＿ method.

Review Questions

1. What are the basic hardware components of a data communications system? What is the primary function of each component? (Learning Objective 2)

2. Name three grades of communications channels, and give an example of each. (Learning Objective 3)

3. What are the three methods for transmitting data? (Learning Objective 4)

4. What is the difference between a single CPU system and a multiple CPU system? (Learning Objective 5)

5. What is the difference between a star network and a ring network? (Learning Objective 6)

6. What are a multiplexor and a concentrator used for? (Learning Objective 7)

Activities

1. Visit a business or other organization in your area that uses computers or terminals (maybe cash registers used as point-of-sale terminals) to communicate with a large computer at another location. Ask the manager, or someone he or she recommends, to explain how their data communications system works. Write an essay about the system you observe, and include sketches. The sketches in the chapter can serve as a guide.

2. Try to obtain a small section (a few inches) of telephone line from your local telephone company. Carefully remove the insulation from around the individual wires. Ask a physics teacher at your school to explain to you how data is transmitted along the wires. Ask the physics teacher to explain, also, how data is transmitted by a fiber optics cable.

3. Visit a computer store in your area. Ask to see a communications software package. Make a list of all hardware and software requirements for running the software package.

4. Visit a local law enforcement agency in your area. Find out if the agency uses computers or terminals to obtain information from the FBI or the state motor vehicle division. If so, request a demonstration. You might also request that an officer visit your school and explain the system to your class.

CHAPTER 14

Database Processing

Learning Objectives

After studying this chapter carefully, you will be able to:

1. Define key terms introduced in the chapter.

2. Explain the purpose of a database management system (DBMS).

3. Identify three popular types of database models.

4. Explain the primary purpose(s) of a back-end processor.

5. Identify the primary purpose of a distributed database.

Chapter Outline

DATABASE MANAGEMENT SYSTEM (DBMS)

TYPES OF DATABASES
Hierarchical Database
Network Database
Relational Database

ACCESSING A DATABASE

BACK-END PROCESSOR

DISTRIBUTED DATABASES

SUMMARY

DATA PROCESSING CAREER:
Database Administrator

Application

Recently a large company made a study of its current data processing function. The company had been using EDP (electronic
data processing) since 1965, and had created and stored an enormous amount of data on magnetic tape and disk. The information
specialists in Figure 14–1 are examining some of the 20,000 tapes
and 200 disk packs contained in the magnetic media library.

The study team found that much of the data on both tape and
disk was historical data that had been stored in many different files
for many different applications. A lot of the data was redundant,
seldom used, and very costly to maintain.

The study revealed that this duplication of data was the result of
the traditional method of data processing in which each computerized application has its own data files that are rarely shared with
any other application. Some of the company's data in unrelated files
was related to more than one application. Different record formats,
however, had prevented the sharing of data.

Figure 14–1
Information systems study team standing in
the magnetic media library.

The company's management decided to convert from the traditional approach of data processing to the newer state-of-the-art database approach of data processing. See Figure 14–2 for a diagram illustrating both systems. The database approach allowed the company to store data one time without duplication and redundancy, except in some instances when there was a need for very fast retrieval of certain frequently used data.

The changeover from the traditional approach to the database approach was gradually accomplished in two years. The company was able to reduce the number of tapes to 10,000 and the number of disk packs to 100. Also, the cost of maintaining the magnetic media library dropped considerably.

In this chapter we will examine the basic database types and concepts. The reader should be aware of the fact that database technology is much more complex than presented in this overview.

Database Management System (DBMS)

A **database management system (DBMS)** is a specific method of storing data on a secondary storage device. Its purpose is to avoid duplication and redundancy of data and to maintain the data independently of the computer programs that use it. In general, the term *database* refers to a group of data necessary to run a business or organization.

A database approach to file organization makes programming easier. It also helps protect the data against unintended user access. Creating and maintaining a database system, such as the one shown in Figure 14–3, is the responsibility of the **database administrator** who is in charge of database administration.

A database is similar to a school library: the library is made up of many independent books sharing the physical space in the library building. Many students check out books on different subjects at different times. The library provides information for many different user needs. Similarly, a database is made up of many independent,

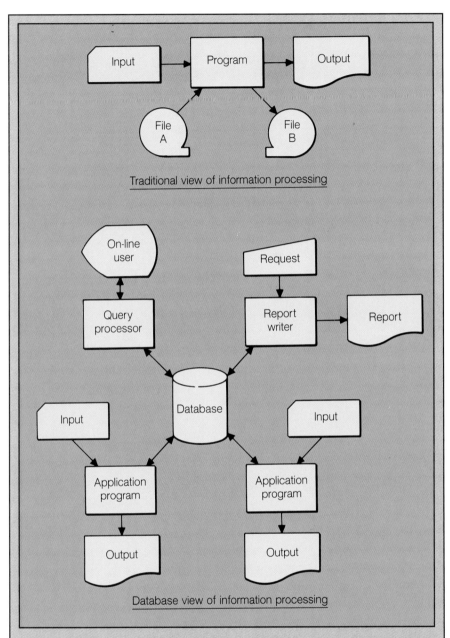

Figure 14–2
Traditional and database approaches to data processing.

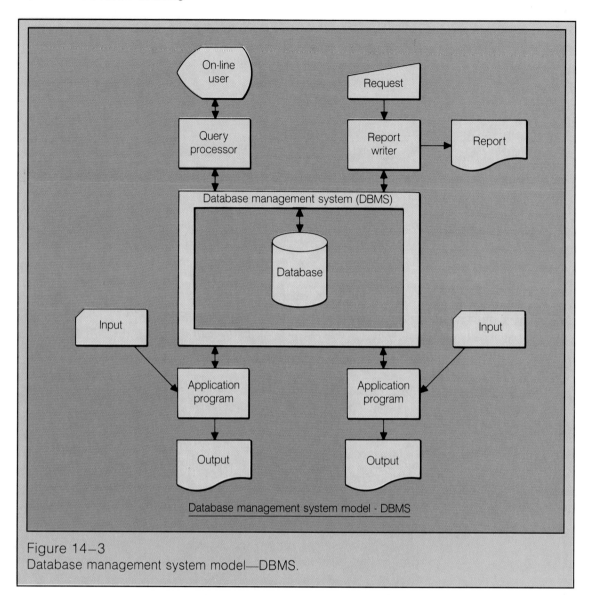

Figure 14–3
Database management system model—DBMS.

but related, files that provide information to different users. An organization may have more than one database to service information requests of users.

The DBMS acts as a file manager (decision maker) between the application program(s) and the data in the database. An application program might request that data be retrieved from a database or be stored in a database. The DBMS supervises and carries out these functions for the application program(s). Levels of user access to specific data in a database are managed and controlled by the DBMS through a security function built into the DBMS software. The person who manages and is responsible for the database function is the database administrator.

DO YOU
REMEMBER

1. . . .The two basic approaches to data processing?

2. . . .The purpose of a database management system (DBMS)?

Types of Databases

There are three frequently used types of databases—hierarchical, network, and relational. Each database consists of three basic parts: structures, operations, and constraints. The structure part deals with the way that elementary items are grouped into bigger units. The operations part includes tools for creating, modifying, inserting, deleting, and retrieving data. The constraints are the rules that control the conditions for creating, modifying, and/or retrieving a specific data element. All three parts—structures, operations, and constraints—must be present in order to have a workable and usable database.

Hierarchical Database

A **hierarchical database,** one of the oldest types of databases, was used as the basis of much early research on database projects. The IBM Corporation's IMS (Information Management System) is well known for being one of the first hierarchical database management systems (DBMS) commercially available in the marketplace.

The hierarchical type is represented by a **definition tree.** The smallest unit of data is called a field. A combination of data fields represents a segment. The relationships among segments are hierarchical, or ranked in relation from most inclusive (biggest) to least inclusive

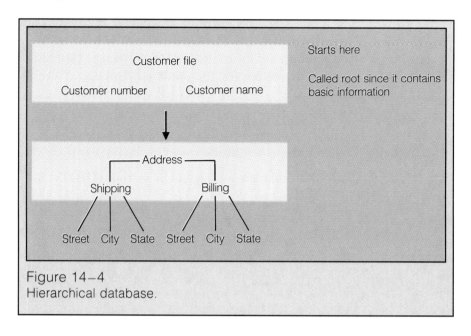

Figure 14–4
Hierarchical database.

(smallest). The segment at the top of a hierarchy is referred to as the root, like a real tree turned upside down (see Figure 14–4).

The hierarchical type of database does have some weaknesses, but it has been improved by many commercial users with their own enhancements. Many of the weaknesses in the hierarchical type have been eliminated in the network and relational databases which will be examined next.

Network Database

A **network database** uses separate data files for each type of data to be stored. In a network database, illustrated in Figure 14–5, the separate data files are linked to each other by pointers. A **pointer** identifies where a particular file and its data are stored. It is an electronic mark in memory that identifies where a file and its data are stored. Although the basic organization of this type of database is not overly complex, the implementation of this approach can be detailed and difficult.

The network database is made up of entities similar to data items that are represented by records. These records make up files that are linked together with pointers. Figure 14–6 illustrates a small part of a personnel skills table file. The pointers show the skill of each employee in the personnel skills table file.

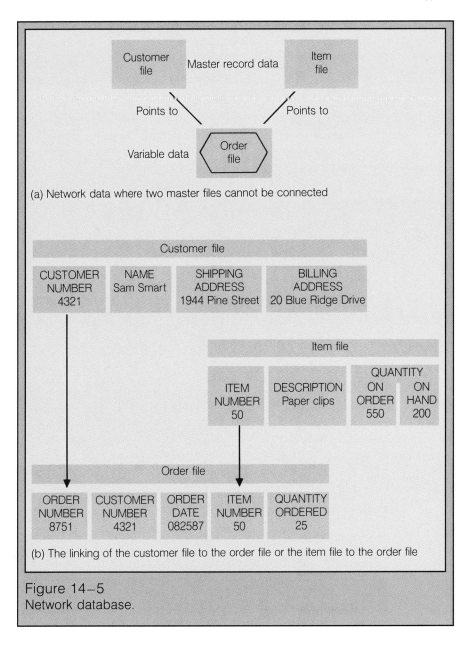

(a) Network data where two master files cannot be connected

(b) The linking of the customer file to the order file or the item file to the order file

Figure 14–5
Network database.

The database software sets up the relationships between different files and data items. User instructions are included in the software manual for indicating which files need to be accessed by which programs. A lot of work goes into planning and setting up the relationships for a network database.

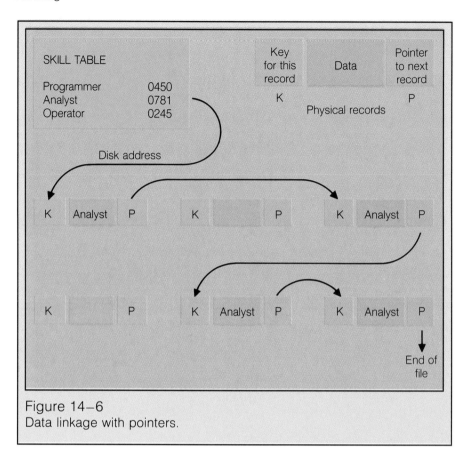

Figure 14–6
Data linkage with pointers.

The network database eliminates the need for duplicating certain records within the database. Also, unlike the hierarchical approach, lengthy searches for connecting record occurrences are not necessary. The network database continues to be used successfully by commercial users.

Relational Database

A **relational database** is the newest and least complex system in appearance, and has become the most popular among available types. As Figure 14–7 shows, the data is represented in table format and is known as *relations*. These relations are used to represent entities and relationships.

A relation is simply a two-dimensional table with overlapping information. One table could contain all the data about students in a

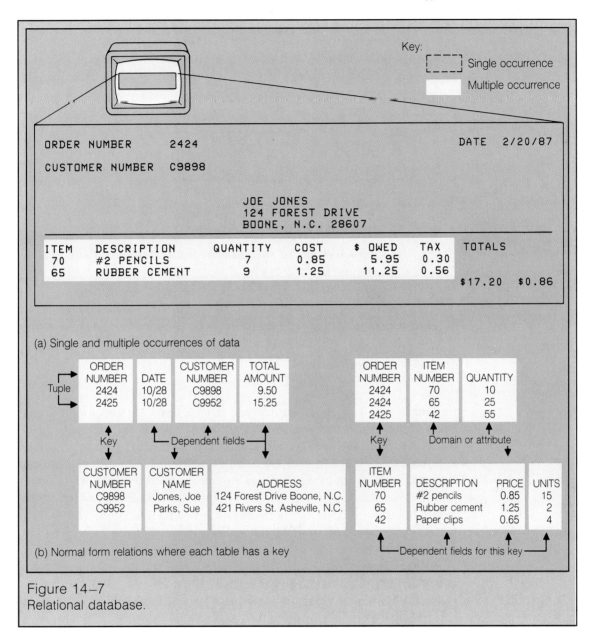

ORDER NUMBER   2424   DATE   2/20/87

CUSTOMER NUMBER C9898

                          JOE JONES
                          124 FOREST DRIVE
                          BOONE, N.C. 28607

ITEM	DESCRIPTION	QUANTITY	COST	$ OWED	TAX	TOTALS
70	#2 PENCILS	7	0.85	5.95	0.30	
65	RUBBER CEMENT	9	1.25	11.25	0.56	
						$17.20 $0.86

(a) Single and multiple occurrences of data

ORDER NUMBER	DATE	CUSTOMER NUMBER	TOTAL AMOUNT
2424	10/28	C9898	9.50
2425	10/28	C9952	15.25

Tuple

Key — Dependent fields —

ORDER NUMBER	ITEM NUMBER	QUANTITY
2424	70	10
2424	65	25
2425	42	55

Key   Domain or attribute

CUSTOMER NUMBER	CUSTOMER NAME	ADDRESS
C9898	Jones, Joe	124 Forest Drive Boone, N.C.
C9952	Parks, Sue	421 Rivers St. Asheville, N.C.

ITEM NUMBER	DESCRIPTION	PRICE	UNITS
70	#2 pencils	0.85	15
65	Rubber cement	1.25	2
42	Paper clips	0.65	4

— Dependent fields for this key —

(b) Normal form relations where each table has a key

Figure 14–7
Relational database.

particular school. Another table could contain all the data about students in different schools in a school system. There is enough common data in both tables to link the different tables together.

In a relational database there are no pointers required between files. Even though some redundancy and duplication of data exist, they serve an appropriate purpose linking tables logically together through meaningful relations. The DBMS software that controls and manages the relational database is complex and normally operates more slowly than other DBMSs. However, the relational database's ease of use and greater ability to handle complex data manipulation offset this weakness of a slower operating speed. The relational database system will continue to gain in popularity with commercial users of database systems.

DO YOU
REMEMBER

3. . . .The three parts of a database?

4. . . .The three types of database systems?

5. . . .The characteristics of the three types of database systems?

Accessing a Database

In a library, information is retrieved from a book by first locating the book needed through the use of a card catalog number that is assigned to each book in the library. The number identifies each book uniquely and indicates where to find the book on a shelf. Once the user knows the card catalog number, he or she can go to the appropriate shelf and remove the book from the shelf. Similarly, a database is accessed through software components within the DBMS package. These software components or modules are called query languages and report writers.

A **query language** is one of the software modules that accompanies every DBMS. DATAEASE, dBASE-III Plus, R-base 5000, and many other DBMSs have their own unique query language built in. A user can configure, or set up, a query quickly by writing a few lines of query language code to specify what he or she wants out of the database. Normally, eight to ten lines of code will produce the desired output for the user.

Query languages are very-high-level, nonprocedural, forth- or fifth-generation languages. These query languages allow the user to request specific information from a database, similar to locating a specific book in a library, without having to go through the formal procedures of writing a traditional computer program. Query languages are easy

Figure 14–8
Executive querying a database using DATAEASE query language.

to learn and use. Many top executives, such as the one shown in Figure 14–8, find it convenient to learn and use query languages to retrieve desired information from a database quickly and accurately for decision-making purposes.

A second way to access a database is through a report writer software component within the DBMS. A **report writer** is similar to

THE COMPUTER DIDN'T DO IT!

The Social Security Administration incorrectly notified a California man of his death and stopped sending his monthly benefits check. It took four letters and three telephone calls for the man to convince the local social security office that he was still alive and his wife was the one who had died.

Figure 14–9
Report query (label format).

a query language. The difference is that the report writer is especially concerned with printed output. It is used to define and specify more detailed and complex reports to be printed. The user must indicate which columns of data are to appear in each output area on a hardcopy report. Once the request for certain information is given, a search for the information is carried out by the report writer software component against the database. After the information is found in the database, it is formatted appropriately and printed. Figures 14–9 through 14–14 give examples of querying and report writing using DATAEASE query and report writer software.

Back-End Processor

A **back-end processor** is commonly called a **database machine.** It is a microcomputer or minicomputer that is attached to a central mainframe computer to handle database requests. The DBMS software is contained in the back-end processor in one of two forms. The DBMS can be stored on regular disk, or it can be placed onto chips within the microcomputer or minicomputer as firmware.

The primary purpose of a back-end processor is to take the database work load off the mainframe computer so the mainframe can do what it is best designed to do—process data. All requests for database processing are handled by the micro or mini back-end processor. A

To produce this output...

```
════════════════════════════════════════════════════════════════
────────────────────────────────────────────────────────────────

Mr. A.B. Anderson
Anderson Tool
11 Anderson Place
Albany NY 12203

Mr. Bernard L. Benson
Benson Engineering
22 Bensonhurst Drive
Baltimore MD 21234

Mr. Douglas Danforth
Carter Pharmaceuticals
44 Danforth Drive
Danbury CT 06810

Ms. Francine Franco
Franco Films
66 Felton St.
Fort Worth TX 76148

Mr. George A. Gates
Geronimo Artworks
────────────────────────────────────────────────────────────────
════════════════════════════════════════════════════════════════
```

...create this report query...

```
for Prospects
;
list records
   President;
   Company;
   Address;
   City;
   State;
   Zip.
```

...and use this special format

```
════════════════════════════════════════════════════════════════
────────────────────────────────────────────────────────────────

.Items
─────────────────────
─────────────────────
──────────────────────────────
────────────────────────────

.end
────────────────────────────────────────────────────────────────
════════════════════════════════════════════════════════════════
```

To produce this output . . .

```
         Company          all      all Activity   all Activity
                        Activity     Type of         Result
                          Date      Contact

Allistor Kennels        05/31/84    Meeting       Qualified
Anderson Tool           05/01/84    Meeting       Qualified
                        06/02/84    Phone Call    Sale
Benson Engineering
Carter Pharmaceuticals  05/04/84    Letter        Sale
                        06/02/84    Phone Call    Disqualified
Elsworth Associates     05/30/84    Meeting       Sale
Franco Films            06/02/84    Phone Call    Qualified
Geronimo Artworks
Harold Signs            05/02/84    Phone Call    Sale
Zycar Autos
```

. . . create this report query . . .

```
for Prospects
;
list records
  Company in groups;
  all Activity Date;
  all Activity Type of Contact;
  all Activity Result.
```

. . . and use a columnar format

```
         Company          all      all Activity   all Activity
                        Activity     Type of         Result
                          Date      Contact

.Items
         _____    _____    _____    _____


.end
```

Figure 14–10
Report query (reporting on related files).

To produce this output...

```
Mr. Douglas Danforth
Carter Pharmaceuticals
44 Danforth Drive
Danbury CT 06810

Dear President:

Thank you for joining our family of clients.

We hope to serve you for many years to come.

Sincerely,

A.B. Cash
Profits Unlimited
```

...create this data-entry form...

```
This report will produce Thank you letters
to companies who have become customers
during the following period:

Beginning Date: _____
Ending Date: _____
```

...and this report query...

```
for Activity
   with Date between data-entry Beginning Date
   to data-entry Ending Date and Result = Sale;
list records
   any Prospects President;
   Company in order;
   any Prospects Address;
   any Prospects City;
   any Prospects State;
   any Prospects Zip.
```

Figure 14–11 (continued next page)

. . .and use a special format.

```
.Items

_____
_____
_____
_____

Dear President:

Thank you for joining our family of clients.

We hope to serve you for many years to come.

Sincerely,

A.B. Cash
Profits Unlimited

.page
.end
```

Figure 14-11
Report query (form letter example).

Figure 14-12
Report query (invoice example).

To produce this output . . .

```
                              INVOICE

 Customer No.001

 Mr. A.B. Anderson
 Anderson Tool
 11 Anderson Place
 Albany NY 12203

 No. of Memberships:    3 at $500    Membership Cost: $ 1,500.00
 No. of Newsletters:    5 at $ 15    Newsletter Cost: $    75.00

                                     BALANCE DUE:     $ 1,575.00
```

. . . create this report query . . .

```
 for Orders
 with Balance Due > 0
 ;
 list records
   Customer No. in order;
   any Prospects President;
   Company;
   any Prospects Address;
   any Prospects City;
   any Prospects State;
   any Prospects Zip;
   Memberships;
   Membership Cost;
   Newsletters;
   Newsletter Cost;
   Balance Due.
```

. . . and use a special format

```
                              INVOICE
 .Items
 Customer No. _____


 _____
 _____
 _____
 _____, _____  _____

 No. of Memberships:    ____at $500    Membership Cost: $_____
 No. of Newsletters:    ____at $ 15    Newsletter Cost: $_____

                                       BALANCE DUE:     $  _____

 .page
 .end
```

To produce this output . . .

Customer No.	Date	PAYMENT
001		500.00
002		500.00
003		1,000.00

. . . create this report query . . .

```
for Cash Receipts
with Posted = no;
list records
   Customer No. in groups;
   Amount of payment.
modify records in Orders
   Amount Paid:= Cash Receipts amount of Payment + Amount Paid;
   Balance Due:= Total Cost — Amount Paid.
modify records
   Posted:= yes.
```

. . . and use a columnar format

Customer No.	Date	PAYMENT
.Items		
.end		

Figure 14-13
Report query (posting transactions).

To produce this output...

```
                        REVENUE REPORT

            Company             Date      Revenue   Memberships
        Anderson Tool         05/15/84   1,575.00        3
        Carter Pharmaceuticals 05/15/84    515.00        1
        Harold Signs          05/14/84   2,725.00        5

        Totals                           4,815.00        9
        Minimum                                          1
        Maximum                                          5

        Average                                      3.0000
```

...create this report query...

```
for Orders
;
list records
   Company in groups;
   Date;
   Total Cost: item sum;
   Memberships: item sum mean max min.
```

...and use a columnar format

```
            Company             Date     Revenue   Memberships
    .Items
                               _____   _____    _____
    .end

    Totals                              _____    _____
    Minimum                                         _____
    Maximum                                         _____

    Average                                        _____
```

Figure 14–14
Report query (statistical example).

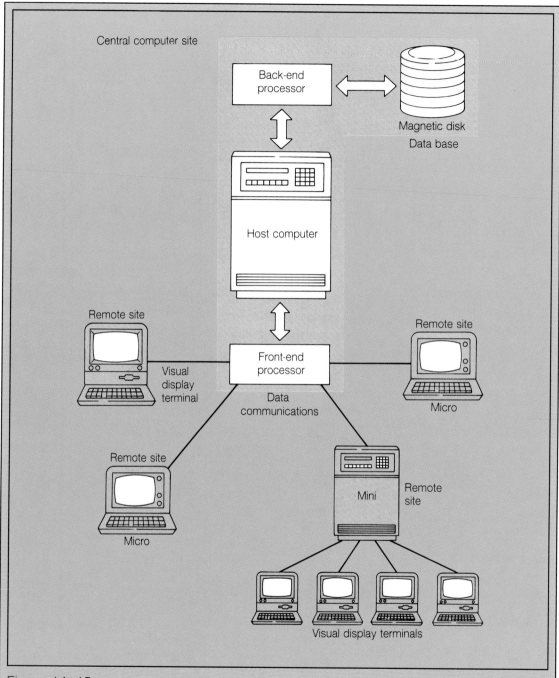

Figure 14-15
Front-end processor, mainframe computer, and back-end processor configuration.

front-end processor, mainframe computer, and back-end processor configuration is illustrated in Figure 14–15.

The back-end processor concept is an efficient and effective way for larger data processing organizations to handle the database function. This concept is interrelated with distributed database technology, explained next.

Distributed Databases

When an organization with many offices needs the local capability to process data, the distributed approach to data processing could be suitable. The **distributed database** approach provides ways of getting the appropriate data to a particular remote site where it is needed. The portion of the corporate, central site database that applies to a particular office can be downloaded (sent back) to that site from the central computer when needed.

A particular remote site would have only the data needed there. Each office would be responsible for keeping the data in its portion of the database secure, and also for updating that specific portion as necessary. The master copy of the overall database would be updated daily at the corporate central site using updates received from the remote sites during the day. This way the central site database would always remain accurate and current. See Figure 14–16 for an illustration of a distributed database environment.

Use of the distributed database approach is made possible through appropriate data communications channels, such as telephone lines, microwave, and satellite delivery systems as presented in Chapter 13. The idea of placing the appropriate data and information at the particular location where they are needed is commonly referred to as **distributed data processing** (DDP). This is one of the fastest growing components of the data processing industry. There are many job opportunities for database and data communications specialists.

6. . . .The process for accessing a database?

7. . . .The purpose and function of a back-end processor?

8. . . .The purpose and function of a distributed database environment?

DO YOU REMEMBER

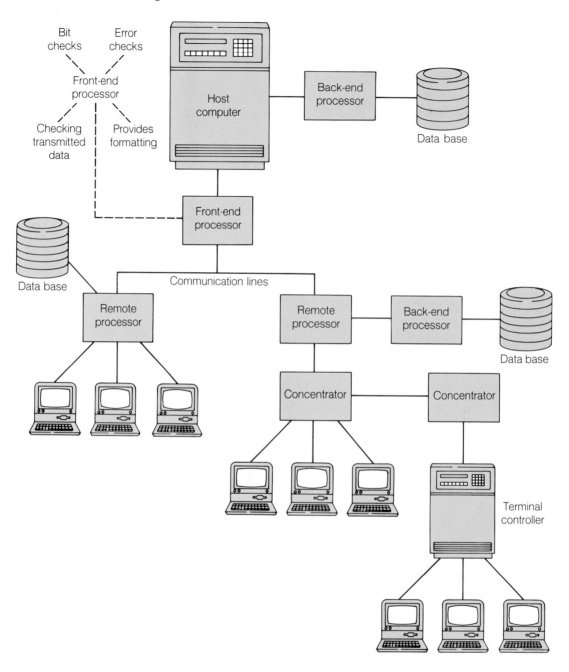

Figure 14–16
Distributed database environment.

Summary

(This summary provides answers to DO YOU REMEMBER. . . questions in the chapter.)

1. **What are the two basic approaches to data processing?**
The two basic approaches to data processing are the *traditional* approach and *database* approach.

2. **What is the function of a database management system (DBMS)?**
The function of a data base management system (DBMS) is to *act as a file manager* between the application program(s) and the data in the database.

3. **What are the three parts of a database?**
The three parts of a database are *structures*, *operations*, and *constraints*.

4. **What are the three types of database systems?**
The three types of database systems are *hierarchical, network,* and *relational* systems.

5. **What are the characteristics of the three types of database systems?**
The *hierarchical* system is represented by a definition tree. The smallest unit of data is called a field. A combination of data fields represents a segment. The relationships among segments are hierarchical. The segment at the top of the hierarchy is referred to as the root.

The *network* system is made up of entities that are represented by records. These records make up files that are linked together with pointers. Pointers show where the data is stored.

The *relational* system is the newest, most popular, and least complex type in appearance. The data is represented in table format and is known as relations. The relations are used to represent entities and relationships. A relationship is simply a two-dimensional table.

6. **What is the process for accessing a database?**
Accessing a database takes place through software components within the DBMS package. These software components are called *query languages* and *report writers*.

7. **What are the purpose and function of a back-end processor?**
The purpose and function of a back-end processor, also referred

to as a database machine, are *to take the database work load off the mainframe computer* so it can do what it is best designed to do—process data.

8. **What are the purpose and function of a distributed database environment?**

The purpose and function of a distributed database environment are to provide ways of placing the appropriate data at a particular remote site where that specific data/information is needed for decision making.

DATA PROCESSING CAREER. . . . .
Database Administrator

CAREER OPPORTUNITY FOR COMPUTER PROFESSIONAL

JOB TITLE:
Database Administrator

JOB DESCRIPTION:
Applicant will be responsible for managing and controlling the information in a database and for keeping it accurate and up to date. The DBA develops controls and standards for creation, modification, security, access, and retrieval functions in a database environment. The DBA works closely with user departments' management in the construction of a database.

EXPERIENCE REQUIRED:
A minimum of three to five years in systems analysis and design and applications programming.

EDUCATION REQUIRED:
A four-year college degree in information systems or computer science.

PERSONAL QUALIFICATIONS:
Applicant must like to work with other people in order to solve problems. Patience, perseverance, and a pleasing personality are necessary qualifications for a DBA candidate.

Key Terms

back-end processor
database administrator
database file organization
database machine
database management system
   (DBMS)
database model
database system
definition tree

distributed database
hierarchical database
network database
pointer
query language
relational database
report writer
traditional data files

Test Yourself

1. A database is a specific method of storing data on a
   _____ storage device in which _____ and
   _____ are minimized, and the data is maintained independently of the computer programs that use it.

2. A database approach to file organization makes
   _____ easier and allows greater _____ to be
   built into user access to the data.

3. A database consists of three basic parts: _____ ,
   _____ , and _____ .

4. The three frequently used database types are _____ ,
   _____ , and _____.

5. A database is accessed through two software components within
   the DBMS that are _____ and
   _____.

6. A _____ processor or _____ machine is a hardware component that normally is a micro or mini computer that
   is attached to the central mainframe computer to handle database requests.

7. The _____ approach provides ways of
   placing appropriate data at a particular remote site.

8. The distributed database approach is made possible through appropriate _____ channels.

9. A _____ is responsible for managing and controlling the data in a database and keeping it accurate and up to date.

Review Questions

1. What is a database? What are the advantages and disadvantages of database processing as opposed to traditional file processing? (Learning Objective 2)

2. What makes up a database management system? What does a DBMS do? (Learning Objective 2)

3. What are the three database types and their basic differences? Which one is the easiest to use? Why? (Learning Objective 3)

4. What is the primary purpose(s) of a back-end processor? How does it fit into a distributed database processing environment? (Learning Objective 4)

5. What is the primary purpose of distributed database processing? How is it accomplished? (Learning Objective 5)

Activities

1. Design a database of your school environment. The database should allow you to answer questions about the classes you have taken, the grade you received in those classes, the rating (from 1 to 10) that you gave the class, the teachers you had, the textbooks you used, and the textbooks' publishers and authors. You should be able to answer questions such as, "Which classes have I taken that were taught by teacher X?" and, "Which textbook was used in class ABC?" You can add additional information requirements of your own.

2. Load the interactive computer-aided-instruction (CAI) software that came with your school's database management system and go through the steps it takes to use the DBMS. Use the learning activities built into the CAI software to test your understanding of how to use the DBMS.

PART VI
Legal and Social Issues

CHAPTER 15

Security, Privacy, and Crime

Learning Objectives

After studying this chapter carefully, you will be able to:

1. Define key terms introduced in the chapter.

2. Identify protection techniques for physical security.

3. Identify protection techniques for data security.

4. Define and explain computer privacy.

5. Define and explain computer ethics.

6. Identify the kinds of computer crime.

7. Define and explain crime prevention.

8. Identify and explain computer copyrights and warranties.

Chapter Outline

Application

A person in Dallas, Texas, used a microcomputer in his home to produce false bills that were sent to small, local government offices throughout the United States. The bills, for services and supplies that were never provided, ranged from $300 to $500, relatively small amounts compared to the normal bills a local government would receive. Due to their small amounts, the bills were not challenged when they were received. The local government agencies routinely produced accounts payable checks for the amounts owed.

When a bill was not paid, the fake supplier's microcomputer automatically created a second notice. Normally, the local government paid the bill after receiving the second notice. The person who created this system collected over $1 million before the scheme was uncovered.

The crime was uncovered when someone in one of the government offices became concerned about receiving two bills for the same amount from two different vendors—the computer criminal had accidentally produced two identical bills. The person involved with this crime was tried, found guilty, and convicted of grand larceny.

Computer Security

Computer security has been a great concern of organizations for many years. The value of any organization's information must be studied carefully in order to determine what types and levels of security measures are needed to protect it. There is no foolproof set of procedures, or security system, that can guarantee a 100-percent secure environment for EDP systems and their data and information. Security is the responsibility of all employees within an organization, not just top management (see Figure 15–1).

385

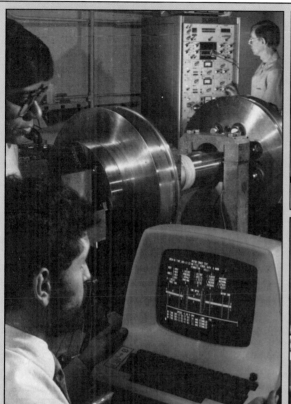

Figure 15–1
The responsibility for computer security belongs to all company
employees.

Physical Protection from Disasters

Physical security deals with providing a certain level of control over physical access to a computer center. Alarms, detection devices, and human guards are used to limit physical access to the hardware and software in a computer center. Other physical devices and techniques often used include badges for authorized personnel; sign-in logs; keys for locking and unlocking terminals; burglar, fire, and smoke alarms; fingerprints and voicewave identification; shredding machines for destroying sensitive file verification lists; electronic card doors; and back-up files for magnetic tape and disk media stored off-site in a vault.

As mentioned earlier, the responsibility for physical security of a computer center belongs to all company employees. The security techniques mentioned above are only as good as the people who implement them. As long as people are involved with computer-based information systems, there won't be such a thing as a 100-percent secure environment.

Security Measures.   There are a number of **security measures** that an organization can use to increase the level of computer center security. The separation of duties within the data processing department helps control the amount of knowledge any one person might have about the operation of the overall data processing function. Rotation of duties within a certain group, such as application programmers, can help discourage any one programmer from tampering with the system. This could be especially important in departments that handle, for example, payroll. Also, rotation of duties periodically within a group can stimulate new ideas and solutions to old and new problems.

Organizations should develop a planned approach to computer security. Normally, more than one procedure, security system, or measure must be used in order to provide maximum security in the overall data processing environment. These mechanisms must be monitored and reviewed on a regular basis by data processing management to be sure that they are functioning properly and still meet the intended need. Management must support maximum security measures and techniques in order for them to be used and enforced.

Disaster Recovery Planning.   **Disaster recovery planning** is a relatively new idea for many data processing organizations. In general, people do not like to think about a natural disaster destroying the physical computer center. However, more computer centers are taken out of operation because of natural disasters such as floods and fires

Figure 15–2
A natural disaster destroyed this computer center.

than because of fraud (see Figure 15–2). A **disaster recovery plan** is a set of documents that describes how, where, when, and who should be involved in establishing a temporary computer center site in the event of a disaster.

If a company loses its computer center, how does this affect the information flow and operation of the organization? The company might be able to continue its operation on a regular basis, or operation of the company might come to a halt. In most cases, a company that uses computers to produce valuable information for decision-making purposes cannot function very long without their computer center. Thus, a back-up site to be used in the case of an emergency should be a mandatory part of the overall management plan for an organization. Every organization should have at least one back-up site that could be used in an emergency. The three types of sites are (1) space shared through reciprocal agreements with like users, (2) shell site facilities, and (3) fully equipped disaster recovery centers. A shell site facility, for example, is a building or room that has been specially equipped with the proper utilities to support a computer operation in the event of a disaster. There is no computer equipment in this facility until after a disaster occurs. At that time, the hardware computer vendor moves the same computer configuration that existed at the original site into this shell site. An organization should invest in at least one of these types of disaster recovery plans. A disaster recovery plan is worth every minute of time and every dollar invested in it. With a disaster recovery plan, an organization could continue to operate. Without one, however, it's doubtful that a company could stay in business more than a few days after a disaster occurs.

Data Security

The data stored in computer files has always been a target for illegal access. **Data security** deals with the controlled access of people to the data. Organizations have developed security measures to restrict access to records in computer files and to recreate destroyed data. A few examples of these security measures are presented in the following sections.

Back-up Data Files.   A simple but effective data security measure is the creation of **back-up files** daily at a specific time. Some organizations make back-up on-line data files twice daily. The first back-up procedure might be done at 12 noon and the second at 12 midnight.

THE COMPUTER DIDN'T DO IT!

A 17-year-old youth nabbed recently in Cleveland for using his Commodore 64 to break into computers in Congress, schools, libraries, and defense contracting companies said he got started hacking about a year ago. "I started tapping lines, then I started getting into bigger and better things, and it got really fun—it got exciting," he told a radio station. "I realized [it was illegal]. When it first started, I was scared. But then it became a daily routine." The youth, charged with two felony counts of wire fraud, said he ran a bulletin board of 100 teen-age hackers' nationwide. The youth's identity was withheld because he is a minor. He is cooperating with local police and met with FBI agents recently. Next, the Secret Service wants to know how he tapped into congressional computers, what he did with White House telephone numbers, and how he got former President Richard Nixon's home number.

Source: *USA TODAY* (July 31, 1986), p. 4B. Copyright © 1986, *USA TODAY*. Reprinted with permission.

Normally, one to three generations of a back-up file are kept at the main computer center, and certain copies are stored in a vault in an off-site building. If a natural disaster at the main computer center destroys the data files, the back-up copies at the off-site location can be used at a back-up facility to continue to process the company's applications. The appropriate disaster recovery procedures for re-creating data files and restoring computer operations are used along with this data security measure.

Passwords for Files.   Another simple and straightforward data se-curity measure is the use of **passwords** with data files. This procedure allows users of specific data files to establish descriptive and appro-priate passwords that are used to gain access to the files. Before access to a passworded data file can be gained, the appropriate password must be supplied. Passwords are filed in a password dictionary. Pass-words should be changed periodically for obvious reasons. Usually, this is a relatively easy and fast process. The password approach to data security is extremely effective if used correctly and monitored regularly by the database administrator.

Level of Data File Access.   **Data file access** can be set up to have access levels of different degrees. The level of access a user would have to data files would be directly related to the user's security clearance and job responsibility. When levels of user security are established [from low level (1) to high level (10)] for a database file, a particular user can gain access only to the portions of the file that his or her job needs. Under this system, most users of the database would not be able to access an entire database record, but only certain portions of a record. This security measure works well in combination with the password security measure.

Internal Security Measures.   **Internal security measures** deal with physical access to the data processing department. As presented ear-lier in this chapter, physical access can be controlled with human guards, electronic doors with appropriate identification devices, alarms, employee badges, keys, and electronic combination locks. Normally, more than one security measure is used in order to max-imize internal security. These physical security measures aid in help-ing to maintain a higher level of data security.

Encryption of Data.   **Data encryption** deals with the translation of normal data into a secret code. This is accomplished through so-

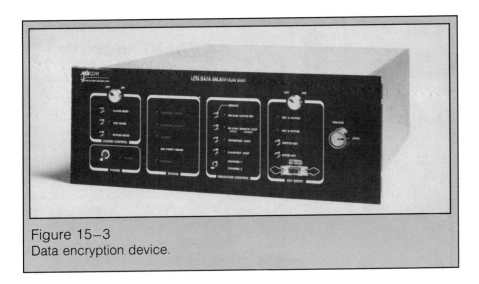

Figure 15–3
Data encryption device.

phisticated coding devices, such as the one shown in Figure 15–3, that scramble the data before it is stored or transmitted to another location. When remote terminals are used to transmit data to and from a central computer site, the data is **encrypted** at one end and transmitted over the appropriate data communication channel to the other end, where it is **decrypted** back into its normal state. Data files can be protected by encrypting the data before it is stored in the file. Then when the data is retrieved from the data file, it is decrypted back into its normal state. Generally speaking, data is encrypted as it exits the computer and decrypted as it enters the computer. Encryption security measures, although somewhat costly, are sophisticated, and very effective.

Detection Devices.   Many organizations use special **detection devices** for identification purposes. See Figure 15–4 for an example of an access control system. Some devices are able to recognize a person's fingerprints or voice waves, and to determine whether a particular person is an authorized computer center employee who is cleared to enter a specific physical area. If a person is not recognized as an authorized data processing employee, then entry is denied and an alarm might go off to notify security guards of an illegal entry attempt. Of course, if a person is recognized, entry is allowed. These detection devices are somewhat expensive and acceptance has been slow by most data processing departments.

Figure 15–4
A computer security system provides for efficient logging of guard rounds from wall box to a central display console.

Developing Computer Security Measures

It is necessary to develop effective and efficient security measures for an organization. As mentioned earlier, security is the responsibility of all company employees, and it is essential that top management supports established security measures.

A well-trained security force is needed to help maintain physical security and data security. These people should be able to detect, at a glance, any security violation. They should be willing to challenge other people concerning security violations when necessary.

When recruiting and selecting persons, such as systems analysts and programmers, to work in a data processing department, careful screening is required. A company should check to be sure that the people selected for employment are ethical and will be loyal to the company. The employees of a company should know that if they are caught violating a security policy, they will be punished according to a set policy.

DO YOU
REMEMBER

1. . . .The two types of computer security?

2. . . .The methods of establishing physical protection from disasters?

3. . . .The methods of implementing data security?

Computer Privacy and Ethics

Computer privacy and ethics are two other major concerns of business organizations. **Computer privacy** deals with controlling personal information and with what, how, and when this information is communicated to another party. Personal information can include, but is not limited to, financial credit, personal employment records, and federal, state, and local taxes. **Computer ethics** deals with individual moral character or standards held with regard to computer use. Laws have been enacted to help control and enforce both privacy and ethics issues.

Privacy

Privacy of data and information stored in electronic form has been a serious problem for organizations since the beginning of electronic data processing. Who should be able to access this data and information, when, and for what reasons are questions that must be answered for each separate situation. The issues of security and privacy of the information are integrated and work in combination with each other. Once information is stored electronically, there is no known foolproof way to guarantee its privacy and security. Even though laws have been established and enacted for the purpose of preventing infractions of personal privacy, the fact remains that as long as people are involved with computer-based information systems, there will always be a threat to personal privacy. The need for information by organizations and the right of individual personal privacy must be balanced, so that privacy can be maintained, but required information can be available to businesses.

Legislation.   The first federally enacted **legislation** concerning personal privacy was the Privacy Act of 1974. The spirit of this legislation is to protect personal privacy of data and information stored electronically in computer files inside and outside a computer. This legislation protected personal privacy at the federal level, but it did not apply to the state and local levels of government. Since the enactment of the Privacy Act of 1974, many state and local governments have established similar laws to protect against the invasion of an individual's personal privacy by business, industry, education, and government agencies at all levels.

Database Issues.   **Database files** allow users to collect and build large data banks of personal records on individuals. This has become a cause for concern among many individuals because of the potential for the invasion of privacy. Easy access to personal data in databases must be controlled. This is done through passwords and authorized levels of access in the DBMS software. Level of access to records in the database is determined on a need-to-know basis, and limits are placed on all users so that security and privacy violations are less likely to occur. Even though software can help limit access to personal and sensitive data and information, it can't guarantee that security and privacy violations will not occur. As long as people work with computers and have access to databases, the risk of security and privacy violations exists.

Ethics

The issue of **ethics** deals with standards of moral conduct in computer usage within an organization. Personal ethics vary, unfortunately, and this can cause an organization severe problems with security and privacy. Most people can be considered basically honest, but there are people who are unethical and dishonest in their dealings with other people. Such people can be a real threat to the security and privacy of the data and software that the organization owns. In the following sections we will examine some of the issues that concern ethics.

Software Piracy and Copying.   Among the greatest problems in the computing industry today are **software piracy** and **illegal copying.** Millions of dollars of income is being lost by software vendors each year because of software pirates. These so-called "pirates" gain access to an organization's software files and simply make a duplicate copy of copyrighted software packages instead of buying their own copies. Most packaged software is copyrighted for the protection of its author and owners. It is illegal to copy this software without appropriate license agreements. Most software vendors allow the purchaser of their software packages to make one back-up copy of the software package to be used in case the original copy becomes damaged. Under no circumstances is it permissible for the original purchaser to make duplicate copies for resale to a third party. It is a violation of the law to copy copyrighted software without written permission from the owner. The best policy to follow when considering whether or not to pirate or illegally copy software is "DON'T DO IT."

Figure 15–5
A hacker at work.

Hacking (Breaking Computer Security).   **Hacking** is the illegal entry
of a person into a computer system for the purpose of breaking computer security and privacy locks protecting sensitive data and information. Hackers are challenged by the excitement of gaining illegal
entry to a computer system and breaking software security measures.
Hacking has become a large and serious problem for the computing
industry. Many of the people who participate in such activities are
young people who are doing it for the excitement of the risk or challenge. The idea, many times, is simply to figure out a way to break
through an organization's security systems; once access is gained,
the fun is over for many hackers. Other hackers like to gain access
and browse through company files just to see what is in them. Sometimes data records in a file are changed by the hacker, causing serious
problems for the organization under attack. Hackers caught in the
act of hacking can be prosecuted for their crimes under existing laws
(see Figure 15–5).

Employee Loyalty.   The subject of **employee loyalty** deals with an
employee's obligations to an employer while in his or her employment. Loyalty is another human characteristic that varies from one

person to another. When a person joins an organization, he or she is normally being hired to work as part of a team with other people in order to conduct the business activities of that organization. These activities normally include a certain level of access to private information for that particular organization. It is expected of employees that they would not give away internal trade secrets, or information, to competing outside organizations. An organization must be very careful when recruiting new employees for data processing related jobs. Employee loyalty is an ethical issue that has come to the forefront of employer's concerns when interviewing and hiring new employees.

Computer Crime

Computer crime has many definitions, and the definition often depends on whom a person talks to. One thing for sure, though, is that it is illegal in any form under the existing laws. Computer crimes, for the most part, are considered to be white-collar crimes. Computer criminals are primarily young, intelligent, well-educated, and technically competent persons. They come from all organizational levels within a business, from the lowest-level employee to the highest-level employee.

Kinds of Computer Crime

There are four broad categories of computer crimes: sabotage, accounting and financial crimes, theft of physical property, and theft of computer services. In the following sections, we will examine each one of these categories in more detail.

Sabotage. **Sabotage** is causing or doing physical harm to computer hardware and/or software. Physical harm can be inflicted, for instance, by taking a hammer and beating the hardware components, causing severe damage. The power supply to the computer might come under attack, or a saboteur might flood the computer center with water from the fire protection system. Software and data files can be electronically damaged by a computer criminal using a magnet to change the state of the magnetic spots on magnetic tape or disks.

Sabotage of computer systems is usually carried out by disgruntled employees or employees fired by an organization. These people want to strike back at the organization in a damaging way because they feel the organization has done damage to them. The sabotage of physical components of a computer system doesn't take place as often as other types of computer crimes do.

Accounting and Financial Crimes.   The accounting and finance areas within an organization are natural areas for a computer-based crime to occur. These areas deal with large amounts of numerical data that represent money. Millions of dollars are lost each year in the United States to computer criminals. Less than 15 percent of these cases are publicized because of the adverse effect this information would have on shareholders and customers of the victimized organizations.

Many computer crimes dealing with money are carried out inside an organization by programmers, systems analysts, and other data processing personnel. A programmer who works with the payroll or accounts payable systems could, and sometimes does, alter certain program statements in order to capture the results of a round-off operation within the program. This small amount is so insignificant for each account processed that it would go unnoticed, possibly, until an audit was made of the system. In the meantime, the computer programmer would be building a computer file with the results of rounding each account placed into it. After processing thousands of accounts over a certain period of time, this computer file could hold thousands of dollars that could be processed unnoticed through the existing payroll or accounts payable system. This type of activity often goes on unnoticed for many years.

To help protect against such illegal activity, periodic system audits should be carried out on all computer-based information systems. An EDP audit would detect many of the illegal activities that might be going on within the system. Accounting and financial crimes are the most costly of all computer crimes and occur rather frequently.

Theft of Physical Property.   Physical property at risk includes the computer hardware, software, and other company property that can be stolen indirectly through computer-based systems. Because of the increasingly small size components, it has become much easier for computer criminals to physically steal hardware. With the introduction of the very compact microcomputers and minicomputers came more physical property crimes. A complete microcomputer system, for instance, will easily fit into the trunk of a small compact car.

Another type of physical property theft is the stealing of a company's manufactured products through the computer-based order entry system. Dummy or false orders can be generated by an inside employee who works closely with the order system. Once these orders have been entered into the system, they can be filled and shipped to someone outside the company.

Software theft is probably the most serious computer crime being committed today. Even though software is not a hardware end-product, it still can be considered as physical property. Most software is stored on a physical magnetic medium that can be stolen easily by computer criminals and copied for personal use or resale. The pirating and copying of computer software is big business and one of the computing industry's biggest problems. Software can also be stolen through remote access to a company's computer facilities. This can be accomplished with a standard dumb CRT terminal, a smart terminal, or microcomputer hook-up tied into the central computer network over standard voice-grade telephone lines. The theft of physical computer property will continue to be a serious problem for computer users.

Theft of Computer Services.   The theft of computer services is a very common activity on most organization's computers. It is especially easy to steal computer time in a time-sharing environment. Even though a time-sharing environment requires passwords to gain access to the computer, it is relatively easy to acquire a password and an appropriate log-on number, particularly for a person who is familiar with the existing computer system. There have been many cases in which computer services have been stolen by hackers, as mentioned earlier in this chapter. Also, many of these thefts occur on college and university campuses where students are learning to use computers. Some students are challenged by so-called "secure systems" and try to break system security just to prove they can.

Employees at all levels within a company steal computer services from their employer periodically. Some organizations allow their regular employees free use of computer facilities at certain times for personal business. Other organizations don't allow employees to use company computers at all. These organizations run a greater risk of employees' stealing computer services. The theft of computer services can be monitored and controlled to a certain degree if appropriate security measures are in place and enforced. System security depends on the honesty and integrity of the persons that use the system. There is no 100-percent secure computer system.

Crime Prevention

Crime prevention means taking specific measures to stop crimes before they occur. Computers can help compile statistical information that actually predicts where crimes might take place and who might be involved. This information is based on historical data that has been collected over many years. From past experiences with certain crimes committed by certain individuals, data can be gathered and used to help predict future trends.

The FBI agent in Figure 15–6 is making an inquiry into the agency's <u>N</u>ational <u>C</u>rime <u>I</u>nformation <u>C</u>enter (NCIC) databases. The NCIC is tied into more than 65,000 federal, state, and local law enforcement agencies. This information center is a central collection and storage facility for crime data and information received from all levels of government. Through using the appropriate statistical models and software, the information center can plot criminal trends from historical data, and predict with some degree of accuracy where the next crime might occur and which criminals might be involved.

Figure 15–6
FBI agent inquiring into the National Crime Information Center's databases.

Using Computer Hardware.   Computer hardware can be used to help prevent crimes by tapping the capabilities of fast processors and mass storage devices. Large mainframes and supercomputers, such as the Cray-1, Cray-2, Amdahl, and CDC Cyber-720, are used to compile statistical information from large database files at very fast speeds. Speed of response is an important characteristic in a criminal information system. Inquirers using the system must be able to receive requested information in an on-line/real-time environment. Response time should be no longer than a few seconds. With the appropriate hardware in place, it can help law enforcement personnel detect and possibly prevent certain types of crimes.

Using Computer Software.   As mentioned above, appropriate hardware can help prevent crimes. Of course, hardware by itself cannot do anything. For these systems, the appropriate criminal software systems must be either written in-house by law enforcement data processing personnel or purchased out-of-house as prepackaged software from a vendor who specializes in law enforcement software packages. Most criminal system software is so confidential and specialized that it must be developed and installed under very strict guidelines set up by the government. Using the appropriate software, law enforcement personnel can search large databases, through high-level query languages, for information concerning a particular crime or criminal. This information can be used to help track the activities of a known criminal and determine whether or not that person might be a potential suspect in a crime.

Using People.   People are the most important element in any system: systems are only as good as the people who design, develop, and implement them. In order for a computer-based crime prevention system to work adequately, there must be hardware, software, and people working together to help detect and prevent crimes. Law enforcement personnel alone cannot detect and prevent all crimes; it takes the involvement of the general public working with law enforcement personnel to successfully enforce the law.

The Law and Computers

An organization must take legal ramifications into consideration when purchasing hardware and software. Warranties, expressed and implied, should be considered when buying the hardware and software components of a system. Copyright laws must be understood when writing software for resale. Many legal questions have arisen over the years concerning the way that the law applies to computers. The laws covering hardware are much easier to work with and understand than are those for the software components of a computer system. The following sections take a basic look at the law and how it applies to computers.

Copyrights

A **copyright** is the registration of a person's written expression of a creative idea filed with the U.S. Copyright Office in Washington, D.C. Software and computer programs have been copyrightable since 1964. Registration is required only to ensure that an individual has the right to sue for copyright violations of published software. Unpublished software is protected by the copyright laws upon its creation. It is not necessary to register unpublished software unless the right to sue for infringement is desired.

Present laws protect copyrighted software against illegal copying only and not against illegal use. It is not illegal to make one back-up copy of most software packages for personal use or to copy a program that appears in a magazine, journal, or newspaper. The back-up copy is to be used only in case the original copy cannot be accessed. Source code can be copyrighted, but object code is questionable because it represents machine language that current copyright laws do not address clearly. Copyrights give the software author limited protection over his or her creation. Although it is hard to detect copyright violators of software products and prove a case, some progress is being made in cases in which outright violations occur with large users of prepackaged software products.

Warranties

Before warranties can be explained effectively, the **Uniform Commercial Code (UCC)** and **common law** must be defined. The UCC is a set of legal guidelines developed and used by lawyers to promote uniformity among state courts of law in cases involving commercial transactions. Article II of the UCC provides the courts with common guidelines concerning the sale of hardware and software products by computer vendors. The common law of the land is based on customs and past legal decisions in similar cases. If Article II of the UCC doesn't apply to a business transaction, then the common law of contracts is used. The UCC is a more precise legal system because it is up to date and does away with the traditional idea of "let the buyer beware."

Implied Warranties. **Implied warranties** deal with contracts for the sale of goods and provide buyer protection. They suggest that a contract for the sale of products automatically contains specific warranties that exist by law. An implied warranty need not be in either written or oral (spoken word) form to be effective.

The two types of implied warranties are **implied warranty of fitness** and **implied warranty of merchantability**. An implied warranty of fitness deals with the specific needs of a purchaser. The purchaser must tell the vendor the specific purpose for which the hardware and/or software will be used. At this point, the purchaser depends on the vendor to use his or her expertise, skill, and common sense to select an appropriate combination of hardware and software to meet the specific need. At a later date, if the hardware and software products do not meet the agreed-upon needs of the purchaser, the vendor has breached the implied warranty and is responsible for damages. The purchaser, however, can only recover a certain portion of the sales price. An implied warranty of merchantability deals with the seller and/or vendor only if he or she is considered to be a merchant. Computer hardware and software vendors are considered to be merchants because they are in the business of selling these products on a continuous basis. The implied warranty of merchantability guarantees the purchaser that the hardware and software systems will operate properly for a reasonable period of time. If something goes wrong with the hardware or software products, within a reasonable period of time, the purchaser can recover part of the cost of the product, but must keep the defective products.

Express Warranties. An **express warranty** is created when the seller of a hardware or software product makes a promise or statement of fact about the performance of the product to the purchaser, and the purchaser uses this information when deciding to buy the product. Express warranties are included in Article II of the UCC. By making such an agreement with the purchaser, the seller is guaranteeing, or warranting, that the product will meet the needs of the purchaser. Express warranties are found in the written contract of sale in which the seller promises to replace products that are defective or will repair a product within a one-year period. An expressed warranty is in written form, and if a breach of contract occurs, the seller of the product must satisfy the damages sustained by the purchaser by lowering the original purchase price, but the purchaser must keep the product. Unless expressly stated in the contract, computer hardware and software products would not have to be replaced, just reduced in price.

Special Problems in Computer Law

Laws dealing with computer hardware and software products have been slow to evolve. This is due in part to a general ignorance about the computing industry. The computing industry is a relatively young industry, and it takes years to develop and write laws for complex environments. The laws that are presently in force in the United States to protect the computing industry against unjust actions and activities are much too general and somewhat weak in structure. There is a great need to develop new laws and modify existing laws to make them more specific and appropriate.

4. . . .The legislation concerning computer privacy and its implications?

5. . . .The issues concerning computer ethics?

6. . . .The kinds of computer crime?

7. . . .How crime prevention can be dealt with?

8. . . .What a copyright is, and what its primary use in the computer industry is?

9. . . .The two types of warranties?

10. . . .The overall situation of computer law today?

DO YOU REMEMBER

Summary

(This summary provides answers to DO YOU REMEMBER. . . questions in the chapter.)

1. **What are the two types of computer security?**
   The two types of computer security are *physical protection* from disasters and *data security.*

2. **What are the methods of establishing physical protection from disasters?**

The methods of establishing physical protection from disasters are *security measures* and *disaster recovery planning*.

3. **What are the methods of implementing data security?**

The methods of implementing data security are back-up data files, passwords for files, levels of data file access, internal security measures, data encryption, and detection devices.

4. **What is the legislation concerning personal privacy?**

The federally enacted *Privacy Act of 1974* was designed to protect an individual's personal privacy of data and information stored electronically in computer files inside and outside a computer.

5. **What are the issues concerning computer ethics?**

The issues concerning computer ethics are *software piracy and copying, hacking* (breaking computer security), and *employee loyalty*.

6. **What are the kinds of computer crime?**

The kinds of computer crimes are *sabotage, accounting and financial crimes, theft of physical property,* and *theft of computer services*.

7. **How can crime prevention be dealt with?**

Crime prevention can be dealt with using computer hardware, computer software, and people

8. **What is a copyright, and what is its primary use in the computer industry?**

A *copyright* is the registration of a person's written expression of a creative idea with the U.S. Copyright Office in Washington, D.C. In the computer industry, it is used to protect against the illegal copying of software packages

9. **What are the two types of warranties?**

The two types of warranties are *implied warranty* and *express warranty*.

10. **What is the overall situation of computer law today?**

There is a great need to develop new laws and modify existing laws to make them more specific and appropriate for the circumstances they will be used in.

DATA PROCESSING CAREER. . . . .
EDP Auditor

CAREER OPPORTUNITY FOR COMPUTER PROFESSIONAL

JOB TITLE:
EDP Auditor

JOB DESCRIPTION:
Applicant will be responsible for performing internal audits on electronic information systems. The results of audits will be communicated to management as written reports.

EXPERIENCE REQUIRED:
A minimum of three to five years on-the-job auditing experience required.

EDUCATION REQUIRED:
A B.S. degree with majors in Accounting and Business Information Systems.

PERSONAL QUALIFICATIONS:
Applicant must like to work closely with other people in various departments and management at all levels.

Figure 15–7
EDP auditor performing an audit.

Key Terms

back-up data files
common law
computer crime
computer privacy
computer security
computer services
copyright
crime prevention
data encryption
data file access
data security
decrypted
detection devices
disaster recovery planning
EDP auditor
encrypted
ethics
express warranty

hacker
hacking
implied warranty
implied warranty of fitness
implied warranty of
    merchantability
internal security measures
legislation
password
physical security
sabotage
security measures
software copying
software piracy
Uniform Commercial Code
    (UCC)
Warranty

Test Yourself

1. Security is the responsibility of all _____ within an organization, not just top _____ .

2. _____ security deals with providing a certain level of control over physical access to a computer center.

3. A _____ plan is a set of documents that describes how, where, when, and who should be involved in establishing a temporary computer center site in case of a disaster.

4. _____ deals with the controlled access of people to the data.

5. _____ deals with the translation of the normal data into a secret code.

6. The _____ conducts periodic audits and/ or examinations of security safeguards for electronic data processing systems.

7. Computer _____ and _____ are two major areas of concern for all business organizations.

8. Legislation concerning personal privacy was first enacted at the federal level of government with the _____ _____ of _____.

9. _____ deals with human variables and standards for moral conduct in computer usage within an organization.

10. Among the greatest problems in the computing industry today are software _____ and _____ by unethical persons.

11. _____ deals with the illegal entry of a person into a computer system for the purpose of breaking computer security and privacy locks on sensitive data and information.

12. _____ deals with an employee's obligations to an employer while in his/her employment.

13. _____ refers to causing or doing physical harm to the hardware and/or software.

14. _____ means taking specific measures to stop crimes before they occur.

15. _____ are the most important element in any system.

16. A _____ registers a person's written expression of a creative idea with the U.S. Copyright Office in Washington, D.C.

Review Questions

1. Explain the differences between physical security and software security. (Learning Objective 2)

2. Discuss the idea that an organization should take a planned approach to computer security. (Learning Objective 3)

3. Why are computer privacy and ethics two major areas of concern for all business organizations? (Learning Objectives 4 and 5)

4. Define hacking, piracy, and software copying. What kinds of problems are created by these three activities? (Learning Objective 6)

5. What are some methods of crime prevention? (Learning Objective 7)

6. Discuss the meanings of a copyright and a warranty. (Learning Objective 8)

Activities

1. Visit a computer center in your area to examine the security measures used and its disaster recovery plan. Write a short paper about your experience.

2. Visit your school's computer lab to see what type of data security is available for student data and program files. Make a list of the types or methods of data security used in the lab.

3. Obtain warranties for several different pieces of hardware and software to compare the wording and meaning of each. Determine if the warranties are valid.

CHAPTER 16

The Future

Learning Objectives

After studying this chapter carefully, you will be able to:

1. Define key terms introduced in the chapter.

2. Identify possible future computer uses in homes.

3. Identify possible future computer uses in schools.

4. Identify possible future computer uses in science and medicine.

5. Identify possible future computer uses in government.

6. Identify possible future computer uses in business, including manufacturing.

7. Briefly explain the meaning of the term *artificial intelligence* as it applies to computers.

8. Identify ways in which computerized robots might serve people in the future.

Chapter Outline

THE FUTURE IS NOW

FUTURE EXPECTATIONS
Computer Hardware
Computer Software
Computers in the Future
Artificial Intelligence and the Fifth Generation
Computer Literacy: Yesterday, Today, and
   Tomorrow!

DATA PROCESSING CAREER: Inventory
   Control Recorder

Application

Jason Rukovick's eighty-one-year-old mother, Mary, was coming to stay with her son's family while recovering from recent surgery. Doctors had cautioned Jason that his mother would need lots of rest in order to recover fully.

Jason's home was already equipped with a computerized monitoring system. A central control panel in the kitchen monitored doors and windows. An infrared camera in the hall, connected by cable to a monitor, could detect an intruder and alert the police automatically by telephone. The system also monitored and controlled household appliances and the central heating and cooling system.

Before his mother arrived from the hospital, Jason contacted the company that installed the system and told the owner, Gerald McKinney, that his mother would be living with the family while recovering from her surgery. Gerald suggested that Jason purchase a newly designed necklace for his mother. The necklace contained a button that, when pressed, activated a small circuit board in the central control panel in the kitchen (see Figure 16–1). When activated, the control panel alerted a nearby ambulance service via telephone. At Jason's request, Gerald immediately installed the new devices.

Several days later, while at home alone, Jason's mother walked to the mailbox, which was a few yards from the house. Returning to the house, she tripped and fell. Unable to get up, she remembered her son's instruction to press the button on her necklace if she needed help. She immediately pressed the button. Minutes later, an ambulance arrived bringing medical help.

Modern computer technology saved Mary Rukovick's life. Too futuristic? Actually, this advanced computer technology is now available.

The names in the story have been changed. However, the story is true, and illustrates the rapid advances being made in computer technology. In one sense, the future is with us now.

Figure 16–1
Gerald explains the features of the necklace and how it should be used by Jason's mother. Gerald explains that pressing the button will alert the emergency medical service.

The Future Is Now

Authors of computer-related articles and textbooks seem to enjoy speculating about the future. Charles McCabe of the *San Francisco Chronicle* once stated that "any clod can have the facts, but having an opinion is an art."

Making accurate predictions is difficult. Many authors have dared to take such risks. Some have had limited success, while others have failed miserably.

Interestingly, most failures have resulted from authors' inability to predict *when* technological advancements would be made, rather than from their inability to predict *what* advancements would be made. Actually, many earlier predictions have come true sooner than predicted. Based on these predictions, it may be said that we are already living in the future. Today, we are surrounded by computer hardware, software, and peripherals that, according to some earlier predictions, should not have been available for another several years.

Future Expectations

In the following sections, speculations will be made about future developments in the field of computing. Each prediction is based on research that is now under way or expected to begin soon. Thus, the predictions that follow are reasonable, and most, if not all, should eventually prove to be accurate. But then again, time alone will tell.

Computer Hardware

Modern computers have enormous capabilities that have resulted from **miniaturization**—that is, the technology that has made it possible to densely pack thousands of tiny electronic circuits together on silicon chips. Present and future research will result in **microminiaturization,** meaning that scientists are developing ways to pack even more circuits onto smaller and smaller chips. This technology will result in new computers that are smaller, faster, and much more powerful than those in existence today. Someday students may carry their own computer to and from school in a pocket or purse. These small computers will have even more capabilities than many personal computers now have. Similar computers will be used by people in their work and at home. Some will have built-in features such as word processing and communications capabilities. Others will have built-in language capabilities such as BASIC, FORTRAN, and Pascal. Potential applications will be limited only by the user's creative imagination. Improvements in production methods will make these computers affordable for most people.

Similar progress will be made with personal computers. By the 1990s, millions of personal computers found in homes today will be discarded. In their place will be personal computer systems having the same, or more, processing power and storage capabilities of many small mainframes in use today. AT&T has already announced a 1 megabyte RAM chip; IBM has made a similar announcement. It is believed that these chips will soon be available in personal computers. These powerful personal computers will be used in education, recreation, and other areas.

Another promising step toward increased computer storage and faster speed lies in the possible development of biologically grown and produced chips, called biochips. Theoretically, a **biochip** would consist of organic molecules assembled into tiny circuits. Should these molecule biochips actually be developed, their closeness and density would result in computers that contain much more storage and are several times faster. Although biochips exist only in theory, remember that theory can, and often does, become reality.

Large mainframe computers in the future will also be smaller, faster, and more powerful, with greater capabilities than present mainframes. Some computer experts predict that in the late 1990s a mainframe about 1 square foot in size may process over 80 million instructions per second. The cost of mainframe systems will also continue to decline. Advances will be made in both primary and secondary storage so that in the next decade, primary storage capacity could increase by as much as fifty times that contained in mainframes today. Optical disk will provide permanent and inexpensive secondary storage: one optical disk, already available, will contain as much data as thirty or more reels of magnetic tape.

Computer Software

A wave of recent technical articles contains predictions about computer hardware. Fewer articles, however, predict advances in computer software. Historically, advances in software have always lagged behind advances in hardware. The reason for this is that computers and other hardware devices must be designed and produced before software can be developed for these devices. The lag between hardware and software development is often a period of several months, and in some cases several years. In the next decade, however, important gains in computer software will be made.

Existing computer languages such as BASIC, FORTRAN, and Pascal will be enhanced with structured versions becoming available. New high-level software packages will be developed that will allow users to solve complex problems. The introduction of new user-friendly computer languages will simplify the writing of computer programs.

Important advancements will be made in existing integrated software packages. Improvements will be made in the integrated programs (word processing, spreadsheets, and graphics, for example). Also, some integrated software packages will be built into the computer's operating system.

Computers in the Future

During the past decade, a flood of computers, peripherals, and software has brought changes in human lifestyles, both private and public. Although it is a subject of debate as to whether all changes have been for the better, the fact that computers have become an important part of society cannot be denied. The following sections will focus on computer applications that will probably be developed during the next decade.

In Homes.   Some homes will be fully computerized by 1995. In these homes, computers will control elaborate security systems and energy-monitoring systems. Computer manufacturers and manufacturers of home furnishings, appliances, and fixtures are already merging their technologies. Together, these companies are designing and producing fascinating home appliances, furniture, and fixtures. For example, General Electric Corporation and American Standard Corporation are designing and building bathroom models with computer-controlled bathroom fixtures. Under control of the computer, the bathtub is automatically filled with water at the exact time and temperature selected by the user. The amount of moisture in the bathroom is controlled by the computer. The computer allows one to raise or lower the commode. Mirrors and windows are defogged by computer-controlled fans.

Today, **videodisk players** can be attached to television sets, enabling viewers to watch movies and other entertainment. The price of a video disk is about the same as the price of a stereo album or tape. Home computer systems in the future will merge videodisk players and powerful computers. This merger will provide users with interactive entertainment, hobby, and educational capabilities including computer programs, sound, and video. Someday, home delivery of videodisks may supplement or even replace newspapers and magazines.

The use of **videotext home systems** that emerged in the 1980s will increase. These systems link microcomputers or terminals with com-

```
CompuServe                    BUSINESS

BUSINESS/OTHER INTERESTS

1 Aviation
2 Business Management
3 Data Processing/MIS
4 Media Services
5 Engineering/Technology
6 Health Professions
7 Legal Services
8 Market Quotes/Highlights
9 Other Interests

Enter choice !
```

Figure 16–2
A videotext system. Subscribers to CompuServe can select from a wide variety of topics.

puterized databases to provide the user with access to information such as news and stock market reports. Notice the variety of topics contained in the videotext system illustrated in Figure 16–2. In the future, these databases will be expanded to provide users with a wealth of other information.

A large percentage of the population will use home computers as telecommuting stations, thus eliminating or reducing travel to and from the office. A **telecommuting station** is a designated location (such as a room in a home) containing the hardware and software needed by a telecommuter. Equipment for the station usually includes a microcomputer or terminal, a modem, and a telephone (see Figure 16–3). Telecommuting will create job opportunities for handicapped and elderly persons, thereby allowing society to benefit from these valuable human resources.

In Schools.   The same videodisk systems that will entertain and educate in the home in the next decade will also be used in schools. Their use will likely lead to the development of innovative educational software. Teachers will be able to prepare educational materials for students with different learning abilities. For homework assignments, students might take their videodisks home and use them on the home system. Private companies will develop challenging educational software materials in all subject areas. Software training programs now

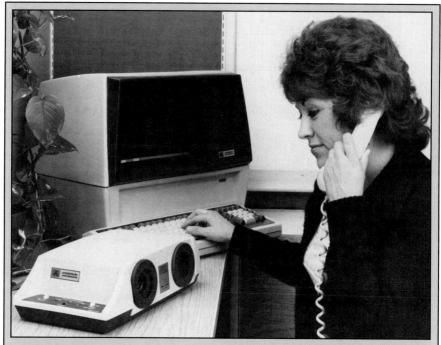

Figure 16–3
A telecommuting station. Many employees can do some, or all, of their work at home using a microcomputer or terminal, other special equipment, and a telephone.

being used by many companies will be adapted for classroom use.

The next decade will bring noticeable improvements in computer equipment (hardware) as well as software. The cost of computers and peripherals will continue to decline. This will enable schools to acquire additional equipment, and bring about changes in the content of computer courses as more students have access to computing equipment. Students will learn how to use the computer for all classes including business, science, art, and English. In the future, students will become more than just *computer literate*. They will become proficient at using this valuable problem-solving tool.

In Science and Medicine.   Potential scientific and medical computer applications are limitless. If advances made during the past decade are an indication, the future of computer technology is indeed mind-boggling.

By 1990, most doctors will have computer systems installed in their offices, and by 1995, most doctors will regularly use computer-as-

1. . . .What *microminiaturization* means and some potential results of this anticipated future technology?

2. . . .What a theoretical *biochip* will consist of, and two important future benefits of this technology, if developed?

3. . . .Some future advancements expected in computer software?

4. . . .Some possible future uses for computers in homes?

5. . . .Some possible future uses for computers in schools?

DO YOU REMEMBER

sisted diagnostic systems. Figure 16–4 shows a baby whose condition is being monitored by a computer.

By the end of the next decade, **microelectronic implants** in humans will control artificial organs such as hearts and kidneys. For some patients, microelectronic implants will restore sight, hearing, and speech.

Someday, computer technology will enable medical scientists to develop procedures for predicting serious illnesses such as cancer

Figure 16–4
A baby attached to a computerized medical monitor. The use of computers in medicine is expanding rapidly. This baby's condition is being monitored by a computerized medical monitor.

and heart attacks, and ways to prevent these and other dreaded diseases. Computer-assisted procedures will aid in the treatment of these diseases.

We can look forward to advances in other scientific fields. Improvements in computer-assisted weather forecasting equipment will result in more accurate long-range forecasts.

By the 1990s, scientists will have perfected ways to allow satellite communications between doctors at urban medical centers and persons living in remote areas. Medical aides living in remote areas will be able to provide medical treatment with information supplied by doctors using computer diagnostic equipment.

In Government.   The federal government is the largest single user of computers in the United States. All government agencies use computers for processing huge amounts of data.

The Internal Revenue Service (IRS), for example, uses computers to audit individual and business tax forms. Because of the large number of tax forms filed each year, the IRS cannot audit all of them. By 1995 however, the IRS will have computers capable of auditing all of the forms that are filed. These powerful new computers will reduce tax fraud by crosschecking information provided by taxpayers and information provided by financial institutions. On the other hand, new computers will make it possible for more taxpayers who overpaid their taxes to get refunds.

Computer-controlled robots are already being used to guard inmates at some prisons. Robots, generally defined as any computer-controlled device, are also used for many other purposes. Millions of automobiles and other products are now made with robotic welders. Robots assemble the parts of many products we buy and use, including refrigerators, televisions, and lawnmowers. As robotic technology improves, more robots will be used as prison guards. Maybe someday robots will keep track of inmates, search inmates and cells for prohibited materials and substances, and even train inmates in various rehabilitation programs.

In Business.   Modern computer technology that we now take for granted was undreamed of just a few years ago. During the past decade, however, many advances have been made in computer hardware, peripherals, and software. Much of this new hardware and software was designed and built for use by businesses—a trend likely to continue. This trend will bring about important changes in businesses, and in the products and services they produce.

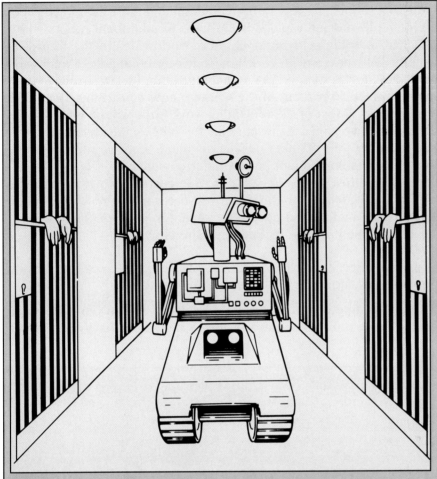

Figure 16–5
A robot guarding prisoners. Computerized robots may someday guard prisoners in their cells by detecting prisoner movements and sounds.

During the next decade, transferring money electronically will become more widespread in the banking industry. Using home computers (or terminals) and telephones, more people will pay their bills by notifying a bank to transfer money from their accounts to those of creditors. By 1990, it is expected that most banks will be connected to a computer network. The network will enable a bank to check a customer's current balance before cashing a check.

Most people already know that computers are used for designing and manufacturing products. In manufacturing, computer-controlled industrial robots are now rather common, and more advanced robots are being developed rapidly. Thousands of additional robots will be installed in manufacturing operations worldwide. In the future, assembly line workers will work alongside robots capable of assembling television and automobile components. Computer-controlled robots might replace 50 percent of the workers now performing small-component work. Most of the remaining work force will be highly skilled engineers and technicians responsible for keeping the automated plants operating. Within the next decade, as much as three-fourths of production technology might be computer controlled.

Soon, utilities companies that provide customers with telephones, electricity, water, and natural gas will use computers and telephone lines to test meters and check the condition of lines. They will also be able to use this new technology to read meters.

Artificial Intelligence and the Fifth Generation

The human-like computers found in science fiction don't exist currently, but fiction sometimes becomes fact. Scientists are trying to

Figure 16-6
Industrial robots in an automobile plant. To be competitive, more companies will use more computer controlled industrial robots to perform repetitive operations like the ones shown here.

THE COMPUTER DIDN'T DO IT!

In the early 1970s, a married couple was having domestic problems. The wife, director of the local draft board, often complained that her husband never helped her with their small children, refused to help with household chores, drank too much, and was cruel to the children and to her. In desperation, she entered her husband in the computer and he was drafted into military service. Revenge comes in different forms!

discover ways in which computers can be used to solve problems that can now be solved only with human intelligence. Using computers to solve problems with human-like intelligence is called **artificial intelligence (AI).** AI combines concepts from such disciplines as psychology, logic, and computer science. Scientists are attempting to learn how to develop computer systems and software programs that can perform tasks never before performed by machines.

Limited success has already been achieved in developing **expert systems.** These software packages include (1) a stored base of knowledge (information) in a specialized area, such as geology, and (2) the ability to probe this knowledge base and make decision recommendations.

As an example, geologists using a computer and an expert system known as **Prospector** were able to locate a rich deposit of molybdenum ore buried deep under Mount Tolman in eastern Washington. They were guided by a computer located more than a hundred miles away. Before this, geologists had tried for more than sixty years to locate the ore.

Present AI applications are limited, but potential applications are not. A joint effort is under way by the Japanese government and several private Japanese companies to develop advanced AI technology. Billions of dollars are being spent for research and development by the Japanese and by American businesses. If successful, the following ''science fiction'' activities might become a reality, and a new **fifth generation** of computers will emerge.

Your artificially intelligent robot defeats you in a game of ''Trivial Questions,'' or plays a game of chess with you (see Figure 16–7). It informs you, in advance, of the final score of a football game you plan to attend that afternoon. Your robot checks your answers for an algebra homework assignment and reminds you about your dental appointment on Thursday. An artificially intelligent computer provides investment bankers with suggestions and information about

Figure 16–7
A human and a robot playing a chess game.

investments that yield the highest return. AI computers help police officers apprehend criminals by analyzing their habits and activity patterns. The potential applications are virtually unlimited.

Many experts are optimistic about the future of artificial intelligence and expert systems. Progress has been slow, but the potential for success is encouraging.

Computer Literacy: Yesterday, Today, and Tomorrow

Many schools now offer courses in **computer literacy** in which students are introduced to computers, their applications, their limitations, and their social impact. Initially, some schools began offering computer literacy courses before actually having computers for students to use. Students were limited to learning what computers are and what impact they have had on society.

The students' inability to use computers severely limited their learning about computers. Many students completed a computer literacy course without ever using a computer, and some without ever seeing one.

The introduction of microcomputers has, of course, brought about changes in computer literacy courses. Most schools now have computers, and students can obtain hands-on experience. Many computer literacy courses now include some programming. Students gain practical experience using prewritten software packages such as word processing, filing, and graphics packages. They are also acquiring problem-solving skills that help them in other subjects.

Some large schools have added additional courses to the computer curriculum. Specialized computer courses such as programming, word processing, and graphics are offered in some schools. No doubt, the list of courses will continue to grow.

Many computer experts believe that the term *computer literacy* now has a different meaning. No longer can a person be considered "computer literate" if his or her knowledge is limited to what computers are and what impact they have had on society. In addition, one who is computer literate should also be able to use a computer as a problem-solving tool. The level of user proficiency will, of course, vary among individuals according to their needs. An office worker, for example, might need more computer knowledge than would a truck driver.

We have seen that computer technology is advancing rapidly, and, in the future, computer use will expand greatly. Education must keep pace with the growing technology. Some schools are expanding computer programs to train students in specialized computer uses such as computerized drafting, accounting, and art. Someday, the computer literate will be those who are well-trained and highly skilled in the use of computers to further their career goals.

---

6. . . .Some possible future uses for computers in science and medicine?

7. . . .Some possible future uses for computers in government?

8. . . .The meaning of the terms *artificial intelligence* and *expert systems?*

9. . . .The modern meaning of the expression *computer literacy?*

DO YOU REMEMBER

DATA PROCESSING CAREER. . . . .
Inventory Control Recorder

CAREER OPPORTUNITY FOR COMPUTER PROFESSIONAL

JOB TITLE:
Inventory Control Recorder

JOB DESCRIPTION:
Large national inventory control corporation is currently seeking high school graduates to train on the job as inventory control recorders. The job consists of working in various locations for clients, recording inventory information by using a handheld micro data recorder device. Persons hired will work along with three to five other people in a team environment. Some travel will be necessary between client locations.

EXPERIENCE REQUIRED:
None

EDUCATION REQUIRED:
A high school diploma

PERSONAL QUALIFICATIONS:
Applicants must be able to produce high-quality and accurate results, enjoy working in a team environment, and be neat in appearance, responsible, and dependable.

Summary

(This summary provides answers to DO YOU REMEMBER . . . questions in the chapter.)

1. **What does *microminiaturization* mean, and what are some potential results of this anticipated technology?**
   Microminiaturization refers to the efforts of scientists to develop ways to pack even more circuits onto smaller and smaller chips. If perfected, this new technology will result in the production of computers that are smaller, faster, and much more powerful than present computers.

2. **What will a theoretical *biochip* consist of, and what are two important future benefits of this technology, if developed?**
   A *biochip* will consist of biological molecules assembled into tiny circuits. The density and closeness of the molecules will result in computers that are much *faster* and *contain more storage capacity* than present computers.

3. **What future advancements are expected to be made in computer software?**

   Several advancements in software are expected, including enhancements in computer languages, structured versions of existing languages, new user-friendly computer languages, new high-level programs for solving complex problems, and more integrated software packages (some of which will be built into the operating systems).

4. **What are some possible future uses for computers in homes?**

   Computers will control elaborate security systems and energy-monitoring systems. Technologies will be merged in the areas of computing and home furnishings and appliances. The merger of powerful computers and videodisk players will provide users with interactive entertainment, hobby, and educational capabilities. Large databases will provide users with a variety of information. Many people will use computers for telecommuting.

5. **What are some possible future uses for computers in schools?**

   The same videodisk systems that will be used in homes will also be used in schools to prepare educational software and other materials. Private companies will develop challenging educational materials in all subject areas. The cost of computers and peripherals will decline significantly, making them more affordable to more schools. In the future, students will become proficient at using computers.

6. **What are some possible future uses for computers in science and medicine?**

   By 1990, most physicians will have computers in their offices for aid in computer-assisted diagnosis and treatment. In the future, microelectronic implants in humans will control organs and even restore sight, hearing, and speech for some patients. Computers will be used for the detection and treatment of serious illnesses such as cancer and heart disease. Computers will result in improved weather forecasting methods and make possible the treatment of patients in remote areas.

7. **What are some possible future uses for computers in government?**

   By 1995, the Internal Revenue Service expects to be able to audit all tax returns by computer. Computer-controlled robots will guard prison inmates and be capable of searching prison cells and prisoners for prohibited materials and substances. These robots also might be involved in rehabilitation programs for inmates.

8. **What are the meanings of the terms *artificial intelligence* and *expert system?***

   Artificial intelligence refers to the use of computers for solving problems, with human-like intelligence. An *expert system* is an accompanying software package for AI that includes (1) a stored base of knowledge (information) in a specialized area, and (2) the ability to probe this knowledge base and make decision recommendations.

9. **According to many experts, what is the modern meaning of the term *computer literacy?***

   Computer literacy now implies that a person is able to use a computer as a problem-solving tool. The level of proficiency will vary among individuals according to their needs.

Key Terms

artificial intelligence (AI)   microminiaturization
biochip   miniaturization
computer literacy   telecommuting station
expert system   videodisk system
integrated software   videotext home system
microelectronic implant

Test Yourself

1. Present and future research will result in _____ , meaning that scientists are developing ways to pack more circuits onto smaller chips.

2. Future computers will be smaller, faster, and much more _____ than those in existence today.

3. Both AT&T and IBM recently announced the production of a _____ RAM chip.

4. New _____ software packages will combine important functions such as word processing, electronic spreadsheets, and graphics that will be built into the computer's operating system.

5. Home computer systems in the future will merge computers with _____ players to provide users with interactive entertainment, hobby, and educational capabilities including sound and video.

6. More people will use home computers as a _____ station, eliminating travel to and from the office. This will create new job opportunities for the elderly and the handicapped.

7. By the end of the next decade, _____ implants in humans will control artificial organs and restore sight, hearing, and speech in some patients.

8. Computer-controlled _____ are already being used to guard inmates in some prisons. In the future, these devices might also be used to search inmates and prison cells.

9. _____ refers to the potential of computers to solve problems with human-like intelligence. The accompanying software is called _____ systems.

10. Many schools now offer courses in _____ . In the future, the content of these courses will probably change in order that students might become more skilled in computer use that will further their career goals.

Review Questions

1. Why do the authors of this textbook suggest that, in one sense, the future is now?

2. What are some possible future computer uses in homes? (Learning Objective 2)

3. What are some possible future computer uses in schools? (Learning Objective 3)

4. How will computers be used in science and medicine in the future? (Learning Objective 4)

5. What are some possible future computer uses in government. (Learning Objective 5)

6. Identify some possible future computer uses in business, including manufacturing. (Learning Objective 6)

7. What is *artificial intelligence?* Do you believe that it is possible to develop this kind of technology? Are there "social issues" that should be considered? If so, what are they? (Learning Objective 7)

8. What are some ways that computerized robots may serve people in the future. (Learning Objective 8)

Activities

1. Magazines and newspapers frequently contain articles describing new and innovative computer technology (both hardware and software). Visit your school and/or local library and find at least three articles that describe newly developed hardware and/or software. Prepare a brief written report about each development to turn in to your teacher or present to your class.

2. Select an area in which you have a particular interest, such as business, weather forecasting, entertainment, or the space program. Using magazines, newspapers, or perhaps by writing letters, obtain information concerning the use of computers in the area you select. Prepare a five-minute class presentation to share what you learn with the class.

3. Write to a computer hardware or software company. Request information about new products being planned or developed. From the information you receive, prepare a written report to turn in to your teacher.

MODULE A

A Guide to Selecting and Evaluating a Microcomputer System

Learning Objectives

After studying this module carefully, you will be able to:

1. Define key terms introduced in the module.

2. Identify the initial considerations before purchasing a microcomputer system.

3. Determine software requirements, availability, and cost for a microcomputer system.

4. Determine hardware requirements, availability, and cost for a microcomputer system.

5. Identify other hardware devices that are used with a microcomputer system.

6. Identify the basic characteristics in selecting a dealer to buy from.

7. Identify the people considerations in purchasing a microcomputer system.

Module Outline

Application

The process of choosing a microcomputer to buy should be taken very seriously by the buyer. This process will involve evaluating many different software and hardware components before selecting the best combination to meet a specific buyer's needs. Good front-end advice to new potential buyers is "buyers beware" of the many different types of software and hardware components available in the marketplace today. Test out and evaluate all software and hardware under consideration before making a selection (see Figure A-1). This is the buyer's responsibility. Know what the software and hardware can and cannot do, and be sure that the software and hardware under consideration will help solve your problems and meet your specific needs.

The following sections deal with how to select and evaluate a microcomputer system. How does a person minimize the risk of choosing the wrong microcomputer system? Let's examine the procedures you should be aware of before buying a microcomputer system.

Figure A–1
A buyer in a computer store.

Initial Considerations

A potential buyer of a microcomputer system should consider a great deal of information before investing in a computer. A good way to obtain much of the information you will need for selecting and evaluating a computer would be to talk to people who already have microcomputers. These people will usually be pleased to give you their opinions on the strengths and weaknesses of their computer systems, and what to look out for before you buy your first computer. What they have already learned will help you gain knowledge about purchasing a computer.

Why Do You NEED a Computer?

The first question to ask yourself is why you need a computer. This is a very important point to consider before any further purchasing decisions are made. A microcomputer can be used for many different purposes, and you must decide what purposes are included in your needs assessment. It might be that you want to use the microcomputer to do word processing or electronic spreadsheet analysis, or perhaps you might want to use the computer primarily to play games. The purposes you have in mind will determine what type of microcomputer you will need. Determining user need is of utmost importance, and will minimize your risk of making the wrong decision.

How Much Do You Plan to Pay?

Once you have determined why you need a microcomputer, then you must decide how much you plan to pay. The two basic categories of microcomputers are personal (less complex units usually costing less than $1,000) and professional (more complex units costing between $1,000 and $15,000 or more).

A potential purchaser must know how much money he or she has available to spend for a microcomputer. After considering budget information, then you must determine how sophisticated the microcomputers that fall within your budget are.

How Sophisticated a System Is Needed?

The personal microcomputer is often a self-contained, one-piece unit with the central processing unit (CPU), the keyboard, diskette drive(s), and video display attached to each other in one cabinet. Other personal microcomputers are made up of separate parts that are attached to each other through appropriate interface cables. Some lower-priced personal microcomputers might consist of only the CPU and keyboard as one unit. The user would then have to use a TV set as the video monitor. Secondary storage devices, such as cassette tape drives and diskette drives would also have to be attached to the computer as separate add-on peripherals.

The professional microcomputer is a more sophisticated and powerful system than the personal microcomputer. Generally, the CPU, video monitor, printer, and disk drives are purchased as separate peripheral devices. In many professional microcomputers, two diskette drives are built into the CPU cabinet and are accessible from the front side. There are many add-on peripheral devices available for professional microcomputers. The professional microcomputer is normally used in a small business environment, but could also be used by individuals as personal computers, or by large corporations as stand-alone systems or smart terminals that interface with the corporate mainframe computers.

After you have familiarized yourself with what makes up a microcomputer system and what types are available, then you must familiarize yourself with what software (programs) is available to meet your needs. Software considerations should always come before hardware selection.

What Kind of Software Is Needed?

The basic reason that software should be considered first is that user software requirements will determine what hardware will be necessary. Most software is developed to run on a particular microcomputer and cannot be used on another type of microcomputer unless it is rewritten. You must research what software is available for the different microcomputers you have under consideration. If to meet your needs, you require a specific word processing package and/or an electronic spreadsheet analysis package, you must determine if these software packages exist for the particular microcomputers you are considering. There may be several word processing and/or electronic spreadsheet analysis software packages available for a particular microcomputer, and you need to examine each package and compare the advantages and disadvantages of each.

Software evaluation and selection should be given ample time and consideration. Remember, what you choose and buy will be what you have to live with for the life of your equipment. Check out all the details before purchasing.

What Kind of Hardware Is Needed to Support Your Software Needs?

After you have considered your software requirements, it is time to consider specific hardware configurations that will run the software you have chosen. There are two types of computer software that must be considered when determining hardware needs. These are Operating Systems (OS) software that tells the microcomputer what to do, and applications software that solves a particular user's problem. The hardware that makes up a basic microcomputer system is the keyboard, the central processing unit, a video display terminal, a printer, and a secondary storage device.

There are other peripheral devices that can be bought and attached to a microcomputer, such as, for instance, a plotter, audio response unit, secondary storage devices, and joysticks. The basic components are described in more detail later on. Figure A–2 illustrates the components of complete microcomputer systems.

Should You Buy Now or Buy Later?

When you decide you need a microcomputer in your business or personal life, it is probably wise to go ahead and purchase one, even knowing that the machine you buy today will become cheaper and better in the future. During the time you wait for a microcomputer to come down in price, you do not have the benefit of its use in the interim period of time. This might end up causing you frustration, and it might cost you money, especially if you are going to use the microcomputer to help in your business.

Clearly, the longer you wait to purchase, the longer it will be before you can gain experience and expertise with microcomputing. If you have a need for a microcomputer and you can justify your needs, then you can feel comfortable with your decision to purchase now.

Determine Software Requirements, Availability, and Cost

Once you have studied the initial considerations, it is time to determine software requirements, availability, and cost. It is recommended that you consider software and hardware together. There can be many microcomputers that will run the software you have chosen to meet

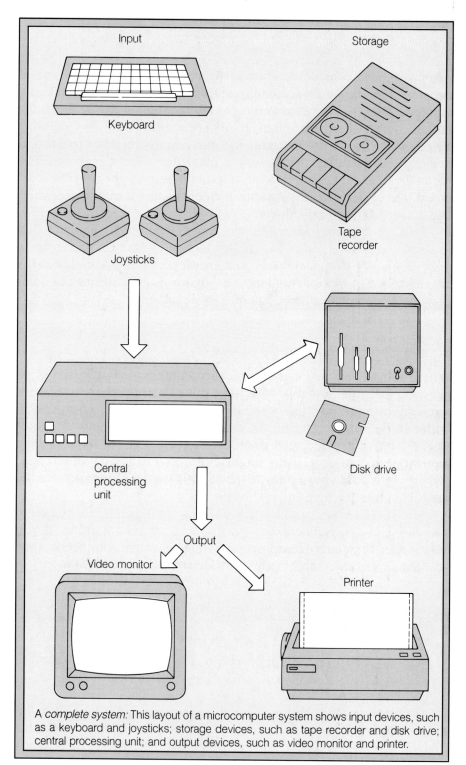

A *complete system:* This layout of a microcomputer system shows input devices, such as a keyboard and joysticks; storage devices, such as tape recorder and disk drive; central processing unit; and output devices, such as video monitor and printer.

your needs, or, on the other hand, there might be only one micro-computer that will run that software.

When thinking about purchasing a microcomputer, the first thing you should understand about microcomputer software is that stand-ardization does not exist. What will run on one microcomputer will probably not run on another because every machine has its own unique characteristics. There are two types of software you should consider: the operating system software and the applications software.

Operating System Software Needs

Operating system software deals with a particular microcomputer's internal system operations. Operating system software determines what applications software you can run on your microcomputer. The differences in operating systems throughout the microcomputing in-dustry causes a great deal of double effort in having to develop the same application programs for many different types of microcom-puters. This is due to the lack of compatibility and standardization in operating systems in the microcomputing industry.

The two most popular operating systems for microcomputers are MicroSoft Disk Operating System (MS-DOS) and Control Program for Microcomputers (CP/M). These two operating systems have had a great deal of applications software written for them. In fact, both have approximately 10,000 available applications programs. Many microcomputers can run more than one operating system. The Texas Instruments Professional Microcomputer, for example, can run four different operating systems (MS-DOS, CP/M, CP/M-86, and p-Sys-tem). The MS-DOS operating system is fast becoming a standard for 16-bit business professional microcomputers. Be careful when con-sidering the operating system(s) for your microcomputer. The oper-ating system is the "brains" of your machine.

Vendor-Supplied Applications Software

When considering applications software you must consider two ways to acquire it. One way is to write it yourself, and the other is to

Figure A–2
A complete system. This layout of a microcomputer system shows input devices, such as a keyboard and joy sticks; storage de-vices, such as tape recorder and disk drive; central processing unit; and output devices, such as video monitor and printer.

purchase already developed vendor-supplied application packages. When you are examining a software package in a microcomputer retail store, such as a game, word processing program, or electronic spreadsheet analysis program, be sure to check what kind of hardware it requires. Normally in the documentation for the software package there will be a page or two devoted to hardware requirements for that particular package. This information may be posted on the outside cover of the binder that holds the documentation.

There are many vendor-supplied application software packages available from prices as low as under twenty dollars to well in the thousands. Before buying any software package, be sure that it is demonstrated to you on the type of hardware you plan to purchase. Ask the salesperson to show and explain all the ordinary and special features of the package. Try it out for yourself to be sure that you understand it and that it will meet your needs. Figure A–3 lists several popular software packages and a comment about each package.

Popular Business Application Software Packages

Rank	Product	Company	Comments
1.	1–2–3	Lotus Development Corp. Cambridge, Mass.	Combines spreadsheet with graphics and database. This integrated product includes limited word processing features.
2.	Wordstar	Micropro International Corp. San Rafael, Calif.	The "Cadillac" of word processing programs. It's known for its sophisticated features that can handle the most demanding scientific writing.
3.	dBase III Plus	Ashton-Tate Culver City, Calif.	This database program demands a lot of user interaction. Nevertheless, it's still leading the pack in this software class.
4.	MultiMate	Softword Systems East Hartford, Conn.	A word processing package that has used some ideas from dedicated word processing minicomputers.

5.	PFS:File	Software Publishing Corp. Mountain View, Calif.	A data handler that allows the user to set up a structured filing system of his or her own design.
6.	MultiPlan	Microsoft, Inc. Bellevue, Wash.	This electronic spreadsheet has become a classic package.
7.	PFS:Write	Software Publishing Corp. Mountain View, Calif.	A simple-to-use integrated word processing program that works well with the PFS data handler program.
8.	VisiCalc	VisiCorp San Jose, Calif.	The original electronic spreadsheet. It allows the user to examine many "what if" questions a business is likely to have.
9.	WordPerfect	Satellite Software International Orem, Utah	A relatively simple-to-use, moderately sophisticated word processing program that provides a broad range of printing capabilities.
10.	PFS:Report	Software Publishing Corp. Mountain View, Calif.	A report generator capable of being used with PFS:File.

Figure A–3
Application software packages.

User-Written Applications Software

Many users of microcomputers wish to write their own applications programs. If this is the case for you, then you must decide what computer language(s) you will need for writing your applications programs. The most common computer language used for microcomputers is Beginner's All-purpose Symbolic Instruction Code (BASIC). BASIC is the most popular language used on microcomputers, but some microcomputers have COmmon Business-Oriented Language (COBOL), FORmula TRANslator (FORTRAN), Assembly, and Pascal languages available.

Once you have decided on the computer programming language you will need, then it is time to develop and write the applications software to solve your problems. This process can take a long time, but the results are programs that will solve your specific problems. You should give deep consideration to whether you should write your own applications software or buy applications software packages. If you can find a software package that comes close to meeting your need, it might be more cost-effective to buy the software package. Most users of microcomputers find themselves developing and writing some of their applications software and buying some applications software packages.

DO YOU REMEMBER

1. . . .The initial considerations when considering a microcomputer system?

2. . . .The three types of software for which software requirements, availability, and cost should be determined?

Determine Hardware Requirements, Availability, and Cost

After software has been considered then it is time to chose the hardware that will run that software. You must decide on the hardware configuration that will best meet your needs. The basic hardware components that make up a microcomputer system are a keyboard, video display, central processsing unit (CPU), secondary storage device, and printer.

Keyboard

The keyboard for a microcomputer system might or might not be attached to the system unit. Many people prefer a detachable keyboard because this flexibility allows the keyboard to be positioned in many different ways to suit the user's needs. Be sure to examine the keyboard with respect to the number of keys it has. Usually, the more keys a keyboard has, the more flexibility you will have. Also, examine the number of function keys, usually found on the top row or left side of the keyboard. Most 16-bit microcomputers will have ten to twelve function keys. In order to use these function keys, the user must have software that will utilize them. They are actually programmed through a particular software package to carry out specific functions within that package. Twenty function keys would probably be too many, for only ten or less out of the twenty would ever be used.

Check to be sure that the keyboard has keys that control the cursor (that little, usually blinking, square on your CRT screen), so you can move it around on the CRT surface freely. Many keyboards have a cursor keypad (see Figure A–4). The cursor keypad normally consists of five keys—home, left, right, top, and bottom—and these keys relate to the direction and position of the cursor on the screen. A second type of keypad is the numeric keypad. The numeric keypad makes it very convenient to enter numeric data. All keys are positioned together in a convenient manner for fast and easy use. The cursor and the numeric keypad are used to speed up and improve the accuracy of data entry.

Because you will be sitting in front of your keyboard for hours at a time, comfort is important. The ergonomic design should be taken into consideration as you examine the keyboard. Many keyboards have been designed around the IBM Selectric typewriter keyboard

Figure A–4
Microcomputer with detachable keyboard.

layout. Check to see that the keyboard is height adjustable. Examine the pitch and angle of the keys on the keyboard. Check the keys to be sure they are concave-shaped so that your fingers will fit on them comfortably without sliding off. The keyboard should have a low profile and a palm rest. Also, there should be an audible click when a key is depressed, and the operator should be able to turn this sound on and off. A keyboard with these features will reduce operator fatigue, and is worth the investment.

The keyboard is a very important component of a microcomputer system. Remember, the keyboard is the component you use to communicate with your microcomputer, so it should be easy and convenient to use.

Video Monitor

The video monitor is referred to as a video display terminal (VDT) or a cathode ray tube (CRT). It is similar to a television screen, but usually has better resolution for displaying characters of data and graphics. The screen can be a full-color or a monochrome (white, amber, or green) screen displaying letters and images on a black background. The monitor can be a specially designed unit used solely for microcomputer video display of data and graphics, or it can be an actual television screen. Many persons choose to use their television sets as a video monitor, especially if they are purchasing a lower-priced microcomputer system. Monitors range considerably in price, depending on their quality and features. Let us examine in more detail some of the basic characteristics of video monitors that you must be aware of and consider before buying one.

You want to consider whether the video monitor can, like the one illustrated in Figure A–5, be tilted, raised or lowered, and turned to minimize glare and provide the best viewing angle. In addition to positioning, consideration must also be given to the color of display (full-color, white, amber, green). Color screens are easier on the user's eyes than white screens, and if you plan to display graphics on your video display, a full-color screen is more desirable for displaying charts, such as bar charts and pie charts.

Readability is a another important factor to consider in video monitors. Questions you should ask include how large are the characters displayed on the screen, what size is the screen, and how many characters can be contained on the screen's surface? The minimum number of characters should be 80 across (horizontally) and 24 lines down (vertically).

Figure A–5
A video monitor. *Movability:* Many video displays tilt and swivel so that your neck does not have to.

Another important consideration is the physical size of the video monitor. You would want to determine how much space on your desk or work area the monitor will take. While some monitors sit on top of the system unit, saving desktop space, other monitors are built into the system unit itself. The detachable monitor normally has cables that attach to the system unit for video input/output and power supply. Be sure the cables are long enough to allow you to position the monitor somewhere else on the desk or work area without being unnecessarily restricted. The cables should be a minimum of 6 feet in length to allow for maximum flexibility in positioning.

Examine the video monitor for capabilities, such as **bit addressable graphics** for displaying charts on the screen. Ask whether the screen works with a light pen and whether it is touch (pressure) sensitive. If you desire to add these features later, will the video monitor have the capability?

These are some of the basic considerations and characteristics that should be taken into account when looking at video monitors. The video monitor is an important component of a microcomputer system. Remember, you might be sitting in front of the video monitor for hours at a time. Thus, it needs to be easy and comfortable to use.

The Central Processing Unit (CPU)

The central processing unit (CPU) is the heart of a microcomputer system. The choice you make about the CPU will determine what you can and cannot do with your computer. Also, the ability to add other peripheral devices to your microcomputer is determined by the type of CPU you choose.

Type of Processor.   The microcomputing industry started out with an 8-bit processor. The processor has served its users well over the years. Thousands of microcomputers have been sold, by hundreds of hardware vendors, with 8-bit microprocessors in them, and the 8-bit microprocessor is still a popular choice. If you are not going to use your microcomputer for commercial applications, but rather for personal use, an 8-bit microcomputer would probably meet your needs. The newer microcomputers have 16-bit microprocessors installed in them. The more bits a microprocessor has, the more power it has. More bits also mean a larger instruction set, and a faster processing speed. A 16-bit microprocessor has more capability and capacity than an 8-bit processer, but it costs more. The same basic application programs can be run on an 8-bit microcomputer as on a 16-bit microcomputer. The major difference in the two types of microprocessors is speed. The 16-bit microcomputer runs the application programs much faster. Notice the microprocessor on a chip in Figure A–6.

Some of the new microcomputers have **coprocessors** installed in them. For example, they may have both an 8-bit and a 16-bit microprocessor contained within the system unit. This allows the user to have access to, and be able to run, thousands of 8-bit and 16-bit prepackaged programs. A microcomputer with coprocessors is not practical for personal use, but it could be practical in a business environment.

The **system unit** is the box that contains the microprocessor, primary memory, the power cord, slots for expansion (parallel and serial ports), floppy disk drives and/or hard-disk drive, graphics plane boards, data communications board, disk drive controller, and internal clock. You want a microcomputer that is expandable, so when your needs change you can add capacity to your microcomputer, or take capacity away. You should be able to add additional primary memory to your microcomputer easily. Be sure your microcomputer can grow with you as your needs change.

Type of Primary Memory.   There are two types of internal memory to consider for your microcomputer. The primary memory for your microcomputer is called Random Access Memory (RAM). This is

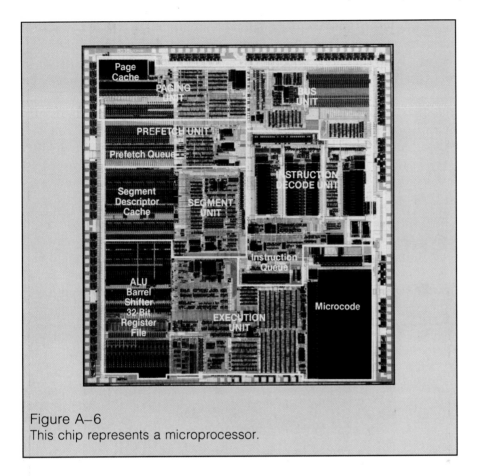

Figure A–6
This chip represents a microprocessor.

where all data is stored temporarily as the processing functions are being carried out by the CPU. Physically, RAM is contained on the microprocessor chip. Another type of internal memory is called Read Only Memory (ROM). This memory can have program instructions in it to carry out certain internal functions, such as instructions to "boot" the system. You can only read from ROM; you cannot write to ROM. This means the user cannot modify the contents of ROM. The contents of RAM can be modified, and usually are, as program execution progresses. Figure A–7 illustrates the basic types of primary memory.

Size of Primary Memory.   After determining the type(s) of primary memory you need for your microcomputer, you should consider and determine how much memory you will need. Memory size is measured in K's. The character K stands for kilo (one-thousand). Usually, memory size is expressed in increments of 2K. In computer mathematics,

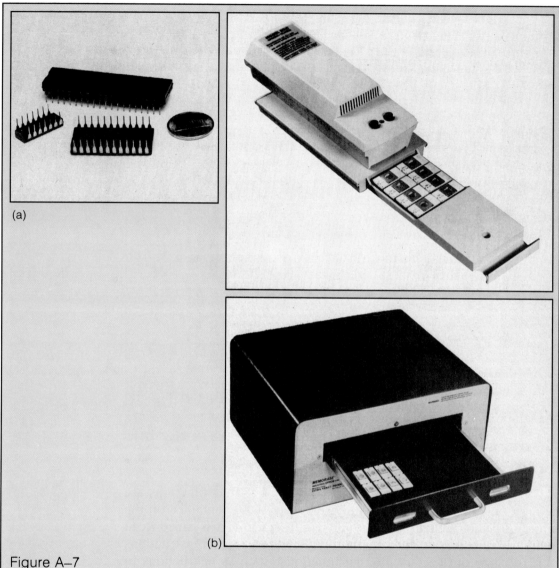

(a)

(b)

Figure A–7
Types of primary memory. (a) ROM and RAM microprocessor chips. (b) Examples of devices for erasing EPROM chips. A high-intensity ultraviolet light source is used for fast erasure of bit patterns.

a kilo is actually 1,024 characters/bytes. The memory size you will need is determined by the software you plan to use. Many prepackaged software solutions require a minimum of 16K of primary memory in which to run. Many sophisiticated software packages require 64K to 256K, or more, of memory. You must be very careful to determine your software needs before determining primary memory size. Many microcomputers will allow you to upgrade memory to accommodate your needs. Remember, all microcomputers are different, and again the buyer must beware. Upgrading primary memory normally involves installing additional memory boards and/or chips. The idea is to buy enough primary memory to run the applications programs you want to run, plus have some to spare.

Secondary Storage

Most users of microcomputer systems have secondary storage capacity for storing data files and program files not stored in primary memory. Secondary storage can be in the form of cassette tape, diskette, or hard disk. All three types can be used by a single user depending on a particular user's needs. Let's examine in more detail these three types of secondary storage.

Cassette Tape Storage.   This type of secondary storage was the first used for microcomputers. The cassette tape is still used today, mostly on lower-priced microcomputers. It is an inexpensive and reliable storage medium, good for backing up on-line disk files. Data is stored on the surface of the tape in magnetic spots according to a predetermined coding scheme. Files are organized sequentially, meaning that the data records are recorded in sequence, one after the other. Files on cassette tape are also accessed sequentially, meaning that the data records must be read one at a time in sequence. Without random access to the data records stored on cassette tape, it takes longer to find specific data records needed for processing. The hardware device used with cassette tape is a standard cassette tape recorder/player (see Figure A–8). It works basically the same way an audio recorder/player works.

Cassette tape secondary storage does allow you to store and retrieve data files and program files that you have created for specific applications. Appropriate consideration should be given to this secondary storage medium by first-time microcomputer purchasers.

Diskette Storage.   This type of secondary storage is sometimes referred to as floppy disk, flexible disk, and diskette (see Figure A–9). Diskettes are available in three basic sizes which are 8-inch, $5\frac{1}{4}$-inch, and $3\frac{1}{2}$-inch. The size you see being used most of the time is the $5\frac{1}{4}$-inch diskette. The 8-inch diskette was the first to be developed and marketed for microcomputers and word processing systems. The second type to be developed and marketed was the $5\frac{1}{4}$-inch mini-floppy

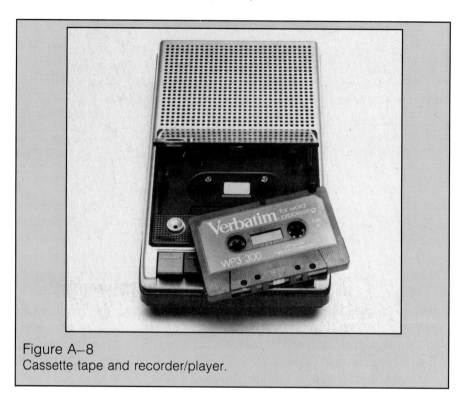

Figure A—8
Cassette tape and recorder/player.

diskette. The third type were the 3-inch, $3\frac{1}{4}$-inch, $3\frac{1}{2}$-inch micro-floppy diskettes. The microcomputer industry has not decided on a standard size for the third type, and all three of the third type are being marketed at this time.

Data is stored on the surface of a diskette as magnetic spots. The data is stored in tracks that are concentric circles running around the diskette surface. The files on a diskette are normally organized in an indexed-sequential, and/or direct, order. This means that the data is stored on the surface in no particular predetermined sequence. Diskette files are accessed randomly, and the data is stored and retrieved in random order as needed.

The hardware device used to store and retrieve the data files and program files from diskette is called a diskette drive. A diskette can be placed into the diskette drive by the user, at which time the diskette is ready to be used. Some diskette drives are built into the system unit, and others are separate units attached to the system unit with an interface cable. A $5\frac{1}{4}$-inch diskette can hold approximately 140 to 150 single-spaced typed pages of information. Diskette secondary storage is reliable and fast.

Figure A–9
Types of diskettes.

Hard-Disk Storage.   This type of secondary storage medium is some-times referred to as a winchester disk. A hard disk can hold large amounts of data, as much as 10–140 megabytes. As with diskettes, the files on hard disks are normally organized in an indexed-sequen-tial, and/or direct, order and are accessed, stored, and retrieved randomly.

The hardware device used with a hard disk storage system is called a disk drive. The hard-disk platters can either be fixed on the drive and not removable, or placed into a disk pack and removable from the disk drive (see Figure A–10). The fixed-disk approach allows for larger amounts of data to be stored on the disk platters. Also, data can be accessed more quickly on a fixed-disk than on a removable disk. On the other hand, removable disk packs give the user the added flexibility of more data storage capacity. Both the fixed disks and the removable disks are reliable and faster than diskettes for secondary storage, but they are more expensive.

Hard-disk storage allows the user to have on-line a large amount of secondary storage for storing data files and program files. If you are anticipating using complex applications software packages, then a hard disk storage system might be a major consideration in your microcomputer choice and purchase.

Figure A–10
A hard-disk drive that uses a 30-megabyte hard disk.

3. . . .The basic hardware components for which hardware requirements, availability, and cost should be considered?

4. . . .The basic hardware components that make up a microcomputer system?

Printers

Hardcopy output devices are another major decision when thinking about the purchase of a microcomputer system. There are many types of printers that produce varying degrees of hardcopy quality. The cost of printers varies considerably. As a first-time microcomputer buyer, you will probably deal with a price in the middle range. In this range, you can get a very good printer that will meet most of your needs for hardcopy output. The speed, reliability, and quality of the printer and its output should be examined carefully before deciding to purchase. Figure A–11 provides a detailed comparison of several printers with regard to use, speed, and cost.

Figure A–11
Comparisons of use, speed, and cost of printers.

Most Frequent Uses of Printers by Applications

	Printers		
Applications	Serial	Line	Page
Bar code printing		X	
Data processing	X	X	X
Electronic mail			X
Graphics	X	X	
Personal computer	X		
Portable terminals	X		
Word processing	X	X	

Minimum and Maximum Speed and Cost Comparisons for Printers

	Characters per second				Lines per minute			
	Minimum		Maximum		Minimum		Maximum	
Type	Speed	Cost	Speed	Cost	Speed	Cost	Speed	Cost
Band					240	$8,000	500	$ 94,000
Belt					300	$4,000	500	$ 5,000
Chain					300	$5,000	2000	$ 69,000
Daisy-wheel	12	$ 800	400	$19,500	150	$4,500	600	$ 15,300
Dot-matrix	1	$ 400	600	$13,500	40	$ 800	1000	$ 10,000
Drum	45	$1,000	4,800	$23,000	20	$3,500	6000	$ 75,000
Electrosensitive	42	$ 400	960	$ 1,000	120	$ 600	18000	$ 53,000
Ink-jet	20	$1,300	270	$ 2,700	50	$ 500	50	$ 500
Laser					1300	$9,000	21000	$315,000
Thermal matrix	2	$ 650	160	$ 1,500	63	$ 600	300	$ 20,000

(continued next page)

Figure A–11 (continued)

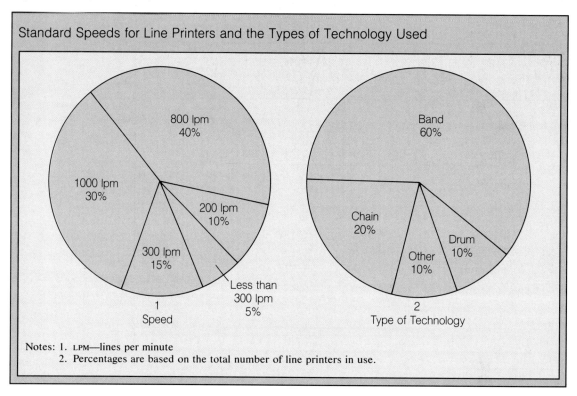

Standard Speeds for Line Printers and the Types of Technology Used

Notes: 1. LPM—lines per minute
       2. Percentages are based on the total number of line printers in use.

Dot-Matrix Printer. The dot-matrix printer, such as the one shown in Figure A–12, is the most popular choice for first-time buyers. The characters are formed from a matrix of pins. The more steel pins in the matrix, the higher quality of the printed characters. To form a particular character, the appropriate pins are positioned in the matrix printhead that is controlled by the CPU. The pins that represent a specific character are fired forward from the matrix printhead against a ribbon that is between the printhead and the paper. A firing action by the matrix printhead pushes the character image onto the paper. A dot matrix printer produces **draft-quality** hardcopy output. Some dot-matrix printers will allow two passes over the same printline to improve the quality of output. When this is done, the image is greatly enhanced and is referred to as double-striking which creates **near-letter-quality** output.

Dot-matrix printers are reliable and can print up to 250 characters per second. This type of printer is highly recommended for first-time microcomputer purchasers.

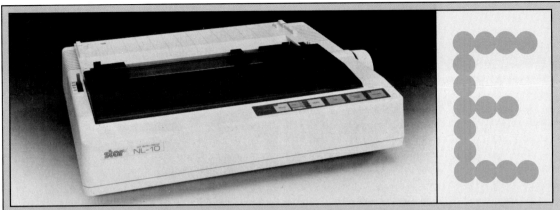

Figure A–12
A dot-matrix printer. The letter E in this example is formed by overprinting—that is, the character is printed twice. When it is printed the second time, the print head is offset just slightly so that the gaps between the dots are filled in. Thus, while the character is still printed using dots, the dots touch.

Daisy-Wheel Printer.   The daisy-wheel printer (see Figure A–13) is considered to be a **letter-quality** output device. When the user's needs require output that is similar in quality to the print on a typewriter, then a daisy-wheel printer is normally selected. The printer works from the principle of a rotating wheel that has a specific font attached to its separated petals. A daisy-wheel printer element rotates on a spindle, and as the appropriate character passes a specific defined point at the printhead, a hammer fires against a specific petal. This causes the character attached to the petal to strike against a ribbon onto the paper on the platen. One big advantage of a daisy-wheel printer is that you can have more than one font style. The daisy wheel is easy to remove from the spindle, thereby allowing the user to use many different daisy wheels of various font styles. The major disadvantages of a daisy-wheel printer are that it prints more slowly than a dot-matrix printer, and that it cannot be used for graphics output. The daisy-wheel printer should be given appropriate consideration if you require high-quality printed output. This printer is nice to have if you have a lot of written correspondence, memorandums, and manuscripts to print.

Ink-Jet Printer.   This type of printer is gaining in popularity because of its high-quality output produced with relatively little noise. The characters are formed by using a template with holes in it. At the

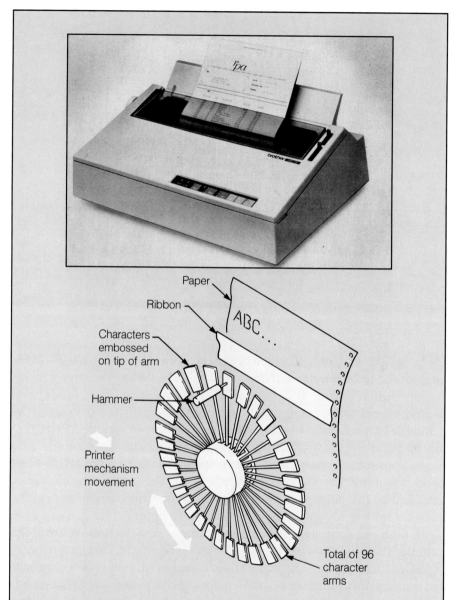

Figure A-13

A daisy-wheel printer. A daisy-wheel printer such as shown here can fit on a desk top. Some daisy-wheel printers allow either continuous form feed or single sheet form feed. The daisy-wheel element itself consists of a number of arms, each with a character on the end. When the printer is running, the wheel spins until the desired character is lined up with the hammer, at which time the character is struck against the ribbon and paper. Since daisy-wheel printers are impact printers, they are fairly noisy when they are printing.

Figure A–14
An ink-jet printer. The color produced from ink-jet printers is of high quality.

time a character is to be printed, a nozzle with a jet-head sprays a fine ink mist into the template that, in turn, forms the appropriate character and sprays it onto the paper. The ink-jet printer is reliable, quiet, and produces high-quality output (see Figure A–14).

Ink-jet printing is a relatively new concept in producing hardcopy output. As you consider this type of printer, be sure to check out all the features and ask for several demonstrations of its capability.

Laser Printers. The laser printer, such as the one the person in Figure A–15 is using, is an almost letter-quality output device. It is fast, reliable, and quiet. However, it is relatively expensive compared to other types of printers. Thus, only if you are anticipating a high volume of output from the applications you will be running on your microcomputer would a laser printer be worth considering. The laser printer uses a laser beam to define and transfer characters of data to

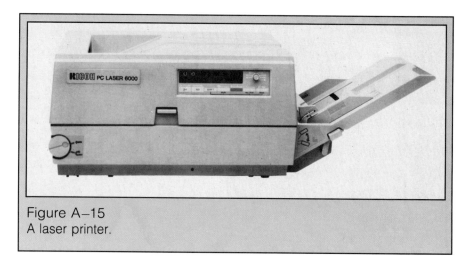

Figure A–15
A laser printer.

a drum that, in turn, transfers the images to be printed to paper using a xerographic process.

Most laser printers print a whole page at a time. Laser printers for a microcomputer can be cost-effective when there are high volumes of output to print. Be sure to ask for a demonstration of each model you might be considering.

Electrostatic Printer.   This type of printer is the most reasonably priced printer in the marketplace. It is a nonimpact printer that operates quietly, but prints slowly and uses a special paper that can be relatively expensive compared to other printer paper. It works on the principle of heat transfer. The printhead forms the characters to be printed electronically, and heats up to a certain temperature. When the appropriate temperature is reached, the printhead transfers the character image to the specially wax-treated paper, whereby the character is printed. The printhead is somewhat like a matrix in that it is made up of dots forming a particular character. The electrostatic printer works well for applications that do not require large amounts of printed output and high-speed printing, such as in writing personal letters with a word processing package. If a printer is a minor concern for your microcomputer system configuration, then you might want to consider the electrostatic printer. The diagram in Figure A–16 shows how an electrostatic printer works.

Figure A–16
Electrostatic printer/plotter. (a) Color plotter diagram.
(b) Electrostatic printer plotter.

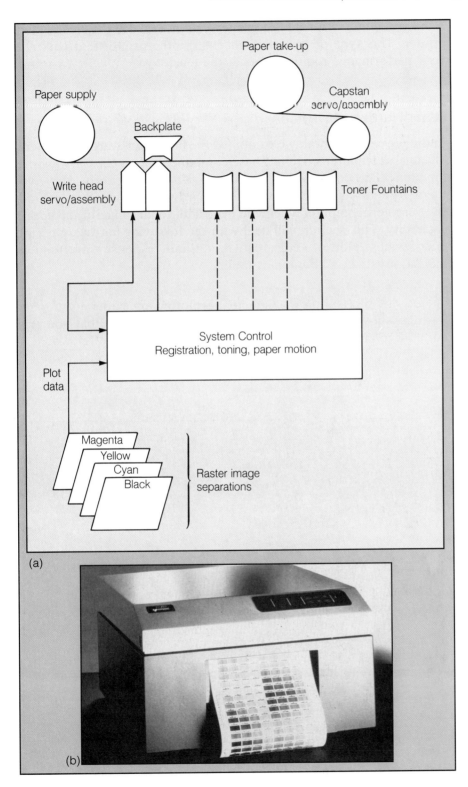

Paper take-up

Paper supply

Capstan
servo/assembly

Backplate

Write head
servo/assembly

Toner Fountains

System Control
Registration, toning, paper motion

Plot
data

Magenta
Yellow
Cyan
Black

Raster image
separations

(a)

(b)

As you conduct a study of printers, do not ignore the electrostatic printer. This type of printer might just be the printer that will meet your performance requirements at the least cost.

Other Hardware Devices

In the previous section, we examined the basic hardware components of a microcomputer system. These components are necessary in order for your microcomputer to be able to function properly. However, there are many additional peripheral hardware devices you can add to your microcomputer when you need additional capacity and special capability. This section will deal with the following hardware peripheral devices: plotter, audio recognition and response unit, modem, mouse, joystick, and graphics tablet.

Plotter.   A plotter allows data to be plotted on paper in graphics form, as shown in Figure A–17. If your needs require that you print out a large amount of data in graph format, then a plotter would be a hardware device worth considering. The output of a plotter is normally plotted in full color.

Figure A–17
Graphics plotters.

Figure A–18
Voice recognition/response unit. A bank teller uses a push-button telephone to call a remote computer and request the status of an account.
After keying the account number and a code for the information desired, the teller receives a voice response. The use of voice synthesizers has made computers more usable by many.

Voice Recognition/Response Unit.   A voice recognition/response unit
allows the user to communicate with the computer through voice input
and voice output. The user actually speaks to the voice recognition/
response unit through a microphone that, in turn, interprets the commands from the user and sends them to the computer for processing.
These units vary in capacity and capability. At present, the vocabulary
is limited. The bank teller in Figure A–18 is using a voice recognition/
response unit to check on the status of a customer's account. The
teller receives a voice response to his request. Also, the telephone
company uses these units to look up a new telephone number when
a customer's number changes, and to recite the new number to the
person who dialed the old number.

Modem.   A modem is a popular hardware peripheral device that allows a computer to communicate with another computer over a data communications link, such as a telephone line, microwave, or satellite hookup. The acronym *modem* stands for *mo*dulate/*dem*odulate. This process involves the conversion of computer electronic signals to data communications signals for transmission of data over a communications link. Both the sending and receiving ends must have a modem in order to convert computer signals to data communications signals, and vice versa. If you plan to link up your microcomputer with another computer, or a computerized information service like Dow-Jones, The

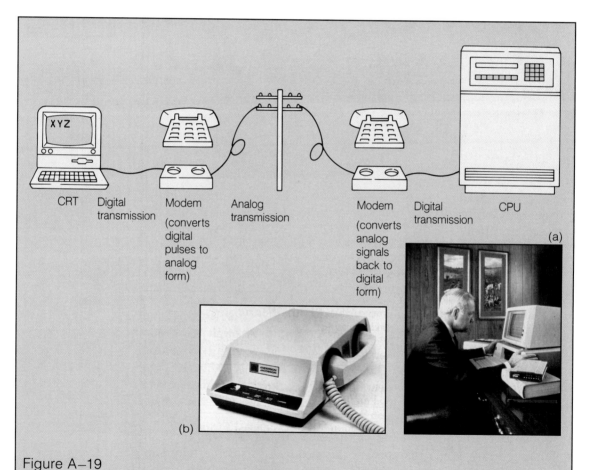

Figure A–19
Acoustic and direct-connect modems. (a) This external direct-connect modem is an example of modems that can be used with personal computers. It transmits data at a rate of 1,200 bits per second. (b) The acoustic coupler allows a portable computer user to communicate with another computer over telephone lines. Note the telephone headset is placed in the molded rubber cups on the acoustic coupler.

Source, or Videotext, a modem will be necessary in order to make the link between computers. There are two types of modems to consider: the acoustic coupler and direct connect, both of which are illustrated in Figure A–19.

Mouse.   A mouse is a hardware peripheral device that allows the user to control the movement of the cursor on the video display by moving the mouse in a certain direction (see Figure A–20). Many vendors produce and sell a mouse for their microcomputer. Instead of controlling the cursor by using the keys on the cursor control keypad, the user holds and moves the mouse in the direction he or she wants to move the cursor on the video display.

Joystick.   Most home microcomputers are used nearly 50 percent of the time for games that need joysticks. A joystick looks similar to the floor stick shift in a car. It allows the user to control the cursor on the video display by moving the stick backward and forward and from side to side. This device is necessary for playing certain games. Figure A–21 shows an example of a joystick.

Graphics Tablet.   A graphics tablet is allowing the user in Figure A–22 to draw designs and pictures on a flat tablet surface and transfer

Figure A–20
Apple Macintosh with mouse.

Figure A-21
A joystick allows the user to control the cursor on the video display by moving the stick backward and forward and from side to side.

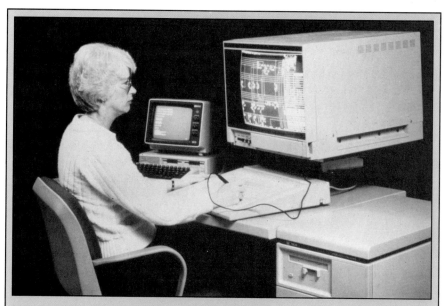

Figure A-22
A graphics tablet.

them to the computer. The image is drawn on the tablet surface using an electronic stylus. The drawing is then digitized by the computer, and the design or picture appears on a video display as graphics output. This hardware peripheral device is very useful for a person who requires hand-drawn design capability and capacity.

5. . . .The different types of printers and how they might be used with a microcomputer system?

6. . . .The other hardware devices that might be used with a microcomputer system?

DO YOU
REMEMBER

Determine the Dealer You Will Buy From

The dealer you buy from is of utmost importance. Some are reliable and honest in their dealings with the public, but others might not be. You should ask yourself these questions when choosing a vendor:

1. Will the vendor be in business next year?
2. Does the vendor know what you are talking about?
3. Can the vendor provide what you need?
4. Does the vendor have a depth of knowledge about microcomputer hardware and software?
5. Can the vendor service your equipment after he or she sells it to you?
6. Can the vendor provide ongoing hardware and software support?
7. Can the vendor provide user training?

You should be sure to get clear answers to these questions before purchasing your microcomputer from any vendor (see Figure A–23).

You can buy your microcomputer from a computer store, such as AMS Computer Store, ComputerLand, Entree Computer Store, or

Figure A–23
Customers checking out a computer dealer. It is important to check out the computer dealer as carefully as you would your computer purchases.

Byte Shop. You can buy from a large merchandiser, such as Sears, K mart, or Penney's. Some manufacturers have their own retail stores, such as Radio Shack, IBM, or DEC, from whom you could buy your microcomputer system. Where you live and what your requirements are for a microcomputer system will determine which source you will choose. You should study each source carefully for advantages and disadvantages.

Financing

Most retail stores do not prefer to finance the purchase of a micro-computer system. There are some retailers, such as Sears, Penney's, and K mart that will allow the purchase of a microcomputer system on approved credit. Some microcomputer stores might be willing to finance the purchase themselves, or make arrangements for financing through a financial institution, such as a bank. Even though these types of arrangements are available from certain retailers, most sellers prefer cash at the time of sale.

Service After the Sale

As you evaluate microcomputer vendors, be careful to determine what type of service after the sale, if any, the vendor provides. A reliable vendor will be able to support your microcomputer hardware and software requirements on an on-going basis. Check to see if the vendor has a repair shop with at least one person, and preferably two persons, who are competent microcomputer technicians. Does the vendor have at least one software specialist who is capable of modifying, customizing, and fixing malfunctioning software? These are important questions, because you need to know where to go when you need hardware and software service after the sale.

Maintenance Contract

As you consider all the various and sundry points before purchasing a microcomputer, don't forget to examine maintenance contracts. There are four levels of maintenance contracts to consider: on-site, courier pick-up and delivery, customer carry-in, and customer mail-in. The least recommended and desirable of the four levels is customer mail-in.

On-site maintenance service means that a microcomputer technician will come to your site to repair your microcomputer within a specified number of hours. This level of maintenance is the most expensive and usually applies to large business accounts. Courier pick-up and delivery maintenance means that a person picks up your microcomputer at your site, and delivers the machine to the service site for repair, and back to you once the microcomputer has been repaired. This level of maintenance is less costly than on-site maintenance, but it can take longer to repair your microcomputer because of handling and transportation time. Customer carry-in service means you take your microcomputer to a microcomputer service center for repair. The vendor you buy from should be able to provide this level of maintenance service. The service center will repair your microcomputer and call you when it is ready to be picked up. This level of maintenance is less costly than either on-site or courier pick-up and delivery. Mail-in maintenance service means that the owner is responsible for sending the microcomputer to the repair shop by mail or via a common carrier. Most microcomputer vendors have a hotline service that can be used by purchasers who have problems with their microcomputer. Normally the person at the other end of the telephone line will help you troubleshoot your problem, but it is left up to you to make the necessary repairs yourself. This level of support is usually provided for hardware and software manufactured by a specific vendor only. Service after the sale is important and must be thought of as a front-end activity in the purchasing process and not an after-the-fact activity.

Used Computers

Used computers might or might not be a bargain. It is hard to determine how much use and what type of use a particular used computer has had. The seller of a used computer might be unloading a particular microcomputer for the wrong reason. Also, watch the pricing of used computers; the seller might be basing his or her asking price on what he or she paid for the computer two or three years ago. If he or she paid $2,000 for the computer and is asking $1,000, this might or might not be a good buy. Check current market prices for new comparable equipment. You could find that a new microcomputer with even more capability and capacity might cost less than that old used microcomputer for $1,000. Remember, "buyer beware," particularly of used microcomputers. You don't want your first experience with a microcomputer to be negative. Be a careful shopper.

People Considerations

People considerations deal with important items, such as user training and documentation. The **user-friendliness** of hardware and software packages must be given serious examination before purchasing. User-friendliness means how easy or how hard is it to work with the hardware and software packages. Most microcomputer systems today require no special training to learn how to operate them. This is basically true also for software packages.

Training

If the hardware and software require special user training before they can be used effectively, you must be aware of that fact. Who will provide such training, and who pays the cost? Most microcomputer systems today require no special user training before using them. The documentation that comes with the microcomputer system is usually adequate to set up the system and get started. However, if training is necessary, where do you get it? Many vendors have training schools for new users of their hardware and/or software systems (see Figure A-24). Vendor school can be rather expensive because of travel and tuition, but normally the quality of instruction is also high. Another alternative for training would be to attend classes that a local micro-

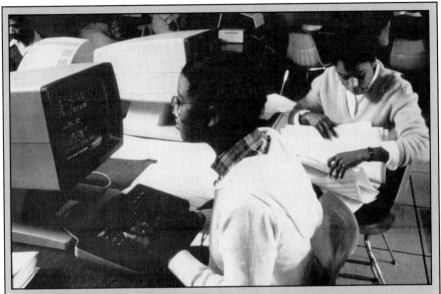

Figure A–24
Types of computer training. *Computer learning:* Classes are offered by dealers and independent sources. *Computer books* teach you about programming and computer operation. *Clear documentation* may be the biggest asset of your new system.

computer retail store might conduct. There is time and money involved with this type of training, but the results can be significant since you will learn what you need to know relatively fast.

Other ways of obtaining training are by taking a formal course at your local community college, reading books and magazines, attending private computer schools, and purchasing private lessons. Many hardware and software systems have tutorials on diskette that will help you learn about specific features of the system. These tutorials teach how to operate the hardware and/or software system by providing examples and hands-on experiences.

Manuals and Documentation

The documentation that comes with hardware and software should be written in such a way that it is easy for the user to interpret and understand. Be sure to examine documentation manuals carefully. Nothing is more important than the documentation that should accompany the hardware and software you purchase. The weakest component in microcomputer systems is the documentation.

Figure A–25
User's manual and documentation.

The manuals should have good examples, demonstrations, and clear diagrams. Check for index tab pages between major sections in the manuals. These tabs help you find specific information faster. Be sure the manuals are attractively packaged, and have been professionally typeset. Remember, manuals will be used a great deal as you learn about your microcomputer hardware and software, so they need to be durable and attractive (see Figure A–25).

DO YOU
REMEMBER

7. . . .How to determine the dealer you will buy from?

8. . . .The people considerations that must be dealt with when purchasing a microcomputer?

Summary

(This summary provides answers to DO YOU REMEMBER . . . questions in the module.)

1. What are the initial considerations when considering a microcomputer system?
One should first determine his or her specific need for buying a microcomputer. The sophistication level of the available microcomputers that fall within a person's budget, the appropriate software packages and hardware devices, as well as knowing when to buy, are also initial considerations.

2. What are the three types of software for which software requirements, availability, and cost should be determined?
The types of software are *operating system, vendor-supplied,* and *user-written programs.*

3. What are the types of hardware for which hardware requirements, availability, and cost should be considered?
The types of hardware are the keyboard, monitor, central processing unit (CPU), secondary storage device, printer, plotter, voice-recognition and -response unit, modem, mouse, joystick, and graphics tablet.

4. What are the basic hardware components that make up a microcomputer system?
The basic hardware components that make up a microcomputer system are an *input device, central processing unit* (CPU), *secondary storage device,* and an *output device.*

5. What are the different types of printers and how are they used with a microcomputer system?
The types of printers are *dot-matrix, daisy-wheel, ink-jet, laser,* and *electrostatic.* They are all used to produce printed (paper) output.

6. What are the other types of hardware devices that might be used with a microcomputer system?
The other types are plotter, voice-recognition and -response unit, modem, mouse, joystick, and graphics tablet.

7. How do you determine the dealer you will buy from?
You determine the dealer you will buy from by examining financing

arrangements, service after the sale agreements, maintenance contract agreements, and used computer agreements.

8. **What are the people considerations that must be dealt with when purchasing a microcomputer system?**
   The people considerations that must be dealt with are *training, manuals,* and *documentation.*

Key Terms

bit addressable graphics
coprocessor
double-striking
draft-quality
ergonomic design

letter-quality
near-letter-quality
resolution
user-friendliness

Test Yourself

1. The first question you need to ask yourself when considering the purchase of a microcomputer system is: Why Do I _____ a Computer?

2. Once you have studied the initial considerations for purchasing a microcomputer system, it is time to determine _____ requirements, availability, and _____ .

3. _____ software deals with a particular microcomputer's internal system operations.

4. Software supplied by software houses is referred to as _____ applications software.

5. Software written by inside programmer/analysts is called _____ applications software.

6. After software has been considered, then it is time to be specific about the _____ that will run the software.

7. The letter **K** stands for _____ which in computer mathematics is actually _____ characters/bytes.

8. _____ devices are a major consideration when thinking about the purchase of a microcomputer system.

9. There are many _____ hardware devices you can add to your microcomputer when you need additional capacity and capability.

10. The _____ you buy from is of utmost importance.

11. Most retail computer stores prefer that you give them the _____ and they will give you the _____ .

12. _____ considerations deal with important items, such as user training and documentation.

Review Questions

1. What are the initial considerations before purchasing a microcomputer system? (Learning Objective 2)

2. Identify software requirements, availability, and cost for a microcomputer system. (Learning Objective 3)

3. Identify hardware requirements, availability, and cost for a microcomputer system. (Learning Objective 4)

5. What are some other hardware devices that can be used with a microcomputer system to enhance its usefulness? (Learning Objective 5)

6. What are the basic characteristics in selecting a dealer to buy a microcomputer from? (Learning Objective 6)

7. What are the people considerations in purchasing a microcomptuer system? (Learning Objective 7)

Activities

1. Visit your local microcomputer store and evaluate it, using the information you have learned about the selection process for purchasing a microcomputer system.

2. Visit your school's library and search current magazines, newspapers, periodicals, etc. for information concerning software for a microcomputer system. Determine software requirements, availability, and cost for a microcomputer system for your school's microcomputer lab.

3. Visit your local microcomputer store to examine microcomputer hardware. Determine hardware requirements, availability, and cost of equipment for your school's microcomputer lab.

4. Research the availability and quality of microcomputer dealers in your area. What does each offer to a potential purchaser? Develop a form to be used in evaluating these dealers on specific characteristics, such as type of financing available, service availability after the sale, maintenance contract availability, training availability, and manuals and documentation availability.

MODULE B

The BASIC Programming Language

Learning Objectives

After studying this module carefully, you will be able to:

1. Define key terms introduced in the module.
2. Name, and distinguish between, the three processing modes in BASIC.
3. Explain the purpose of DOS system commands, and give examples of system commands introduced and explained in the module.
4. Explain how a BASIC statement, a new program, and an old program are entered into a computer.
5. Explain the main difference between using **INPUT** statements and **READ** and **DATA** statements for entering data in BASIC.
6. Explain briefly the various BASIC statements introduced in the module, and give an example of how each can be used.
7. Distinguish between a conditional and an unconditional branch in a program.
8. Explain how the **TAB** function and the **PRINT USING** statements can be used to format output.
9. Write, enter, and execute BASIC programs using statements introduced in this module.

Module Outline

INTRODUCTION TO THE BASIC
/ LANGUAGE

OVERVIEW OF BASIC
Compilers and Interpreters
Processing Modes
Structure of BASIC Programs
Using BASIC
Constants and Literals
Variables
Order of Mathematical Operations

BASIC PROGRAMMING STATEMENTS
REM (REMark) Statement
PRINT Statement
END Statement
LET Statement
INPUT Statement
GOTO Statement
READ and DATA Statements
TAB Function
PRINT USING Statement
IF/THEN Statement
GOSUB and RETURN Statements
FOR . . . TO . . . NEXT Statement
FOR . . . TO . . . STEP, NEXT Statement

We have learned that many problems can be solved using computers (see Chapter 9). We also learned the importance of using a structured approach in the problem-solving process that includes the following steps:

1. Defining the problem.

2. Planning and designing the solution.

3. Writing the program.

4. Testing the program.

5. Documenting the program.

6. Maintaining the program.

In the first step, Defining the problem, a problem should always be analyzed using the idea of the basic flow of all data processing—**input, processing, output.** The programmer should first determine the desired **output.** Next, the programmer must determine the kinds of **input** data needed to produce that output. Finally, the programmer needs to determine the **processing** to be performed on the data in order to obtain the desired output.

The second step, Planning and designing a solution, requires the programmer to develop a series of logical instructions for the computer to follow. A **flowchart** is normally used for this purpose. A well-prepared flowchart provides good documentation for the programmer to follow when writing a computer program (step 3). When preparing flowcharts, a programmer should use standard ANSI flowchart symbols (see Chapter 9). Flowcharts accompany sample programs in this module. For convenience, some of the more widely used ANSI flowchart symbols are shown again in Table B–1.

If the problem has been clearly defined (step 1) and the solution carefully designed (step 2), writing the program should be relatively easy. At this point, the programmer should be able to translate the flowchart into a computer program—that is, a series of step-by-step instructions the computer can easily follow. The programmer must, of course, choose a particular language to write the program in and must be familiar with the **rules** and **syntax** of the language. This module provides information about the BASIC programming language. After learning this information, a programmer should be able to write programs for a variety of computer applications.

After a computer program has been written, it should be tested thoroughly. A thorough testing helps assure that the program does what it is supposed to do.

Table B–1
Frequently Used ANSI Flowchart Symbols

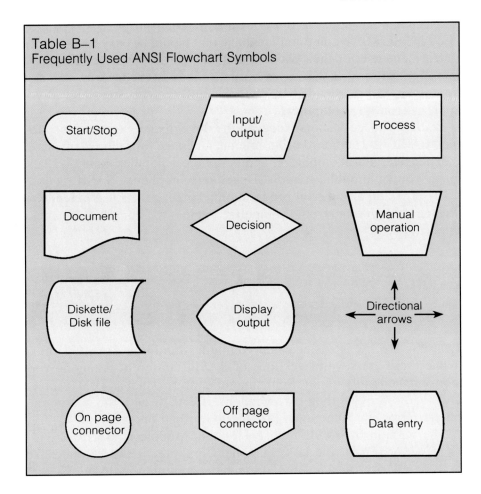

Throughout program preparation, the programmer should retain all documentation pertaining to the program, including the flowchart and a listing of program instructions. In the event that changes in the program are needed later, the programmer will realize the value of the documentation. Up-to-date documentation always includes changes that have been made in the program.

Introduction to the BASIC Language

BASIC, an abbreviation for **B**eginner's **A**ll-purpose **S**ymbolic **I**nstruction **C**ode, was developed in the 1960s by Professors John Kemeny and Thomas Kurtz at Dartmouth College. Their purpose was to produce an interactive computer language that would be easy for students to learn and use for their classes, and for a variety of other programming applications. BASIC uses words, called **reserved words,** that can be quickly comprehended by the user and that produce logical responses from the computer.

BASIC's success soon exceeded the developers' expectations. Today, BASIC is a standard programming language for millions of small, inexpensive microcomputers, and is the most popular computer language course in public schools. Despite its simplicity, BASIC is both a versatile and a powerful programming language. Its use extends to writing everything from computer games to complex business applications.

Overview of BASIC

Learning BASIC is easier when you understand how BASIC works. While there are several versions of BASIC, differences among versions are generally minor. Some manufacturers (such as IBM, Apple, and Tandy) provide their own versions of BASIC with the microcomputers they sell. Some even provide more than one version.

The version of BASIC chosen for this Module is BASICA (Advanced BASIC) for the IBM Personal Computer (IBM–PC) because of its popularity and widespread use in the computer industry. Several sample programs are presented in this module to illustrate the topics covered; all of them were written using BASICA. Where there are significant differences between the BASICA version and other popular versions, the differences will be noted for each program. Otherwise, it can be assumed that there are no differences in the versions.

Compilers and Interpreters

Computers are designed to read and execute instructions in machine language. A program written in a high-level language, such as BASIC, must be translated into machine language before the computer can carry out the program's instructions. This translation process is performed by compilers and interpreters.

A **compiler** translates an entire program into machine language at one time. For this reason, a compiler is fast and efficient. A compiled program will execute more quickly than an interpreted program. However, when any changes are made to a compiled program, the program must be recompiled before the program can be run.

An **interpreter** translates a high-level program into machine language, one instruction at a time. Thus, an interpreter is slower and less efficient than a compiler. An advantage of an interpreter, though, is that it allows a program to be changed easily. Most versions of BASIC use an interpreter.

Processing Modes

For convenience, several versions of BASIC offer the user three processing modes: immediate mode, program mode, and edit mode. This combination of processing modes increases BASIC's versatility and offers valuable advantages to the programmer.

In **immediate mode,** an instruction is entered into the computer and immediately executed. In this mode, many computer operations can be performed without writing a complete computer program. An immediate mode instruction is typed without a line number. When the computer receives a command without a line number, it recognizes that the command is not part of a program but is to be executed immediately.

In the following example, a keyboard is used to type the word "PRINT" followed by the mathematical expression "(4 + 5 + 6)/3." Next, a designated key called a *carriage return key* is pressed to enter this statement. On the IBM–PC, the designated key pressed to enter something into the computer is the bent arrow ◄┘ key, or ENTER key. On other microcomputers, a different key such as the ENTER or RETURN key performs this function. For convenience, the symbol <CR> is used in this module to indicate when the user should press the designated carriage return key, hereafter referred to as the <**CR**> key, to enter something into the computer. The <**OUTPUT**> symbol is used to show the results of processing that appear on the screen. In the example below, when the expression is entered and the designated key pressed, the computer will perform the calculations immediately and PRINT (display) the output "5" on the screen, as shown below:

```
PRINT (4+5+6)/3     <CR>
5                   <OUTPUT>
```

This same calculation can be done in program mode, as shown in Program B. 1. The primary differences are that in **program mode** each instruction is part of a program and each must be preceded by a **line number.**

Program B.1

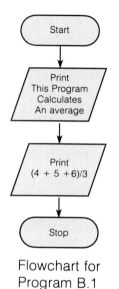

Flowchart for Program B.1

```
10    REM *** ILLUSTRATION OF "PROGRAM MODE" ***
20    PRINT "THIS PROGRAM CALCULATES AN AVERAGE"
30    PRINT (4 + 5 + 6)/3
40    END

RUN
```

OUTPUT

```
THIS PROGRAM CALCULATES AN AVERAGE
   5
```

BASIC Version	Differences
Apple	None
IBM-PC	None
TRS-80	None
GW-BASIC	None

Notice that in program mode each instruction is preceded by a line number. This tells the computer that the instruction is part of a program and is not to be executed until told to do so by the programmer. Typing the word **RUN** on the keyboard and pressing the <CR> key tell the computer to begin executing instructions in the program in numerically ascending order (beginning with the lowest-numbered instruction).

Most microcomputer versions of BASIC also include an **editor** that allows a user to make changes in a program and to correct errors easily. For example, assume that after typing the above program, you discover you should have instructed the computer to divide by 5 instead of 3 in line 30. BASIC's editor allows you to correct this error easily by retyping line 30 correctly, as shown in Program B.2.

Program B.2

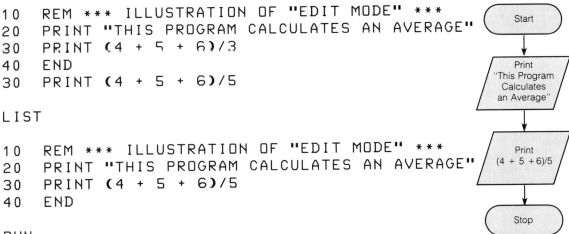

```
10   REM *** ILLUSTRATION OF "EDIT MODE" ***
20   PRINT "THIS PROGRAM CALCULATES AN AVERAGE"
30   PRINT (4 + 5 + 6)/3
40   END
30   PRINT (4 + 5 + 6)/5

LIST

10   REM *** ILLUSTRATION OF "EDIT MODE" ***
20   PRINT "THIS PROGRAM CALCULATES AN AVERAGE"
30   PRINT (4 + 5 + 6)/5
40   END

RUN
```

Flowchart for
Program B.2

```
                OUTPUT

   THIS PROGRAM CALCULATES AN AVERAGE
     3
```

BASIC Version	Differences
Apple	None
IBM-PC	None
TRS-80	None
GW-BASIC	None

Notice that the word **LIST** was entered in Program B.2 after the new line 30. This instructs the computer to replace the first line 30 (with the error) with the new line 30. Thus, the line containing the error is erased from memory and replaced with the correct line. Some versions of BASIC allow the programmer to correct an error by retyping only the error.

The **edit mode** makes it easier for programmers to correct errors and to make changes in a computer program. The user's manual that accompanies the version of BASIC you are using provides information about the editor. Knowing this information will be valuable as you prepare and enter BASIC programs on your computer.

Structure of BASIC Programs

A BASIC program consists of a series of instructions, called statements. A **statement** instructs the computer to perform some action, such as calculating a value, comparing two values, or printing output. Most, but not all, BASIC statements consist of three main parts: a line number, a command, and the remainder of the statement. Below is an example of a BASIC statement:

$$10 \ \text{LET} \ X \ = \ 10$$

In the above example, the line number is 10, followed by the word LET, followed by the remainder of the statement. In BASIC, the only rule for line numbers is that the first statement in a program must have the lowest number, the second instruction must have the second lowest number, and so on. This is because BASIC statements are executed in order, from the lowest to the highest number. Statements are often numbered in increments, called **gaps,** of 10 (10, 20, 30, and so on), so that additional statements can be added to the program without having to renumber the statements. For example, line 15 can easily be added between line 10 and line 20. When added, BASIC places line 15 between line 10 and line 20.

The command part of a statement instructs the computer to perform some action. In the example above, the LET statement assigns a value to a variable (the variable X is assigned a value of 10). This and other statements are explained in more detail later.

DO YOU REMEMBER

1. . . .The primary difference between a compiler and an interpreter?

2. . . .The three processing modes available with BASIC?

3. . . .The three primary parts of a typical BASIC statement?

Using BASIC

Large computers usually require a formal start-up procedure before BASIC can be used. With microcomputers however, the start-up procedure is easier. Some microcomputers allow the user to simply turn on the computer to use BASIC, because BASIC is permanently stored in ROM memory inside the computer. On others, BASIC must be loaded into memory from floppy disks. Some microcomputers allow either method to be used. On the IBM–PC, the user must enter a command such as "BASIC" or "BASICA," after loading the disk operating system, to activate the BASIC interpreter. The procedure for loading BASIC varies among computers, and specific instructions are provided in the computer's manual. These instructions should always be followed carefully.

The procedure for loading BASIC using the IBM Personal Computer, for example, is explained below. The actual procedure for loading BASIC can vary for other microcomputer brands. Again, the user should follow instructions in the manual for the particular microcomputer when loading BASIC.

Loading BASIC: An Illustration.   On the IBM–PC, the BASIC language is contained in ROM. Instructions for accessing ROM BASIC are contained on the accompanying disk operating system (DOS) disk. Turn on the monitor. Find the disk labeled DOS, and insert it in drive A. After inserting DOS in drive A, turn on the computer by flicking the red switch on the right side of the computer. After a few seconds, the following message, called a prompt, appears in the upper left corner of the monitor screen:

```
Current date is Tue 1-01-1986
Enter new date:
```

Using either hyphens (-) or slashes (/) to separate the month, day, and year, the user now enters the date and presses the <CR> key. The display now appears as follows with a new prompt, this one for time:

```
Current date is Tue 1-01-1986
Enter new date: 09-01-1987
Current time is 0:16:35.44
Enter new time:
```

An IBM Personal Computer operates on a 24-hour military clock. For example, the time 4:35 P.M. should be entered as 16:35. Colons should be used to separate the hours, minutes, and seconds (seconds are optional).

Entering the data and/or time is optional. Either, or both, can be omitted by simply pressing the carriage return <CR> once to omit entering the date, and again to omit entering the time.

Whether the date and/or time is entered or omitted, the following display should appear:

```
The IBM Personal Computer DOS
Version 3.0 (C) Copyright IBM Corp 1981,
1982, 1983, 1984
```

```
A>
```

The **A>** symbol is the DOS prompt. The **A** indicates that the computer is set to read data from, or write data to, the floppy disk in drive A. When the DOS symbol A> appears, a user can enter any one of several system commands (explained later), or the command to load BASIC. To load the BASICA version, simply type BASICA following the A> symbol as follows:

```
A>BASICA
```

After typing BASICA and pressing the <CR> key, the following will be displayed on the monitor:

```
The IBM Personal Computer Basic
Version 3.00 (C) Copyright IBM Corp
1981, 1982, 1983, 1984
60887 Bytes free
```

```
Ok
```

The **Ok** message indicates that the BASIC interpreter has been loaded and that the user can now enter a BASIC program.

In addition to BASIC, the disk operating system (DOS) contains several other programs that allow the user to accomplish other important tasks such as formatting a new blank disk or copying files to another disk. Each of these tasks is accomplished by entering a specific command following the A> symbol. Several of these important system commands are explained in the following sections.

NOW TRY THIS!

Read carefully the instructions for loading BASIC in the DOS manual for the particular microcomputer you are using. Following the instructions carefully, load BASIC. Make notes of all information displayed on your monitor. In your notes, indicate the exact meaning of all displayed information. Practice loading BASIC until you can do it without having to refer to the manual.

DOS (Disk Operating System) Commands.   DOS commands differ from BASIC language statements. BASIC language statements (explained later) are executed when an entire BASIC program is run. A DOS command (usually one or a few words) executes in immediate mode as soon as the command is entered and the <CR> key is pressed. DOS commands govern the operation of the BASIC program, but are not statements in the program. Thus, a DOS command does not require a line number. Specific DOS commands vary depending upon the type of computer and the version of DOS used. See Table B–2 for a summary of the frequently used DOS commands—DIRECTORY, FORMAT, COPY, NEW, LOAD, SAVE, LIST, and RUN—that are discussed below.

DIRECTORY Command. A DIRECTORY is a program that displays a list of programs and/or files on disk. By typing the command **DIR** (an abbreviation for DIRECTORY) and pressing the <CR> key, a list of the user's file names of programs and data is retrieved from the disk and displayed on the computer's monitor. The actual command to list a directory varies with different versions of BASIC.

FORMAT Command. Before a new blank disk can be used, it must be prepared for use. Preparing a disk for use is called **formatting** or **initializing** the disk. A new disk needs to be formatted only once—and not each time it is used.

COPY Command. Every DOS system includes a program that allows a user to copy data from one disk to another. The copy command enables a user to make a back-up copy of important data in case the original disk is damaged or lost.

NOW TRY THIS!

Insert the DOS in the disk drive of your computer. Turn your computer on to load the operating system. After loading DOS, follow instructions in the manual and execute each of the following activities:

1. Execute a DIRECTORY to see DOS programs.
2. FORMAT a blank disk.
3. If your DOS disk is not copy protected, make a back-up copy of the DOS disk.

NEW Command. The **NEW** command is used to clear (erase) any program or data currently in the computer's memory, a procedure that should be done before a new program is entered. Using this command ensures that instructions from a previous program will not affect the new program.

LOAD Command. Most computer systems allow the user to load a program from secondary storage, such as magnetic disk or tape, into primary storage by typing the command **LOAD** followed by the name of the program to be loaded. After loading, the program can be run or modified by the user.

For computers having more than one disk drive, it is sometimes necessary to tell the computer which drive is being used to load the program. The usual procedure is to type the command **LOAD,** the file name, a comma, and then the drive number. For example, the command "LOAD Payroll, D2" tells the computer to load the Payroll program from the disk in drive 2.

SAVE Command. A program can be saved (on disk or tape) by typing the command **SAVE,** followed by the name of the program being saved. When a program is first entered into the computer, the program is in primary storage. Unless the program is saved (written onto disk or tape by the computer), it will be lost when the power is turned off. Therefore, when entering a large program or large amounts of data into a computer, a good practice is to save your work at frequent intervals (such as every 4 or 5 minutes). The possibility of losing several hours of unsaved work will cause the user to take this warning seriously.

When a program is saved, it is known as a **file.** When using the SAVE command, the file name (program name) must be specified.

LIST Command. The **LIST** command instructs the computer to display the BASIC program currently in the computer's memory on the computer screen. Typing LIST, followed by pressing the <CR> key will display the program in numerical order. If one or more statements in a program have been retyped, listing the program causes the program instructions to be displayed in correct numerical sequence, as illustrated earlier in Program B.2.

RUN Command. After a complete BASIC program has been entered, the program can be executed by typing the word **RUN** and then pressing the <CR> key as shown in previous programs. The computer immediately runs (executes) the program and displays the output on the computer screen. After completing this task, the computer stops and waits for the user to give it something else to do.

Table B–2
Summary of Common System Commands
[All commands are entered by pressing the <CR> key]

System Command or Activity	Apple IIe DOS 3.3 APPLESOFT	IBM–PC DOS 3.0 BASICA	TRS–80 III–IV BASIC	Computers Using GW–BASIC
To load the disk operating System (DOS) (BASIC is on the DOS disk)	Insert DOS 3.3 disk in disk drive. Turn computer on. Follow instructions on screen.	Insert DOS 3.0 disk in disk drive. Turn computer on. Follow instructions on screen.	Insert TRSDOS disk in disk drive. Turn computer on. Follow instructions on screen.	Insert DOS 2.11 disk in disk drive. Turn computer on. Follow instructions on screen.
To assess BASIC	BASIC is ready when] prompt is displayed. Use upper case only.	Type BAS-ICA when A> appears. BASIC is ready when **OK** is displayed.	Type BASIC when **TRSDOS Ready** message is displayed.	Type BASIC when **A>** appears. BASIC is ready when **OK** is displayed.
DIRECTORY command	When] prompt appears, type **CATALOG** and press **RETURN.**	When **A>** prompt appears, type **DIR** and press <CR> key.	When > prompt appears; type **DIR :0** and press <CR> key.	When **A>** prompt appears, type **DIR** and press <CR> key.
FORMAT command	When] prompt appears, type **INITIALIZE** and press **RETURN.**	When **A>** prompt appears, type **FORMAT** and press the <CR> key.	When > prompt appears, type **FORMAT** and press the <CR> key.	When **A>** prompt appears, type **FORMAT** and press the <CR> key.
Copy command (for two-drive system)	When] appears, type **RUN COPYA** and follow instructions on screen.	At **A>** prompt, type **DISKCOPY A: B:** and follow instructions on screen.	Refer to instructions in manual for specific model and version.	At **A>** prompt, type **DISKCOPY A: B:** and follow instructions on screen.

(continued)

Table B–2 (continued)
Summary of Common System Commands
[All commands are entered by pressing the <CR> key]

NEW command	Type **NEW** and press **RETURN.**	Type **NEW** and press <CR> key.	Type **NEW** and press <CR> key.	Type **NEW** and press <CR> key.
LOAD command (from disk)	Type **LOAD** (**file name**) and press **RETURN.**	Type **LOAD** (**file name**) and press <CR> key.	Type **LOAD** (**file name**) and press <CR> key.	Type **LOAD** (**file name**) and press <CR> key.
SAVE command (to store on disk)	Type **SAVE** (**file name**) and press **RETURN.**	Type **SAVE** (**file name**) and press <CR> key.	Type **SAVE** (**file name**) and press <CR> key.	Type **SAVE** (**file name**) and press <CR> key.
LIST command	Type **LIST** and press **RETURN.**	Type **LIST** and press <CR> key.	Type **LIST** and press <CR> key.	Type **LIST** and press <CR> key.
RUN command	Type **RUN** and press **RETURN.**	Type **RUN** and press <CR> key.	Type **RUN** and press <CR> key.	Type **RUN** and press <CR> key.
Sign-off procedure	Turn power off.	Turn power off.	Turn power off.	Turn power off.

Note: The manual accompanying a particular microcomputer identifies the carriage control <CR> key for the microcomputer.

NOW TRY THIS!

After loading DOS and BASIC in your computer, perform the operations below:

1. Enter the statement, "How are you?" and **SAVE** the statement on your newly formatted disk.
2. Enter a **LIST** command and observe what happens.

Using Function Keys.   The keyboards on some, but not all, microcomputers have special **function keys** that make it possible for the user to enter commands with just one or two keystrokes. When using BASIC on one of these computers, numbers and commands appear at the bottom of the screen. These identify special function keys and how they are used. The first function, for example, says "1LIST."

This tells the user that pressing the **F1** key means the same thing to the computer as typing the word **LIST.** Thus, to list a program, the user needs only to press **F1** key, then type the file name, and finally press the carriage return <CR> key. Other function keys and their uses are explained in the owner's manual.

Entering BASIC Statements.   Most computer systems allow a user to enter BASIC statements by simply typing them in at the keyboard. Remember that in immediate mode a BASIC statement does not require a line number, but it does in program mode. Thus, each statement that is part of a BASIC program must have a line number. No two statements can have the same line number. By numbering statements in increments of 5 or 10, for instance, additional statements can be added to the program later.

After the statement has been typed, the <CR> key is pressed. If only the number of an existing line is typed and the <CR> key is pressed, that line will be deleted from the program. Remember to save the program if you want to retain it permanently on disk or tape.

Entering a New Program.   A new BASIC program is entered the same way as a BASIC statement—by typing it in at the keyboard. Program statements are entered one at a time until all statements have been entered. All statements in the program should be numbered (and arranged in numerical sequence), because statements will be executed in numerically ascending sequence when the program is run.

Loading an Existing (Stored) Program.   One of the most important features of a computer is that a program can be saved (stored on a secondary storage medium such as disk or tape), and re-entered into primary memory any time it is needed. To enter an existing program from secondary storage, the user types the command LOAD, the name of the program, and presses the <CR> key. This command retrieves the program from secondary storage and loads it into primary memory where it can be run or modified.

---

4. . . . .What the DOS commands are?

5. . . . .How a BASIC statement is entered into the computer?

6. . . . .How a new program is entered into the computer?

7. . . . .How an existing (stored) program is entered into the computer?

DO YOU
REMEMBER

Constants and Literals

A **constant** is an item of data that does not change in value during program execution. A **literal** is any combination of characters entered between quotation marks. Notice in Program B.3 that when the program is run, the output consists of exactly the words and numbers entered **between the quotation marks.**

Program B.3

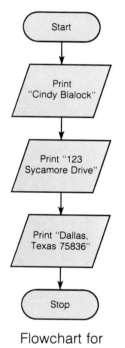

```
10   REM *** ILLUSTRATION OF "LITERALS" ***
20   PRINT "CINDY BLALOCK"
30   PRINT "123 SYCAMORE DRIVE"
40   PRINT "DALLAS, TEXAS 75836"
50   END
```

RUN

```
                         OUTPUT

CINDY BLALOCK
123 SYCAMORE DRIVE
DALLAS, TEXAS 75836
```

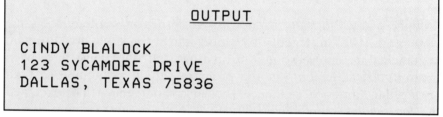

BASIC Version	Differences
Apple	None
IBM-PC	None
TRS-80	None
GW-BASIC	None

Flowchart for Program B.3

Variables

One of the most useful properties of a computer is its ability to manipulate variables. A **variable** is a name that represents a value that can be created or changed. In a computer, a variable is a named storage place in the computer's memory. A variable name (such as PAYRATE or NETPAY) is assigned by the programmer to store data in the computer's memory. A variable name used in a BASIC program will not change, but the data assigned to the variable name might change. In a payroll program, for example, the variable name PAYRATE will not change, but the pay rate amount for individual employees will probably be different. Keep in mind that, as a computer program is being run, various data can be stored in this named memory location. In BASIC, there are two kinds of variables: numeric variables and character (or string) variables.

Numeric Variables.   A **numeric variable** is a storage place in memory for a numeric value that will be created or changed while the program is being executed. Examples of numeric variables in a payroll program include hours worked, pay rate, gross pay, and net pay. The following format is used to assign a value to a variable:

```
line # LET variable name = value
```

For example, to assign the variable Y the value of 10, the instruction

```
30 LET Y = 10
```

may be used. When the program is run and line 30 is executed, the variable Y in primary memory will be assigned the value of 10.

Memory locations may be thought of as mailboxes for temporarily storing variable values. In the statement above, 10 is stored in mailbox Y, as illustrated below:

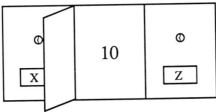

As the name implies, variables can change in value. The storage location of a variable in primary memory, however, can hold only one value at a time. For example, if the value assigned to the variable is changed to 25, as shown in the statement

```
30 LET Y = 25
```

the value in the Y mailbox will change from 10 to 25, as shown below.

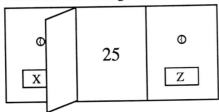

Once a new value is assigned to a variable location, the old value is erased and lost from memory.

In your study of mathematics, you learned that one numeric variable can be defined in terms of another. For example, when the instruction Y = 5 * X is executed by the computer, the results will be 30 if X is assigned the value of 6. The instructions and the way the variable values may be stored are shown below:

```
10 LET X = 6
20 LET Y = 5 * X
```

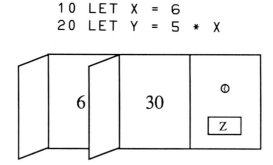

Different versions of BASIC vary in their ability to handle numeric data. Some versions handle only **integers** (whole numbers), while other versions have the ability to handle decimal numbers, called real numbers or floating-point numbers. Most versions, however, are designed to handle and process real number data.

Character (String) Variables.   Character (string) variables are used to store alphanumeric data. For example, student data such as name and courses the student is enrolled in are stored in character variables.

A character variable ends with a dollar sign ($). A numeric variable does not have a dollar sign after the name of the variable.

Variable Names.   Variable names begin with a letter of the alphabet, but other characters in the name can be letters or numbers. When assigning names to variables, a programmer might find it helpful to assign names related to the kinds of data to be stored in the variable. For example, if the programmer is going to store student names, naming the variable STUDENT$ makes it easier for the programmer to remember the kind of data stored in the variable.

One potential problem in assigning names to variables is that the version of BASIC being used might restrict the length of the variable name. Tables B–3 and B–4 show that some versions limit variable names to a few characters, while other versions allow as many as forty characters. Obviously, versions allowing more characters give the programmer greater flexibility in naming variables.

Table B–3
Numeric Variable Names

BASIC Version	Number of Unique Characters Recognized	Additional Characters Allowed
Applesoft BASIC	2	Yes
IBM-PC BASIC/ BASICA	40	No
TRS-80 BASIC	2	Yes
Microsoft GW– BASIC	40	Yes

Table B–4
Character Variable Names

BASIC Version	Number of Unique Characters Recognized	Additional Characters Permitted
Applesoft BASIC	2 (plus $)	Yes[a]
IBM-PC BASIC/ BASICA	40 (plus $)	No
TRS-80 BASIC	2 (plus $)	Yes[a]
Microsoft GW– BASIC	40 (plus $)	Yes

[a]The last character must be a dollar sign ($) when additional characters are used.

Order of Mathematical Operations

Computers are designed to perform mathematical operations in the same order as mathematicians. To avoid incorrect output, the programmer should be familiar with this order when writing program instructions.

Suppose, for example, that you write the following instruction to calculate the average of two test grades of 80 and 90:

40 PRINT 80 + 90/2

Will the computer add the two test grades and then divide the sum by 2, or will the computer divide 90 by 2 and add the result to 80? The latter is true because division is carried out before addition. In this example, the calculated average will be 125, which is incorrect! The correct average will be calculated if the two test grades are enclosed in parentheses because the operations in the innermost parentheses are completed first. Thus, the instruction 40 PRINT (80 + 90)/2 will cause the correct average 85 to be calculated.

Below is the order in which mathematical operations are performed by a computer. You should immediately recognize this as the same order you learned in your study of mathematics:

1. Quantities in parentheses are evaluated first, starting from the innermost parentheses.

2. Next, quantities raised to a power are evaluated.

3. Next, multiplication and division are performed.

4. Finally, addition and subtraction are done.

5. Operations of equal value are performed from left to right.

In the following example, mathematical operations are performed in the same order as listed above:

50 LET X = (6 + (12 + 4)/8) + 20 ^ 2

Order of Operation	Explanation
(1) $12 + 4 = 16$	Innermost parentheses first
(2) $16 / 8 = 2$	Next priority
(3) $6 + 2 = 8$	Process rest of outer parentheses
(4) $20 \char`^ 2 = 400$	Next priority
(5) $8 + 400 = 408$	Process lowest priority

8. . . .The meanings of *constant, literal,* and *variable* in **BASIC?**

9. . . .Why variable names are used?

10. . . .The primary difference between numeric variables and character (string) variables?

11. . . .The order in which mathematical operations in a BASIC statement are performed?

DO YOU
REMEMBER

BASIC Programming Statements

In the following sections, BASIC statements and new keywords are introduced. Learning how they are used will enable you to begin writing simple programs using BASIC. The manual for the version of BASIC you are using contains other, more advanced statements and keywords. By studying the manual, you will learn to write more powerful and advanced programs.

It has already been pointed out that every line in a BASIC program begins with a **line number,** followed by a **BASIC statement.** Another important rule to remember is that every BASIC statement begins with a reserved word. A **reserved word** is a word that has a special meaning to the computer. BASIC, like other programming languages, has its own set of reserved words, some of which are explained next. For both convenience and emphasis, BASIC reserved words in this module will be printed in upper-case letters.

REM (REMark) Statement

REM (for REMark) statements allow a programmer to introduce explanatory remarks in the body of a program. They can be inserted anywhere in the program, but have no effect on program execution. When the program is run, everything to the right of the word REM is ignored. The following is an example of a REM statement:

```
10  REM *** This Program Calculates an Average ***
```

In the above statement, notice the reserved word **REM** following the line number. To the computer, this means that the programmer has merely inserted a remark in the program. When the program is listed, the statement will be printed as part of the program, but it will have no effect on program execution.

REM statements can be used to document a program, to explain program segments, and/or to define variables used in the program. Thus, they allow the programmer to include valuable information such as copyrights, program ownership, and updated documentation in BASIC programs.

PRINT Statement

In BASIC, the **PRINT** statement produces output. In program mode, the PRINT statement includes a line number, the command PRINT, and a value or list of values. The value(s) to be printed can be constants, variables, or expressions.

The PRINT statement causes output to be displayed on the screen or sent to a printer. Some versions of BASIC for microcomputers use the word PRINT to display output on the screen, and the word LPRINT to send output to a printer. Some send output to a printer with the statement PR# followed by the slot number where the printer cable is connected to the computer. The general form for the PRINT statement is

line # PRINT (constant, variable, expression)

The PRINT statement can cause any value or combination of values to be printed. PRINT statements can be used to print constants, variables, both constants and variables, and strings (like those shown in the program below). Thus, a BASIC program can include any number of PRINT statements. In Program B.4, several PRINT statements are included to illustrate the versatility of the PRINT statement. In the program, notice the PRINT statement in line 30 that includes only the line number followed by the word PRINT. This causes the computer to leave a blank line in the output. These PRINT features are illustrated in Program B.4.

Program B.4

```
10   REM *** ILLUSTRATION OF "PRINT" STATEMENTS ***
20   PRINT "THIS IS A PROGRAM"
30   PRINT
40   LET A = 5
50   LET B = A * A
60   PRINT "A =",A
```

```
70   PRINT "A SQUARED =",B
80   END
```

RUN

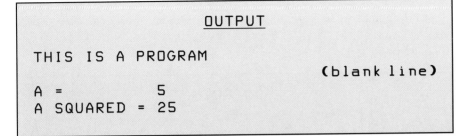

```
                    OUTPUT

THIS IS A PROGRAM
                              (blank line)

A =           5
A SQUARED = 25
```

BASIC Version	Differences
Apple	None
IBM-PC	None
TRS-80	None
GW-BASIC	None

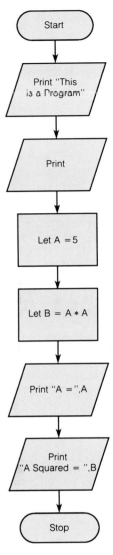

Flowchart for Program B.4

In Program B.4, line 20 causes the character string "THIS IS A PROGRAM" to be printed. Line 60 causes the string "A =" plus the value of A (5) to be printed. Line 70 causes the string "A SQUARED =" plus the value of B (25) to be printed. The purpose of the LET statements in lines 40 and 50 will be explained later.

A complete explanation of the PRINT command is beyond the scope of this module. As with all BASIC commands, the user should become familiar with the manual for the version of BASIC being used.

END Statement

The **END** statement signals the end of a program, and terminates program execution. An END statement is usually placed at the end of a program, although it can be placed anywhere to terminate program execution. The general form for the END statement is

line # END

Some interpreted versions of BASIC omit the END statement, but it is a good practice to include it because it identifies the end of the program. Program B.5 illustrates the use of the END statement.

Program B.5

```
10    REM ***ILLUSTRATION OF "END" STATEMENT ***
20    LET Z = 10 + 19 + 27/3
30    PRINT "VALUE OF Z =",Z
40    END
```

RUN

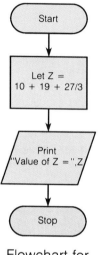

Flowchart for
Program B.5

OUTPUT
VALUE OF Z = 38

BASIC Version	Differences
Apple	None
IBM-PC	None
TRS-80	None
GW-BASIC	None

Program B.5 performs a mathematical calculation and prints the output. Line 20 divides 27 by 3 and adds the result (9) to the sum of 10 plus 19. Line 30 prints the string "VALUE OF Z =", and the actual computed value of Z which is 38. The END statement identifies the end of the program.

LET Statement

The **LET** statement is an **assignment statement,** one of the more important and useful statements in BASIC. This means that a LET statement can be used for any, or all, of the following purposes:

> **1.** *Assign a constant to a variable.* The general form for this LET statement is
>
> > line # LET variable = constant

The following LET statements illustrate how constants are assigned to variables:

```
10 LET A = 5
20 LET B = 8
30 LET C = 7
```

Recall that a variable is a storage location in computer memory. After the above LET statements are executed, each of the constants (5, 8, and 7) is stored in memory as illustrated below:

Memory Locations		
A	B	C
5	8	7

2. *Assign one variable to another variable.* The general form for this kind of LET statement is

line # LET variable 1 = variable 2

The variable that receives the new value loses its previous value and, instead, contains the new value. In the form for the LET statement above, the value of variable 1 (left of the equal sign) loses its previous value as it receives the value of variable 2. The value of variable 2 (right of the equal sign) does not change. For example, notice in the following group of LET statements that line 40 causes the value of variable A to change from 5 to 6:

```
10  LET A = 5
20  LET B = 8
30  LET C = 7
40  LET A = A + B - C
```

After the above statements are executed, the

contents of the variables in memory can be illustrated as follows:

	Memory Locations		
A	B	C	D
6	8	7	

3. *Assign character (string) constants to character (string) variables.* A **string constant** is any combination of characters a user wishes to identify in a program as a variable. The group of characters is always enclosed in quotation marks, but the quotation marks are not part of the value assigned. The general form for this LET statement is

line # LET character variable = character constant

Below are examples of this kind of LET statement and an illustration of how they might appear in memory:

```
10   LET B$ = "Robert Boswell"
20   LET C1$ = "374 Elmwood Drive"
```

Memory Locations	
B$	C1$
Robert Boswell	374 Elmwood Drive

4. *Assign the result of a calculation to a variable.* The LET statement can be used to calculate the value of a mathematical expression and then assign the resulting value to a variable. The general form for this type of LET statement is

line # LET variable = mathematical expression

The mathematical expression is always to the right of the equal sign and can include both variables and constants. BASIC processes the expression and assigns the resulting value to the variable on the left of the equal sign. The mathematical expression can be long and complex. In BASIC, there are five **operators** that can be used in mathematical expressions. These operators are shown in Table B–5.

Table B–5
Mathematical Operators

Operation Performed	Keys Used to Perform Operation			
	Applesoft BASIC	IBM-PC BASIC	TRS-80 BASIC	MICRO-SOFT GW–BASIC
Addition	+	+	+	+
Subtraction	–	–	–	–
Multiplication	*	*	*	*
Division	/	/	/	/
Exponentiation	^	^	^	^

NOW TRY THIS!

Load DOS and BASIC into your computer. Using a combination of **REM, PRINT,** and **LET** statements, write a short program illustrating all of the mathematical operators shown above. Check your output to make certain your program is correct.

12. . . .The primary purpose of *REM* statements in a BASIC program?

13. . . .Why *PRINT* statements are used in a BASIC program?

14. . . .The uses for *LET* statements in a BASIC program?

DO YOU REMEMBER

INPUT Statement

Before data can be processed, it must be entered into the computer. One method is to enter data using INPUT statements. The general form for the INPUT statement is

line # INPUT variable data

An **INPUT** statement in a BASIC program allows data to be entered from the keyboard after the RUN command is given. As shown in Program B.6, the program will stop when it reaches the INPUT statement in the program, display the message ENTER PRICE = and wait for the user to enter the data. The question mark prompt on the next line is the computer's way of asking what data (price) the user wishes to enter.

<u>Program B.6</u>

```
10   REM   * ILLUSTRATION OF "INPUT" STATEMENT *
20   REM
30   REM      THIS PROGRAM COMPUTES THE PRICE
40   REM            INCLUDING THE SALES TAX
50   REM
60   REM                    VARIABLES
70   REM
80   REM            P = Product price
90   REM            T = Sales tax
100  REM
110  REM
120  INPUT "ENTER PRICE =",P
130  LET T = P * 1.05
140  PRINT "PRICE WITH TAX =",T
150  END

RUN
```

<u>OUTPUT</u>

```
ENTER PRICE = 1.00
PRICE WITH TAX =                          1.05
```

Start

Input
"Enter Price =",P

Let T = P * 1.05

Print "Price
with Tax =",T

Stop

Flowchart for
Program B.6   RUN

```
                    OUTPUT

ENTER PRICE = 24.00
PRICE WITH TAX =                       25.20
```

BASIC Version	Differences
Apple	Use semicolon in line 120 before P
IBM-PC	None
TRS-80	None
GW-BASIC	None

INPUT statements permit the user to enter different values each time the program is run. In Program B.6, each value (price) entered will be multiplied by 1.05, giving the price with the tax.

Each time the program is run, line 120 tells the computer that you will enter the price when you are reminded to do so by the message "ENTER PRICE =" displayed on the screen. Each time the message is displayed, the user enters the price and presses the <CR> key. The program is then executed and the price (including tax) is displayed on the screen.

NOW TRY THIS!

Assume that your company has ten employees and that each employee's gross pay is calculated by the formula

Gross pay = Hours worked * Hourly pay rate

Assume, also, that you are required by law to withhold a total of 27 percent of each employee's gross pay for taxes and Social Security.

Prepare a flowchart showing the logic of your problem solution. Next, write and enter a BASIC program to compute each employee's net pay using **REM, PRINT, END, LET,** and **INPUT** statements. (Use different hours worked and a different hourly pay rate for each employee.)

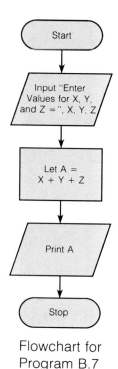

Flowchart for
Program B.7

GOTO Statement

The sample programs shown thus far have been executed in sequential order—that is, one instruction after another in numerical order. In many programs, however, it is necessary to alter the order in which instructions are executed. This alteration of program execution is known as **branching,** and a statement that alters the execution is known as a **branch.** An example of a branch is a GOTO statement. A **GOTO** statement causes an **unconditional transfer** of control to the statement indicated in the GOTO statement, because the computer does not have a choice. When a GOTO statement in a BASIC program is encountered, the computer must immediately GOTO and execute the statement specified in the GOTO statement. The general form for the GOTO statement is

line # GOTO new line #

The GOTO statement form above shows that whenever a GOTO statement is encountered, control is automatically (unconditionally) transferred to the new line specified in the GOTO statement. Notice the purpose for the GOTO in line 50 Program B.7.

Program B.7

```
10   REM   *** ILLUSTRATION OF "GOTO" STATEMENT ***
20   INPUT "ENTER VALUES FOR X, Y, AND Z =", X,Y,Z
30   LET A = X + Y + Z
40   PRINT A
50   GOTO 20
60   END

RUN
```

OUTPUT	ENTER
ENTER VALUES FOR X, Y, AND Z =	5,4,3
12	
ENTER VALUES FOR X, Y, AND Z =	12,7,89
108	

BASIC Version	Differences
Apple	None
IBM-PC	None
TRS-80	None
GW-BASIC	None

In Program B.7, each time the computer reaches line 50, the computer branches back to line 20, which instructs the user to enter new values for X, Y, and Z. This feature, which allows a section of a program (a series of instructions) to be executed repeatedly, is called **looping,** a feature that can be quite useful to a programmer.

An important caution is in order! The GOTO statement does give the programmer more control over the logical flow of a BASIC program. However, unconditional changes in program flow can result in BASIC programs so complex that the logic is difficult to follow. Thus, the use of GOTO statements should be minimized, and even avoided if possible. For this reason, other control statements are introduced later that are preferable to GOTO statements.

READ and DATA Statements

We learned earlier that using INPUT statements is one method for entering data into a computer. Another method is to use a combination of READ and DATA statements that allows data to be entered from a BASIC program. **READ** statements are usually inserted near the beginning of a program, and **DATA** statements near the end.

The general form for a READ statement is

line # READ variable 1, variable 2, . . .

The general form for a DATA statement is

line # DATA item 1, data item 2, . . .

READ and DATA statements work together to enter data into the computer. Consider Program B.8 which is similar to Program B.7 but has been modified slightly.

Program B.8

```
10    REM ** ILLUSTRATION "READ" AND "DATA" STATEMENTS **
20    READ X,Y,Z
30    LET A = X + Y + Z
40    PRINT A
50    GOTO 20
60    DATA 5,4,3,12,7,89
70    END
```

RUN

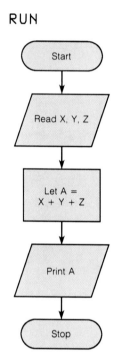

Flowchart for
Program B.8

OUTPUT

```
12
108
Out of DATA in 20
```

BASIC Version	Differences
Apple	None
IBM-PC	None
TRS-80	None
GW-BASIC	None

Line 20 in Program B.8 instructs the computer to READ and assign data values in the DATA statement to the corresponding variables X, Y, and Z in the READ statement. The computer automatically finds the data values (numbers) in the DATA statement in line 60 and assigns the values in the order they appear in the READ statement (from left to right). Thus, the number 5 (in the DATA statement) is assigned to the variable X (in the READ statement), the number 4 is assigned to the variable Y, and the number 3 is assigned to variable Z, as illustrated below:

Memory Locations		
X	Y	Z
5	4	3

Earlier you learned that a LET statement, like the one in line 30 in Program B.8, can be used to assign the result of a mathematical expression to a variable. Line 30 tells the computer to add the data values assigned to variables X, Y, and Z and to assign the result to variable A. After execution, variables X, Y, Z, and A might appear in memory as illustrated below:

Memory Locations			
A	X	Y	Z
12	5	4	3

After the first loop has been completed, the next group of values (12, 7, and 89) is read and processed. Notice the output (108) for this group of values.

After all data values have been read and processed by the computer, the message "OUT OF DATA in 20" will appear on the screen. If too many data items are included, the computer will READ only enough to fill the variables and ignore the remaining data items.

15. . . .The purpose of *INPUT* statements in a BASIC program, and how data is entered into a computer when an *INPUT* statement is used in a program?

16. . . .The purpose of *GOTO* statements in a BASIC program, and why a *GOTO* statement is said to cause an unconditional branch?

17. . . .The primary purpose of *READ* and *DATA* statements in a BASIC program?

DO YOU REMEMBER

NOW TRY THIS!

Using a combination of the BASIC statements already introduced, including **READ** and **DATA** statements, write, enter, and execute a program that produces a hypothetical list of student names, addresses, and telephone numbers. Leave a blank line between each line of output.

TAB Function

Earlier we learned that the PRINT statement produces output. The PRINT statement, however, provides little control of the output format, and users often want to format the output produced. BASIC provides various methods for formatting output. One method is to use the TAB command in a PRINT statement to cause output to be printed in a particular column. **TAB** advances the PRINT statement to the column indicated in parentheses after the TAB statement. The general form of the TAB command is

line # PRINT TAB (expression)

Program B.9 uses the TAB function. Notice that TAB commands can be used to display headings as well as the data under the headings.

<u>Program B.9</u>

```
10   REM           *** ILLUSTRATION OF "TAB" FUNCTION  ***
20   PRINT TAB(3);"COL1";TAB(9);"COL2";TAB(15);"COL3";
     TAB(21);"TOTAL"
30   READ A,B,C
40   LET T = A + B +C
50   PRINT TAB(3);A;TAB(9);B;TAB(15);C;TAB(21);T
60   IF A = -99 THEN 90
70   GOTO 30
80   DATA 512,127,750,626,405,860,-99
90   END
```

RUN

```
                         OUTPUT

        COL1    COL2    COL3    TOTAL
         512     127     750     1389
         626     405     860     1891
    Out of DATA in 30
```

BASIC Version	Differences
Apple	Limited to 40-column display
IBM-PC	None
TRS-80	Limited to 40-column display
GW-BASIC	None

In Program B.9, the word TAB in line 20 instructs the computer to print four column headings (COL1, COL2, COL3, and TOTAL), and to begin printing each in the column indicated in the parentheses following each TAB. Thus, the "COL1" heading will be printed beginning in column 3, and so on. Line 30 tells the computer to read the first three data values from the DATA statement (line 80). Line 40 instructs the computer to add (horizontally) the values of A, B, and C to obtain the horizontal total (T). Line 50 prints the values of A, B, C, and T in their respective columns. Line 60 terminates program execution when the value −99 is read. Line 70 returns the computer to line 30 to read more data values for A, B, and C.

Notice the semicolons separating the TAB functions in Program B.9. The semicolons assure that headings will be printed in the positions indicated in parentheses following the TAB statement. Separating them with other punctuations, such as commas, can cause headings and data to be printed in columns other than those specified in parentheses. Notice, also, that commas are used to separate data values in the DATA statement. The presence of a comma between data items indicates to the computer that another data value follows the last one read.

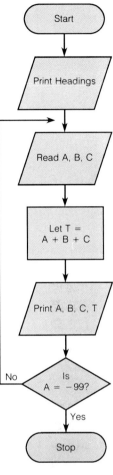

Flowchart for Program B.9

NOW TRY THIS!

Using **PRINT TAB** statements to format your output, write and enter a BASIC program that produces a list of employee names, pay rates, number of hours worked, and gross pay for each employee in column format. Use column headings.

PRINT USING Statement

Some versions of BASIC, including the IBM-PC and TRS-80 versions, offer a PRINT USING statement as a method to format output. Other versions, however, do not allow the use of this statement. Because some versions do not allow PRINT USING statements, the programmer should refer to the manual before attempting to include them in a BASIC program.

The **PRINT USING** statement allows the programmer to specify the format of both numeric and character (string) output. The general form for the PRINT USING statement is

line # PRINT USING format string, or variable data

The format string in the PRINT USING statement includes certain characters that specify how the output of the data is to be formatted, or edited, as shown in Program B.10.

Program B.10

```
REM *** ILLUSTRATION OF "PRINT USING" STATEMENT ***
PRINT USING "  \       \            \     \    \        \";
"ITEM","TOTAL","SALES"
PRINT USING "\           \            \     \    \        \";
PURCHASED","PRICE","TAX"
READ B$,X
LET Z = X * .05
PRINT USING "\          \              $$##.##      $$##        .##";B$,X,Z
GOTO 40
DATA SHIRT,22.50,SOCKS,3.75,SWEATER,39.95
DATA SCARF,14.50,COAT,69.00,BELT,12.50
END
RUN
```

```
                        OUTPUT

        ITEM              TOTAL        SALES
     PURCHASED            PRICE         TAX
     SHIRT               $22.50       $1.13
     SOCKS                $3.75       $0.19
     SWEATER             $39.95       $2.00
     SCARF               $14.50       $0.73
     COAT                $69.00       $3.45
     BELT                $12.50       $0.63
     Out of DATA in 40
```

BASIC Version	Differences
Apple	PRINT USING not applicable
IBM-PC	None
TRS-80	None
GW-BASIC	None

Program B.10 uses PRINT USING statements to format the output. The quotation marks and pairs of left slashes specify the columns in which output is to be printed. Number characters (#) are used to specify the format for numeric values. Each number character (#) stands for a digit. The decimal between the second and third number characters indicates that the numeric data displayed will have two digits to the right of the decimal and two digits to the left.

Additional characters can be included in a PRINT USING statement to specify the format of the output. Versions of BASIC that allow PRINT USING statements make the preparation of output easier and the presentation more attractive. Most versions of BASIC allow the use of the characters listed in Table B–6.

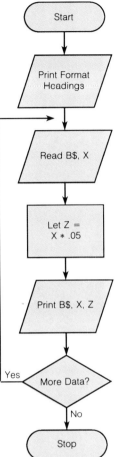

Flowchart for
Program B.10

Table B–6	
Selected **PRINT USING** Characters and Their Functions	

Character	Function

#	Number signs specify the format for numeric values. Each # represents a numeric digit, and decimal points and commas can be used. For example, the statement
	
	`40 PRINT USING "###.##;38.12`
	
	will print
	
	`38.12`

$	A dollar sign at the beginning of the string prints a $ at that position. For example, the statement
	
	`40 PRINT USING "$###.##;38.12`
	
	will print
	
	`$ 38.12`

$$	Two dollar signs ($$) at the beginning of a numeric format string will cause a floating decimal point with a dollar sign ($) placed adjacent to the numeric value. For example, the statement
	
	`40 PRINT USING "$$####.##";38.12`
	
	will print
	
	`$38.12`

(continued)

Table B–6 (continued)
Selected **PRINT USING** Characters and Their Functions

!	An exclamation mark (!) causes the first character in a string to be printed. For example, the statement
	
	`40 PRINT USING "!"; "JOHN"`
	
	will print
	
	`J`

//	Two slashes specify the format for character strings. Some versions of BASIC require left slashes. For example, the statement
	
	`40 PRINT USING "/      /";`
	`    "ROBERT"`
	
	will print
	
	`Robert`

Some versions of BASIC provide other important uses for PRINT USING statements. The manual for the version being used should be studied carefully to learn the various ways PRINT USING statements can be used. Special attention should also be given to learning the characters that particular version of BASIC allows.

DO YOU
REMEMBER

18. . . .The purpose of using one, or more, *TAB* functions in a program?

19. . . .The purpose of using *PRINT USING* statements in a BASIC program?

IF/THEN Statement

Statements like PRINT and GOTO are called unconditional statements because the computer will always execute them. In contrast, the **IF/THEN** statement is **conditional** because the action taken depends upon whether the condition is found to be true. The simplest form of the IF/THEN statement is

line # IF condition THEN line #

NOW TRY THIS!

Write and enter a BASIC program that produces the following output. Use **PRINT USING** statements to format your output like that shown below:

```
       NAME          TELEPHONE NUMBER
   Adams, Joel       (205) 374 5185
   Baker, Cathy      (205) 374 2215
   Carter, Mel       (205) 374 8876
   Dixon, Diane      (205) 374 9834
   Epley, David      (205) 374 1881
```

The condition portion of the statement compares two values that must be separated by one of the following symbols:

SYMBOL	MEANING
=	equal to
>	greater than
<	less than
>=	greater than or equal to
<=	less than or equal to
<>	not equal to

Below is an example of an IF/THEN statement:

30 IF X > 10 THEN 70

When the condition in line 30, X > 10, is true, the computer immediately goes to, and executes, line 70. When the condition is false— that is, when X is less than or equal to 10, the computer proceeds to the next line of the program.

IF/THEN statements have many important uses in programming. One such use is illustrated in Program B.11 in which an IF/THEN statement is used to notify a user inputting payroll data if, and when, too many hours are entered for an employee.

Program B.11

```
 10    REM *** ILLUSTRATION OF "IF/THEN" STATEMENT ***
 20    REM
 30    REM                    "VARIABLES"
 40    REM
 50    REM              H = HOURS WORKED
 60    REM              R = RATE OF PAY
 70    REM              W = GROSS PAY
 80    REM
 90    REM
100    PRINT "ENTER HOURS WORKED AND PAY RATE = "
110    INPUT H,R
120    IF H > 40 THEN 160
130    LET W = H * R
140    PRINT "GROSS PAY =",W
150    GO TO 100
160    PRINT "TOO MANY HOURS ENTERED = ",H
170    END
RUN
```

```
                        OUTPUT

    ENTER HOURS WORKED AND PAY RATE =
    ? 40,4
    GROSS PAY =        160
```

RUN

```
                        OUTPUT

    ENTER HOURS WORKED AND PAY RATE =
    ? 45,4.50
    TOO MANY HOURS ENTERED = 45
```

BASIC Version	Differences
Apple	None
IBM-PC	None
TRS-80	None
GW-BASIC	None

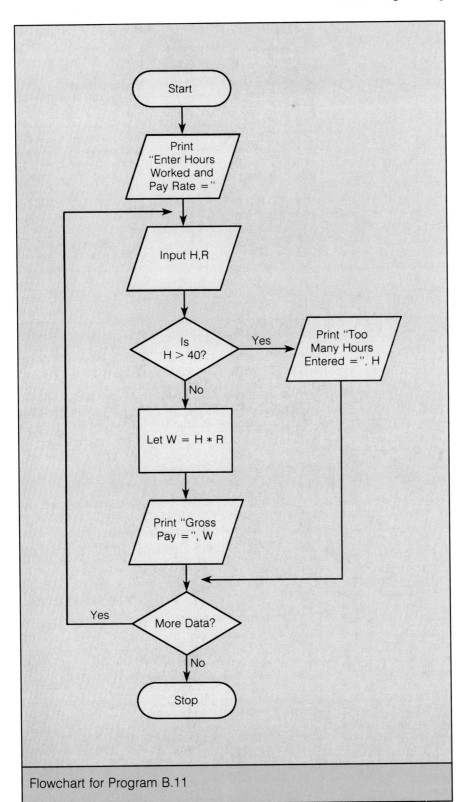

Flowchart for Program B.11

When Program B.11 is run, the user is prompted by the message "ENTER HOURS WORKED AND PAY RATE = ", and a question mark prompt to enter the number of hours the employee has worked and the pay rate. When the computer executes line 110, if the number of hours entered is greater than 40, control is transferred to line 160 which causes the computer to display message "TOO MANY HOURS ENTERED = " followed by the number of hours entered for the employee. If the number of hours entered does not exceed 40, the number of hours entered is multiplied by the hourly rate giving the employee's gross wage (line 130). The purpose of the IF/THEN statement in Program B.11 is to prevent a user from entering too many hours for an employee.

There are even more advanced uses for IF/THEN statements that are beyond the scope of this module. As always, programmers wanting to write more advanced programs using IF/THEN statements should become familiar with the manual that accompanies the version of BASIC being used.

NOW TRY THIS!

Refer to Program B.11. Rewrite the program so that 10 percent (10%) of each employee's gross pay will be withheld for taxes. Make the necessary changes that will produce each employee's net pay after the 10 percent tax is withheld.

GOSUB and RETURN Statements

In BASIC, a **subroutine** is a series of program statements that is branched to and executed, after which control is returned to the point where the branch began. Frequently, it is desirable to alter the order of program execution to allow the execution of a subroutine.

In BASIC, a subroutine can be implemented by using a combination of two statements: a GOSUB statement and a RETURN statement. A **GOSUB** statement transfers program control to the line where the subroutine begins. A **RETURN** statement inserted at the end of the subroutine returns control to the statement immediately following the GOSUB statement in the program.

The general form for the GOSUB statement is

line # GOSUB line #

The reserved word GOSUB causes the computer to skip to the line number specified after the word GOSUB. When the computer reaches a GOSUB statement during program execution, control will pass to the line specified in the GOSUB statement. The statement in that line will be executed next, followed by successive statements in order until a RETURN statement is reached.

The general form for the RETURN statement is

line # RETURN

When the computer reaches the RETURN statement, control is transferred back to the statement immediately following the GOSUB statement. The remainder of the program statements are then executed in order unless other statements are reached that also transfer control.

A word of caution! Do not confuse the GOSUB statement with the GOTO statement. Program B.12 illustrates the correct use of GOSUB and GOTO statements:

<u>Program B.12</u>

```
 10    REM *** ILLUSTRATION OF "GOSUB" AND ***
 20    REM ***      "RETURN" STATEMENTS        ***
 30    REM
 40    REM
 50    REM                  "VARIABLES"
 60    REM
 70    REM      N$ = EMPLOYEE NAME
 80    REM       H = NUMBER OF HOURS WORKED
 90    REM       R = PAY RATE
100    REM       G = GROSS PAY
110    REM       S = SOCIAL SECURITY
120    REM       I = FEDERAL TAX
130    REM       D = TOTAL DEDUCTIONS
140    REM       N = NET PAY
150    REM
160    REM
170    REM
180    READ N$,H,R
190    IF H < 0 THEN 340
200    GOSUB 270
210    LET S = G * .075
220    LET I = G * .20
230    LET D = S + I
240    LET N = G - D
250    PRINT N$,"$",N
260    GOTO 180
```

```
270    IF H > 40 THEN 300
280    LET G = H * R
290    GOTO 310
300    LET G = (40 * R) + (H - 40) *(R * 1.5)
310    RETURN
320    DATA BILL SMITH,40,4,JANICE WONG,44,5.25
330    DATA DEBRA MADISON,45,4.40,KIM FONG,38,4.60,-99
340    END
RUN
```

OUTPUT

BILL SMITH	$	116
JANICE WONG	$	175.0875
DEBRA MADISON	$	151.525
KIM FONG	$	123.395

BASIC Version	Differences
Apple	None
IBM-PC	None
TRS-80	None
GW-BASIC	None

Program B.12 shows how GOSUB and RETURN statements can be used to branch to subroutines within a program, execute the subroutines, and return to the main part of the program. After the computer reads an employee's name, the number of hours worked, and the pay rate (line 180), the computer determines in line 190 if the number of hours is less than zero. If so, the computer skips to line 340, which ends program execution. If not, the computer continues to line 200, which instructs the computer to begin executing the subroutine that starts at line 270. Line 270 is a conditional statement that tells the computer to execute line 300 if the number of hours worked exceeds 40. Line 300 calculates the employee's gross pay if (and only if) the number of hours worked exceeds 40 using the formula in the statement. Then line 310 is executed, which tells the computer to return to the line immediately following the line containing the GO-SUB statement. Thus, the computer will return to line 210 and begin calculating the employee's net pay (lines 210–240). After this, the

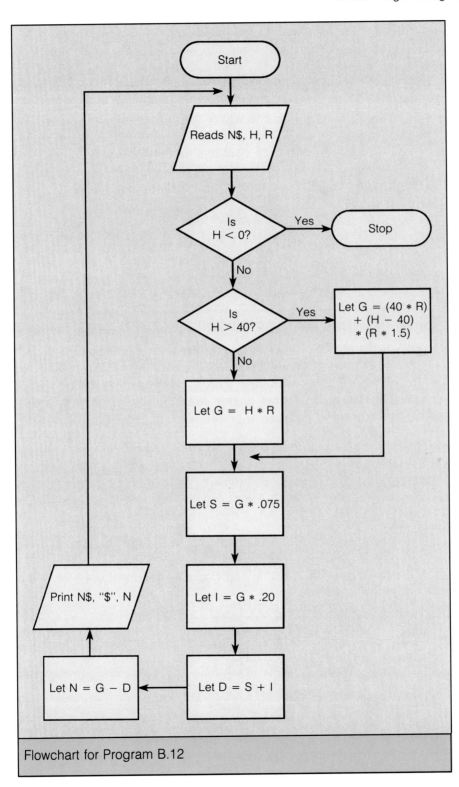

Flowchart for Program B.12

desired output is printed by line 250. After printing the output, line 260 tells the computer to go to line 180, which reads data for the next employee.

Notice, however, that if the condition specified in line 270 is not true (that is, if the number of hours worked does not exceed 40), the computer continues to line 280 where a different formula (G = H * R) calculates the employee's gross pay. The following line (290) sends the computer to line 310 which contains the RETURN statement that sends the computer back to line 210. Then lines 210–240 calculate the employee's deductions before printing output according to line 250.

GOSUB and RETURN statements are potentially powerful programming statements in BASIC. Using these statements, along with others previously explained, a programmer can write complex, yet valuable, programs.

FOR . . . TO . . . NEXT . . . Statement

Earlier you learned that a GOTO statement can be used to establish a loop. Another easy method for establishing a loop is to use FOR . . . TO . . . NEXT . . . statements, often called simply FOR/NEXT statements. These statements enable the computer to repeat a task any number of times, as shown in Program B.13.

<u>Program B.13</u>

```
 10    REM  *** ILLUSTRATION "FOR...TO...NEXT" ***
 20    REM  ***              STATEMENT           ***
 30    REM   *                                     *
 40    REM
 50    REM
 60    REM                  "VARIABLES"
 70    REM
 80    REM         N$ = STUDENT NAME
 90    REM         T1 = 1ST TEST GRADE
100    REM         T2 = 2ND TEST GRADE
110    REM         T3 = 3RD TEST GRADE
120    REM         T4 = 4TH TEST GRADE
130    REM         A  = FINAL AVERAGE
140    REM
150    REM
160    REM
170    PRINT "STUDENT NAME","FINAL AVERAGE"
```

```
180    FOR N = 1 TO 4
190    READ N$,T1,T2,T3,T4
200    LET A = (T1 +   T2 + T3 + T4)/4
210    PRINT N$,A
220    NEXT N
230    DATA CINDY FULLER,92,90,98,88
240    DATA MIKE FULLER,96,82,86,98
250    DATA ANDY MILLER,80,84,94,78
260    DATA BOB TOSH,74,68,82,90
270    END
RUN
```

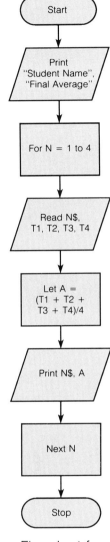

Flowchart for
Program B.13

```
                    OUTPUT

STUDENT NAME      FINAL AVERAGE
CINDY FULLER      92
MIKE FULLER       90.5
ANDY MILLER       84
BOB TOSH          78.5
out of DATA in 190
```

BASIC Version	Differences
Apple	None
IBM-PC	None
TRS-80	None
GW-BASIC	None

Program B.13 illustrates one possible use of FOR . . . TO . . . NEXT statements. Line 180 tells the computer to repeat the loop four times (FOR N = 1 to 4), because the final average is to be calculated for each one of four students. Each time the loop is repeated, the computer is instructed to read a student's name (N$) and four test grades (T1 through T4) from the data statements. Next, line 200 privides the formula for calculating each student's average. Finally, each student's name and average are printed before the next loop is executed. Notice that line 220 returns the computer to line 190 to read data for the next student.

NOW TRY THIS!

Refer to Program B.13. Assume your teacher uses this program to calculate student grade averages, and wants you to rewrite the program so that the final exam score (T4) will count twice as much as each of the other test scores. Make the necessary changes, and enter and execute the new program.

There are many other useful applications for these statements. For example, FOR. . . TO. . . NEXT statements are also useful for incrementing numbers, as shown in Program B.14.

Program B.14

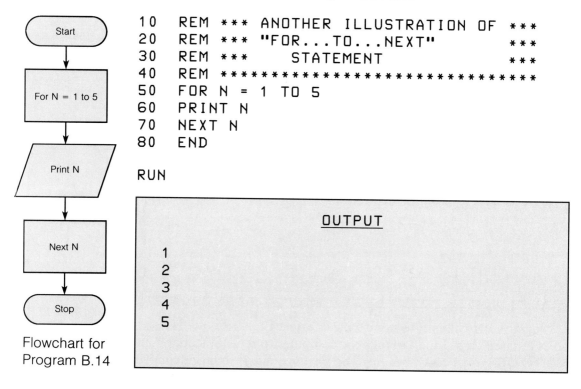

```
10    REM *** ANOTHER ILLUSTRATION OF ***
20    REM *** "FOR...TO...NEXT"         ***
30    REM ***      STATEMENT            ***
40    REM *******************************
50    FOR N = 1 TO 5
60    PRINT N
70    NEXT N
80    END

RUN
```

OUTPUT

```
1
2
3
4
5
```

Flowchart for Program B.14

BASIC Version	Differences
Apple	None
IBM-PC	None
TRS-80	None
GW-BASIC	None

Program B.14 instructs the computer to print the numbers 1 through 5 beginning with the number 1. Many different mathematical operations can be performed with only minor changes in the above program.

FOR. . . TO. . . NEXT statements are often used in programs with TAB functions to format the output in table format. Program B.15 illustrates this combination in a BASIC program.

Program B.15

```
 10    REM * ILLUSTRATION OF "FOR...TO...NEXT" STATEMENT*
 20    REM *          USED WITH "TAB" STATEMENT          *
 30    REM ***********************************************
 40    PRINT TAB(5);"COL1";'TAB(16);"COL2";TAB(28);"COL3";
       TAB(40);"TOTAL"
 50    FOR N = 1 TO 4
 60    READ X,Y,Z
 70    LET T = X + Y + Z
 80    PRINT TAB(5);X;TAB(16);Y;TAB(28);Z;TAB(40);T
 90    PRINT
100    NEXT N
110    DATA 484,521,336,765
120    DATA 403,552,111,348
130    DATA 689,987,650,768
140    END
```

RUN

In program B.15, line 40 formats the four column headings. Line 50 specifies the number of times the loop is to be executed. Line 60 reads three values from the DATA statements. Line 70 tells the computer how to calculate the total for each row. Line 80 specifies the format for printing the data values in the columns. Line 90 causes a blank line to be left between each output row.

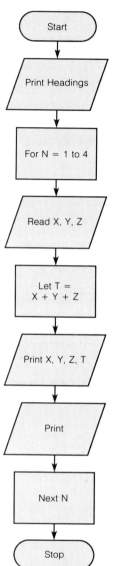

Flowchart for
Program B.15

```
                    OUTPUT

COL1         COL2         COL3        TOTAL

   484          521          336         1341

   765          403          552         1720

   111          348          689         1148

   987          650          768         2405
```

BASIC Version	Differences
Apple	Limitation of 40 columns causes output in the TOTAL column to "spill" to next line
IBM-PC	None
TRS-80	Possibly the same as Apple
GW-BASIC	None

FOR . . . TO . . . STEP,NEXT Statement

FOR . . . TO . . . NEXT statements provide an easy way to establish a loop for incrementing values. Program B.14 illustrated how FOR/NEXT statements can be used to increment numbers one at a time. But suppose that a programmer wants to generate a sequence of values in which each number in the sequence differs from its predecessor by a constant amount. This can be done using **FOR . . . TO . . . STEP,NEXT** statements as illustrated in Program B.16.

Program B.16

```
10    REM   ***        ILLUSTRATION OF        ***
20    REM   ***   "FOR...TO... STEP,NEXT"   ***
30    REM   ***           STATEMENT           ***
40    REM   ********************************************
50    FOR N = 1 TO 5 STEP 2
```

```
60    PRINT N
70    NEXT N
80    END

RUN
```

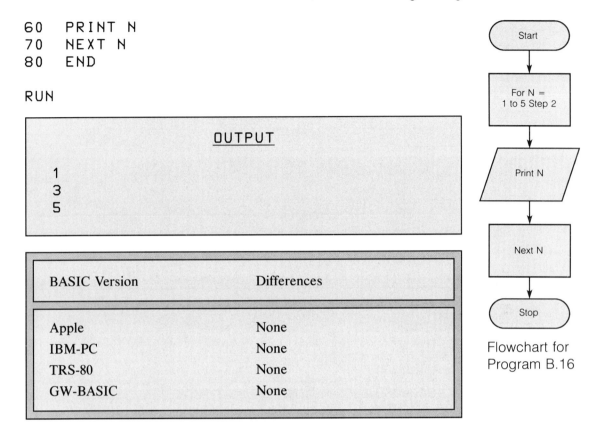

```
                        OUTPUT

    1
    3
    5
```

BASIC Version	Differences
Apple	None
IBM-PC	None
TRS-80	None
GW-BASIC	None

Flowchart for
Program B.16

Program B.16 instructs the computer to increment (or change) and print a range of numbers (1 to 5) in increments of 2. The computer first prints the number 1. Next, the number 1 is incremented by 2, and the result, 3, is printed. Finally, the number 3 is incremented by 2, and the result, 5, is printed. The **STEP** part of the statement merely indicates to the computer the amount by which each number printed should be incremented (or changed).

Numbers can also be changed in a negative direction. In such cases, the negative direction must be indicated in the FOR and STEP parts of the statement, as illustrated in Program B.17.

Program B.17

```
10    ***    ILLUSTRATION OF "FOR...TO...STEP,NEXT"    ***
20    ***              STATEMENT INCREMENTING            ***
30    ***            IN A NEGATIVE DIRECTION             ***
30    ***************************************************
40    FOR N = 5 TO 1 STEP-2
50    PRINT N
```

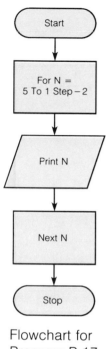

Start

For N =
5 To 1 Step − 2

Print N

Next N

Stop

Flowchart for
Program B.17

```
60   NEXT N
70   END
```

RUN

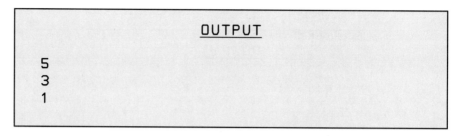

OUTPUT

5
3
1

BASIC Version	Difference
Apple	None
IBM-PC	None
TRS-80	None
GW-BASIC	None

NOW TRY THIS!

Using Program B.16 as a guide, write, enter, and execute a BASIC program that produces a list of fifty numbers, each number incremented by 5, beginning with the number 1.

DO YOU
REMEMBER

20. . . . .The purpose of an *IF/THEN* statement in a BASIC program, and why this statement is said to cause a conditional branching?

21. . . . .The purpose for which *GOSUB* and *RETURN* statements are used in a BASIC program?

22. . . . .The purpose of the *FOR. . .TO. . .NEXT* and the *FOR. . .TO. . .STEP,NEXT* statements, and the primary difference between them?

Summary

(This summary provides answers to DO YOU REMEMBER. . . questions in the module.)

1. **What is the primary difference between a compiler and an interpreter?**
   A *compiler* translates an entire program into machine language at one time. An *interpreter* translates a program into machine language one instruction at a time. Most versions of BASIC use an interpreter.

2. **What are the three processing modes available with BASIC?**
   Several versions of BASIC include three processing modes. In *immediate mode,* an instruction is entered into a computer and executed immediately. In *program mode,* each instruction in a program is given a line number, and all instructions are entered into the computer before the user instructs the computer to process the program by typing the RUN command. Following the RUN command, instructions are processed in numerical order. *Edit mode* allows the user to easily correct errors and/or modify the program.

3. **What are the three primary parts of a typical BASIC statement?**
   The three primary parts of a typical BASIC statement are the *line number,* the *command,* and the *remainder of the statement.*

4. **What are the DOS commands?**
   The DOS commands are **DIRECTORY, FORMAT, COPY, NEW, LOAD, SAVE, LIST,** and **RUN.**

5. **How is a BASIC statement entered into a computer?**
   A BASIC statement is entered into the computer by typing the statement and pressing the RETURN or ENTER key, or a special key designated for entering instructions and data into the computer.

6. **How is a new program entered into a computer?**
   A new program is entered into a computer in the same way a BASIC statement is entered—by typing the statement in at the keyboard and pressing the RETURN or ENTER key. Program statements are entered one at a time until all statements have been entered.

7. **How is an existing (stored) program entered into the computer?**
An existing program can be entered into the computer from a secondary storage device. The medium containing the program is inserted into the device, and the system command (such as LOAD) and the file name are typed using the keyboard. Pressing RETURN, or another appropriate key, will cause the program to be loaded into primary storage.

8. **What are the meanings of *constant, literal,* and *variable* in BASIC?**
A *constant* is a value that does not change. A *literal* is a string of alphanumeric characters used for headings and remarks. A *variable* is a value that can be changed by the programmer.

9. **Why are variable names used in BASIC?**
Variable names are used to reserve storage locations in memory for values that might be changed. The variable name will not change during program execution, but the values can change.

10. **What is the primary difference between numeric variables and character (string) variables?**
A *numeric variable* is a storage place in memory for a numeric value that will be created or changed while the program is being executed. Numeric variables can contain only numbers and decimals. A *character (string) variable* is used to store nonnumeric data (data that does not contain numbers).

11. **In what order are mathematical operations in a BASIC statement performed?**
Mathematical operations are performed in BASIC as follows: parenthetical expressions are evaluated first, beginning with the innermost parentheses; then quantities raised to a power; then multiplication and division are performed; and, finally, addition and subtraction are performed.

12. **What is the primary purpose of REM statements in a BASIC program?**
REM statements allow a programmer to introduce explanatory remarks (or comments) into a BASIC program. This type of statement has no effect on program execution.

13. **Why are PRINT statements used in a BASIC program?**
PRINT statements in a BASIC program cause output to be displayed on the screen. In immediate mode, the *PRINT* statement can be used to perform calculations and display the result. *PRINT* statements are also used to produce blank lines in output.

14. What are the uses for LET statements in a BASIC program?

LET statements in a BASIC program can be used to assign a constant to a variable, to assign one variable to another variable, to assign character (string) constants to character (string) variables, and to assign the result of a calculation to a variable.

15. What is the purpose of INPUT statements in a BASIC program, and how is data entered into a computer when an INPUT statement is used in a program?

An *INPUT* statement allows data to be entered from a keyboard after the *RUN* command is given. When the computer reaches the *INPUT* statement, the computer will stop, display a question mark prompt, and wait for the user to enter the data.

16. What is the purpose of a *GOTO* statement in a BASIC program, and why is a GOTO statement said to cause an unconditional branch?

A *GOTO* statement causes control to be transferred to another line in the program, specified in the GOTO statement. When a GOTO statement is encountered, the program automatically (unconditionally) branches to the line specified in the statement.

17. What is the primary purpose of READ and DATA statements in a BASIC program?

The primary purpose of *READ* and *DATA* statements is to allow data to be entered from a BASIC program, READ and DATA statements must be used together in a program.

18. What is the purpose of using one, or more, TAB functions in a BASIC program?

The *TAB* function can be used in a *PRINT* statement to format output. It can be used to print headings in certain columns and to display data in those columns, for example.

19. What is the purpose of using PRINT USING statements in a BASIC program?

The *PRINT USING* statement allows the programmer to specify the format of both numeric and nonnumeric output.

20. What is the purpose of an IF/THEN statement in a BASIC program and why is this statement said to cause conditional branching?

An *IF/THEN* statement allows conditional branching in a BASIC program. The condition specified in the statement compares two values; if the condition specified in the statement is true, a certain action is taken, but if it is false, a different action is taken.

21. Why are GOSUB and RETURN statements used in a BASIC program?

A *GOSUB* statement in a BASIC program causes control to be transferred to a subroutine. A *RETURN* statement at the end of the subroutine causes control to be transferred back to the statement immediately following the GOSUB statement.

22. What is the purpose of the FOR. . .TO. . .NEXT and FOR. . .TO. . .STEP,NEXT statements, and what is the primary difference between them?

A *FOR. . .TO. . .NEXT* statement in a BASIC program enables the computer to repeat a task, and display the output the number of times specified in the statement in increments of one. A *FOR. . .TO. . .STEP,NEXT* statement allows the computer to repeat a task, and display the output in increments specified in the STEP portion of the statement. This allows the programmer to generate a sequence of values in increments of any amount.

Key Terms

BASIC	literal
compiler	LOAD
constant	PRINT
edit mode	PRINT USING
END	program
FOR/NEXT	program mode
FOR. . .TO. . .NEXT	READ
FOR. . .TO. . .STEP,NEXT	REM
function key	reserved word
GOSUB	RETURN
GOTO	RUN
IF/THEN	SAVE
immediate mode	statement
INPUT	system command
interpreter	TAB function
LET	variable
line number	
LIST	

Test Yourself

1. Three modes for processing data in the BASIC language are
   _____ mode, _____ mode, and _____
   mode.

2. When processing data in program mode, every instruction must
   have a (n)_____ .

3. A(n) _____ in BASIC instructs the computer to perform some action such as calculating a value, comparing two
   values, or printing output.

4. A(n) _____ command governs the operation of a
   BASIC program and is not a statement in the program.

5. A(n) _____ is a program that supplies a complete list
   of a user's file.

6. The _____ command instructs the computer to display
   a program currently in the computer's memory on the computer's screen.

7. The _____ command tells the computer to begin executing instructions in the program in numerically ascending
   order.

8. A(n) _____ is a storage place in memory for a numeric
   value that will be created or changed while the program is
   being executed.

9. An instruction in a BASIC program includes a _____ ,
   a BASIC _____ , and _____ .

10. A(n) _____ statement allows a programmer to insert
    comments in a BASIC program.

11. A BASIC program is terminated by the _____ state-
    ment, which is the last statement in the program.

12. One purpose of the _____ statement is to assign the
    result of a calculation to a variable.

13. A(n) _____ statement allows data to be entered into a
    computer from a keyboard after the RUN command is given.

14. Two statements that are used together in a computer program
    to allow data to be entered into the computer from the program
    are the _____ and _____ statements.

15. The _____ statement produces output on the computer's screen.

16. A(n) _____ can be used with a PRINT statement to format output.

17. The general form for a PRINT USING statement is the line number, followed by PRINT USING, followed by _____ .

18. A(n) _____ statement enables control to be transferred to a subroutine that is executed, after which a RETURN statement returns control.

19. A(n) _____ statement is said to be conditional because the action taken depends on whether or not the condition specified in the statement is true.

20. _____ statements provide a simple way of establishing a loop by allowing a task to be repeated any number of times.

Review Questions

1. What are the three processing modes that can be used with BASIC and the primary advantage of each to a user? (Learning Objective 2)

2. List the DOS system commands used in BASIC and describe the primary purpose of each. (Learning Objective 3)

3. How are a BASIC statement, a new program, and an existing program entered into a computer? (Learning Objective 4)

4. Instructions and data are entered into a computer by using an INPUT statement and by using READ and DATA statements. What is the primary difference between these two methods? (Learning Objective 5)

5. Since they have no effect on program execution, what is the value of REM statements? (Learning Objective 6)

6. Identify four purposes of the LET statement in BASIC. (Learning Objective 6)

7. What are the primary purposes of PRINT statements? (Learning Objective 6)

8. What is the primary purpose of a PRINT USING statement in BASIC? (Learning Objective 6)

9. Explain why GOTO statements cause an unconditional transfer of control and IF. . .THEN statements cause a conditional transfer of control. (Learning Objective 7)

10. What is the primary reason for using a TAB function? Give an example of its use. (Learning Objective 8)

Access mechanism The mechanism in a direct-access secondary storage device (disk drive) that positions the read/write head over a particular track.

Accurate Free from error.

Acoustic coupler modem A type of modem that uses a telephone hand set to connect a computer to telephone lines by means of sound.

Ada A programming language developed by the U.S. Department of Defense and named in honor of Lady Ada Augusta Byron.

Address A primary storage location identified by a unique identifier.

Algorithm An outline of a logical problem solution containing the logic patterns and calculations to be used in a computer program.

Alphanumeric video terminal A television-like output device used to display alphabetic, numeric, and special characters sent from a computer.

Analog computer A computer that measures continuous physical or electrical conditions, such as temperature or density, rather than operating on digits like a digital computer.

Application software A sequence of instructions written to solve a specific problem using a computer.

Applications programmer A person who writes application programs.

Arithmetic/logic unit (A/L unit) The part of the CPU that executes mathematical calculations and logic operations.

Artificial intelligence (AI) The capability of computers to solve problems that require imagination and intelligence; research on this concept is currently under way.

ASCII An abbreviation for American Standard Code for Information Interchange. A standard binary code (7-bit or 8-bit) for representing data and/or program instructions.

ASCII–8 An 8-bit version of ASCII.

Assembler A language translator program that converts an assembly language program into a machine language program.

Assembly language A symbolic programming language that uses symbols (mnemonic codes) rather than 0's and 1's.

Back-end processor A small computer serving as an interface between a large computer and a database stored on a direct-access storage device.

Back-up copy A second copy of important programs or information (usually stored on another disk).

Back-up data files Copies of original files that can be used if original copies of files are damaged or destroyed.

Band printer A type of impact printer in which a rotating band of characters is used to print images on paper.

Bandwidth A measure of the capacity of a communications channel expressed in bits per second, or bauds.

BASIC An abbreviation for Beginner's All-purpose Symbolic Instruction Code; an interactive programming language developed for use by beginning programmers.

Baud rate A communication rate referring to the number of bits transmitted per second.

Binary coded decimal Positional notation in which individual decimal digits representing a number in decimal notation (base 10) are each represented by a binary number. For example, the decimal number 12 is represented by 0001 0010 using the standard 8 4 2 1 method of binary coded decimal notation and by 1100 in binary notation. Abbreviated BCD.

Binary system A number system with a base of 2 used to encode any data through the use of 0 or 1, with 0 representing an off condition and 1 representing an on condition.

Biochip A theoretical primary storage chip that uses groups of molecules to form a circuit. None has yet been developed.

Bit A binary digit, either a 0 or a 1.

Booting The process of entering software (system and/or application) into a computer in preparation for processing data.

Branch pattern A programming statement to by-pass or alter the normal flow of program execution.

Broadband channel Any data communication channel capable of handling (carrying) more data than a voicegrade channel. Examples are microwaves and fiber optic cables.

Business analysis software Software programs written to solve specific problems such as accounting and inventory management.

Byte The number of bits (8) required to store one character.

C language A programming language developed by AT&T for use with its UNIX operating system and AT&T computers.

Calculating Performing arithmetic operations on data such as adding, subtracting, multiplying, or dividing.

Cathode ray tube (CRT) The display tube contained in video monitors and television sets.

Cell A specific location in an electronic spreadsheet at which a particular row and column intersect.

Central (host) computer A large computer to which other smaller computers or terminals are connected.

Central processing unit (CPU) The electronic "heart" of a computer system that processes data; it contains the primary storage unit, the arithmetic/logic unit, and the control unit.

Chain printer A line-at-a-time printer that uses a chain to position characters to be printed.

Character printer A printer that prints a single character at a time.

Classifying Arranging data according to predetermined characteristics. For example, students may be classified as "male" or "female."

Coaxial cable A communications channel capable of handling large amounts of data at very high speeds.

COBOL An abbreviation for Common Business-Oriented Language; a programming language used primarily for business applications.

Coding Writing a computer program in a programming language for the computer to perform a particular task.

Collecting Gathering or assembling data that is to be entered into a computer for processing.

Command area An area shown at the bottom of some spreadsheets that displays the commands available to the user.

Communication The transferring of data or information to the user in a form that is understandable.

Communications adapter A special circuit board installed inside a computer that allows data to be sent over a communications channel such as telephone line.

Communications channel A medium for carrying data from one location to another, such as a telephone line or coaxial cable.

Communications satellite An earth-orbiting device capable of relaying communication signals over long distances.

Communications software Computer programs that allow computers to communicate through a modem.

Compare To evaluate two data values to determine their equality or difference.

Compiler A translating program stored in computer memory that translates instructions in a programming language into machine language.

Complete That which has nothing missing—for example, complete information.

Computer-assisted design (CAD) The use of computers to design, analyze, and refine products.

Computer-assisted diagnosis Using a computer as a diagnostic tool to save doctors time and to assist in fast, accurate diagnosis. The computer evaluates medical data to show variations from the normal and suggests a diagnosis.

Computer-assisted instruction (CAI) The interaction between a computer and a student whereby the computer serves as the instructor.

Computer-assisted manufacturing (CAM) The use of a computer to simulate steps in the manufacturing process.

Computerized-axial tomography (CAT scan) A medical testing device that uses a combination of x-ray and computer technologies to provide accurate patient diagnosis.

Computer crime A criminal act that is accomplished by using a computer.

Computer engineer A computer professional responsible for the design and development of computer equipment.

Computer generation An era in the history of computing distinguished by the introduction of improved computer technologies.

Computer graphics A chart, drawing, or picture produced using a computer.

Computer literacy A broad knowledge and understanding of computers, their use, and their societal implications in our world.

Computer output The data that has been processed

by a computer and sent to an output device such as a video monitor or printer.

Computer output microfilm (COM) Miniature photographic images of output placed on photographic film rather than on paper.

Computer privacy The personal rights of an individual pertaining to the collection, processing, dissemination, and evaluation of personal data using a computer.

Computer program A set of instructions for the computer to follow in order to perform a task.

Computer security A program of methods designed to safeguard computer hardware, software, data, and information.

Computer services The services performed by computer personnel for the benefit of users.

Computer system All computer hardware, software, and personnel needed to perform the desired computing tasks.

Computer user Anyone who uses a computer or the output from a computer. Almost everyone is a computer user, either directly or indirectly.

Concentrator A device that allows a number of input/output devices to use a single communications channel.

Concise Characterized by an absence of unnecessary words, sentences, or other data. Information is concise when it contains only that information needed by the user.

Control statement A computer program instruction or statement that terminates the sequential execution of instructions by transferring control to an instruction elsewhere in the program.

Control unit The part of the CPU that directs the sequence of operations in a computer system.

Converting Changing data or information in a computer into a form understandable by the user during the output phase of the information processing cycle.

Coprocessor An additional microprocessor in a computer.

Copy protection A method of preventing users from making unauthorized copies of software programs.

Copyright The legal rights of the owner that prevent other persons from making illegal reproductions of the product.

Cost of storage The cost of storage per one byte of data.

Crime prevention Actions to prevent criminal activities such as the intentional destruction of computer hardware or software.

Cylinder An imaginary vertical line extending through a disk pack that intersects the same number track on each disk—for example, a vertical line extending through track 5 on every disk in the pack.

Daisy-wheel printer A letter-quality printer that uses a plastic disk (wheel) to which characters are attached, resembling a "daisy" flower.

Data Unprocessed facts that may be in the form of numbers, characters, or words.

Data communications The transmission of data between computers and/or terminals via communications channels such as telephone lines.

Data communications specialist An individual trained in the specialized area of data communications.

Data communications system The hardware, software, and personnel needed to perform data communications.

Data density The amount of data that can be stored on a secondary storage medium.

Data encryption The conversion of data into a specially coded form to prevent its unauthorized use.

Data entry The entering of data into a computer for processing.

Data file *See* File.

Data file access The process of obtaining access to stored computer files.

Data hierarchy A pyramid-shaped diagram showing different kinds of storage (primary, tape, and disk) and the tradeoffs of choosing one kind versus another in terms of cost, speed, and amount of storage.

Data processing teacher A person who has obtained the education needed to teach data processing to students.

Data security Measures taken to protect data and programs stored in a computer system.

Database A systematic arrangement of data that can be retrieved by a computer.

Database administrator A manager responsible for all data in a business or organization.

Database file organization The method selected for organizing and storing data in a database.

Database machine A specially designed machine that contains a database.

Database management system (DBMS)   A program for creating and using data stored in a database.

Database model   A design for a database.

Database system   A complete system including the hardware, software, and personnel needed to create and manage the storage, access, updating, and maintenance of a database.

Debug   To find and correct errors in a computer program.

Decimal numbering system   A base 10 number system.

Decision-logic pattern   An instruction in a computer program that may, or may not, alter the normal flow of the program.

Decrypted   Retranslated back after having been encrypted for security purposes—for example, decrypted data. *See also* Data encryption.

Definition tree   A hierarchical structure that defines the data in a data base, starting at the root level, or main part, and branching out from that point.

Demodulation   An action performed by a modem in which data signals are converted from analog to digital form.

Density   See Data density.

Desk-checking   The process of visually and mentally reviewing the syntax and logic of a computer program before entering the program into a computer.

Detection devices   Hardware devices that monitor and detect certain invalid conditions within a security system. They are capable of taking corrective action against specific security violations.

Digital computer   A general-purpose computer capable of processing alphabetic and numeric data.

Digitizer   A pressure-sensitive tablet having the same coordinates as the video monitor that allows a user such as a draftsman or engineer to produce highly technical drawings.

Direct access   The capability to read or write a record in any order without having to read an entire file.

Disaster recovery plan   An overall organizational plan for recovering from a computer disaster such as fire.

Disk drive   A direct access (random access) secondary storage device.

Disk pack   Several magnetic disks arranged together in a unit.

Diskette (floppy disk)   A thin, flexible disk used with microcomputers for direct-access secondary storage.

Distributed database   A database approach that places databases at local or regional sites and provides access to computing resources.

Documentation   A written report containing details of how a program or system was developed and how it should work.

Dot-matrix printer   A printer that uses rows and columns of small dots to form characters on the paper.

Double-striking   A feature available on some dot-matrix printers allowing characters to be printed twice to form clearer characters.

Downloading   Transferring data from a large central computer to a smaller remote computer.

Draft-quality   Normal quality print produced by a dot-matrix printer.

Drum printer   An impact printer consisting of a metal cylinder with rows of characters engraved on the surface. One line is printed with each rotation of the drum.

EBCDIC code   An abbreviation for Extended Binary Coded Decimal Interchange Code, which is a popular code for representing data in a computer.

EDP   *See* Electronic data processing.

EDP auditor   A professionally trained individual capable of verifying the accuracy of information processed by a computer system such as financial records and reports.

Educational software   Computer programs developed for use by schools.

Electronic data processing (EDP)   Processing data using computers.

Electronic mail   Special software that allows computer users to send messages back and forth to each other's computer monitor.

Electronic spreadsheet   A computerized matrix containing rows and columns into which data can be entered. Individual matrix cells can be updated instantly by the computer when new data is entered. Often used by business analysts.

Encrypted   Translated into a secret code for security reasons—for example, encrypted data. See *also* Data encryptions.

Entertainment software   Computer programs such as computer games developed to entertain the user.

EPROM   A ROM chip that can be erased and reused; its name is an abbreviation for Erasable Programmable Read Only Memory.

Erase   To remove data from a storage medium.

Ergonomic   A term used to describe computing equipment and furniture that is designed to be comfortable to use and that results in increased productivity.

Expert system   A software program designed to simulate how a professional person thinks through a problem to determine the correct solution.

Express warranty   A warranty created when a seller makes any promise or statement of fact concerning the product being sold, if the buyer uses the promise or statement as a basis for purchasing the product.

External direct-connect modem   A modem located outside the computer but connected to the computer by cable.

External information   Information generated from external sources, such as information from vendors, goverment agencies, or lenders.

Fiber optic cable   A data communications channel made of tiny glass strands capable of carrying huge amounts of data at the speed of light.

Field   A group of related characters treated as a unit such as a person's name, address, or telephone number.

Fifth generation   The next generation of computers are expected to use artificial intelligence techniques to produce machines capable of simulating human logic.

File   A group of related records treated as a unit.

Firmware   A term that refers to software programs that have been permanently stored in memory, usually in Read Only Memory (ROM).

Fixed disk   A non-removable magnetic disk used in microcomputers that is in a sealed unit. It has a large storage capacity and is reliable, inexpensive, and small.

Flowchart   An outline of the steps to be followed in a computer program.

Flowchart symbols   Specific symbols used to prepare a flowchart developed by the American National Standards Institute.

Font   A particular formation of characters printed.

Forth   A structured programming language for writing system and applications programs.

FORTRAN   An abbreviation for FORmula TRANslator, a programming language popular among mathematicians, scientists, and engineers.

Full-duplex   A communication method that allows data to be sent in both directions at the same time.

GIGO   An abbreviation for Garbage In—Garbage Out. This means that if incorrect data is entered into a computer, the output will be incorrect.

General-purpose computer   The most commonly used type of digital computer capable of solving a wide variety of problems.

General-purpose language   Any programming language suitable for a variety of data processing applications.

Generation   *See* Computer generation.

Graphics   Images, such as charts and pictures, that can be displayed on a monitor.

Graphics display monitor   A monitor with special capabilities for preparing detailed scientific and engineering drawings.

Graphics software   Special programs that allow a user to create and produce detailed drawings.

Graphics tablet   A device that allows the user to create designs on a video monitor screen by drawing on the device.

Graphics video terminal   A terminal that can display pictures, drawings, graphs, charts, and other images in a variety of formats and colors.

Hacker   A dedicated and often compulsive computer programmer. Hackers sometimes attempt to gain unauthorized entry into other computer systems.

Half-duplex method   A communication method that allows data to be sent in both directions, but in only one direction at a time.

Hard disk   A direct-access secondary storage medium made of rigid material capable of storing large amounts of data.

Hardcopy   Printed output on materials such as paper, microfilm, or plastic.

Hardware   The physical components that make up a computer system: input, processing, and output devices.

Head crash   The potential destruction of programs and data caused by physical contact between read/write heads and storage disks.

Hierarchical database   A type of database in which data is always entered at the base of the structure.

Hollerith card   An 80-column punched card developed by Herman Hollerith in the late 1800's.

Hollerith code   A code for storing data on punched cards developed by Herman Hollerith.

Illegal copying   The electronic copying of copyrighted software for personal use or for resale.

Impact printer   Any printer that prints by physically striking print elements against paper to produce images, like a typewriter.

Implied warranty   A warranty that provides for automatic incorporation of specific warranties in a contract for the sale of products.

Information   Data that has been processed so that it is useful.

Information processing center   A department that provides computing services to an organization.

Information resource management (IRM)   A system designed specifically to manage an organization's information.

Ink-jet printer   A printer that produces images by spraying ink onto the paper.

Input   The phase of the information processing cycle during which data is entered into a computer for processing. Input activities include collecting, verifying, and coding the data.

Input device   Any device used to enter data into a computer, such as a keyboard.

Input/output control system (IOCS)   Programs in an operating system for handling all input and output.

Integrated circuit   The electronic circuitry etched on a silicon chip. Computers contain integrated circuits capable of processing data and storing data temporarily.

Integrated software   Two or more software programs designed to work together.

Interactive processing   A processing method whereby a user can interact directly with the computer during program execution.

Interface   A point of contact, or meeting, between a computer and an external entity, whether a user, a peripheral device, or a communications medium.

Internal information   Information generated from within a company and used by the same company.

Internal modem   A modem that plugs directly into expansion slots inside the computer.

Internal security measures   Measures and procedures established by a company to control internal protection of data.

Interpreter   A translator program that translates one instruction at a time into machine language for immediate execution.

Interrecord gap   A space separating records on magnetic tape allowing the tape to be stopped and restarted, if necessary, in the gap.

Joystick   An input device in the form of a stick which, when moved about, causes objects on the monitor screen to move; often used for computer games.

Key-to-disk   A device containing a keyboard used to record data on magnetic disk for later entry into a computer.

Key-to-tape   A device containing a keyboard used to record data on magnetic tape for later entry into a computer.

Keyboard   An input device that sends data to the computer when the keys are pressed.

Large-scale integrated circuit (LSIC)   An integrated circuit containing thousands of microscopic transistors on a silicon chip.

Laser printer   A nonimpact printer that uses laser beams and electrophotographic technology to produce images on paper.

Lasers   Tightly packed, narrow beams of light formed by the emission of high-energy molecules that are used to send data as light signals through strands of fiber optic cable.

Leased line   A dedicated communications channel leased from a common communications carrier, such as a telephone company.

Letter-quality   A high-quality print produced by a printer comparable to that produced by a typewriter.

Librarian   A person responsible for maintaining all magnetic tapes and magnetic disks used at a computer installation.

Light pen   A pen-like device containing a photoelectric cell in the tip used to produce drawings on a video display or graphics monitor.

Line printer   A printer that prints one line at a time.

LISP   A programming language often used for research in the area of artificial intelligence; its name is an abbreviation for LISt Processor.

Local area network (LAN)   A network linking together computers in nearby offices and buildings allowing communication between the computers.

Local system   A computer system located at one's own location, such as at one's own business.

Logic error   An error in the design of a problem solution resulting in incorrect output. Although the program may execute, the output will be incorrect.

LOGO A high-level programming language designed for students that teaches them to draw geometric patterns and other images on a monitor screen.

Logic patterns An instruction or combination of instructions in a computer program that directs the computer to perform a task.

Loop pattern An instruction in a computer program that causes the repeated execution of a group of instructions.

Machine language The only language a computer can execute directly without it's being translated. Machine language consists of instructions using only 1s and 0s.

Machine-dependent language A computer language that can be used only with a specific computer.

Machine-independent language A computer language that can be used on various computers.

Magnetic disk A disk coated with magnetic recording material that allows data to be stored on the disk as magnetized spots.

Magnetic ink character recognition (MICR) A technology in which a device called a magnetic ink character reader reads characters.

Magnetic tape A secondary storage medium consisting of a long strip of plastic material coated with a thin layer of magnetic particles. It is the most widely used sequential-access secondary storage medium.

Mainframe computer A large, multiple-user computer.

Main menu A listing of program names and functions on the screen of a terminal or microcomputer.

Memory Another name for storage.

Membrane keyboard A flat, pressure-sensitive keyboard activated by pressing a marked location rather than by pressing a particular key.

Menu-driven User-friendly software that gives the user a list of choices and prompts from which selections can be made.

Microcomputer A small, single-user computer with circuits that consist of tiny integrated circuits on silicon chips.

Microcomputer consultant A computer professional who is experienced and knowledgeable about microcomputer systems, and who provides a variety of microcomputer services to clients.

Microelectronic implant A tiny electronic device surgically implanted in a person to help restore a particular body function, such as hearing or speech.

Microminiaturization A term implying very small size, even smaller than miniaturization.

Microprocessor Miniature integrated circuits on a silicon chip.

Microsecond One-millionth of a second (0.000001).

Microwave system A system that produces very high communications signals, allowing huge amounts of data to be sent at very high speeds.

Millisecond One-thousandth of a second (0.001).

Miniaturization The technology that makes it possible to manufacture tiny integrated circuit chips without decreasing the efficiency of the circuits.

Minicomputer A computer smaller and less powerful than a mainframe computer, but larger and more powerful than a microcomputer.

Mnemonics A code that uses easy-to-remember abbreviations for words, such as DVD for divide.

Model A representation of a real world system, such as an architect's model of a building to be constructed.

Modem A device used to connect communications equipment with a telephone line; its name is an abbreviation for MOdulator-DEModulator.

Modularization A programming method in which computing tasks are arranged in segments or modules.

Modulation The conversion of digital signals to analog signals by a modem in order to communicate data over a telephone line.

Module A series of instructions in a computer program that causes the computer to perform a particular task.

Monitor A display device used in almost all computer systems, large and small.

Mouse A desk-top device that controls cursor movement on a video monitor; it can be used in place of a keyboard.

Multiple CPU system A computer system that uses two or more computers in the system.

Multiplexor An electronic device that allows several input/output devices to use a single communications channel at the same time.

Multiprocessing A multiple CPU configuration that allows several programs to be processed at the same time.

Multiprogramming A technique whereby several programs are placed into primary storage at the same time for processing, thereby increasing CPU efficiency.

Music synthesizer Special computer equipment and software that converts digital signals into sound.

Nanosecond One-billionth of a second:
(0.000000001)

Narrowband channels A communications channel capable of carrying only small amounts of data at relatively slow speeds.

Near-letter-quality A high-quality print feature available with some printers.

Network A group of computers and terminals that are linked together to serve several users at one time.

Network database A type of database in which pointers are used to make connections between data stored in different files.

Nonremovable disk pack A type of disk pack in which disks cannot be removed from the pack.

Nonimpact printer A printer that forms characters on the paper without actually striking it.

Nonvolatile storage A type of storage that retains the stored information if the power supply is turned off. Examples are magnetic tape and magnetic disk.

Object program A machine language program generated from a source program by a translating program.

Office automation The integration of computers and communications technology with traditional office procedures to increase the productivity of office workers.

Off-line A term that describes any computer or peripheral device that is not immediately accessible by the CPU.

On-line A term that describes any computer or peripheral device that is immediately accessible by the CPU.

Operating system A group of computer programs that directs the operations of a computer system.

Optical bar code recognition (OBCR) A technology that converts data represented as bars into a form suitable for processing; used by supermarkets.

Optical character recognition (OCR) A technology in which a device reads characters, numbers, and symbols, and transforms them into data that can be processed by a computer.

Optical (laser) disk storage A relatively new storage technology in which data is stored on a plastic disk as microscopic holes burned into the disk by a laser beam.

Optical mark recognition (OMR) A technology in which a device called a scanner senses the position of marks on a page and converts the marks into data for processing.

Output Useful information that comes from the computer as the result of processing raw data.

Output device A device that produces the results of computer processing (output) in understandable form.

Owner's manual A manual accompanying a piece of computer equipment, providing detailed instructions for using the equipment.

Parallel interface A peripheral card inside a computer that allows data to be sent 1 byte at a time.

Parallel transmission A method of sending data in which the bits used to represent a character are all sent at the same time (side by side).

Parity A means of detecting erroneous transmissions of data in which the number of 1 bits is odd or even.

Pascal A structured, high-level programming language particularly useful for mathematical and graphics applications. Named in honor of Blaise Pascal.

Password A word that identifies a particular user of a computer system as an authorized user.

Peripheral card A card containing electronic circuitry installed in a computer that allows peripheral devices to be used with the computer.

Peripheral device A device that can be attached to a computer but is not essential to the computer's operation, such as a printer.

Personal microcomputer A small computer designed for use by an individual user.

Physical security A system developed to prevent physical damage to computer hardware and software.

Picosecond One-trillionth of a second:
(0.000000000001)

Pixel A position on a computer monitor or terminal; an acronym for picture element.

Plotter A device capable of producing hardcopy output of computer graphics.

Point-of-sale devices Electronic devices capable of capturing sales data immediately and used by retail stores at checkout locations.

Pointer A data field in a disk record or index file that stores the address location of another disk record. Sometimes called a chain address.

Pressure-sensitive keyboard A type of keyboard

that is sensitive to touch. It has a membrane surface with switches underneath the key positions.

Primary storage   Internal storage in a computer.

Printer   An output device that produces a hardcopy of data or information from a computer after processing.

Private area network (PAN)   A computer network available only to users within a private business or organization.

Processing   The electronic manipulation of data to produce information.

Professional microcomputer   A microcomputer designed for use by small businesses or other professional users such as accountants.

Program   *See* Computer program.

Program disk   A magnetic disk containing one or more computer programs.

Programming language   A language used to write computer programs.

Program maintenance   The periodic modification of a computer program to retain its usefulness. For example, a payroll program might be modified because of changes in the tax laws.

Program mode   A processing mode in which an entire program is entered into a computer before any instructions are executed.

Programmer   One who writes computer programs.

PROLOG   A computer language used primarily for artificial intelligence research.

PROM   A type of ROM that can be programmed by the user or the manufacturer; its name is an abbreviation for Programmable Read Only Memory. After it has been programmed, a PROM chip cannot be changed.

Pseudocode   A series of English-like statements showing the logic used in designing a problem solution.

Punched card   A paper card used to encode data for processing by a computer.

Query language   A unique language used with a database.

RAM   An abbreviation for Random Access Memory, volatile internal computer memory that can be reused.

Read/write head   An electromagnetic device that reads, writes, or erases data stored on the surface of a magnetic storage medium such as disk or tape.

Read/write notch   A small opening on the side of a diskette jacket that allows data on the diskette to be read, written, or erased. By covering the notch, data cannot be written on the diskette and existing data cannot be erased or altered.

Record   A group of related fields of data treated as a unit—for example, a person's name, address, and telephone number, as well as additional fields of data.

Register   A location in primary storage for storing data and instructions currently being processed.

Relational database   A type of database in which data is stored in the form of related tables of data.

Relations   The linkage records in related files have to each other through common attributes or characterics. Relies on external tables or indexes for storing and retrieving information.

Relevant   Only that which is needed by the user—for example, relevant information.

Removable disk pack   A disk pack that can be removed from a disk drive and replaced when needed.

Removable storage media   Media that can be removed from a storage device, such as magnetic tape and disk.

Remote system   A computer system in which some computers, terminals, and other hardware components are located at sites physically removed from each other so that communications channels are required for the system.

Report writer   A computer language that allows the user to instruct the computer to produce various reports (without the user's having to write a program).

Resolution   The quality of the image on a video monitor.

Retrieve   To obtain data or information from a computer system.

Ring network   A computer network without a central computer. All computers in the network are interconnected by a communication channel.

ROM   An abbreviation for Read Only Memory, internal computer memory in which instructions and programs are permanently stored and cannot be changed.

Run-time error   A program error that, when detected by the computer during program execution, stops program execution. It is often caused by telling the computer to do something it cannot do.

Sabotage   The deliberate and unlawful damaging of computer hardware and software.

Save A command to store data or information somewhere other than in the computer's primary storage, such as on tape or disk, so that the data can be used again later.

Secondary storage External computer storage, usually on magnetic disk or tape, that provides for permanent storage of data and programs.

Sector A segment of a magnetic disk or diskette.

Sequential-access storage Secondary storage from which records must be read in order, one after another, until the desired record is read. An example is magnetic tape.

Serial interface A peripheral card allowing for serial transmission of data to certain devices or over a communication channel.

Serial transmission A method of sending data in which a group of bits representing a character is sent one at a time.

Shut-down procedures A series of steps followed in shutting down a computer system.

Silicon chip A specially treated material containing computer circuitry.

Simple-sequence pattern A series of program instructions executed one after another in sequence.

Simplex method A communications method that allows data or information to be sent or received, but not both.

Simulation model A mathematical representation, or model, of a real system. It can be manipulated and studied to better understand the real system it represents and to make predictions about the effects of potential changes.

Single CPU system A computer system having only one computer.

Softcopy Computer output displayed on a video display monitor.

Software The instructions used by a computer to process data.

Software copying The process of making a copy of computer programs, data, or output.

Software piracy The unauthorized copying or using of computer programs, data, or output.

Software vendor A private company that produces and/or sells computer software.

Sort To arrange data or information on the basis of a predetermined sequence, such as in numeric or alphabetic order.

Source program A program written in a programming language prior to translation into machine language.

Special-purpose computer A computer with limited capabilities that can perform only one, or a few, tasks.

Special-purpose language A computer language used only for a special purpose, such as producing reports.

Speed The time required to store data on, or retrieve data from, a secondary storage medium such as tape or disk. Also, the rate at which a computer can execute instructions and process data.

Spreadsheet *See* Electronic spreadsheet.

Staging The process of retrieving data from a mass storage device, storing the data on magnetic disk, and returning the processed data from disk to mass storage.

Standard keyboard A keyboard identical or similar to that of a typewriter.

Standard magnetic disk A magnetic disk normally used with large computers.

Star network A computer network in which terminals or small computers are connected to a central computer as if they were points on a star.

Start-up procedures A series of actions taken to ready a computer for use.

Status area A message line shown above or below the text area in an electronic spreadsheet that shows the position of the cursor and the data that was entered into a particular cell.

Storage capacity The amount of data that can be stored using a particular kind of storage, such as primary storage, tape, or disk.

Storage hierarchy The range of storage options from which users select the most appropriate storage medium, based on the cost of storage and the speed at which data can be retrieved.

Store To save data, text, programs, or information for future use.

Stored-program concept The capability of modern computers to store instructions in primary storage and to follow the instructions to process data without human intervention.

Structured programming The preparation of a computer program following an approved set of standards for planning and writing a program that is more accurate and efficient.

Summarizing Condensing or reducing large amounts of data into a smaller and more useful amount.

Supercomputer The most powerful and most expensive type of computer available. Examples are the Cray-II and the Cyber 205.

Syntax A set of rules governing the way instructions in a program are to be written.

Syntax error A violation of the rules of a programming language (similar to an error in the English language) that prevents a program from executing.

Synthesizer *See* Music synthesizer.

System command A operating command given by a user instructing the computer to do something, such as save (store) data on magnetic disk.

Systems analyst A specialist who evaluates the goals, objectives, and information needs of an organization to devise a better method of operating, such as a better method of managing inventory.

System software Programs that manage the efficient operation of a computer system and aid in the development of application programs.

Tape cartridge mass storage system A system that uses magnetic tape cartridges to store huge amounts of data.

Tape cassette A small reel of magnetic tape housed in a plastic container; used for secondary storage with some microcomputers.

Tape density The amount of data that can be stored per inch of tape.

Tape drive A hardware device that moves magnetic tape past read/write heads to record and/or retrieve data.

Tape player/recorder A small sequential-access storage device used with some microcomputers.

Telecommunications The transfer of data from one location to another over communications channels.

Telecommuting Using terminals and telephone lines to allow a user working at home to communicate with a computer at his or her office.

Teleconferencing Using electronic equipment to communicate, thereby eliminating the need to travel to a conference.

Terminal An input/output device used to input programs and data to the computer and to receive output from the computer.

Time-sharing system A computer system that allows multiple users access to computer resources by means of telephone hook-ups.

Timely A characteristic of useful information, meaning that a user must have information at a particular time if it is to be useful.

Top-down programming A method of problem solving in which the main functions are defined first, followed by subfunctions that are defined in more detail.

Track On disk, a circular path on which data are recorded; on tape, a continuous path extending the full length of the tape on which data are recorded.

Traditional data files Files that are stored using file cabinets and file folders.

Transistor A tiny complete electronic system made up of electronic circuitry on a silicon chip.

Translating software Computer programs that change instructions in a high-level language program into machine language.

Turnaround time The time required for a program to be sent to a computer and executed, and the results (output) returned to the user.

Uploading Transferring data from a user's computer to another computer, such as a central computer.

User *See* Computer user.

User's Manual A manual (usually provided by the manufacturer) that provides information on how to use computer hardware or software.

User-friendly A term that refers to a computer, peripheral device, or software that is easy to use.

User-written program A computer application program written by a programmer for his/her own use or for use by the employer of the individual.

Utility software Software programs written to perform frequently needed processes such as sorting data and merging data.

Vendor-written program A computer program, such as for word processing, written for sale to computer users.

Verifying Checking to make certain the data or output is accurate and complete.

Video display monitor A commonly used output device that displays softcopy output on a television-like screen.

Videodisk system A secondary storage system.

Videotext A service available to subscribers that provides two-way information capabilities using computers.

Voiceband channels A grade of communications channels used to carry data that are normally used for telephone (or voice) communications.

Voice input A technology that allows users to give instructions to a computer by voice.

Voice output A technology that allows the output of a computer to be produced in voice-like sounds.

Voice recognition system The input part of a communications system that allows the computer system to receive voice input from a user.

Voice response The technology that allows a computer to produce output in voice sounds.

Volatile storage Any type of storage that loses its data if the power supply is turned off.

Warranty A legal commitment by a seller who warrants (assures) the buyer that the product purchased is free from defect or damage.

Windowing software Special software programs that allow the user to view and/or work with more than one program at a time.

Word processing A computer program that allows the user to create, edit, and manipulate text data, such as a letter or report.

Word size The number of bits required to represent a character in primary storage; varies with the type of computer.

Word-wrap A feature of a word processor that formats words near the right margin of text. A word that does not fit into the available space at the end of a line of text is automatically moved (wrapped) to the next line.

Xerographic printer A type of nonimpact printer that uses a printing method similar to that used by many copying machines.

ACKNOWLEDGMENTS AND PHOTO CREDITS

Contents vii Charles Feil/Stock, Boston; **viii** Courtesy of IBM; **ix** (*left*) Courtesy of Hewlett-Packard; **ix** (*right*) Courtesy of General Electric Research and Development Center; **xi** (*left*) Courtesy of NASA Photos; **xi** (*right*) Courtesy of Lawrence Livermore National Laboratory; **xii** Chris Gilbert

PART I 1 Charles Feil/Stock, Boston

Introduction 3 (*counterclockwise from top left*) Chris Gilbert; Chris Gilbert; Courtesy of Radio Shack—A Division of Tandy Corporation; Courtesy of National Semiconductor; **4** (*top*) David Burnett/Woodfin Camp & Associates; (*bottom*) Courtesy of Apple Computer, Inc.; **5** (*counterclockwise from top left*) Brian Payne/Black Star; Courtesy of Hayes Microcomputer Products; Mathew Naythons/Black Star; Dennis Brack/Black Star; **6** (*top*) Courtesy of Wright State University; (*bottom*) Courtesy of General Motors; **7** (*top*) Courtesy of NASA Photos; (*bottom*) Courtesy of Nissan Motor Company

Chapter 1 8 Courtesy of IBM; **11** Joseph Nettis/Photo Researchers; **12** Courtesy of IBM; **13** Courtesy of Hewlett-Packard; **17** Courtesy of IBM; **19** Courtesy of IBM; **20** Courtesy of IBM Archives; **21** Courtesy of Cruft Photo Lab, Harvard University; **22** Courtesy of Unisys

Chapter 2 32 UPI/Bettmann Newsphotos; **34** The Bettmann Archive, Inc.; **35** Courtesy of The Science Museum of London; **36** Courtesy of IBM; **37** Courtesy of IBM; **38** Courtesy of IBM; **39** Culver Pictures, Inc.; **40** Courtesy of the Picture Collection/The Branch Libraries/The New York Public Library; **42** Courtesy of The Institute for Advanced Study, Princeton, NJ; **44** Courtesy of Unisys; **48** Courtesy of IBM

PART II 57 Courtesy of IBM

Chapter 3 58 Peter Menzel/Stock, Boston; **69** Courtesy of AT&T Bell Laboratories; **83** Courtesy of Cray Research, Inc.; **84** Courtesy of IBM; **85** Courtesy of Prime Computer, Inc.; **86** Courtesy of Apple Computer, Inc.; **89** Courtesy of GTE

Chapter 4 93 Owen Franken/Stock, Boston; **95** Courtesy of IBM; **97** Courtesy of IRS/National Computer Center; **103** (*bottom*) Courtesy of SCANTRON; **106** (*bottom*) Courtesy of Hewlett-Packard; **110** Courtesy of Albert-son's, Inc.; **111** Courtesy of Texas Instruments; **112** Courtesy of Wang Laboratories, Inc.; **113** Courtesy of Lear Siegler, Inc./Data Products Division; **114** (*left*) Courtesy of Houston Instrument; (*right*) Courtesy of IBM; **115** (*top*) Courtesy of Combustion Engineering; (*bottom*) Courtesy of Rockwell International; **117** Courtesy of Hewlett-Packard

Chapter 5 121 Richard Pasley/Stock, Boston; **122** Chris Gilbert; **123** Courtesy of Hewlett-Packard; **124** Courtesy of IBM; **128** Courtesy of Xerox Corporation; **129** Courtesy of IBM; **133** Courtesy of Xerox Corporation; **136** (*left and right*) Courtesy of Hewlett-Packard; **137** Courtesy of Hewlett-Packard; **138** (*top*) Courtesy of Apple Computer, Inc.; (*bottom*) Courtesy of Los Alamos National Laboratory; **139** (*top*) Jim Harrison/Stock, Boston; (*bottom*) Courtesy of Electronic Arts; **140** (*top*) Courtesy of Commodore Electronics, Ltd.; (*bottom*) Courtesy of Lear Siegler, Inc.; **142** Courtesy of Bell and Howell; **144** Courtesy of Hewlett-Packard

Chapter 6 147 Courtesy of Laser Magnetic Storage International Company; **169** Courtesy of IBM; **171** Courtesy of Laser Magnetic Storage International Company

PART III 177 Courtesy of Hewlett-Packard

Chapter 7 178 Courtesy of IBM; **179** Chris Gilbert; **180** Courtesy of IBM; **182** Chris Gilbert; **183** Courtesy of IBM; **185** Courtesy of IBM; **186** Hank Morgan/Rainbow; **187** Courtesy of General Motors; **188** Courtesy of Hewlett-Packard; **189** Chris Gilbert; **190** Courtesy of Apple Computer, Inc.; **193** Courtesy of Apple Computer, Inc.; **195** Courtesy of Hewlett-Packard; **196** John Blaustein/Woodfin Camp & Associates; **197** Courtesy of G.E. Calmo Company; **199** Courtesy of Radio Shack—A Division of Tandy Corporation; **200** Courtesy of Maxtor Corporation

Chapter 8 209 Charles Feil/Stock Boston; **211** Courtesy of Apple Computer, Inc.; **213** Courtesy of Apple Computer, Inc.; **214** Courtesy of Apple Computer, Inc.; **215** (*left and right*) Courtesy of Apple Computer, Inc.; **218** Courtesy of Software Publishing Corporation; **222** Courtesy of Texas Instruments; **223** Chris Gilbert

Part IV 231 Courtesy of General Electric Research and Development Center

Chapter 9 232 Courtesy of Hewlett-Packard; **234** Chris Gilbert; 246 Courtesy of IBM; **248** Courtesy of IBM

REGISTERED TRADEMARKS AND COPYRIGHTS